Otis L. Graham, Jr.

Associate Professor of History
University of California
Santa Barbara

THE GREAT CAMPAIGNS:
Reform and War in America, 1900-1928

PRENTICE-HALL INTERNATIONAL, INC., London
PRENTICE-HALL OF AUSTRALIA, PTY. LTD., Sydney
PRENTICE-HALL OF CANADA, LTD., Toronto
PRENTICE-HALL OF INDIA PRIVATE LIMITED, New Delhi
PRENTICE-HALL OF JAPAN, INC., Tokyo

E
7 43
G72

85052

© 1971 by Prentice-Hall, Inc., Englewood Cliffs, New Jersey

Printed in the United States of America

C—13–363572–4

P—13–363564–3

Library of Congress Catalog Card No: 79–135756

Current printing (last digit):
10 9 8 7 6 5 4 3 2 1

contents

DOCUMENTS

I. Reform: 1900-1916

II. War: 1914-1918

III. Reform: 1917-1928

foreword

The opening of the twentieth century seemed an appropriate time for self-congratulation. If some doubted the extent of American ingenuity and technological progress, they had only to attend the Pan-American Exposition at Buffalo, New York, and marvel over the new wonders of electric lighting. The United States had just emerged from a popular war with Spain, and with spoils which included the Philippine Islands and a semi-protectorate over Cuba. (There was no need to linger over the costly and brutal suppression of the Filipino insurgents, whose principal crime had been to demand independence rather than Anglo-Saxon tutelage.) The prosperity which the Republican Party had promised was now apparently at hand—it was sufficiently impressive, at least, to turn the heads of commercial farmers from notions of free silver and third parties to business ledgers, business organization, and pressure politics. The labor wars of Homestead and Pullman, and that ugly spectacle of a march of the unemployed on Washington, D.C., were all but forgotten; indeed, it seemed almost certain that the "labor agitator" was on his way to becoming an extinct species. And, best of all, William McKinley was President of the United States. His very face and demeanor suggested a nation at peace with itself. "I can no longer be called the President of a party," he proclaimed in 1900. "I am now the President of the whole people." That he was—surely the most popular President since Abraham Lincoln. The new Vice-President, Theodore Roosevelt, reconciled himself to four years as "a dignified nonentity." But Leon Czolgosz, a self-professed anarchist, decided otherwise. On September 6, 1901, he shot and mortally wounded the President. "It is God's way," McKinley murmured. "His will, not ours, be done." It was an ominous note on which to usher in the new century.

There was good reason to be concerned about the health, the moral integrity, and the destiny of the American Republic, whatever the outward signs of equanimity and the apparent prosperity. The danger was sufficiently obvious: a growing fragmentation of American society, made urgent by an accelerated and unregulated industrialization and urbanization, and the distinct possibility that a brutalized and radicalized proleteriat would fulfill Jack London's apocalyptic vision in *The Iron Heel*. Yet, Americans remained confident that their society was sufficiently durable, flexible, and liberal to handle any social crisis. What emerged in the early years of the twentieth century was "a wave of reform, the mounting of a thousand campaigns of all shapes and sizes to intervene, to bring under control and redirect, the forces that were at work with such alarming result in modernizing America." This is the central concern of Otis Graham's *The Great Campaigns*. To explain the nature of that movement called Progressivism, to comprehend the varied and often contradictory banners which it unfurled, is no easy task. It demands inquiries into motivation—the kinds of impulses that moved men and women from a state of apathy and indifference to become indignant Christian crusaders. "Progressives liked to run under the flag of generosity and conscience," Graham argues, "but what they were usually about was something quite legitimate but less angelic, group economic and cultural self-interest. This should not make progressivism the less interesting. Indeed, it makes it more interesting because it becomes thereby believable."

To study the Progressive Era is not simply to explore political clashes, legislative debates, political personalities (though Roosevelt and Wilson afford a veritable bonanza for the amateur psychologist), or the various doings at city hall and the state house. This is the stuff of which most textbook accounts are made, but it fails to illuminate the diverse forces at work in this period. It tells us little, for example, about the crucial role of business and professional groups in reform activities, the kinds of attitudes which infused the Progressive mentality, the obsessions with "efficiency," "rationalization," and "orderly procedure." We have reached a point in historical scholarship, Graham states, when "we need no longer rely upon rhetorical evidence in reconstructing what was being proposed and done by whom to whom in this tumultuous period." These are precisely the kinds of issues that he sets out to clarify.

It is customary to view World War I as a chapter in American diplomacy and as the bridge between the reformist Progressive Era and the conservative, complacent Twenties. But the War was also a significant and suggestive chapter in the history of Progressive reform—indeed, in some ways, its finest hour. This is not to argue that Progressives had an affinity for war. Graham rejects this notion. But the ways in which Progressives mobilized for the War, the kind of unity they sought to impose on American society, the rhetoric they used in the prosecution of the War, and the wartime lessons in business-government cooperation are most instructive for an understanding of this many-sided movement. The War, for example, perverted the idea of the regulatory state and virtually crippled the humanitarian side of reform. "No historian," Graham writes, "has described this process in full detail, for it involves matters of mood and spirit as well as the traditional pull and haul of politics." Although protest was by no means absent in the Twenties, the dominant spirit was clear enough, and wartime Progressivism was to reap a rather strange harvest— prohibition, Americanization, immigration restriction, and white supremacy. This "triumph of the reactionary spirit," Graham notes, was not the result of a sinister plot hatched in Wall Street. It was eminently American—"a national phenomenon expressing the ultimate decision of the great bulk of the American people that they would not tolerate any further disturbance or uncertainty, and were in no mood for idealism." It reached its apogee, in fact, in the very home of American reform, when the State of Massachusetts executed two

Italian aliens and anarchists, Nicola Sacco and Bartolomeo Vanzetti, on the most circumstantial kind of evidence.

What Otis Graham has described so well is essentially the American reform mentality—its changing moods, aberrations, triumphs, and far-reaching consequences. That his analysis departs from some traditional views of Progressivism is abundantly clear. "We see social control where older histories described liberation, we attribute reform measures to professional and commercial elites rather than the indignant rhetoricians of Congress, pulpit, and magazines, and we describe the goal as the rationalization and centralization, not the democratization, of American society." Graham's Progressivism may not be the Progressivism described in most textbooks but it becomes more believable, precisely because it is so characteristically American.

The objective of each volume in The History of the American People series is to encourage the student to think critically about how we got to where we are. There is no attempt to be definitive—that is, to treat every aspect of American society in its historical development or to describe every legislative act and presidential election. Each of the participating authors will make his own choice of emphasis, seeking thereby to illuminate what is most significant about a particular historical period. The documentary and photographic sections are essays in themselves. They are intended not as appendices but as integral and essential portions of the author's total presentation. They are aimed, too, at involving the student in the mood and spirit of the period. There is no conscious attempt in this series to present either "Revisionist" or "Counter-Revisionist" history. We have simply invited some thoughtful, critical, and skeptical minds to address themselves to the history of American society. And it is precisely to that kind of audience that we dedicate these volumes.

Leon F. Litwack

preface

Leon Litwack and Robert Fenyo spoke to me about this volume some three years ago. Just about that time I was feeling more than usually tentative about the things I was telling students about the reform experience at the beginning of this century, and I welcomed the opportunity to rethink the period and its problems. If one is interested in liberal reform, I discovered, one is lured into the war years and the 1920s. The design of this book reflects that discovery. The decision to end the study at the eve of the Depression was not made on historical grounds. My interest remained, and there was more to the story, but the book began to encroach on another in this series.

Readers will note the critical attention paid to the work of four men—Samuel P. Hays, Richard Hofstadter, Gabriel Kolko, and Robert Wiebe. It was these men (Hofstadter in the 1950s, the others in the 1960s) who unsettled my settled views and finally left me no alternative but to attempt a synthesis of my own.

Some of my extensive debts to other authors are acknowledged in the Bibliographic Essay. Citations to direct quotations are also included in this essay, which takes the form of a running bibliographic commentary on the text. It could easily be four times as long, for the shelves are full of indispensable studies.

Special thanks go to Leon Litwack, Henry Adams, Barton J. Bernstein, David Burner, W. Elliott Brownlee, A. Russell Buchanan, Maurice Conway, George Dangerfield, Alexander DeConde, Carroll Pursell, and Roger Williams for critical readings. Samuel and Sherrill Wells went to unusual lengths to talk me out of some of my errors, as did my brother, Hugh D. Graham. All of these scholars deserve the thanks of myself and my readers, and must not be blamed for flaws of style or content. My greatest debt is to my best friend, to whom I dedicate this book.

Otis L. Graham, Jr.

part one

REFORM: 1900-1916

I.

In that melancholy, fascinating, inconclusive book, *The Education of Henry Adams* (1906), a weary descendant of the nineteenth century's greatest American family brooded his way into the new century, trying to perceive what lay ahead for his country. Henry Adams was personally inclined toward a strong sense of the apocalypse, but his feeling that the nation was in a unique crisis was shared by many thoughtful people. The turn of a century naturally produces a good deal of introspection, but well before 1900 American intellectuals began to express a growing consensus that the United States, if not the entire Western world, was entering a time of unprecedented peril and opportunity. Josiah Strong's popular book *Our Country* (1886) judged the end of the nineteenth century to be a time in human affairs second in importance only to the time of the birth of Christ, a "fateful moment" of fluidity in which the national destiny was being shaped by forces only half understood.

The air of crisis was a compound of confidence and foreboding. The signs of the times were mixed, and individuals came to varying conclusions about the future. There were grounds, of course, for that well-entrenched American confidence. The war with Spain was successfully concluded, the flag had been planted in Puerto Rico, Hawaii, and the Philippines, and the threat of Bryan and his angry millions seemed well in hand. The country was in the middle of a fabulous economic expansion, with the national wealth nearly doubling between 1890 and 1900. New marvels were appearing yearly, among them electric lights and trolleys, X-rays, wireless transmitters, autos, and even rumors of flying machines. With such sure signs of progress there were many whose rising excitement at the turn of the century was untroubled by serious doubts. "Laws are becoming more just," orated the Reverend Newell Hillis in 1900, "rulers humane; music is becoming sweeter and books wiser; homes are happier, and the individual heart becoming at once more just and more gentle." The popular novels of the day, such as Gene Stratton Porter's *Freckles,* Charles Major's *When Knighthood Was in Flower,* or John Fox, Jr.'s *The Little Shepherd of Kingdom Come,* while they were not untouched by the general excitement and sense of big things impending, reflected a remarkable absence of any feeling that what was going on in the Western world at the turn of the century might disturb the verities of God, home, family, neighborliness, and a safe return on investments. In addition to clergymen of sunny disposition and those novelists who were in touch with the mood of middle-class ladies, others here and there in the social structure greeted the new century with considerable confidence. A biographer of J. P. Morgan wrote of him in 1900: "His married children and grandchildren were all well and happy...his friends were near by. The people in his social world were of his own kind....New York was a friendly, neighborly city....He was looking forward with the eagerness of a much younger man to the great possibilities of the century that was about to begin."

But for many contemporaries the dynamic epoch just ahead was awaited with a good deal of anxiety. The novel may have been largely immune to pessimism until the eve of the World War, but many general books at the juncture of the centuries expressed fears that the times were out of joint—Strong's *Our Country,* Henry Demarest Lloyd's *Wealth Against Commonwealth* (1894), William T. Stead's *If Christ Came to Chicago* (1894), Walter Rauschenbusch's *Christianity and the Social Crisis* (1907), Homer Lea's *The Valor of Ignorance* (1900). Journalist Mark Sullivan, surveying the popular mood in his *Our Times: The Turn of the Century,* found a prevailing "irritation," a feeling that "some force or other was "crowding" the average man, that he was "being circumscribed in a tightening ring."

The grounds for such a volume of pessimistic thoughts, unprecedented since the dark, doubtful days of the 1780s and 1790s, were everywhere to see. The 1890s had been a frightful decade. Contemporaries noticed that immigration of undesirable ethnic groups from Europe had mounted alarmingly, and were further shaken by the news, extrapolated from the Census of 1890, that the supply of free land was on its way to exhaustion and that a continuous frontier line no longer existed. Agrarian radicalism had been massing ominously even before the economic slump of the mid 1890s, and the depression produced a high level of industrial disorder, of which the most visible episodes were the Homestead strike of 1892, the Pullman strike of 1894, and the march of Coxey's rabble in the same year.

By 1900, it is true, a returning prosperity had at least for the moment removed the threat of actual armed uprisings by the labor force. But other problems had appeared and intensified. Shortly after the turn of the century the volume of social criticism and warning reached a point where contemporaries recognized that a national movement of self-criticism was under way, and they called it, in Theodore Roosevelt's term, muckraking. The exposure movement in journalism cannot be accounted for without mention of the new mass audience hungry for both shock and a more personalized news; a new class of publishers unhampered by the old literary tastes; and the arrival in the ranks of journalists of a class of ambitious, moralistic, and talented college graduates. But it was grounded in real and mounting social problems, and reflected the widespread social uneasiness at the opening of the twentieth century. From this muckraking literature, supplemented by autobiographical material and the record of corrective action, we can reconstruct the leading concerns of that vocal segment of the public which had detected disturbing developments and tendencies in the dynamic society that was *fin de siècle* America.

II.

Lord Bryce had said in 1888 that the governing of cities was the United States's most conspicuous failure. Contemporaries understood without consulting a sociologist that the country was industrializing, that industrialization meant urbanization, and that the cities, and in and around them the factories, were attracting and using people too fast for decent standards to be maintained. Too many people moved to the cities, and too many different kinds of people, straining urban public services, the peace of the streets, and the older residents' peace of mind. We are at the core of the matter when we know, for example, that Seattle had a population of 80,000 in 1900 but 237,000 in 1910, that as many as 50,000 people tried to settle in Chicago every twelve months through the 1890s, that between 1880 and 1910 the total of urban-dwellers in the nation trebled. These masses came to urban centers not only because employers offered good money to those who would man the lathes and looms, carry and cook, draft and file; they came also because young men (and women, although they were less mobile) wished to be where the action was, and defined this more broadly than merely economic opportunity. Commercial schemes and new pleasures beckoned, limitless and undreamed-of vistas opened to farm-born boys who were tired of the tempo of Iowa afternoons.

As a result of this population shift, governmental problems proliferated in America's bulging cities, taking familiar forms of waste and inefficiency, ineptitude, and outright scandal. Municipal governments in those days did not have extensive duties, but where they functioned—providing police services, granting utility franchises, cleaning the streets—they did not seem to function according to reasonable standards of honesty and efficiency, according to the best magazines. Readers learned that in virtually every large city the city government was more or less openly bought and sold by the "interests" which their few functions affected. This situation was objectionable because it was expensive and immoral—and, quite probably, in that order. The classic account of these conditions, Lincoln Steffens's report on six cities in his series, "The Shame of the Cities," appeared in *McClures' Magazine* in 1904 and 1905. At this distance it is too easy to shrug at the "bit of graft" that seems to have been the central feature of the misgovernment that aroused Steffens and his upper-middle class readership, but for one thing we forget the size of the stakes. The franchises granted to the public service corporations in New York City in 1903, although appraised at 235 million dollars, were actually worth half again as much, and returns on this investment were not taxed. This untaxed local monopoly engaged the cupidity of enterprising men who thought little of purchasing a city council or board of aldermen for what Cleveland reformer Fred Howe called "a possession fairly regal in its proportions."

State governments were equally susceptible to purchase because the functions they shouldered—granting urban charters, corporate charters, franchises, permits in resource management, and deciding who should and should not be taxed—had to do with allocating advantages of a very lucrative sort. Naturally, men with much at stake did not leave such things to chance. Frank Norris's novel *The Octopus* described a simple case: the government of California at Sacramento was owned outright by the Southern Pacific Railroad. In a state like LaFollette's Wisconsin, a number of interests—railroads, lumber, and mining companies—had always used the state government as the pathway to public lands and untaxed franchises. What was new at the turn of the century was not the increased occurrence of such arrangements, although there may have been some of that as industry expanded, but the spreading awareness that such lavish attention to private interests did not automatically forward the public interest.

These functions and malfunctions had to do with spending the public's money and with dispensing rights to the public domain, not with any question of the range of public services. Misgovernment in the former areas was objectionable enough, but was probably insufficient to generate a sustained, nationwide protest. Yet the same process of industrialization and urbanization that brought city and state governments to such venal arrangements created additional problems of a different type. Misgovernment that took the form of fiscal dishonesty or subservience to a few transit corporations and extractive industries came about primarily because the scale of operations of these quasiutilities had grown so great that the interests involved felt it both necessary and possible to purchase their host governments in order to gain security and stability. But industrialism did more than place strains upon elected officials, strains that, in a newly impersonal environment, usually proved too much for their integrity. It affected the conditions of life and work for millions in the cities, and affected them in a way that added to the sense of wrong that was growing in the country.

Conditions of life and work for most of humanity, even in America, had always been hard and unattractive; but as Americans packed into cities and around factories in the years after the Civil War the human price of modernization ran very high. While the farm population showed some increase, the cities grew three times as fast. Most of that growth reflected immigration from rural America, but the most visible part of it in the largest cities came off the boats from Europe. Nearly nine million immigrants entered between 1900 and 1910, until a city like New York recorded 76 percent of its population (in 1910) as foreign born or their children, and even the small cities off the seaboard averaged one-third immigrants or first generation Americans. Whatever the combination, the cities choked on the numbers. Wards in New York and Chicago groaned under a greater mass of humanity than the center of Bombay, India, and millions packed into tenements if they were lucky, into rows of shanties if they were not. Basic municipal services, inadequate at the beginning of the period, could not cope with the growth. Two-thirds of Chicago's streets in 1900 were mud; cities like Rochester and Pittsburgh were at best half sewer and half privy, and Baltimore and New Orleans had no sewers at all. Water, both in quantity and quality, was everywhere a problem. In Washington, D.C., the water pressure was so low in the eastern portion of the city that half the city schools had no operative toilets at all.

Some could buy relief from such conditions, but a sea of people could not. America, even then the world's wealthiest society, was a poor country. Robert Hunter estimated in 1904 (in his book *Poverty*) that ten million Americans were so poor that they were slowly starving to death, and his estimate excluded the entire agricultural population, for whom figures were nonexistent. Wages for the American worker were in a slow ascent, as they had been since the Civil War, but still pressed close to the subsistence level: track hands on Southern railroads earned 47.5 cents a day, unskilled packinghouse workers averaged $7.40 a week in the seasons when they worked, and the Triangle Shirtwaist Fire investigation revealed that the girls worked seventy hours a week at top speed to earn $4–5. The nutritional level permitted by such earnings, added to the abominable housing available in the industrial centers, meant staggering health problems, of which tuberculosis and anemia were the most common, with typhoid and bubonic plague not unheard of. Occupational diseases such as lead poisoning, respiratory diseases among miners, "Phossy Jaw," and so on, were largely uncompensated, as were the industrial accidents that statistician Frederick Hoffman estimated at 1,664,000 (fatal or near-fatal) in 1900. The strains and hazards of industrial labor broke the health of many adults, and widespread child labor brought the most vulnerable class of employables into brutal contact with the factory regimen. And the human beings who endured these social arrangements for such meager rewards now lived without the supports of community life, largely unknown to employer and fellow-employee alike. Those who could not keep up, the old, the blind, the injured, the epileptic, the orphaned, the feeble-minded, or merely the unemployed, had previously found some small havens in the interstices of community—family, church, neighborhood. The industrial order, harsh for even the healthy wage earner, had no use at all for the others. Woodrow Wilson provided an apt summary in his first inaugural address: The nation was too busy becoming an industrial power to

> count the cost of lives snuffed out, of energies overtaxed and broken, the fearful physical and spiritual cost of the men and women and children upon whom the dead weight and burden of it all has fallen pitilessly the years through.

These accompaniments of industrialism were of concern not only to those who endured them but also to the middle class, who narrowly escaped the worst of them. For the American who did not directly experience such conditions of life, they were deplorable not only because they made for the degradation and unhappiness of those on the bottom, but also for what they threatened to provoke. Men who were subjected to such torments might, like the barbarians within the gates of the city, rise up and destroy the comfortable folk around them either by riot or by plague.

The threat of riot has received the greater attention. And one is struck by the frequency, in both the public addresses and private remarks of men of that generation, of expressions of fear of a radicalized lower class. The industrial unrest of the 1880s and 1890s continued only slightly abated in the new century, and more ominous than strikes was the jump in union membership, from 800,000 in 1900 to over 2,000,000 in 1904, and the Socialist Party's steady growth after its founding in 1901. While some concerned middle-class people dallied with socialism, most of them, like Theodore Roosevelt, became sympathetic to reform so that a way might be found to preserve the system against the twin horribles of plutocratic revolution and socialist revolution. T.R. equated his reformism with antisocialism many times in public and more often in private, and he has been frequently quoted. Editor Joseph Pulitzer said it just as well in a letter in 1907, in which he praised Roosevelt's efforts to bring corporations into line: "The greatest breeder of discontent and socialism is lack of confidence in the justice of the law, the popular belief that the law is one thing for the rich another for the poor."

This concern with the political threat constituted by a depressed urban lower class is familiar to any student of this period. But it seems to me after reviewing the literature on urban reform, and urban biographies in general, that we have too often undervalued the fear of the unsanitary impact of the urban mass—what today most educated people would call the urban ecological problem. When urban reformers like Charles Loring Brace called the slum dwellers "the dangerous classes" they had in mind the problems of germs and sewage fully as much as muggings or socialist assemblymen. James Crooks, in his biography of Baltimore during this era, for example, reminds us that extensive efforts in that city from 1895 to 1911 to improve public health, to revise housing codes, and to enlarge recreation facilities were motivated at least as much by fear of disease among the poor, packed into their reeking, dank quarters in an unsewered part of town, at they were by humanitarianism or civic pride. The rhetorical evidence from other cities and the pattern of urban reforms suggest that Crooks's judgment has broad validity. Urban citizens from the middle and upper walks of life developed in large numbers a broad sense of social urgency over these issues, and whether they thought of the working class as suffering or threatening or both, they were adopting a broad view of society which might move them to action in matters beyond immediate and accustomed interests and formerly left to Fate.

This same generation of Americans also became aware of a menace that transcended state lines and that had developed at the apex rather than the bottom of the social order. The consolidation movement in industry was a long-term trend, but a burst of mergers from 1897 to 1904 more than tripled the number of so-called trusts, establishing effective control of the market in a number of areas, among them sugar, tobacco, oil, steel, and railways. A similar centralization took place in investment banking. While we now know that the concentration movement was brought to a monopolistic conclusion only in certain areas and that continuing invention and new entries into the market kept competition fierce in most sectors of the economy, contemporaries took the revelations of monopoly such as those of Ida Tarbell on Standard Oil, Charles Edward Russell on the beef trust, or Louis Brandeis on the financial empires of Wall Street as accurate descriptions of a general process that was overtaking and revolutionizing American life.

The average citizen could think of any number of reasons to dread the continuation of this trend. Monopoly closed off economic opportunity, stifled the spirit of new enterprise, and threatened to end the social mobility which had been America's chief appeal. Another and more immediately visible result of economic concentration was the production of huge fortunes, opening an intolerable gulf between the classes. Andrew Carnegie earned 23 million dollars making and selling steel in 1900 (tax free), while the girls at the Triangle Shirtwaist Company were working six days for their five dollars a week. The largest American fortune, estimated to be about one billion dollars, was equal to the savings of the poorest 2.5 million people; the top 2 percent of the population held 60 precent of the country's wealth. The fortunes piling up in the hands of a few men and families represented immense power, and America had no defense against it comparable to the constitutional defenses erected by the Founders against political power. But the threat to liberty posed by economic monopoly went beyond the creation of limitless private fortunes. The owners and managers of the corporations that had eliminated the chastening force of competition in their economic area held important powers that were quite beyond challenge. They could force consumers to eat beef that was in too large part made up of suspect portions of cows and other mammals (including the immigrants who worked about the vats); their only alternative was not to eat canned meat at all. Most important, they could force consumers of staples like sugar and steel to pay prices that had no relation to costs—except the costs of maintaining the captains of industry and their wives and daughters in their fullest opulence. Pricing power was the mightiest weapon of all, the key to national economic health, the arbiter of every man's consumer decisions. Men trusted such a power only to the impartial and invisible hand of the marketplace, and were appalled to see it fall into the grasp of a few men selected not for their wisdom but for their ambition and cunning. A general inflation from 1897 to 1913 supported suspicions that pricing power was in fact in such hands and was being used to exploit the consuming public in the most shameless way. And if quality deterioration and price-fixing were not enough, economic monopoly permitted unrestrained entrepreneurs in the extractive industries to scar the earth, poison the air and water, and waste the treasure of the planet, passing on to future generations a part of the price of their present enjoyment.

There were a number of other social ills that darkened the new century, such as the use of liquor, prostitution, the inferior legal and social position of women (too few worried about blacks for this to be listed as a general concern), expensive armaments and the threat of war, poor public education, and so on. But the leading concerns were as we have reviewed them: misgovernment; the state of life of the urban lower classes, their uncontrolled increase and political instability; economic concentration and all forms of unfair economic advantage. The contemporary sources are clear enough on these matters. But of the larger, overarching fear they contain only hints, multitudinous but nowhere fully developed. This might be stated as a fear that the social order was breaking apart, that the binding commonalities could no longer be sure of mastering the centrifugal, disintegrative forces which were lately gathering momentum.

Of course, America had always been an unruly, individualistic society, perhaps especially in the nineteenth century, and patriots long dead—Hamilton, Emerson, Hawthorne, Lincoln—had worried about its divisive tendencies. But there had always seemed to be enough cultural consensus, enough common purpose in expansion and physical survival, to hold the society together. It was only toward the end of the nineteenth century that anxiety about the very existence of the social order became widespread, and it served as the common denominator of the various maladies that beset modernizing America at the hinge of the centuries.

The concern over social cohesion was far from unwarranted. The sources of authority that had held the nation together were visibly eroding. Any contemporary conservative could have catalogued the problems of order: neither God, the family, the ethical prohibitions of the Protestant clergy, nor the social constraints of respectable community opinion were holding their own against the doubts, heresies, and temptations of modernism. As these loyalties of a village culture began to dissolve in the acids of science, geographical mobility, and that school of cultural relativism, the city, there was exposed to view the lack of national institutions for social integration. There was no national church, nor any consensus really on the value of religion, let alone the true denomination; there were no national universities, no national media, an enfeebled army and navy with thin traditions, and only poorly connected local elites to pose as a national aristocracy. There was little sense, either, of a national cultural inheritance, In place of a historic and viable national literature, art, music, or drama, there were only ethnic and regional survivals from European cultures, and on the whole a society too busy to define itself in cultural terms.

Most important, there was only a tiny, feeble national government, without the means and without the inclination to offer authority, vision, direction. Lord Bryce devoted one of his chapters in *The American Commonwealth* to the subject, "Why the Best Men Do Not Go Into Politics," describing for his English audience how the American national government, enervated by laissez-faire doctrines and the absence of constitutional power, adequate revenues, and a trained and aggressive civil service, was quite rightly not regarded in the late nineteenth century as a proper place for young men of energy and promise. Why should the best men have served the public? Government had no mandate to play a large role, and if it had, it did not possess the resources for sustained management. The executive staff at the White House in the 1890s numbered ten people, of whom four were bookkeepers and messengers. The president had access to no economists, no statisticians, no planning staff for either foreign or domestic questions. The secretary of agriculture complained in 1900 that more men worked for George Vanderbilt on his North Carolina estate than worked for the entire Department of Agriculture. When the European scholar M. I. Ostrogorski published his observations of American government in 1902 (*Democracy and the Organization of Political Parties*), he summed up the relation between American government and the larger society:

> From one end of the scale to the other, the constituted authorities are unequal to their duty; they prove incapable of ensuring the protection of the general interest, or even place the power which has been entrusted to them by the community at the disposal of private interests. The spring of government is weakened or warped everywhere.

"The weakened spring of government"—an incisive description of the frailty of national institutions of social cohesion at the end of the nine-

teenth century. And just at the time that the exuberances of industrialism and urbanism began their historic and apparently permanent
undermining of the authorities of community life, which in the absence
of strong national institutions provided all of the bonds between individuals in a fiercely competitive society, the forces of division began to
be augmented. The tide of immigrants from eastern and southern
Europe, the steady northward migration year after year of 10,000 or
more blacks from their invisible existences south of the Potomac,
threatened to fragment what seemed a homogeneous Yankee culture
into a babel of tongues, colors, and customs. The increase of tensions
between economic classes projected a disintegration of another sort,
probably more violent and lethal than the cultural conflicts which
were intensifying between nativists and others. "The present assault
upon capital," spoke the gloomy Justice Stephen J. Field, "is but the
beginning. It will be but the stepping-stone to others, larger and more
sweeping, till our political contests will become a war of the poor
against the rich; a war constantly growing in intensity and bitterness."

It was only natural that as men began to suspect that social antagonisms were multiplying beyond the capacities of the old processes of
reconciliation, they would begin to sense total disorder in the wings.
And so we detect beyond their fears of ethnic and class conflict a
general fear of forces building off somewhere in the surly ranks of
labor, among ruthless industrialists with continental schemes and unlimited capital, in the laboratories of scientists with their revolutionary
probes into matter and energy. "The shadow of force lay over the
period," wrote Alfred Kazin, and while he knew this by reading the
novels of Jack London, Theodore Dreiser, Frank Norris, and many
others, we find it everywhere in the written record. Contemporaries felt
themselves entering an age of power—not restrained power, but uncoordinated aggregations of power in a setting of deep social antagonisms. In the words of Henry Adams:

> The citizens were crying, in every accent of anger and alarm, that
> the new forces must at any cost be brought under control.... Prosperity
> never before imagined, power never yet wielded by man, speed never
> reached by anything but a meteor, had made the world irritable,
> nervous, querulous, unreasonable, and afraid.

The response of others was more ambiguous, since the rising level of
tension and the new concentrations and techniques of power engendered in younger men a sense of zest and excitement as well as forebod-

ing. But the foreboding went deep. It was not power alone which so set the nerves on edge, but the feeling that power seemed no longer harnessed toward a common vision, that it was instead hoarded by unseen men in whom one had no trust, for some deadly thrust against the rights of citizens. Power massed, not where the community willed it, but in private, irresponsible hands. Social change accelerated, out of control.

Such a catalogue of worries might have sent an older society into fatalism and a scramble for private sanctuary. But America in 1900 felt herself a young nation, bursting with energy and an instinctive confidence. Even though men doubted the future, almost none of them doubted that the future was worth a fight. The big news of the inter-war period (1898–1917), therefore, was the emergence of a wave of reform, the mounting of a thousand campaigns of all shapes and sizes to intervene, to bring under control and redirect, the forces that were at work with such alarming result in modernizing America. Were her cities foul, their governments inept and criminal? This was intolerable; they must be cleansed. Were her people suffering, brooding upon foreign ideologies? They must be uplifted, given hope in the American system. Was the society being pulled apart by the mounting pressures of materialism, distrust of strangers, the unpredictable and selfish conduct of irresponsible private groups? Then we must at once discover effective principles and techniques of order, and a strengthening of our common purpose. Just at the beginning of the century, but near the end of his life, Henry Adams wondered if he could come back in 1938, on the one hundredth anniversary of his birth, and, "for the first time since man began his education among the carnivores, ... find a world that sensitive and timid natures could regard without a shudder." Even as he wrote, young men and women were stirring themselves for the efforts necessary to answer his question in a proud affirmative.

III.

Mere hardship and accelerating social change, of course, do not always produce a reform movement. Men must not only become collectively aware of social troubles, but do so in a spirit of indignation, which means imagining that things could and should be better than they are. It is well to remind inhabitants of a dissident, reformist, even revolutionary century, that such social activism is not typical of human life. Docility and privatization have been more general, interrupted occasionally by outbursts of dissatisfaction, which have been brief and atypical. The emergence of social protest is what must be accounted for, not apathy, and it makes a fascinating study. The problem may be approached in the aggregate, asking what group or groups are making an uprising and for what ends, or it may be approached individually. In the latter case it becomes the problem of accounting for the making of a reformer, of learning how a man came to hear the fire bell of progressivism in the night, when those around him slept. The approaches are complementary: biography is also history.

Earlier writers did not always think this a difficult or particularly interesting problem. The task was to account for the awakening of altruism and enlightened self-interest—in that order. The answer seemed obvious, especially to readers of progressive manifestos, speeches, and autobiographies. First, social conditions had worsened abruptly, and then a few talented and sensitive souls saw what was happening around them. They were the early theorists and the muckrakers, and they awakened the nation. The nation—or a large part of it—become converted to social concern and reform because these persuasive writers touched its conscience and alerted its sense of self-interest.

But how were these early harbingers themselves shaken from lethargy? It seems that the prime incubator was the chaotic city of turn-of-the-century America, with its sweaty ghettos, its crime and unhealthiness, and its feeling of being out of control. Most of the muckrakers were from small-town environments, and the city shocked them by contrast to the neighborly, orderly world they had known. They were too spirited and principled to witness these social conditions with anything but sustained indignation, and it was to be they who alerted the millions who could not witness urban social problems firsthand, either because they still lived in little New England or Midwestern towns, or because their urban careers—unlike those of journalists—did not take them on the other side of the tracks and did not encourage social observation. Thus we account for the muckrakers and early writers, and they account for the others.

There is vast evidence in autobiographical accounts to support the claim that progressivism was launched by a few mighty books. Countless reformers report that they were transformed originally by one of the early indignant classics of progressivism, books like Edward Bellamy's *Looking Backward* (1888), William T. Stead's *If Christ Came to Chicago* (1894), Jacob Riis' *How the Other Half Lives* (1890), Charles Sheldon's *In His Steps* (1896), or a book that made more reformers than any other since *Uncle Tom's Cabin,* Henry George's *Progress and Poverty* (1886).Tom Johnson, for example, the great reform Mayor of Cleveland (1901–09), was converted from the aggressive pursuit of wealth to the sacrifices of the reform effort (which cost him his health and his fortune) by reading *Progress and Poverty* on a train to New York. Johnson returned to Cleveland and a life of reform when a lawyer he hired for the purpose could not prove to him that George was wrong. Once converted, men like Johnson, and Chicago's John Peter Altgeld, Wisconsin's Robert LaFollette, and especially Theodore Roosevelt and Woodrow Wilson, men of charismatic power whose lives were dedicated to a cause beyond self, turned thousands of young men to reform by the power of their personalities and their rhetoric.

One of the problems with the account just offered is its heavy reliance upon altruism. Once aroused, reformers spoke of justice, of sacrifice, of duty, of service. Their literature is saturated with such terms, and with an intensely moralistic temper. This is because that generation was a religious—primarily a Protestant—generation, and the only language they knew to express their aroused feelings was the hortatory language of the Gospel—Uplift, Redemption, Conversion, Battles for the Lord, Forces of Evil, Crusades, and so on. Not only was their language drawn straight from the pulpit (to which most of them had been subjected two or three times a week since early youth, unlike our own generation), but most of their campaigns resembled revivals. In 1912 the Progressive Party of Theodore Roosevelt, with some of the most advanced and sophisticated minds of the era in the auditorium, stood and sang without reserve "We Stand at Armageddon and We Battle for the Lord."

While some of the leading ideas of progressivism were in the long run hostile to both Puritanism and Christianity, the great bulk of the movement was unaware of these ideas or at least of their implications, and confronted the problems of the era with the familiar mental attitudes and rhetoric of the Puritan tradition. Historians by the nature of their work have reread this rhetoric and have usually allowed themselves to believe that all of this language drawn from the Gospel of the prophet of love suggests that progressivism was chiefly about altruism. But they were misled by more than language. There was an element within progressivism for which altruism is the only appropriate descriptive term: the social work and social settlement element, supplemented by the Social Gospel clergy (some of them), and a few general intellectuals or professional reformers—one hardly knows what to call them—who worked, not just talked, for the underdog..

But altruism thins out quickly when one moves from these circles outward to areas of progressive effort that were far more typical. The language, admittedly, was the same. But when progressives outside these small groups used the word "justice," its primary meaning had to do not with benevolence or with wrongs done by society to its helpless victims. Most of those in hot pursuit of justice were calling for more advantages for themselves and less for their economic competitors. This is not a question of "sincerity" but of determining exactly what people meant by certain terms. Actually, some measure of justice and equity was often involved when a group in revolt sought to advance its own ends, but such motivation should not be confused with altruism. Few movements of any size are ever mounted by men disturbed primarily by the plight of others—and progressivism was a large, complex, national movement. As we shall see, most progressives were brought to rebellion by pain experienced directly, by some setback to their own interest. Aware that his taxes were high, a citizen joined the Municipal Voter's League of Chicage to eliminate graft and put the city on a more frugal footing. Angry at what seemed to be exorbitant rates for shipping goods to market, a farmer or grain shipper would work for a state regulatory commission or a strengthening of the Interstate Commerce Commission. Shocked by Upton Sinclair's description (in *The Jungle,* 1906) of what he had thought was good, clean ham, a citizen become a T.R. supporter in the fight for federal regulation of meatpacking. Such motivation was thoroughly American, quite proper and natural, and often actually coincided with the broader public interest. It was the motivation behind the vast bulk of progressive pressures. Progressives liked to run under the flag of generosity and conscience, but what they were usually about was something quite legitimate but less angelic, group economic and cultural self-interest. This should not make progressivism the less interesting. Indeed, it makes it more interesting because it becomes thereby believable.

Those not of a speculative turn of mind may doubt the value of inquiries into motivation, especially in view of its complexities. That would be a mistake. The most entertaining argument in recent years was started by a man who was dissatisfied not only with suggestions of the motivating power of sheer altruism, but was also skeptical that the force of ideas was a sufficient cause of a man becoming a reformer. Ideas, of course, are indispensable to any reform movement, and we have the testimony of innumerable progressives that they were transformed by a book, a speech, a sermon. But what accounts for the selective effect of ideas—for their striking sparks in some who encounter them, and not in others? In *The Age of Reform* (1955), Richard Hofstadter noted evidence gathered by other investigators indicating that progressives were drawn inordinately from a special segment of society, essentially the young, well-to-do, and well-educated sons and daughters of the older American families that some like to call WASPs. They and their fathers generally belonged to social and occupational groups—clergy, small-town lawyers, doctors, merchants, and small manufacturers—who were not quite so prestigious at the turn of the century as they had formerly been, for a number of complicated reasons. Hofstadter suggested that the thunderbolt of reform struck most frequently where certain relative (not absolute) losses in personal status had begun to irritate, preparing the ground for great exertions which would be somewhat misleadingly labeled as aimed at improving others' lives.

This thesis, widely acclaimed, has also been widely resented. To some, Hofstadter seemed to be saying that progressives only *thought* they were awakened by the condition of the country and the plight of disadvantaged groups, and only *thought* they pursued altruistic ends. Actually they were awakened by personal discomforts having nothing or little to do with trusts or poverty, and they pursued psychic relief. Hofstadter was not saying exactly this. His argument was complex, comprehensive, and brilliantly stated, and ought to be sampled in the original—but to some readers who knew *they* were altruists he seemed to be excessively cynical. Such readers might well have cited Jane Addams on this point: "It is natural to feed the hungry and care for the sick, it is certainly natural to give pleasure to the young, comfort the aged, and to minister to the deep-seated craving for social intercourse that all men feel."

Thus it has been felt by some that the study of motivation is risky ground for historians; and historians like Hofstadter and Christopher Lasch (*The New Radicalism in America,* 1965) who wrote about what motivated the modern reformer, and others like David Donald who wrote about the motivations of the abolitionists, have not been universally welcomed. The critics are correct about the risks, since psychology and sociology are inexact sciences, especially when the people under study are no longer alive. But historians of reform movements that parade under the banner of crusades for altruistic goals must and will critically compare the announced aims of such reform movements with any evidence, sociological or psychological, they can find. This is so because it is decidedly *not* natural, Jane Addams notwithstanding, for most people to go beyond their minimal and convenient philanthropies and sacrifices.

I do not mention the Hofstadter book because the thesis has proven "true," for some damage has recently been done to it by historical investigation, and the argument is far from resolved. The most important result of this controversy has been the stimulation of dozens of studies of the sociological profile of progressivism. Such studies provide a broad range of data on who the reformers were in the various areas of activity, and some attention has also been paid to the "conservatives." Such studies are invaluable. We need no longer rely upon rhetorical evidence in reconstructing what was being proposed and done by whom to whom in this tumultuous period.

IV.

However it came about, indignation replaced complacency in the minds of thousands of Americans around the turn of the century, and prospects began to brighten for some sort of disturbance of the status quo. But even with social maladjustments identified and condemned as scandalous and intolerable, there still remained intellectual barriers to corrective action. One was a traditional laissez-faire attitude which, while often violated in practice, had been greatly talked of as a virtue, especially after the Civil War. Its constitutional counterpart, strict construction, in the hands of skilled judges like Stephen J. Field, had drawn a tight circle around political power in order to leave unfettered such "natural" forces as the acquisitive geniuses of John D. Rockefeller, Henry Clay Frick, Judge Elbert Gary, "Buck" Reynolds, and their like. A scientific version of laissez-faire, "social" or "hard" Darwinism, was imported from England and adapted to American conditions by men such as William Graham Summer. They saw it as Nature's way that some should visit morally invigorating but often fatal hardships upon others so that Nature could at length locate those she shouldn't have created in the first place and repair her error by eliminating them. These were the major intellectual barriers to reform, and a man could hardly move from indignation to action without first removing them, for they were widely held ideas. A few recent immigrants, due to their defective European educations, held none of these theories and could proceed to collective action at once, but this was thoughtless in more than one sense of the word. Had everybody behaved so without premeditation and soul-searching as did the simple socialists from Europe, the very livelihood and certainly the joys of the American intellectual historian would be in jeopardy.

The process of reeducating a generation is an interesting one to follow, especially for those who enjoy books and ideas as much as the progressives themselves enjoyed them. What was needed to liberate men from laissez-faire and social Darwinism, with their view of the social system as some sort of natural machine that men should not tamper with since they had not built it, was a general skepticism about the sanctity of current relationships, a confidence in the tinkering impulse, and a social theory that made social control no violation of some cosmic law. The skepticism was provided by any number of irreverent thinkers, the most effective being Thorstein Veblen (*The Theory of the Leisure Class,* 1899; and *The Theory of Business Enterprise,* 1904), and two professional satirists who are less appreciated by historians, Mark Twain and Peter Finley Dunne. The confidence in deliberate, rational manipulation of a complex social order, always latent in the American character, was given powerful expression by William James and John Dewey, who provided philosophical arguments why men should trust more in their intelligence—trained, scientific intelligence, not hunches—than in traditional wisdom or habit. The social theory that rebutted Sumner's reading of Darwin was also the work of many hands, among them the economist Richard T. Ely, who found no economic law prohibiting economic reform, and religious thinkers like Washington Gladden, John A. Ryan, and Walter Rauschenbusch, who testified as theologians that God had no objection if men did not meekly accept their temporal fate. The most comprehensive rebuttal of social Darwinism came at the hand of the sociologist Lester Frank Ward (*Dynamic Sociology*, 1883), who proved to all but the most hardened readers that Herbert Spencer and Sumner were wrong to assume that progress for human society could best be achieved by abdicating the directional function to fate. Ward was emphatic that fate was in no way superior to the guidance of intelligent men, and that anyway the control of social change had never been left to fate but had always been exercised by men—currently the more aggressive industrialists and financiers.

Men who were ready to act found the new theories persuasive and unshackled themselves from the old. This was not simply done; men cherished their old ideas more fondly than their wives, and discarded them with a good deal more anguish than any divorce. Among all the old theories that delayed and obstructed reform, undoubtedly the most hampering—because it was institutionalized—was a body of jurisprudence built up laboriously during the nineteenth century and designed to defend the rights of property from competing claims such as humanity, mercy, or the public good. That jurisprudence was intricate and in its way fascinating. It was also infuriating to Populists, Grangers, and progressives of all types who from time to time tried to expand the police powers of the state or build on the general welfare clause of the Constitution. Such efforts were almost invariably struck down or circumscribed by some canon of conservative jurisprudence—usually the due process clause of the fifth and fourteenth Amendments, or, when conservative judges were tired of being confined to constitutional language and were in a sporting mood, "freedom of contract."

What was needed to dissolve the bonds of conservative legal theory was another legal theory that emphasized the necessity for the law to be alert to changing circumstances and also to the fallibility of judges, indeed the fallibility of the Constitution makers themselves. Such a new view of the law was provided by Oliver Wendell Holmes, Jr., an activist in trying to get the Court to adopt a more passive role toward legislative experimentation. Holmes was inclined toward judicial self-restraint even though he usually thought the laws of reform-minded legislatures to be socially misguided, and he was skeptical of many of the "constitutional principles" that his brethren on the Supreme Court had discovered in and between the lines of the Constitution. He once rendered his judicial philosophy as follow: "Long ago I decided I was not God. When a state came in here and wanted to build a slaughter house, I looked at the Constitution and if I couldn't find anything in there that said a state couldn't build a slaughter house I said to myself, if they want to build a slaughter house, God-damnit, let them build it." In 1918 the Supreme Court struck down the Keating-Owen Child Labor Law on the ground that among the vital Fifth Amendment liberties was "freedom of contract," in this case the solemn right of eight-year-old Homer Dagenhart of North Carolina to either agree or not agree to work twelve hours a day. "When my brethren talk of 'freedom of contract'," Holmes said philosophically, "I compose my mind by thinking of all the beautiful women I have known." Holmes' doctrine of judicial self-restraint, along with Louis D. Brandeis' insistence that judges examine not only the law but the facts of social life (see his "Brandeis Brief" in *Muller* v. *Oregon,* 1908), helped squeeze a few modest reform measures past hostile courts. The work of these judicial thinkers, along with Charles A. Beard's *An Economic Interpretation of the Constitution of the United States* (1913), a history of the writing of the Constitution that painted the warts of self-interest on the faces of the Founders themselves, helped to inform and justify a popular suspicion of the courts, where conservatives were accustomed to take up their last stand.

These were the liberating theories of what Eric Goldman calls "Reform Darwinism," acting as corrosives of established belief and practice and as encouragement to innovation. They were warmly welcomed by men tired of the incantations of their elders, but still men of an essential conservatism despite their new plans, who wished first of all to assure themselves that they did not break some rule of the universe before they went about their renovations. Such theories put into the hands of a generation about to undertake collective action against existing arrangements the intellectual tools they needed to denounce things as they are, to discredit the idea that "things as they are" are as they have to be, and to justify rearrangements in social affairs based on reason, science, justice. The central features of these new modes of thought were a passion for the concrete, a confidence in human nature, human reason, and an aroused majority. They were formidable convictions. History was to treat them roughly. It was also to reveal significant differences and variations, among reformers themselves, in the weight given to democratic participation as against scientific expertise. But this is to anticipate the story.

V.

While it is true that the chief significance of progressivism is undoubtedly the resort to the state for a number of purposes, from arranging a different distribution of economic rewards and burdens to enforcing correct moral behavior, a large part of the reform effort took nonpolitical forms. Though scholars have a tendency to skip over these forms in order to get to the political battles, the nonpolitical aspects of reform deserve careful attention. Socially concerned people today believe in the efficacy of going down to Mississippi delta shacks and Chicago slums to share the situation of the poor and try to improve it. The progressive counterpart was settlement work. Modeled on London's Toynbee Hall, the first American settlement houses were established in the 1880s—Neighborhood Guild in New York, Hull House in Chicago—and at the turn of the century there were over a hundred. The intent of the settlement was to "fill the gap" that was opening between the urban lower class and the rest of society. Settlement workers did not think of themselves as simply uplifting the poor, although this was unquestionably involved. The best of them saw settlement work as a chance for the sons and daughters of comfortable, old-stock families to take advantage of contact with peoples whose culture had a number of things to offer. The spirit of the settlements, unlike the earlier charities movement, was not paternalistic; individual improvement in standards of behavior seemed less important than a pragmatic concern for improvement in standards of living. The routines were roughly similar in all the settlements; they may be followed in Jane Addams' *Twenty Years at Hull House* (1910), in Mary Simkhovitch's *Neighborhood: My Story of Greenwich House* (1938), or in Lillian Wald's *The House on Henry Street* (1915). They included day nurseries, counseling, clinics and visiting nurses, classes in hygiene, cooking, and spelling, the formation of clubs for all ages around interests such as athletics or Great Books or singing, the establishment of art museums and libraries, the serving of meals at all hours of day and night.

There has never been a satisfactory attempt to measure the effect of the settlement. Without doubt the settlement movement, like the Peace

Corps currently, had more beneficial effects upon those who came to serve than on those who received the attention of these lay missionaries. After observing the social roots of poverty, a few settlement workers left the settlement and stormed city hall, demanding better housing, sewage and sanitation, and factory laws. But although the settlements contributed people and ideas to the political wars of progressivism, the heart of the work was nonpolitical, the work of volunteers, people-to-people, in the ghetto.

The social ills that produced the progressive revolt, especially the problems of economic concentration and the problems of social inefficiency and disorder, suggested another nonpolitical remedy to reformers. This was functional organization, the organization of one's occupational interest against competitors or potential intruders. Actually, the word should be counterorganization, since those Americans who federated along functional lines in the progressive years saw themselves as driven to it by the prior organization of enormous corporate interests.

Railroads were consolidating, or being consolidated by financiers, until by 1900 six large systems controlled 95 percent of the nation's mileage; therefore, belatedly and indignantly, shippers organized to seek some control of rates affecting their region, usually in businessmen's leagues, chambers of commerce, or farmers' commodity groups and cooperatives. The same process went forward in professional circles, where rising occupational groups vital to the new technology combined in associations to improve salaries, upgrade standards, regulate entry into the field, and improve public relations. The labor force continued its slow self-organization after the depression of the 1890s had interrupted unionization, with union membership jumping from 868,500 in 1900 to 2,000,000 in 1904. Employers, alarmed at any workforce organization and exaggerating its extent (union membership grew very slowly after 1904, and was only about 2.5 million when the war began), formed hundreds of local employer organizations and three national groups, the National Association of Manufacturers (1895), the National Civic Federation (1896) and the Citizens' Industrial Association (1903).

This wave of counterorganization which followed the industrial combinations of the 1880s and 1890s may be sketched by consulting the *National Organizations of the United States* (Encyclopedia of Associa-

tions vol. 1.) : The Farmers Union, 1902; The International Brotherhood of Teamsters, 1903; The American Astronomical Society, 1899;
The American Association of Agricultural Engineers, 1907; The Federal Council of Churches, 1908; The American Federation of Teachers,
1905; The American Association of State Highway Officials, 1914;
The New England Fish Exchange, 1908; The American Landscape
Architects Association, 1899; The Society of Automotive Engineers,
1905; The Anti-Defamation League of B'Nai B'rith, 1913; The American Institute of Chemical Engineers, 1908; The American Association
of Petroleum Geologists, 1917; The American Chamber of Commerce,
1912. Admittedly many such organizations learned to exert political
pressure when the need arose, but they were founded primarily to gain
group ends through economic pressure upon larger power blocs, or by
controlling entry into the field of their activity. A secondary interest,
especially among the professional groups like doctors, architects,
engineers, and the like, was to secure some control over group standards
and practices by consolidating to control the licensing process.

Some years ago this development would not have been seen as a part
of progressivism, since the formation of trade and professional organizations had nothing to do with elections and was not conspicuously
altruistic. And indeed I am not arguing that the simple fact of organization was a sign of progressivism; voluntary organization long predated the progressive era. What we perceive as distinctive in this period
is not the fact of organization but the scale and frequency of it. Americans of that generation, in numbers which allow us to speak of a mass
movement, turned to group organization to defend themselves against
economic rivals, rationalize disorderly and unpredictable business and
professional practices, and pursue a vision of an expanded role in
society. And while there were exceptions, there was about much of this
organizing binge a fervor and a sense of social responsibility which are
a second distinctive feature of the group life of the prewar years. Of
course this was true of the civic groups, the ministerial associations, and
the charity organization societies. Their purpose was altruistic, and we
expect them to talk like saints and go on crusades, which they did. A
familiar part of the progressive movement were the voluntary organizations formed to advance the consumer interest. They were not many
and they were never powerful; but to some the consumer seemed the
truly forgotten man of a period when every other conceivable interest
was being protected by federation; organizing the consumer allowed

full play to the progressive preference for activities that could be designated as in the public interest. The best known of the consumer organizations was the National Consumer's League, established by Florence Kelley in 1899 as a federation of state leagues. But other groups established at that time also adopted the consumer interest as part of their charge—for example the People's Lobby, formed by Samuel Merwin of *Success* magazine in 1906, and the American Home Economic Association, established in 1909.

While such groups have always been recognized as signs of progressivism, voluntary organization of a distinctly progressive cast was taking place among commercial and professional groups not normally thought of as participating in, for want of a better term at this point, uplift movements. The rhetoric that accompanied much of this organization marks it as sharing not only the era but also the spirit of progressive reform. In conventions and meetings among engineers, doctors, architects, and others, the talk, after the middle nineties and especially between 1910 and 1916, was likely to be not only about strength of materials and medicine and design, but also about the social crisis and the social responsibility of men whose considerable talents had previously served only self. The engineering profession, to take only one example, had organized into its four Founder Societies in the 1870s and 1880s in order to upgrade standards and regulate practices. But the rise of a sense of group responsibility occurred in the early twentieth century, appearing in the presidential addresses delivered at annual conventions of the Founder Societies (American Institute of Mining and Metallurgical Engineers, American Society of Mechanical Engineers, American Institute of Electrical Engineers, American Society of Civil Engineers), in the establishment by Morris L. Cooke and others of the Committee on Public Relations of the ASME in 1910, in the founding in 1917 of the Engineering Council, a federation of engineers interested in social action. Here in the organizational life of a commercial group one finds a part of the story of progressivism—not only a wave of organization so that control might be imposed on some area of confusion and waste in the economy, but the high-minded language of social responsibility. Admittedly, everybody talkin' 'bout Heaven ain't goin' there. Progressive engineers hoped to achieve the good society by running industry the way it should be run, namely, to produce goods, not profits; but the bankers and managers whom circumstances had regrettably placed in charge of the productive system proved too dull to see the logic of this. In the end, progressivism in the engineering profession produced some elevated language (such as the statement by President E. D. Meier of ASME in 1912, "the golden rule will be put in practice through the slide rule"), energetic subcommittees which framed denunciations of financiers and monopolies, and a study, *Waste in Industry,* published in 1921. But whatever the accomplishments of reformers in this area, no account of progressivism is complete if it examines only City Hall and the halls of Congress and ignores the group life of many commercial groups and virtually all of the professions in the years between the Spanish-American War and World War I.

One could extend the mention of areas outside politics where the progressive spirit stirred. All three major faiths in America, Protestant, Catholic, Jewish, experienced internal questioning and a realignment toward a greater sense of social relevance, at least in the urban areas and among religious writers and thinkers. Painting and literature reflected social themes, often critically. Legal and Constitutional thought developed a strong interest in social facts, relied less on precedent. Old professions such as medicine, engineering, and the law reverberated with calls to duty, to social activism, to community as well as client service. New professions sprang up—social work, city planning, public health—where young people could prepare technical solutions to pressing moral problems. Psychotherapy emerged within psychiatry, behavioralism within psychology, and attacked their enervated parent disciplines for their lack of fervor, their lack of interest in improved human behavior, their lack of appreciation of the malleability of man and his future.

The most quickened profession, the most altered social institution outside politics, was surely education. Citizens and administrators banded together for more schools and better teachers. Progressive educators sought the improvement of society by sweeping aside the old, rigid, classical curriculum in favor of an education relevant to life and directed toward freeing the creative potentialities of the student. Thinking of education in a broader sense, virtually the entire muckraking literature, most of the general books written by reformers from Edward Bellamy to Herbert Croly, and all of the sermons preached by the reform-oriented clergy of the Social Gospel were efforts to solve the social crisis by educating and exhorting the public. It is with good reason that Rush Welter, in *Popular Education and Democratic Thought* (1963), sees progressivism primarily as an effort in public education, not in political action. Many men thought that it would be enough to speak out, breaking the silence that concealed the social crisis; individual enlightenment would follow, and wrongs would be voluntarily corrected. Many a progressive novel showed that all that was needed was the conversion of some wealthy but unenlightened factory owner who would then with a word eliminate all the selfish practices that had grown up while his conscience unaccountably slept. Such writers had no intuition that the state and its coercive powers would play such a large role in the action that followed their exposures.

VI.

Much, doubtlessly, was accomplished by these nonpolitical activities, especially if one's goals were modest. But it is a characteristic of modern life that before long every issue becomes politicized, and in due time the progressives found, if they had not realized it at the beginning, that the changes they wished could best, or only, be achieved through a resort to government. The power of law was quicker than education, more permanent and reliable than group counterpressures.

The first resort was usually to the most immediate level, municipal government. The progressive movement really began there, in a series of battles that are the skirmish line of a long war—Chicago, 1896; Toledo, 1897; Detroit, 1899; Cleveland 1901; then too many to count. While municipal reform involved reformers of quite diverse origins and aims, the predominant type was the Good Government progressive, a citizen from the comfortable classes who dropped his law practice or took time off from his business in order to sweep the grafters out of city hall. The "Goo Goos" resented the waste and inefficiency of the typical ward-based machines, whose careless ways seemed not only immoral but inadequate to the governance of booming cities. So these civic reformers counterattacked to restore—or to secure for the first time—both honesty and rationally organized government.

The pattern was similar from city to city. First came the formation of a City Club or Municipal Voters' League, then the launching of a campaign to replace the existing Irish mayor with a son of one of the better families.[1] Subsequently, seeing the need for structural rather than personnel changes, there would be a remodeling of city government, encompassing perhaps the city manager or commission from, and a new city charter allowing the city to own its utilities and exercise broader functions in a number of areas. And always there was the establishment of new agencies staffed with engineers, city planners, statisticians and other professionals to administer the vital health, crime prevention, and welfare functions of the metropolis. Great rhetorical efforts accompanied all these innovations, identifying reform with Democracy, The People, and so on. But the few close studies we have indicate that these municipal reformers were usually drawn from a narrow segment of society, the upper-middle business and professional classes. As Samuel P. Hays writes, they were "a small elite segment of society," businessmen whose interests were not focused in the street corner but were city-wide, and the lawyers who saw things as did the broader-visioned businessmen.[2] Since the groups they ousted were representative of social classes lower on the economic and social scale, municipal reform, according to the most recent and best evidence, should be seen as a shift of power upward in the social pyramid. This is not the only time in this century when the word *democracy* was borrowed by a movement that the unbiased observer might see as elitist.

The foregoing summary of the activities of municipal reformers slights the excitement, color, and difficulty of these crusades. The Goo Goos must have been making some headway, since in every case the "machine" and its allied business interests (usually the existing franchise holders in utilities) fought back as if capitalism itself were at stake. It was not safe to be a municipal reformer: Francis Heney was shot in the head in San Francisco and Fremont Older was kidnapped,

---

[1] While there was usually one large "Citizens' " alliance formed to guide the city's reform energies, when the moment finally came for a city-wide political campaign, American cities in the progressive era fairly teemed with businessmen's leagues, women's groups, and other organizations formed to advance the civic good. Zane Miller tells us that in Cincinnati in 1909 there were 40 civic groups, all tugging and talking Cincinnati upward.

[2] S. P. Hays, "The Shame of the Cities Revisited: The Case of Pittsburgh," in *The Muckrakers and American Society,* ed. Herbert Shapiro (1968). Hays found the opponents of reform to be small businessmen, white-collar workers and skilled workers, and other middle and lower-middle class elements. Less than a quarter (24 percent) of these "ins" (conservatives would be the wrong word) were drawn from the larger business and professional groups, whereas *all* of the reformers were from this elite.

and in Chicago Raymond Robins was brutally beaten by hired thugs.[3] Politics, as Mr. Dooley reminded onlookers, "ain't beanbag." The risks the municipal reformers took, their herculean exertions, their appealing rhetoric, these earned them the acclaim of subsequent writers. But in recent years we have not thought entirely well of this type of reformer. Some of this shift of opinion came when it became understood that the "bosses" usually came back after a few years, bringing the bad old days back to city hall. But a more basic critique has emerged, in part stimulated by the discovery of exactly which classes the Goo Goos represented. The civic reformer was property oriented, and typically offered greater efficiency in government and a stricter accounting for the public monies. But honesty is a less valuable virtue than compassion, which the old machines actually possessed in large degree. Although there was graft in the unreformed system, it made some efforts to minister to the needs of the lower classes, while the reformers were trying chiefly to reduce the taxes paid by property.

In this sort of reassessment the hazards are romanticizing the old machines on the one hand and regarding too lightly the improvements in the way of efficiency on the other. But when the right balance is struck, it seems that the gains of efficiency were made at the expense of removing government a few steps from the more needful and numerous people of the city and turning it over to the experts. The 1960s have sharpened the realization that such a shift is not entirely beneficial. The current mood seems to favor the compassionate local democracy, with its easy standards and sticky fingers, to the efficiency experts in city hall.

But municipal reformers were not all honesty-oriented. Some of them were services-oriented, and some of these had a lower-class bias even though they were usually themselves of upper-middle class origin. Of course there were municipal services that benefitted all classes, such as an aggressive public health service, prompt collection of garbage, smoke abatement, and lower water and electricity rates. But many progressives also worked for services of special benefit to the

---

3 Of course, there are forms of retaliation more dread than violence—excommunication, for example. Melvin Holli tells us (in his *Reform in Detroit: Hazen S. Pingree* and *Urban Politics* (1969)) that after Mayor Pingree's attack on the transit interests he was deprived of his pew in the Woodward Avenue Baptist Church.

crowded, working-class sectors—parks and recreation areas, lower streetcar fares subsidized by general taxation, humane criminal treatment, free or low-cost clinics, tenement inspection, and the like. Where these functions were successfully pursued by a reform administration, as in New York City, it generally meant that the Goo Goos had been joined in their insurgency by elements from the immigrant or working-class community. But whether the municipal reformers' efforts benefitted their own class or the one beneath it, at their best they followed a vision that combined the interests of all—a vision of a beautiful city on a hill, the twentieth century embodiment of that refuge envisioned by the Puritans who crossed the Atlantic to the new world.

VII.

At about the time that urban reform movements were increasing and becoming commonplace, progressives opened a second front at the state level. This order was no accident. In the nature of things, urban reform drew attention to inadequacies in state constitutions and administrations. Urban experimenters were everywhere hampered by state constitutions and codes, and it soon appeared that the way could not be cleared for thorough urban housecleaning without some preliminary renovation at Sacramento, Columbus, or Albany. At first the urban reformers' demand was merely for greater home rule, but the difficulty in achieving this at the capital brought them to see the need for substantial changes in the personnel and structure of state government. State legal arrangements not only fastened impotence upon the cities, but state governments were if anything more venal than city governments—they were found to be veritable Sodoms and Gomorrahs of lobbyists and graft, machines, cliques, and indifference behind which a few vested interests looted undisturbed.

When this was learned by urban reformers the progressive movement broadened to the state level, and a series of "honest" governors led angry citizens' movements in state after state. Here were produced some of the great figures of progressivism, men like Robert LaFollette, Hiram Johnson, Charles Evans Hughes, and Woodrow Wilson. The pattern of housecleaning was standard: after the election of a Peoples' Governor, there would be procedural reforms to sweep away the electoral arrangements that had been so complicated and slow that they had encouraged voter apathy—the most familiar of these reforms being the initiative, referendum, and recall, the direct election of senators, the short ballot, direct primaries, shorter terms for elective officials, and the like. Government was brought closer to the "public" and parties were diminished in power. The virtue of such changes of course depended upon the willingness of the public to exercise such powers as had been wrested in their behalf from the party apparatus, public officials, and the judiciary. The public was to disappoint its self-appointed champions, but the dearly-won victories of the Direct Democracy reformers were an important experiment and one that had to be tried.

As with urban reform, state progressivism was a coalition of diverse callings. The middle-class reformer described in George Mowry's study of California progressives was called by duty to the purgation and democratization of state politics, and he saw his role largely in negative terms. He would take the government away from the railroads and other special interests and return it to "the people," or, as he sometimes put it, "set it free." But there were other types jostling in the ranks of state reform. Many had something substantive to achieve once government was in purer hands. They were of two general types, the champions of their own group interests and the champions of the unrepresented and the disadvantaged. Both of these took up when and where the Goo Goos left off. They had lent a hand when the fight was being made for direct primaries and the other Direct Democracy measures, but such changes of the electoral rules were to them only preliminary.

The best-reported of the "positive" accomplishments of state reform were the social justice measures. In this category came the child labor laws, the statues regulating hours and wages, factory working conditions, and the like. While measures of this sort were secured in some cases with the self-interested help of organized labor, most of the pressure came from middle-class groups like the American Association for Labor Legislation, the National Consumers' League, or the General Federation of Women's Clubs. Cooperation between such groups and the representatives of organized labor was never extensive, and this was only partially because Sam Gompers preferred not to divert labor's attention from collective bargaining by allowing these costly and wearying forays for some small legislative advantage. It was also because middle-class reformers did not enjoy working with the representatives of labor, whom they found materialistic, unrefined, and hopelessly mired in a very narrow social perspective. In a book like Irwin Yellowitz' *Labor and the Progressive Movement in New York State, 1897–1916* (1965), for example, one sees these hostilities at work in a period and place of considerable class tension and can understand why a labor-progressive coalition for social legislation rarely became more than a theoretical possibility.

The entire body of child labor law passed in the South, for example, was secured by pressure from middle-class reformers in the child labor leagues, interested clergy (the head of the child labor movement was the Reverend A. J. McKelway), women's clubs, and the PTA. For such a coalition based primarily upon altruism, the passage of child labor laws in thirty-one states, of minimum wage laws (for women) in fifteen states and maximum hours (for women) in thirty-nine states, was a remarkable display of the power of appeals to conscience, factual studies, and sheer persistence. Most of these laws were watered down in passage and the funds appropriated for their enforcement were invariably skimpy, but advocates could ignore these things in their enthusiasm for the precedents they were setting.

But the social justice forces accounted for only a part of those enlarged state functions resulting from progressive pressure. Among the legislation-minded newcomers to the state capitals were angry businessmen of various sorts. Usually they were producers or shippers with freight rate grievances against the railroad, and they hoped to replace the intractable railroad traffic manager with a state rate commission. In small states like New Hampshire progressivism was a businessman's revolt against a railroad, and little else. Even in California, which ultimately produced a comprehensive reform experience including labor legislation and conservation measures, the origin of the movement was in an uprising of businessmen and publishers against the Southern Pacific Railroad. Other businessmen demanding state reform legislation were industrialists who had found the costs and uncertainties of the employers' liability system burdensome, and who saw in workmen's compensation a way to make the costs of industrial accident more predictable. Workmen's compensation laws have been taken to be a part of the social justice side of progressivism, but their chief support came from the manufacturers (through the National Association of Manufacturers especially) and insurance companies, who wished, in Roy Lubove's words, "to substitute a fixed, but limited charge for a variable, potentially ruinous one."

To be sure, the professional altruists of the social welfare camp also worked for workmen's compensation, but the laws bore the stamp of their business sponsors. In three out of four instances the laws provided that reserve funds be held by private insurance companies rather than by the state, and in the central matter of the level of compensation the victory of the employers was graphic in the meager extent of benefits. But whether employer or employee benefitted most, these laws were the embodiment of progressivism—passed in the teeth of apathy and indifference, designed to secure through state power some measure of predictability and control over the costs of industrialism.

VIII.

Even before progressivism at the state level had reached its apogee, reformers began to think of Washington. Note the grievances that required federal action. Only national legislation could satisfy the businessmen of the South and Midwest, who hoped to break the grip of eastern interests by tariff reduction and national banking reform. Only federal action could remove the constitutional barrier against a graduated income tax. Only the national government could effectively "do something about the trusts." Only the federal government could curb local pressures on the public domain and inaugurate satisfactory conservation policies. Only in Washington could those businessmen whose national interests and aspirations were blocked by confusing and overlapping state laws secure sensible and safe regulation of industrial enterprise. Only in Washington could farmers secure adequate credit for their seasonal needs, and only there could those determined ladies who wished to vote in federal elections secure their inalienable rights.

All of these goals—tariff reform, banking and industrial regulation, effective antitrust action, an income tax, conservation—required national legislation. A number of other reforms might be secured piecemeal through the states, such as woman suffrage, child labor reform, or wage and hour laws. But in the case of the labor legislation especially, the forces behind them were weak, and their progress through the states was retarded by the reluctance of individual states to raise the operating costs of industry while neighboring states did not. Such considerations led these social justice reformers with their chronically weak constituencies to turn their eyes toward Washington where the assistance of an enlightened president might enable them to win the measures their numbers could hardly hope to secure. Prohibition and woman suffrage were also for a time pushed in the individual states, but a federal solution was seen to be quicker, and these reforms also were brought to Washington for fulfillment.

Thus reform rose to the national level primarily because certain tasks could best, and in some cases only, be accomplished there. There was, too, the allure of national action. Men of ambition and energy could see no reason why the entire nation should not share in their enlightened leadership. Out of this complex field of hundreds of progressive groups and interests, there emerged in a little over a decade an altered and enlarged national state that bridged the years between laissez-faire and the welfare state of Franklin Roosevelt.

The legislative landmarks of national progressivism are familiar enough, but the story of who was actually getting what is only now becoming clear. Progressivism came to Washington in the days, and some say in the person, of Theodore Roosevelt, and we remember a number of events that appear as battles between the forces of reform and the forces of standpat-ism. These battles seem to have eventuated in victories for T.R. and his followers, usually in victories over business. One of the early signs of a new spirit at the apex of government was the antitrust prosecution of the Northern Securities Company (1902–4). This was clear evidence of a zeal for antitrust that previous administrations had conspicuously lacked, and reformers were heartened when the government secured a dissolution decree in the case. But this opening gun of the progressive antitrust campaign was one of the last moments of unanimity among reformers. Although the balance of the national progressive experience had largely to do with federal action involving large business enterprise, nothing was ever very clear again. What should be done about monopoly, and when something finally was done, who had done what to whom? The Northern Securities Company case heralded a reform administration, but it gave no clues as to the complexities inherent in the relation of large industrial operations to justice, the public interest, or the reasonable demands of interested parties in the world of commerce.

On this question, T.R., searching for what was politically safe before he decided what was morally right, pursued several lines at once.

His attorney general instituted a few suits against conspicuous trusts, such as Standard Oil and the meat-packing combine. But the courts had no clear notion of what was wise or of the precise meaning of the Sherman Act (they thought about it in that order), and these cases dragged out past T.R.'s departure from office with no clear result. While the president thought dissolution of large corporations was indicated in some cases, he leaned toward regulation of practices and standards in others. Leading examples of the latter were the meat-packing industry and the food and drug industries, where the administration sought regulatory power. That power was conferred in 1906 after two bitter legislative battles, and most accounts give the impression that Roosevelt had forced the public interest upon reluctant packers, processors, and drug manufacturers.

Such was not the case. The packers themselves were eager for stricter federal regulation (cursory inspection had been begun in 1891) to reassure their European buyers. The mere passage of the meat inspection act was no sign that the industry had been reformed, at least as T.R. and his supporters used that word. It might, on the contrary, be a sign that the government was being used. Everything depends upon a comparison of what the industry wanted in such an act, what was wanted by the advocates of regulation who had the public rather than the industry good in view, and what the legislation eventually provided. There was indeed an uproar from the industry as the government moved toward some sort of resolution of the matter in early 1906, but the uproar was largely against further exposures like those of Upton Sinclair (*The Jungle,* 1906) and of T.R.'s two investigators, Neill and Reynolds. The packers favored regulation, but protested agitation and the threat of the wrong kind of regulation. With regard to the important issues on which there was dispute, Senator Beveridge and other reformers argued that the cost of regulation should be placed upon the packers, insuring a stable source of funds for administration and enforcement. If the funds did not come from such a levy on the industry, Beveridge pointed out, Congress might emasculate any law by making piddling appropriations. He was perhaps recalling that the Congress had appropriated *no money* to enforce the Sherman Act during the first twelve years after its passage.

The packers opposed carrying this charge, and they won. The president and the reformers wished to date the cans; the packers had this stricken from the bill. T.R. also resisted close court supervision of Department of Agriculture orders issued under the law, and the result here was a draw. In summary, the meat-packing law of 1906 was a law the packers shaped to a large degree, and with which they were content. As Senator McCumber, a friend of strict regulation, commented: "We have met the enemy and we are theirs." The industry could easily live with the degree of federal supervision the law entailed, and all it really yielded to T.R. was the principle that the meat-packing industry was affected with the public interest and that the guardian of this interest was the federal government. Little was changed in the processing of canned meat; certainly nothing was changed for the workers, about whom Upton Sinclair had been most concerned.

This same general assessment holds also for the Pure Food and Drug Act of 1906, banning misbranded or adulterated food and drugs. Its leading advocate, Dr. Harvey Wiley of the Department of Agriculture, saw the struggle for regulation as one between Good and Evil, but it is more accurate to see it as a struggle between some food and drug interests and others. True, the strongest opposition to the law of 1906 came from food and drug companies, either patent medicine firms or canners and packagers whose interests would be hurt if certain preservatives were banned. And the General Federation of Women's Clubs, the public-spirited doctors of the young American Medical Association, and the implacable bureaucrats from the state food and dairy departments led by Edwin F. Ladd of North Dakota and Robert M. Allen of Kentucky composed the noisy, resourceful lobby for the public that colored the bill a bit pink. But decisive support and influence came from businesses that would be subject to regulation under a new federal law—established firms with an interest in stability and good public relations, which looked with more than mild approval upon a law that drove their unscrupulous, fly-by-night competition to the wall. The president of the Proprietary Association, a patent medicine group that helped shape the law after an early opposition, said in 1928: "Many of us remember the days when the business was laughed at. Today it is a most substantial, firmly established, constantly growing industry." And it was this Association, according to a trade journal, that deserved primary credit for having secured the law of 1906.

The popularity of that law among drug companies is easier to understand when one observes how a combination of weak provisions and lax enforcement diluted its effect. Enforcement was hampered by small appropriations and extensive court review, and even when convictions were obtained the penalties were low. The maximum fine under the act was $300, and the average fine levied from 1907 to 1933 was only $66. The first case brought by the Bureau of Chemistry under the 1906 law was an expensive, carefully drawn indictment of a company producing Cuforhedake Brane-Fude. The government won the case, and by a combination of fines was able to relieve a Mr. Harper, one of America's truly brilliant captains of industry, of the sum of $700. Lest the modern reader either laugh at the nomenclature of the medicine involved or take satisfaction at the victory of the watchdogs of the public health, it should be pointed out that Mr. Harper merely subtracted the $700 from the $2 million a leading scholar estimates as having been his take from sales of Brane-Fude. A firm determined to bottle and sell such questionable potions could afford to regard such a sum, which was rarely imposed anyway, as a virtual licensing fee. The bottling, advertising, and selling of useless and even poisonous substances continued, as Americans were to learn in the early 1930s when a small revival of muckraking searchlighted the food and drug industries.

T.R.'s leadership had been important in getting any law at all through a divided Congress, but he had inherited reform pressures in both meat-packing and food and drugs that went back almost twenty years. Similar pressures had been building since the 1880s to take the power of rate-making out of the hands of railroad traffic managers. Rail transportation was often a monopoly, with no effective competition from rival roads or water transport to discipline those who made the rates. Theodore Roosevelt put himself at the head of forces who wished to reform the making of rates, bringing them under public control. The Hepburn Act of 1906 seemed to bring the reformers victory over the railroads. Certainly the battle was hard enough, with the parliamentary maneuvering against Senator Aldrich and the "conservatives" consuming over eighteen months and taking all Roosevelt's skill. But again it is enlightening to look closely at the details.

The Interstate Commerce Commission, established in 1887, had been ineffective from the start. The Supreme Court ruled in a series of cases that the ICC could only *invalidate* rates through a tortuously slow process, but could not set binding ones. The Court also held that the legal basis for "long–short haul" equalization and rebate control was inadequate. The Hepburn Act was the centerpiece in a set of four reform laws that finally gave the ICC effective power to control the rate-making process. The Elkins Act of 1903 outlawed rebates, the Hepburn Act of 1906 conferred power to set maximum rates; and a major weakness of that act—that the courts could choose between ICC and railroad judgments as to what was a fair or an unfair rate—was remedied by the Physical Valuation Act of 1913, allowing the ICC's estimate of a fair return to prevail. Power to overrule long–short haul differentials came with the Mann-Elkins Act of 1910. The Hepburn Act may properly stand as a symbol of this legislative record, representing the substitution of public for private control over a vital service— rail transportation.

But public control, of course, is not synonymous with democracy, justice, or the public interest—although it *is* reform. What the progressives had done with regard to the railroads was to make a procedural change whereby an area of important decision-making was regularized, rationalized, and opened to the political pressures of more of the affected groups (but not all or even most of them). The changes were urged not by "the people" but by shippers from geographical areas whose natural economic advantages were nullified by the basing-point system, or by shippers of commodities in economic difficulties who attributed this to high rates on the only railroad available, or by railroad managers themselves who preferred predictability to the rate wars and ill-feelings of private rate-making. Where was the public interest in all this? Neither the Congress nor the ICC could discover it, and they have not to this day. How was one to set rates so as to advance the public interest? Often a long haul to centers of population received lower rates than shipments to closer points, but this was because of the economies of heavy traffic. A rate system that charged strictly by the mile might seem fairer to short-haul shippers, but its effect would be to eliminate the advantages of heavily populated areas and to decentralize industry. The South and rural areas generally would gain, but at the expense of efficiency. The South would also gain if the basing-point system were overturned by the ICC, but in this case the result would probably be *more* efficiency. What is clear is that the existing rate structure that the newly empowered ICC inherited, with its built-in differentials, rewarded established economic advantage and penalized aspiring competitors. But it required the wisdom of Solomon to discern where in these questions lay the general good.

Another divisive question had to do with a fair return. Presumably a fair return—and no more—was in the public interest, and years of litigation had placed a "fair return" at somewhere between 6 percent and 8 percent of invested capital. But who was to assess the physical worth of the sprawling railroad empires? These were questions of the most technical nature, and in the process of considering them it was impossible to keep clearly in mind the good, beautiful, and true. But there *was* a solution, and the progressive generation found it. The Congress, pressed by angry groups of shippers and by the railroad men themselves, passed these impossible questions on to a commission. Machinery was evolved to somewhat stabilize a situation that was chaotic. Experts now decided in an atmosphere charged with political pressure what railroad rate-makers had decided in an atmosphere of economic pressure. The process was more open than in the days when John D. Rockefeller powered his way to a favorable rate, and it allowed the consultation of more interests before a decision was reached. No man can demonstrate with exactitude that justice was the end result of the progressive regulation of railroads, but regularity of procedure was accomplished, and this was close to the heart of progressivism. And when formerly private decisions are politicized, whether aggrieved groups actually improve their position or not, the new procedure reduces the feeling of powerlessness among the unconsulted, which is a clear gain for any democratic society.

These were the leading progressive achievements of T.R.'s two terms: the establishment of regulatory agencies in the areas of rail transportation, meat-packing, food and drugs, and a reputation for antitrust action. One recalls the T.R. years also for conservation, another area where The People are supposed to have mastered The Interests, and another area where this was not at all the case. Progressive conservationists were primarily scientifically oriented men, like the forester Gifford Pinchot or the geologist W J McGee, who wished to bring rationality and a national perspective to resource exploitation. To such men a scientific use of America's resources required an immediate control over access to and disposition of these resources, a control that could only be exercised by men such as themselves. In addition to far-sighted and ambitious federal bureaucrats, such a program appealed to those larger extractive industries already on the resource site. It tended to infuriate small operators and those contemplating entry into the public domain, who felt they could not control the remote eastern bureaucracies under Pinchot and Roosevelt, and could not stand to have their costs raised by any shift to "scientific management." The conservation movement was thus primarily the promotion of an elite of scientists, their few sympathizers in Congress, and the larger corporations involved in resource exploitation. The "little people" at the grass roots in the West and elsewhere were more often than not suspicious and opposed to the centralization that conservation implied.

These general remarks do not do justice to the complexities of the conservation movement. Conservation involved forests, mineral reserves, irrigation and water rights, grazing, flood control, and recreation. No single legislative battle clarified the issues. The only significant legislation was the Newlands Act of 1902 establishing the Bureau of Reclamation, and the Weeks Act of 1911 providing federal grants for fire prevention in the forests, and neither act caused major debate or produced major consequences. The story of conservation in the progressive era may be a simple story of good and evil in T.R.'s speeches, but behind the rhetoric the story was one of obscure bureaucratic struggles to control the policy of one or more of the twenty-six government agencies having cognizance over public resources. Some of these struggles—most notably the Ballinger-Pinchot contest of 1910—were invested with the usual the-people-vs.-the-interests rhetoric, but the progressive conservation movement could not be accurately described by the progressives' own words, certainly not by the word *democracy*.

If anything, conservation was antidemocratic in that it sought to gather "rights" from thousands of private hands—from miners, lumbermen, ranchers—and centralize them in the hands of experts in Washington. That the movement was not democratic in the simple sense of the word should not discredit it, since the little people fully intended to continue to rape the land in the way they always had. Those who wished to put access to resources on a scientific basis may perhaps be seen as the trustees for the many unborn, a silent majority. They claimed, at any rate, to be acting in the interests of some larger public when they overrode the wishes of a majority of local resource users. Whatever they claimed, they usually lost. The story of progressive conservation efforts is the story of a wave of general publicity and a few specific proposals like the Inland Waterways Commission Report of 1907, all followed by legislative inaction or outright hostility. Congress refused to set up the permanent Inland Waterways Commission through which Pinchot and T.R. hoped to establish multiple-purpose resource planning, and when T.R. asked for funds to continue his National Conservation Commission, that request, too, was refused.

Another aspect of conservation was preservation, itself a minority movement and quite antithetical to Pinchot's emphasis upon scientific use. But the prophetic dreamers of the preservation movement, men like John Muir, were if anything less successful than the elite that wanted scientific control over exploitation. Their chief effort came in the fight to save Hetch Hetchy valley for aesthetic enjoyment, and they lost the valley to San Francisco's water needs in 1913. Presumably some public education was accomplished by both wings of the progressive conservation movement. But both were disappointed in their immediate goals, since the destructive exploitation of both the wilderness and of cultivated land went on, as the brown cargo of the Mississippi River attested daily, and the dust storms and floods of the 1930s were to prove dramatically and conclusively.

IX.

While the national progressivism of the T.R. years primarily involved efforts to bring order and rationality to certain sectors of the economy, pressures for direct democracy measures and for labor legislation were gathering strength. Roosevelt's last Annual Message (1908) spoke of the unfinished business ahead: improved regulation of industry, abolition of child labor, shorter hours for all labor, a federal workmen's compensation act, a progressive inheritance tax, an inland waterways commission, and perhaps even old-age insurance. He was never given the chance he sought in 1912 to advance toward these goals. Some well-informed people have doubted that he would have achieved much along these lines, or that he really wanted to. Certainly his priorities after 1912 were weighted toward national unity, and social justice measures were divisive issues. But Roosevelt's accomplishment by 1908 was not negligible, and it satisfied his sense of what was possible. Those who were in sympathy with the man who was the American President from 1961 to 1963 will appreciate T.R.'s largest achievement: a young president with style and ideas came into office, bringing fresh vistas and attracting young and talented people into public service, all in contrast to an earlier, more sluggish leadership. Of course, as with John F. Kennedy, nothing much happened along the lines laid down in the speeches. But who can say that such revivals of simple faith in national leadership, faith that forces are being brought under the control of decent men, are not in certain circumstances worth more than the scornful radical ever imagines?

But the animation died under Taft, and a sense of being thwarted returned to those who wished to master their environment. Actually, Taft was as honest as any reformer, and more interested in antitrust and efficient government than most. Yet he did not like movement and change, and was soon on good terms only with the conservatives. The pressures for additional federal action grew on a number of fronts, and were strong enough to produce a few victories even if Taft would not lead. The thrust for direct democracy brought on a successful fight to curb the powers of Speaker of the House Joseph Cannon, and secured the Seventeenth Amendment requiring senators to stand for election before the registered voters rather than before state legislatures. Foes of the existing pattern of economic advantages worked for a lower tariff, and while they were unable to reduce it noticeably in the Payne-Aldrich Tariff of 1909, they got out of the effort a sense of solidarity and a momentum toward further change. Conservationists brought about the removal of Secretary of the Interior Richard Ballinger, suspected (unfairly, it now appears) of granting excessive rights in the public domain to corporate interests that rewarded him personally. The trust issue was still unresolved. Some men still seemed to be getting too rich by methods that were questionable. Women and children still worked under inhumane conditions for unhealthful periods. By the beginning of the second decade of the century virtually all intellectuals, many preachers, undetermined numbers of businessmen and lawyers, and large blocs of Congressmen were in an urgent, indignant mood. The year 1912 saw a skirmish for positions, an alignment of the heterogeneous forces of reform behind presidential candidates, and the stage was set for the culminating surge of national progressivism.

It appeared from the talk of the central figures that the many elements of progressivism had fused into two coherent schools in

1912.[4] The leading question seemed to be what to do about the Trusts. The second question was what would be the relation of government to disadvantaged groups. Behind T.R. one could see gathered those who felt that industrial concentration ought to be welcomed but regulated, and that it was now the responsibility of government to intervene on behalf of those social groups too weak to defend themselves under the new conditions. T.R.'s New Nationalism further held that no narrow construction of the Constitution, no property claims, ought to stand in the way of federal power as it coerced entrenched oligarchies and unified the nation. Behind Woodrow Wilson were to be found those who trusted to a vigorous antitrust policy and a lowered tariff to make such a medding state unnecessary.

Had Roosevelt won, it would have been discovered that his following was as varied and contradictory as progressivism itself. Grouped uneasily under his banner were big industrialists like George Perkins and Dan Hanna, for whom Roosevelt's attitude toward size in business had a welcome and enlightened ring; social workers who had a number of specific tasks to suggest for T.R.'s active and humanitarian state; antitrusters like Amos Pinchot and George Record, who were either confused (they should have been with Wilson on doctrinal grounds) or would not relinquish their faith that T.R. was still the trustbuster of 1902; and an assortment of "out" politicians, admirers of T.R., and anti-Taft Republicans. Some theoretical unity was imposed by T.R.'s campaign speeches, in which the New Nationalism was reasonably coherent, but his talk only papered over serious divisions in program and emphasis not only in the Bull Moose party but also in T.R.'s mind itself. Progressivism' contained innumerable faiths, and even under the campaign pressures of 1912 it could not be fused into only two schools.

Wilson's following had somewhat more theoretical unanimity. His New Freedom speeches represented fairly well the things his party believed to be true at the end of their intellectually sterilizing sixteen years

---

[4] A small number of progressives preferred the Socialist candidate Eugene Debs in 1912, but it simplifies matters to ignore both these and that small group that voted for Taft. Whether one judges by numbers or by doctrine, Wilson and Roosevelt spoke for progressivism in 1912.

out of power. But the results of his administration were also to show how many voices were raised in the tents of reform. Wilson's following included agrarians who, while far from being advocates of big government, hankered after the special favors which the New Nationalism had promised. Agrarian pressures were among those that drove Wilson from the negativism of the New Freedom in the transitional year of 1915.

But for a time the new Democratic administration acted as it had talked. Both tariff reduction by the Underwood Tariff of 1913 and the Federal Reserve Act of the same year were plainly legislative products of the New Freedom philosophy, which enjoined the removal of barriers rather than compensatory favors. To reduce privilege by bringing down the tariff was a first priority among many reformers but especially among Democrats, and the Underwood Act brought rates down from an average of 40 percent to an average of 29 percent. Enough populism remained in the Democratic Party to produce a move to add a progressive income tax to the tariff bill, and conservatives saw revolution in such taxation. In fact, the Democratic progressives passed the tax not to redistribute income but to make up for revenue lost by a lower tariff. They were out to balance the budget, not to soak the rich. The rates ran from 1 percent to a towering maximum of 7 percent. Nonetheless the battle for tariff and tax reform had been hard, with the intervention of Wilson himself required to defeat the swarms of lobbyists who resented losing control of the government on this issue for the first time since the 1870s.

The antimonopoly bent of Wilson's party also suggested action to break the "money trust" discovered in the Pujo investigations, and Wilson's political skills were adequate to that task, gaining the Federal Reserve Act after a fierce congressional struggle in 1913. Democratic rhetoric and many accounts have called the act a victory for The People over the bankers. It was not that, and it was very nearly the reverse. Bankers small and large had hoped for banking "reform" since the panic of 1907. The existing banking system (or lack of system) permitted no fluid reserves to cover local crises, provided for no national currency, no coordinated check clearance. These deficiencies needed to be remedied, but they had nothing to do with democracy or social justice, only with efficient banking. Some bankers and the few reformers who understood banking also wished central control over the supply of money (essentially, control over credit), a useful power that might or might not advance the public good. Western and southern commercial and agricultural interests simply wished credit decentralized so that they might have more of it than Wall Street had been willing to supply. Out of these conflicting pressures came the Federal Reserve Act of 1913, the first national banking reform since Lincoln's day.

Who had done what to whom? The New York bankers had offered the Aldrich bill, which would centralize credit controls in the hands of a committee of bankers. Wilson stood firmly for the principle (he later lost sight of the substance) of public control of the supply of money. His supporters divided between those who wished public control lodged in Washington, and those provincial supporters who wished a more decentralized, "democratic" system allowing each region of the country to control its own monetary destiny. The form of the Federal Reserve Act suggested a victory for the latter interests, for it set up twelve reserve districts, which were empowered to pursue independent credit policies up to a point, and it was expected that each district—governed largely by locally appointed businessmen and bankers—would be responsive to local needs. A Federal Reserve Board in Washington retained some monetary powers and was appointed by the President. This paper decentralization represented a legislative victory for western and southern voices (some of them bankers' voices) over the eastern money managers, and a symbolic victory for public control of banking. Both victories soon proved illusory. The New York Reserve Bank (one of the twelve) came quickly to dominate the system, giving New York bankers more power than they had possessed before 1913. The nonbanking interests which were supposedly built into the Federal Reserve Board simply never emerged. The Federal Reserve Board appointments of Wilson and subsequent presidents were men subservient to the eastern banking community and without much vision or courage. Anyway, the board's powers were not extensive. Oddly enough, the New York branch under Benjamin Strong in the 1920s (until Strong's death in 1928) more effectively pursued policies that conduced to the public interest than those favored either by the parochial bankers in the other eleven branches or by the Federal Reserve Board in Washington.

That the bill did not actually democratize the important banking decisions in America, despite its twelve districts, turns out in retrospect to have been no disaster. To bring more bankers into the decision-making process would not have produced wiser policies. Monetary powers should certainly be in public hands, and the Federal Reserve Act was a small step in that direction, but a very, very small step. Even had Wilson not staffed the Board with ex-bankers and conservative economists, there was in the country little understanding of what a banking policy in the public interest might be.[5] Had that understanding existed, the Board possessed insufficient powers to pursue it and what was worse, insufficient will. The collapse of 1929 demonstrated this, and the search for both went on in the 1930s. Like most other progressive regulatory measures, the banking reform of 1913 replaced uncoordinated strivings with an orderly, more centralized apparatus very friendly to the industry it was mandated to guide. The gain for efficiency was immediate, but the gain for other social goals took years and a different climate to materialize.

On the final issue on the New Freedom agenda, the trusts, there was the most embarrassing confusion. Progressivism had never spoken clearly or in one voice on the issue. Mr. Dooley expressed the prevailing ambivalence from his saloon on Halstead Street: "Th' trusts, . . . are heejous monsthers built up be th' inlightened enterprise iv th' men that have done so much to advance progress in our beloved country. . . . On wan hand I wud stamp thim under fut; on th' other hand not so fast." While all reformers were sure something ought to be done, only a few—like Senator Gilbert Hitchcock from Nebraska, where there were few trusts—wanted the courts to accept the literal line of the Sherman Act, making illegal all combinations or firms large enough to exercise market control, or in the law's words, to "restrain trade." Yet the Court, left without further guidance after the law of 1890, had decided by 1911 in the Standard Oil case that restraint of trade had to be "undue" restraint, the word *undue* inviting the

---

[5] It is quite clear from the brief congressional debate on the bill and from the accounts of the few interested and economically competent contemporaries that Congressman Glass and Senator Owen were probably the only men in the 531-member U.S. Congress who understood either the problem or the Federal Reserve bill, and one has doubts about Glass. One clue to the confusion of that body, a confusion that is thoroughly understandable, lies in the final vote in the Senate—the bill passed on 22 December, 1913 by a vote of 43–25. Since all 25 Nays were cast by Republicans, it is clear that the Senators were doing what they always do when the technical details of a matter are obscure, i.e., repairing to the firm ground of partisanship.

judges to refer to their own "standard of reason." In concrete cases, this meant that the Sherman law would be construed generously in favor of the corporations before the dock. Rather than leave the trusts to friendly judges, progressives produced innumerable proposals designed to create firm legal and moral ground somewhere between dissolution of all industrial combinations and the leniency of the Court. Before Wilson had time to clear up his thinking on the matter the congressional hoppers were full of proposals, and his own Attorney General, James McReynolds, had boldly added a drastic one of his own.

Wilson, in addition to being pledged to act on the monopoly question, was not a man who enjoyed confusion, and he set himself to think the matter through during a vacation in December, 1913. Of course he was not alone in wishing clarification. While a few businessmen felt comfortable with the issue in the hands of the Court, most did not like to pursue their schemes for expansion in a state of legal uncertainty. Administrations came and went, attorneys general came and went even more often, and no businessmen could be sure what would be thought reasonable and legal at any given time. This uncertainty inclined such men to prefer either a governmental commission to advise them in advance as to disputed portions of the law, or additional legislation spelling out what was permitted and what was proscribed.

But more than legal uncertainty brought businessmen into the camp of those wishing something done about the monopoly question. Despite the competitive ideal, the business community itself had for years spawned ingenious plans for avoiding "destructive" competition —competition that disordered the market and prevented anyone from planning intelligently. The "Gary dinners" were only the most civilized of these. Inevitably, a legal remedy appeared most appealing. The Congress could formulate a law specifying unfair practices in business, thus making illegal those forms of competition that disrupted plans and shortened tempers—and presumably making legal all those things businessmen wished to do toward bringing the market under control.

Wilson ultimately agreed with those, whether businessmen or aroused reformers, who counseled action rather than delay. He thought for a time that a law could be drafted explicitly prohibiting wrong ways of doing business, and the Clayton bill introduced in April, 1914, was

his chief proposal. But it soon became clear that it was permanently
unclear what was legal and what was not, since no law could keep
abreast of entrepreneurial inventiveness. Congressmen closest to the
question, the members of the Senate Interstate Commerce Committee, were cool to the idea of writing a permanent list of Thou-
Shalt-Nots, and they pressed Wilson to drop the Clayton approach.
Seeing no way to frame a law whose language alone would forever
demarcate monopoly from legitimate interfirm cooperation and planning, Wilson allowed himself to be persuaded by Brandeis, the lawyer
George Rublee, and a number of senators that the problem was best
passed on to a strong commission with a broad congressional mandate.
The commission could then search for the elusive public interest and
punish transgressors. Ignoring the New Freedom philosophy he had
articulated with such clarity, he cut the Clayton bill adrift and
placed his faith in regulation.

Once again, the progressives turned to the experts. The Federal
Trade Commission was established in September, 1914, and was
thought by business generally to have been a happy inspiration. There
was now an agency to advise businessmen what was legal and what
was not, before their (to them) well-meaning efforts landed them in
an expensive lawsuit. It was important to them that the commission
be staffed with men of large experience (in business) and friendly
disposition. They were not disappointed in Wilson's appointments, nor
in the spirit of the Federal Trade Commission and Justice Department
regulation during the war years and the 1920s. There were some
disgruntled New Freedom progressives who muttered about having
voted for Wilson and instead getting Roosevelt's New Nationalism,
but it was equally fair to say that the New Freedom philosophy had
never been adequate and that Wilson had been flexible enough to
see it. The important question was, had Wilson capitulated to the
interests of large business or had he provided the machinery by which
the national interest would henceforth prevail? As events were to
work out—many of them, such as the war, beyond Wilson's control—
the suspicions of the jilted New Freedomites were amply justified.
Wilson spoke the truth when he declared, after signing the bill establishing the FTC, that "the road at last lies clear and firm before
business."

After years of ambivalence and confusion over the issue of business
combination, the progressive generation had reached a decision of

sorts. The government would permit that stabilization that established business interests sought, but it was pledged to police the game so that flagrant collusion was not allowed to anesthetize the market. Experts were hired to look after a matter that had proven too intricate for the representatives of the public. A predictable commission replaced a variable Department of Justice and changeable Congress, a gain for order but not necessarily for the competitive ideal or the claims of small business. As to the public interest, there was no agreement on what had become of it or into whose hands it had been delivered. But since much of progressivism had to do with imposing order on confusion, this third achievement of Woodrow Wilson's first administration was one of the culminating moments of progressivism.

The hard fight for these measures occupied an exhausting eighteen months, and Wilson declared the end of progressivism in a letter to McAdoo in November, 1914. A business recession of that year reinforced his feelings that enough had been done to clear the road and that clearing the road was enough. Wilson announced his contentment with the reformed status quo. Legislation to aid special groups was not progressivism to him, and in 1914–15 Wilson killed long-range agricultural credits, fought off organized labor's demands for exemption from the antitrust laws, resisted a national child labor bill and a Constitutional amendment permitting women to vote in federal elections. He continued to ignore the few reformers such as Oswald Garrison Villard, who pressed the cause of the American Negro on him, and his administration extended racial segregation in the federal services.

But a number of pressures, about which historians disagree, forced Wilson to gradually abandon his principled objection to an active, paternalistic role for the government. He signed the LaFollette Seaman's Act in March of 1915, although it obviously conferred upon one sector of the citizenry a boon denied to others, a precedent sure to excite a clamor from other aggrieved groups. He had breached his New Freedom position again, just as in the struggle for a monopoly law, and moved further toward the New Nationalism. The approach of the election of 1916 finished his education in the virtues of a more active government. Proving himself more a political leader than an ideologue, Wilson moved to befriend those groups who stood to make his reelection possible.

Historians have called this 1916 burst a radical phase, and in some sense it was. Wilson appointed the liberal Jew, Louis D. Brandeis, to the Supreme Court, an act that sent fear and fury through those Arthur Link calls "the masters of capital." Their dismay was understandable, as the high court had always belonged not only to Anglo-Saxons but to conservative ones. A system of federal farm loan banks was established with Wilson's blessing in 1916 to provide the long-sought rural credit. Wilson now supported a workman's compensation bill for federal workers and the Keating-Owen child labor bill, and both were enacted. He signed into law a measure establishing the U.S. Shipping Board, an agency empowered to build or charter vessels and to regulate rates on the ocean. Social Justice progressives were sure their hour had come.

But the hour was only partially allotted to them. The decision to commit the government to the aid of pressing special interests was not radical. It seemed so because some of these groups were underdogs, and to aid them appeared to force justice upon the system. But the willingness to pass special legislation was neither radical nor conservative. Everything depended upon the groups aided. Count as evidence of radicalism, or at least advanced progressivism, the prohibition of child labor, workman's compensation for federal workers, and perhaps —some argument is possible—the rural credits bill. The Adamson Act granting an eight-hour day to railroad workers is hard to categorize, since with the help of the ICC the costs were passed on to consumers. But now that the government was answering to pressures there were sure to be gains for those already strong. Wilson backed a tariff commission that would be friendlier to protection than the Congress (Wilson's biographer Arthur Link called the Tariff Commission "a victory for protectionists"), an emergency tariff protection for chemical industries threatened by German dumping, legislation allowing firms in the export trade to violate the antitrust laws and a businessman's advisory group to establish early control over the imminent mobilization process.

True, 1916 was a big year for reform forces, for the Democratic Party had jettisoned its Constitutional scruples. But it was also a big year for those already wealthy and powerful, for they could do as well—even better—in an open struggle for governmental benefits as the do-gooders on leave from Hull House. The progressive era by 1916 had brought an active, intervening government. Which groups this government would favor remained still a matter of pressure, luck, and politics. As much as advanced Social Justice progressives complained about Wilson's capitulations to businessmen, it was clear from the way they voted in 1916 that the president was thought to have a leaning toward using government for afflicting the comfortable and comforting the afflicted, all things being equal. In this they read his mind correctly, to his eternal credit. But a war he did not seek diverted Wilson from this phase of advanced progressivism toward another type of reform—the remaking of international relations. In the process—and it was a complicated process—most of the progressive hopes of 1916 were rudely disappointed.

part two

WAR: 1914-1918

On 4 August, 1914, a war started in Europe, and before it was over on 11 November, 1918, men had shot, stabbed, gassed, and drowned each other, finally killing 8–10 million of each other—the bulk of the young, educated elites in each participating country. The survivors carried away memories of months and years of mud, boils, diarrhea, fear, and mutiny. It was a performance for which it was hard to devise proper adjectives, owing to the inadequacies of words like *insane, barbaric, meaningless,* and so on. For the first three years the war was almost entirely a European affair, and it raised some fundamental doubts about Europeans, about mankind, indeed about God himself. Americans could make little sense of it at all and almost unanimously assumed that such an irrational orgy had nothing to do with their country, where life was going forward so satisfactorily.

Their newspapers invented euphemisms like "fronts," "advances," "barrages," utilized maps and arrows, and in these forms provided the reading public with a minimal dose of information about the situation. Belligerent propaganda services attempted to supplement this with pictures of actual violence and indecently graphic stories of the crimes of soldiers, but these glimpses of the horror of Europe produced no widespread feeling that the war had any meaning for neutral America. We had nothing to do with such things. In the words of the American President, Woodrow Wilson, America must be "neutral in fact as well as in name...impartial in thought as well as in action."

Thirty-two months after the carnage had begun, on 2 April, 1917, this man went before a joint session of Congress and asked the nation to join in the war. Of some, more would be asked than of others. It was "a message," he frankly admitted to a friend, "of death for our young men." Within the week the Congress sent a war declaration to the president for his signature. For the country at large, this meant that the U. S. government would over the next eighteen months require the bodily service of 5 million men, would requisition some $33 billion of the national wealth, would exercise the right to allocate resources, fix prices, wages, and standards, and imprison men for improper speech and publication. For some 130,000 young males, the demands of our foreign policy were translated into a very compact sacrifice. The burdens of national defense are always distributed unevenly. Walter Hines Page, age 60 in 1914, and American Ambassador to Great Britain, wanted very much for "his country" to join the war against Germany. On 25 June, 1918, his nephew Allison Page was shot dead in a scrubby forest near the French village of Belleau.

Early death is always thought provoking. Young Page's curiosity about the ends to which he was being put, if he was ever curious, ended in a ditch in northern France. And there were some, including his uncle, who never doubted the worth of this and other sacrifices distributed somewhat unevenly among the people. But a great disillusionment set in after the war. Perhaps such sacrifices had been in vain. This note was strong in postwar literature, as for example in George Santayana's *The Last Puritan:*

> I should be glad to die now, if I could find something to die for. These poor recruits are told that they are dying for their country. That's sheer cant. Nobody knows whether he's doing his country any

good by dying for it, or whether his country is better worth dying for than any other. And what is one's country, anyhow? A piece of land? How is a piece of land in danger? Institutions and ideas? But institutions and ideas are always changing; by dying to preserve one set you will be creating another.... It's a blind current that sweeps us on, we don't know for how long or to what issue.

Historians, naturally, were more specific. Many of them in the 1920s and 1930s became revisionists, critical of the decisions reached by American leadership in the neutrality period. They piled up a literature of condemnation, told a story of unofficial selfishness and official folly. The years, however, have brought a new attitude. We have no more taste for angry condemnation. Problems of policy-makers seem staggering. Having seen no president shape an entirely successful foreign policy, our standards are more realistic. It now appears to many scholars that we would do better to understand the interplay of events and the process of decision-making than to search for fools. In the words of Ernest May, Harvard's respected diplomatic historian, one leaves the study of American policy in the years 1914–17 with "a sense that it could not have ended otherwise."

A strong note of historical determinism seems just the antidote for the runaway indignation of revisionists, who, through no fault of their own, were not yet educated by the unfolding years of unmanageable foreign relations and the enormous pressures for a broader American involvement in world affairs. But surely policy-makers in the 1914–17 period had some choices. If so, and if, after choosing, their hopes were disappointed, then possibly their choices were wrong. Granting this, the study of such errors might help reduce disappointment and social cost in the future. John F. Kennedy was of this mind when he tried to apply what he had learned from reading Barbara Tuchman's *The Guns of August* to the Cuban crisis of the autumn of 1962. Secretary of State Dean Rusk reflected on the Munich Agreement of 1938, and it led him to advise the commitment of American troops in Vietnam. I do not cite these applications of historical study with uniform approval, but one must approve of the effort to discipline the decision-making faculties through a thoughtful study of the past. And if historians will not help, busy public figures will do it for themselves.

Such a purpose for historical study involves a dispassionate attempt to understand how things happen (and, as Lewis Namier said, how they don't happen), but also implies that one look hard for errors as well as success. But it is no invitation to unrestrained moralists. Let them find their therapy elsewhere. It constitutes a legitimate and valuable effort, methodologically imperfect and usually futile, to fend off tomorrow's disasters.

In August, 1914, there seemed to be no chance that any American would be a combatant in the war. Indeed, most English and German boys had reason to expect to miss the thrill of combat, as a short war was universally predicted. Modern armies were irresistible, and they were also so expensive that the struggle could not be supported for more than a few months. In addition to the short life expectancy of this European quarrel, American males who were over seventeen and under forty were protected from any involvement by the broad agreement in the country that the war and its outcome were no concern of ours, and—there were a few dissenters here—that war was repugnant and pointless wherever it occurred. As a final comfort to those who might have worried about American life and limb, the American president, whose Constitutional and traditional powers over foreign policy had over the years become almost total, was a near-pacifist whose considerable personal talents were enlisted squarely behind the maintenance of neutrality.

Despite these conditions, the peace of the nation, if one looked quite closely, stood in a certain jeopardy. The country was in large cultural and ethnic debt to Great Britain, and a strong undercurrent of sympathy for the Allies soon developed and was sure to complicate the government's desire to be officially neutral. As for the government, where foreign policy is concerned the word refers to the president and those officials in a position by function, political power, or friendship, to influence or advise him. The composition of this part of the United States government, the decision-making part of it in the field of foreign policy, cast a slight and at that time unsuspected shadow over American neutrality. While almost any newspaper editor or large contributor to the Democratic Party might influence the president, Wilson was unusually independent and the group of real influentials was quite small. Secretary of State William Jennings Bryan was in fact impartial, but State Department counselor Robert Lansing (to be Secretary after Bryan's resignation in June, 1915) wished Britain to win, as did Ambassador Walter Hines Page in

London, Wilson's personal secretary Joseph Tumulty, and most (in the end, all) of the Cabinet, including the potent figure William G. McAdoo, Secretary of the Treasury and Wilson's son-in-law. The president himself, although a man of mixed feelings, was pro-Ally. In addition to these officials, the president took advice from his friend colonel Edward M. House of Texas, and from his wife (after December 18, 1915) Edith Bolling Galt Wilson, both of whom were strongly pro-British. The chairmen of the Senate and House Committees on Foreign Relations and Foreign Affairs (Sen. William J. Stone and Rep. Henry D. Flood) were both impartial, but either they did not try or were not allowed to influence policy. Thus the people with whom the president discussed policy, and from whom he regularly received news and advice, with the one exception of Bryan, saw to it, some consciously and some unconsciously, that his patience was encouraged in one direction and his inflexibility and suspicion in another. This did not mean there must be war with Germany. It simply meant that American policy would be shaped by men who were partial to the Allies.

But more important than pro-Ally sympathies in the nation at large and in the president's circle of advisers, American neutrality was menaced by the geographic, military, and economic facts of life. When the war was not won by land armies in a few weeks, the sources of supply became all-important. The United States, industrially advanced and organized at all levels for profit, grew rather quickly into a major supplier to a Europe whose demands for steel, brass, cotton, and other materials had suddenly increased. Both belligerent blocs would try to interdict goods bound for the other, but Germany, her surface naval forces soon swept from the seas, would interdict by submarine and torpedo, while the Allies would interdict by edict, surface capture, docking, and confiscation. Death by drowning was the frequent consequence of the former; the irritations of delay and property loss, along with some very distant German nutritional problems, were the consequence of the latter. The naval and geographic facts of life arranged that the Allies purchase most of the trade, and the Central Powers deal out most of the violence. The pressure that ultimately shattered American neutrality came from these circumstances, which were little appreciated at the beginning. For two and a half years Wilson, with the help of the German Chancellor and Foreign Office, sought to alter or evade these circumstances. These were the most fateful years in the history of American diplomacy since Adams, Franklin, Madison, and Jay had navigated clear of the perils of Europe.

August 1914–December 1914

Serious problems concerning the American relation to the war arose only in 1915, and it was not until 1916 that the concentration of the president and the Congress on questions of foreign policy came to overshadow all other national business. Yet in the early months of the war, in the summer and fall of 1914, fateful decisions were made, often without extended consideration and by second-rank officials, which were to permanently narrow the range of American alternatives. The first decision had to do with the Declaration of London, a convention drawn up at British insistence in 1909 (which Commons but not the Lords had ratified) that offered reasonably clear guidelines as to rights of neutrals on the seas. The declaration left certain important American export products, such as cotton and copper, on the free list (no interference permitted), and in general provided such broad rights of neutrals as to make an ocean blockade ineffective. The British navy under an Order in Council of 20 August had set aside the contraband categories of the declaration and the rights therein guaranteed to neutrals, and on 26 September the U. S. government demanded that the British observe the Declaration of London, which the lawyers in the State Department regarded as the most definitive statement of international law. Before the British had time to reply, the United States began to yield. House, aided by the British Ambassador Sir Cecil Spring-Rice, persuaded Wilson to send a telegram softening the 26 September note, and Page in London took the rest of the sternness out of the note in his amicable discussions with Foreign Secretary Sir Edward Grey. A tone of conciliation was established, and for four weeks the two governments disagreed, the Americans urging observation of at least the "free list" portions of the Declaration, the British adamant that the present war could not be conducted by the old rules, especially if they were found in unratified treaties. On October 22, State Department Counselor Lansing gave up the struggle and abandoned the Declaration, and nothing was heard from Wilson. The American government would flounder for more than two years in an effort to establish some other clear definition of a line between those British harassments that were permissible and those that were intolerable infringements of neutral rights.

In the same autumn three other important decisions were made at various levels in the government, none of them engaging the full attention of the president, whose wife had died in August. The British Admiralty announced a mine blockade of the North Sea, and the United States acquiesced.[1] When the Americans later protested the German declaration of a war zone around the British Isles, the comparison with our acquiescence in the North Sea blockade suggested unneutrality to men from central Europe who did not appreciate the subtleties of international law. A second decision had to do with armed merchantmen. It was the duty of a neutral to prevent its ports from serving as naval bases for belligerents, but "defensive" armament against pirates remained an archaic provision of the international legal system, such as it was. When British merchantmen began to arrive in New York with mounted guns, the German government protested that they were warships intended for aggressive use and should be impounded by the United States. Counselor Lansing secured the permission of Bryan and Wilson to issue a ruling on September 19 differentiating between defensive and offensive armament, a ruling that generally permitted merchantmen to mount guns of less than six-inch caliber aft. It was a fateful decision. Six months later such defensively armed merchantmen were under Admiralty orders to open fire on submarines at sight, but they used American ports as privileged vessels of innocent commerce. Technically, Lansing had a case. Under traditional law the British merchant fleet had the right to arm itself against lurking pirates. The Germans were apparently not very good lawyers. They thought the ruling unneutral. Whatever they thought, the Armed Ship circular of September 19 was to cause endless trouble later in the war.

A third decision concerned war financing. In October, both Wilson and Bryan, under extreme pressure from bankers, allowed it to be known that the government's disapproval of private loans to belligerents, expressed on August 15, did not extend to credits, of which the government promised to take no notice. The difference between loans and credits seemed a major one to the principled men in the

[1] A weak protest was finally dispatched on December 28, and nothing was heard of it again.

executive branch, but a minor one to bankers with good European clients, and the financing of American trade with belligerents—which in effect meant the Allies—went forward at once.

By the end of 1914 the American government had made several fateful decisions, most of them by secondary officials. It had been decided that neutral rights, whatever they did include, did not include the rights specified in the Declaration of London, and that neutrality was not compromised by expanding trade on a deficit basis with the maritime belligerents. In each case the government was acquiescing in developments that had tremendous pressure behind them, and opposing ideas and interests were neither intellectually nor politically mobilized. If one expects of government that it respond to the existing pressures, it may be admitted that the course taken in these cases was not surprising. But in the anguished days of spring, 1917, Wilson would surely have given much for the chance to live the autumn of 1914 over again.

January 1915–September 1915

As 1915 opened, few Americans doubted that their country should, and would, wait out the war in official neutrality. In five months we were at the edge of war, with a new respect for the mighty, impersonal currents of events and interests that pulled a peace-loving people toward what still appeared to most of them a pointless war. In view of the inability of the German army to win a quick victory on land, the German Admiralty convinced their emperor, sometimes called "The All-Highest" (he was really a middle-aged man named William Hohenzollern) to inaugurate submarine warfare against allied shipping. The announcement was made to neutrals on February 4, and the twenty-eight German submarines were to commence what the admirals hoped would be their deadly work on February 18. The Germans not only did not know precisely what to expect from the U-boats, but were also unsure of the attitudes of neutrals carrying on commerce with the Atlantic ports. They were surprised at the general vehemence of neutral comment, but especially by the stern tone of Woodrow Wilson, who declared that Germany would be held to "strict accountability" for any infringement of neutral rights. Wilson's warning hardly clarified the situation. Neutral rights, uncertain in the face of the unprecedented de facto (but never, by anyone's claim, "legal") blockade such as Britain was gradually tightening around Germany, were even less clear in the event of a submarine campaign. At first thought it might seem that neutrals would not be affected by U-boat warfare against Allied shipping, but both Wilson and the German leadership had a vision of what was coming. U-boats crept along under the sea, their periscopes washed by brine and fog, their crews tense and cramped. If they surfaced to identify, board, inspect, and order passenger removal, all before attack, they were vulnerable to gunfire and ramming; if they did not, the job of identification, especially if Allied ships ran neutral flags, could not be accomplished without mistakes. Hence the danger to neutrals, and, if there was such a thing, neutral rights.

America's problems with England were real enough, with ships stopped and towed to port for delays and confiscation, mails interrupted, and endless arguments about what constituted contraband. But there were no deaths, and the incidents were spaced, tedious, and clouded in legal complexity. A U-boat campaign, in lurid contrast, would bring large numbers of men to their deaths, trapped screaming in iron hulls breached by the icy Atlantic. The strain of any such atrocities, which were sure to be displayed in all their horror on the front page of newspapers, might prove too much for sentiments of neutrality.

Wilson and his advisers saw this and hoped a way might be found to lift both the blockade and the submarine campaign before either became fixed. The days of February and March, 1915, were full of diplomatic activity, as befitted men who knew themselves to be at a turning point. Communications were sent to determine if the belligerent governments might retrace their steps. The German government seemed willing to call off its submarines if Britain would allow food into Germany. Secretary Bryan, sensing deliverance, persuaded Wilson to appeal to both sides for a modus vivendi—no submarine attacks without warning, in return for no misuse of neutral flags, no arming of merchantmen, and the entry of noncontraband into Germany. Germany agreed in a note of February 20, but seemed to wish the category contraband shrunk back to something like the Declaration of London limits. This meant the British would be allowed to intercept only the obvious implements of war, effectively eliminating their blockade. The British, never for a moment considering trading their stranglehold for the recall of twenty-eight submarines of doubtful effectiveness, ignored the Wilson-Bryan offer and declared a total blockade on March 11 in "retaliation" for the submarine campaign inaugurated three weeks earlier.

The Bryan modus vivendi failed, but it appears in retrospect to have been one of those moments when events might have been altered. Strong American pressure at this time might have forced both sides to strictly limit their naval war—although admittedly it was Britain, the nation we wished least to antagonize, who was required to yield the most. There were political materials inside each bloc that American diplomacy might have catalyzed against unyielding governments. The British government actually felt their position vulnerable even after the decision of March 11, and as late as June was not willing to refuse discussions of Bryan's idea. The Germans, understandably, were even closer to some arrangement whereby the submarines might be traded for supplies. Such an arrangement, or even long talks about such an arrangement, would have avoided the sinkings of April and the resultant tie-up in German-American relations, which prevented Wilson's mediation efforts from getting underway until the fall. But admittedly any mutually acceptable limits on the naval war faced great odds, and American diplomacy was far from being sufficiently resolute to capitalize on the scurrying opportunities of that spring. Soon the sinkings started, preoccupying Wilson's government through murderous months with their hardening effects on the spirit of compromise.

The mistakes that had been feared were not long in coming. On March 28 the *Falaba* went down with one American death; the *Cushing* on April 29; the *Gulflight* on May 1. Then on 7 May, 1915, the Cunard liner *Lusitania,* fast and modern, came carelessly close to Ireland, and Lt. Schweiger was able to gain a great victory for Germany and for all those fine things for which she selflessly fought, killing with one torpedo 1,198 men, women, and children (among them 128 Americans).

The American press inflamed itself in a ritual of patriotism and Christian indignation, helping to force Wilson, who turned out to be very cautious where actions were concerned, to make it clear what he had meant by "strict accountability." Had he meant a strict postwar financial accounting, as he apparently had in mind in the case of British violations of neutral rights, or would he press for satisfaction now? And would he settle with the Germans separately, or link the sides together in their crimes, not holding the one to proper behavior if he could not hold them both? Bryan advised the safest course in both instances—no showdown with Germany now, and a joint demand upon both belligerents. Wilson chose to insist that Germany repudiate her tactics at once (Britain would be given more time), and chose to deal with the belligerents one at a time, Germany first. Over these issues Bryan resigned and took up opposition on the peace wing of American opinion.

Despite Wilson's hard line, the negotiations with the Germans over the *Lusitania* dragged out. The Germans decided secretly to insure the safety of passenger liners but were unwilling to apologize. Wilson, while insisting on a curb on U-boats, gradually retreated from his early insistence that submarine warfare be discontinued altogether. Then on August 19 a submarine sank the *Arabic* with two American deaths, an act that generated more American pressure and led the German government to issue the *"Arabic* Pledge" of September 1. Germany would not attack liners, whatever their flag, without warning. The status of merchantmen was unclear; they were not included in the pledge to observe cruiser rules. But Wilson had at least forced the Central Powers to modify their tactics and leash the Admirals. There would be no more *Lusitanias*.

The War Hawks—Theodore Roosevelt, Henry Watterson of the Louisville *Courier-Journal,* and others—were unhappy with Wilson's patient diplomatic style. But most of the country could hardly have failed to reflect with some sobering effect upon how close the country had come to a break with Germany, and therefore possibly even to war, over the right of American citizens to sail into the war zone on ships of any flag carrying any form of contraband. Many were aware that the *Arabic* Pledge had settled little and that there would be more trouble with the submarine if the administration adhered to its broad definition of American rights. Wilson would find in the next round of crisis diplomacy that the dissenters were prepared to take the reins of diplomacy from his hands if he ran risks that they thought unjustified.

September 1915–December 1915

Just as the year 1915 brought no decision in the war in Europe, so it brought no resolution of the problems of the United States as she

attempted to profit from the war without being inconvenienced by it.
During the fall both sides continued in one form or another to injure
American feelings in undramatic but irritating ways; but Wilson
produced no ultimatums and passed the weeks in a kind of smouldering
disagreement with both European blocs. A note of October 21 finally
informed the British that we completely denied their right to institute
the sort of blockade they had declared in March, but said nothing
about retaliation. The principal problems were still with Germany,
but here also there were nagging doubts and disagreements without
any resolution. Wilson had won a respite from German attacks on
passenger liners of all flags, but the status of belligerent merchantmen
was uncertain. Relations with Germany were strained in November by
the revelations in the *New York World* of German efforts to foment
strikes or outright sabotage efforts in munitions industries, and by the
November 7 sinking of the Italian liner *Ancona* with heavy loss of life.
A satisfactory disavowal and indemnity had not yet been obtained
from Germany regarding the *Lusitania,* and the exchange of irritating
notes on that issue strung out through the final months of 1915.

One of the most important decisions of 1915 was made almost by
default. While Bryan's loan ban had been relaxed to permit interbank
credits, the disapproval of outright loans set a limit upon the amount
of financing that American banks could offer the Allies. Informed
of a British financial crisis in August, 1915, Secretary McAdoo pled
with Wilson for an explicit governmental permission to the banking
community to extend loans of large size to the Entente powers, even
if this meant public bond drives. Wilson was hesitant, but was under
pressure from Lansing, McAdoo, and the bankers, and finally responded to Lansing's argument that to refuse loans would dry up the
U. S.-British trade and produce "industrial depression, idle capital
and idle labor, numerous failures, financial demoralization, and
general unrest and suffering among the laboring classes." In October
Wilson transmitted to Wall Street an oral acquiescence (he would
not put anything in writing on the subject) in an expanded loan program. Although the first public loan did not go well, credit was no
longer a problem to the Allies, and the trade with them accelerated.
Business was stimulated, as all had predicted, and Wilson owed his
reelection in 1916 in part to the economic health generated by the
war trade. In March, 1917, American loans to the Allies would total
$2,262,827,544 (as against German loans of about $27 million).

Yet the situation was not without its price. Wilson's desire to mediate between the belligerents was fatally handicapped, as far as the Germans were concerned, by the fact that the United States was supplying the Allies with the implements of war. Wilson had not planned this development, but reasoned that it would have been unneutral to interfere, through an embargo on arms trade or on loans, with a natural economic development of this sort. But one suspects he would have approached this problem differently had he foreseen how the economic ties with the Allies would destroy his potential as a mediator in the desperate days of 1916.

While at the end of 1915 the state of American foreign policy, the mind of the president, and public opinion itself were all confused and unresolved, the year had revealed some things with reasonable clarity. The American president was not treating the antagonists in similar ways, in part, but only in part, because the antagonists were not treating American commerce in similar ways. With Germany, while Wilson permitted delays, he seemed bent upon forcing a humane naval war even if the land war were totally without rules. With Britain he argued American rights less insistently and seemed willing to accept postwar adjustment of claims. "We are face to face with something they are going to do," Wilson wrote Bryan after the British announced their blockade, "and they are going to do it no matter what representations we make." When the United States protested the blockade in a note of 30 March, 1915, the British were allowed an undisturbed three months in which to reply, and the State Department answered their July note in late October. Robert Lansing explained the process in his *War Memoirs:*

> The notes that were sent [to Britain] were long and exhaustive treatises which opened up new subjects of discussion rather than closing those in controversy. Short and emphatic notes were dangerous. Everything was submerged in verbosity. It was done with deliberate purpose. It insured continuance of the controversies...

There were many reasons for this dual diplomacy, among them the difference in naval methods, the pro-ally sympathies of Wilson and his advisers, the economic involvement of the country with the Entente, the adroitness of British diplomacy, and the occasional ineptitude of the German government. But while American diplomacy came to bear with more firmness upon the Central Powers than upon the Allies, American belligerency was yet far off. The American public was still overwhelmingly against military involvement, even if the

Lusitania incident had shifted public sympathies considerably. And almost equally important among those factors tending to block or delay American belligerency was the fact that the American president was not yet committed to an Allied victory, not yet convinced that both sides were not in some respects in the wrong, not willing to forgive the Allies forever for their maritime affronts—in short, still far from possessing any consistent desire to maneuver this country toward intervention.

1916

Wilson was acutely aware of how close America was to war as 1916 opened, and he worked to enlarge and activate those alternatives that history and his own decisions had left him. He was attracted, early in the year, to a proposal made by Lansing aimed at reducing the loss of life incident to submarine warfare. Wilson's demands upon Germany came down essentially to the requirement that submarines operate on the surface by cruiser rules. This idea had little appeal for the Germans, not because they preferred to lurk out of sight to satisfy some defect in their national character, but because the Allies began arming ships—usually in concealed bays—and firing on submarines that came considerately to the surface. Craft called Q-boats, gunboats disguised as dumpy merchantmen, began to operate around the British Isles in 1915. On August 19, for example, the submarine U-27 was surprised and sunk by the tramp steamer (under an American flag) *Baralong* as she was in the act of legally searching a halted vessel. The *Baralong,* which became the British Q-boat *Baralong* seconds before opening fire, made the occasion more memorable in the German navy by firing on the submarine crew in the water after the sub itself was sunk. So long as submarine commanders could expect such incidents, they would tend to attack from below surface; so long as they attacked with only periscope identification, mistakes would occur—neutral vessels, even liners, might innocently attract an undeserved and unintended torpedo.

The president was aware of this problem and was therefore enthusiastic when on January 7 Lansing suggested a modus vivendi by which the United States would force the disarmament of commercial vessels by impounding any armed vessels putting into American ports. Germany, for her part, could then observe cruiser rules. The

American government sent the proposal to the Allied capitals on January 18 for their reaction.

It seems in retrospect to have been a promising step for a president who wished to stay out of the war. The Germans appeared to welcome the idea, and the United States could have adopted such a modus vivendi whether the Allies liked it or not. Other neutrals, such as Holland, had done so from the beginning. But Wilson abandoned the modus vivendi when the British response was a bitter negative, not because he agreed with their argument that his proposal was unneutral, but because their attitude toward the modus vivendi imperiled his other and to him more important effort of 1916—mediation. To mediate he must be regarded as a true neutral by the British, and to achieve this position he was willing to sacrifice all secondary lines of strategy.

Wilson had hoped to mediate a compromise peace since the first days of the conflict. He had tendered his services as conciliator in August, 1914, and had encouraged both Bryan's mediation inquiry of September and Colonel House's exploratory trip to Europe in the Spring of 1915. Wilson had little grasp of the details of territorial demands, the military situation, or special treaties that bounded the areas of real negotiation. But he saw with clarity what only a few Europeans kept in view, that the best outcome for everyone concerned was an end to the war without victory for either side. And he had a powerful—and a very natural—desire to be the personal agent of such a healing settlement. The *Lusitania* and *Arabic* incidents lent urgency to his thoughts of mediation, and he cast about for an effective form for his diplomatic intervention.

It appeared that he had found it in a bold proposal of House, broached to the president in October, 1915. House had for some time been worried that the country might drift into war with Germany over some technical infraction by a submarine, and would in such circumstances lack the national unity and intellectual conviction that House thought necessary to carry the nation through to a proper culmination. He therefore offered the following plan: the United States would propose a peace conference when it received an Allied signal that their arms were successful and they were confident of the results of peace negotiations; the Germans would either accept the American invitation to talks, in which case there would be peace (favorable to the Allies), or if they did not the United States would enter the war on the side of the Allies. In the latter case the American people would be united by the knowledge that Germany was irredeemably warlike and insatiable.

The president was at first stunned by the boldness of House's idea (and probably also by its blatant unneutrality), but House took his silence for acquiescence, and there followed one of the strangest and most confused episodes in the records of American diplomacy. House drafted a letter to British Foreign Secretary Sir Edward Grey, sketching his plan briefly and suggesting further discussions in Europe. Grey and the British seemed interested, if cautious, and House set sail on December 28, never suspecting how cool they were both to him and to any talk of a negotiated peace. The Colonel made the rounds of the European capitals, engaging in earnest after-dinner talks with wary heads of state and foreign ministers who trusted neither him, Wilson, nor the enemy, and who knew all along that their war-embittered publics would never agree to any settlement that brought them so little advantage that the enemy could be induced to sign it. The desire to end the war short of victory was almost nonexistent in governing circles in January and February of 1916 when House made his rounds, for each side dreamed of the massive blows their armies would deal to the foe when the weather improved. But House, who avoided precise territorial details and did not sense the gap between the demands of the rivals, pressed hard for the agreement. Grey was amiable enough over the matter. He saw to it that the memo contained no action date and could be invoked only by the British when they were ready. Grey saw no risks for Britain, and there were none; the risks were in a rebuff. A delighted House returned on March 6 to present Wilson with an agreement initialed by the British Foreign Secretary.

The House-Grey Memorandum stipulated that the president, upon hearing from Britain and France that the time had arrived (meaning the Allies were winning and would deal from strength in negotiations), would propose peace talks. When the Germans did as expected and refused to consider negotiations, the United States would *probably* (Wilson inserted the word, making British doubts about the whole arrangement virtually total; Wilson, considering congressional and public opinion, could hardly have done otherwise) enter the war on the side of the Allies. To House, the agreement meant an end to the American dilemma. To the British it meant nothing at all. Yet upon it Wilson fastened his great hopes for impartial mediation; and to it he sacrificed the Lansing modus vivendi when Britain made it clear that she thought the modus vivendi grossly unfair and destructive of Wilson's status as a true neutral. Lansing withdrew the modus vivendi on February 15, and House was able to bring home his vague and meaningless agreement. Thus as March arrived America was if anything closer to the war the president did not want than she had been in September when Germany gave the *Arabic* pledge. The submarines were active again, American trade with the Allies was increasing, and all the president had for five months' effort was a note signed by a Texan of independent means but no official position, and a skeptical British Foreign Secretary.

At this point another alternative offered itself, one in many ways more promising than the two Wilson had been trying. When the modus vivendi collapsed, leaving Wilson's strict accountability policy unaltered, and with Germany intensifying her submarine warfare, a large number of Congressmen with independent ideas about foreign policy could no longer be restrained. Since the fall of 1914 congressional hoppers had never been empty of proposals to insure American neutrality, most of them involving some form of embargo on munitions or a passenger ban or both. But foreign policy is traditionally as well as Constitutionally a presidential function, and Wilson, usually engaged in close negotiations to pressure a belligerent to alter its tactics, had successfully discouraged these bills as signs of moral infirmity that undercut his diplomatic efforts. He also shunned them as being reminiscent of the Jeffersonian embargo which was so politically disastrous a century before.

But by late February, 1916, Wilson faced a Congressional revolt. Ranking Congressional Democrats learned from the president on February 21 that he would go to any length to defend the right of American citizens to travel safely even on armed belligerent merchant ships, and the House was swept by a war panic. Sentiment for a passenger ban ran three to one by some estimates, and it threatened to mass behind the McLemore bill in the House and the Gore resolution in the Senate. It is hard not to see in these bills a line of policy that surrendered nothing that was vital to the American national interest, and yet that promised to virtually eliminate the chance of an inflammatory incident. Unfortunately, this healthy initiative came from what Wilson saw as a dangerous source—the Congress. Although he had earlier toyed with the idea of a passenger ban, the president now felt that his leadership was jeopardized, and that the passage of any important foreign policy measure at all that was not initiated by the administration would be not only an intolerable Constitutional affront but would damage his influence in European capitals. Afraid that he could never mediate if his authority were in question—it was proving difficult enough as it was—Wilson committed his full resources to crushing the Gore-McLemore proposals. Presidential conferences with leaders of both parties, intensive lobbying by McAdoo and Post-master General Burleson, and a strong presidential letter to Senator Stone made public on Feburary 24 brought many Congressmen to see another side of the issue, and support for the passenger ban fell off.

Wilson had shown again that, when fully aroused, he had no peers at the arts of politics—or perhaps some would prefer to say the arts of demagoguery. The letter to Stone must have taught any number of petty politicians and small-bore evangelists how it was done by one of the masters. In view of the long list of humiliations Wilson had found ways to live with since 1914, the most delicate thing a historian can say about such phrases as "once accept a single abatement of right and many other humiliations would certainly follow, and the whole fine fabric of international law might crumble under our hands piece by piece" is that they are embarrassing. Wilson here appears more rigid than he actually was, but talk of this sort exacts its price. While the letter and the entire presidential counterattack were suc-cessful in preserving the president's control of foreign policy, he found it hard to retreat from such principled peaks once his passions had cooled. And of course the largest part of the price was the loss of a promising alternative on the road to 2 April, 1917.

All the proposals and explorations of the fall and winter having changed nothing, the inevitable crisis promptly developed. The French packet *Sussex,* an unarmed passenger vessel, was torpedoed in the English Channel with the loss of fifty lives. Although this might sound callous to the souls of the fifty, what made the attack regret-table were injuries suffered by four Americans, who would not have been aboard (or would have been disavowed) had earlier measures to warn American citizens off ships in the war zone been enacted. Other attacks without warning on liners were reported in the days after the *Sussex* incident, and Wilson, despite reports that the public was not yet ready for a break with Germany, felt himself obliged by his entire line of diplomacy since the winter of 1915 to accept all risks and force Germany to choose between a modification of tactics and war with the United States. His note to Germany of April 18 was an ultimatum, demanding an end to submarine attacks on neutral as well as enemy commerce. The German government went through an intense struggle, and finally replied on May 4 with the *"Sussex* Pledge," promising to visit and search all vessels prior to attack. Since some vessels were armed, this meant a drastic curtailment of submarine warfare.

The president had a diplomatic victory, and the war once again seemed far away. But Wilson knew enough of the pressures within Germany—a navy with an extravagant pride in its submarines and its strategic judgment, an army stalemated, a public opinion frustrated at the leashing of the ultimate weapon in the midst of a protracted struggle—to know how fragile was the pledge of May 4. And while he had taken no official notice of it, he had read the concluding paragraph of the German pledge, which declared that if the United States did not "demand and insist that the British government shall forthwith observe the rules of international law universally recognized before the war," that the pledge would no longer be binding. Thus the German note was a kind of time bomb. In the time remaining, American neutrality rode with three historical possibilities, all of them to varying degrees improbable: a successful American effort to raise the British blockade, a quick peace through the victory of one side or the other, or a mediated peace without victory.

Wilson knew the first to be virtually impossible, and the second to be unlikely and also undesirable, since it would lay the seeds of another conflict no matter which side won a clear victory. With time running out, he tried to find the wisdom and the resolve that he might combine with the powers of his office (which he held subject to a November election) to try to bend the wild forces of European war and American domestic politics toward a type of settlement for which he and Colonel House had found no enthusiasm in two long years of probing. To be sure that Wilson understood the need for urgent action, Imperial Chancellor Bethmann-Hollweg dictated a message to the president through Ambassador Gerard on May 11, reporting that he was under extreme pressure from the Right and the Center parties in Germany as well as from the press and that he could not long restrain the admirals.

May 1916–January 1917

From May to July Wilson pressed the Allies to implement the House-Grey agreement, gradually becoming aware that they would never ask for a mediated peace, from which little territory could be gained (or regained), so long as military victory seemed possible. Allied war aims were far beyond what could be expected from any negotiated settlement, and their political leaders declined to suggest to their respective publics that the time had perhaps come to trade hopes of vengeance and territorial compensation for nothing more than an end to the killing. There are signs that the German government, and certainly the war-weary Austrian government, might have actually gone to a peace table and acknowledged that the war was unwinnable. Yet the war aims even of the relatively moderate coalition held together by Bethmann were sufficiently ambitious that talks with the Allies would probably have led nowhere. And groups with more annexationist goals were gaining strength within Germany. It is hard to see how Wilson, even had he arranged some sort of exploratory talks, could have brought about an actual settlement. We see now what he could not see, the irreconcilability of even the minimum war aims of the opposing blocs. The Allies would insist on their rights to Alsace-Lorraine, Russian control of the Dardanelles, and the restoration of Belgium, to mention only their leading requirements. If they submitted to talks in the summer of 1916, Germany, which held Belgium, northern France, and most of eastern Europe, would inevitably secure a settlement leaving her stronger than before the war and presumably unchastised. And even if they chose to trust Wilson to fight for more acceptable territorial arrangements—and few Allied leaders had such faith in Wilson—they could not be sure he would be president after 1916. As for the Central Powers, while they were moderately interested in talks, they had no intention of allowing Wilson to be present as mediator. In short, Wilson in the summer of 1916 sought to bring about a peace between governments that wanted peace less than they wanted some other things.

But surely the *people* of Europe were ready for an end to killing, even if it meant a compromise on war aims. Wilson finally saw that his only course was to abandon the House-Grey agreement, which forced him to wait in silence until the Allied governments were ready to negotiate, and to make a general public appeal such as he had made in August of 1914, and such as Bryan and the peace groups had urged many times in the interim. While it might embarrass certain governments (i.e., the Allies, whose military position made them hostile to a general appeal, which is why Wilson never made one), Wilson was sufficiently desperate to bring to bear upon them the pressure of their own domestic public opinion to force them to some response. If he could but get a statement of war aims in print, perhaps the terms would be bridgeable.

But to bridge the gap between belligerent war aims, given their present mood, would require his active participation; and he could not participate if either side thought him unneutral. He must prepare the ground by moving to an indisputably neutral position and then time his appeal so that neither side, faltering on the battlefield, would be able to charge that the appeal was a hostile act coming when it did. We may summarize in terms that seem accurate in retrospect but, if Wilson had summed up his chances thus, would have chilled his spirits and caused the young American males who did not yet pant for war to begin to wind up their affairs: the memories of German-American conflicts since 1914 would have to be erased by an effective attack upon the British blockade; the right wing in each country must yield to its enemies on the left sufficiently so that moderate war aims might come forward; the press in each nation must reverse themselves and begin to educate the public to accept a no-win policy; generals and admirals must lose confidence in one final land battle or undersea superweapon; and the situation on the battlefront must be so thoroughly stalemated, after a German retreat to the territorial status quo ante bellum, that neither side went to a conference with a significant geographical advantage. But Wilson did not see these obstacles as he looked ahead. He saw only, as he campaigned for reelection in the fall, that the American people did not want war, that time was running short on German forebearance, and that he must somehow bring peace or face national humiliation, division, or war, and perhaps all three.

The president therefore executed a remarkable diplomatic flanking maneuver and began to put serious pressure on friendly, democratic, heroic Britain. The British blockade, vexing even in its early stages, was by the summer of 1916 one constant interference. American ships were searched at sea or towed to harbor, mail was confiscated, American firms blacklisted, coaling facilities denied. These practices had been protested before, but by a State Department preoccupied with submarine crises. Now, in the late summer of 1916, there took place a sharp change in the volume and tone of American notes to London. And in September, going beyond protests for the first time, Wilson obtained from Congress legislation (which he never used) to deny port facilities to ships of any nation that discriminated against American commerce, and urged the Federal Reserve Board to restrain bankers who were financing the Allied war trade. The British blockade was not altered by such methods, but Wilson hoped the Germans would take his new tone as proof of an independent and neutral spirit. With the election out of the way in November he began to give thought to the drafting of a peace appeal.

He was unusually slow, but he had little reason to know that the most fortuitous moment (in an admittedly unpromising venture) had already passed. Bethmann was eager for a Wilsonian peace overture in August, when Germany faced a Rumania in revolt (not knowing she would be victorious there in December), the Reichstag had recently passed a peace resolution, and the relatively moderate Falkenhayn had not yet been replaced as Chief of Staff by the aggressive team of Hindenburg and Ludendorff. But Wilson refused to make his appeal before the election, possibly because of a scrupulous regard for political fairness, possibly because he was preoccupied, possibly because he knew the Allies were furious at the idea,[2] or out of some combination of the three. After the election he was delayed by a cold, a session of Congress, and the reorganization of the British government. On December 12, his own note nearly ready, he was surprised by the release of Germany's own peace overture to the Allies. He quickly issued his own message on December 18, asking all belligerents to state their terms, and expressing confidence that the objects of all nations were actually similar. Although he had toned down his note from his first draft, which clearly threatened American action against whichever bloc did not respond properly, Wilson's December 18 message nonetheless was, as Ernest May puts it, "the most dangerous document that Wilson approved since the House-Grey memorandum and the *Sussex* ultimatum." Preceded as it was by a German peace offer, it ran a very high risk of bringing Germany and America into

[2] Lloyd George, British Minister of War, in an interview with American newspaperman Roy Howard on September 28, denounced any talk of stopping short of a fight "to the finish—to a knock-out."

sympathetic alliance, a possibility that shocked Wilson's advisers and disquieted the president, but a possibility that he was willing to face rather than drop the idea of a peace move altogether.

But if in December there seemed the chilling possibility that Wilson's action would sour Anglo-American sympathies, there was by then no chance that it would actually bring about a compromise peace. This is not to say that American intervention was inevitable, since a few reasonable alternatives still seemed open; but bringing about a peace was not really one of them, despite the time spent on it in the closing days of 1916. This may be said today because we know more about belligerent war aims than Wilson could possibly have known, even if he had been deeply interested in the wearisome study of military and geographical details, which he was not.

It is possible to make too much of war aims. Many readers of Fritz Fischer's important book, *Germany's War Aims in the First World War,* have concluded from the sweep of Teutonic visions that Germany was totally and permanently beyond reason and her complete defeat was necessary for any sort of sensible outcome to the war. But Fischer's book is not about what the German government insisted upon at a conference called in a lull of a stalemated war; it is about the terms Germans used in arguing with each other about what the Fatherland deserved, all against the background of an optimistic military outlook (the military was always optimistic) and the efforts of various groups to demonstrate more patriotism (which meant annexing more territory) than their rivals. War aims in all countries were always in flux. They functioned in part as debating points against an enemy negotiator and were accordingly inflated to permit room for compromise.

They were also inflated because they were formulated by conservative political and military leaders in a setting of fierce political conflict between Right and Left, where it was understood that annexationist war aims strengthened the Right, and vice-versa. Instead of differing openly over the real issues between them,[3] i.e., property rights and constitutional reform, the Right and the Left in Germany (and everywhere else) fought a somewhat suppressed battle over whether to terminate the war in victory or in partial compromise, in

[3] Chancellor Bethmann practiced a policy he called "Burgfrieden," or putting domestic quarrels on ice. He discouraged all airing of divisive issues, including war aims, to keep his majority coalition intact.

huge annexations or modest ones. The Right was annexationist and victory-minded, the Left somewhat less of both, and each was sure that if it did not win on war aims the jig was up for its postwar political power and the economic interests it represented. So long as war aims were invested with such domestic political importance the terms of any discussion of them—internally, or between governments—were sure to be irrational and diplomatically misleading. This is not to say that there were important groups in Germany, out of power but capable of organizing a government, that held *moderate* war aims. War aims of the Left were simply less immoderate than those of the conservatives. But any shift of political power towards the Left would have altered German negotiation terms so as to favor Wilson's hopes for a compromise peace; so would a deterioration of the military situation, or the weakening of a principal ally. One can conceive of events that might have transformed German war aims from an insuperable barrier to merely a formidable one. The outrageous lists of territories to be annexed and indemnities to be paid that were circulated inside the German government do not, to my mind, foreclose the possibility of a negotiated settlement.

Yet even when we discount some of the discussion of war aims, which scholars now dig out of Foreign Office memos, letters, and position papers of general staffs, one has to admit nonetheless that the two sides were very far apart when Wilson made his plea. German officialdom was talking in terms of annexations including Alsace-Lorraine and indemnities against France, various territories in the East, concessions in Belgium which would make her a ward of Germany, colonial annexations in central Africa, the Azores, Tahiti, and annexation of parts of Serbia, Rumania, and Italy. The Allies were equally generous to parts of the world they deemed in need of liberation. When the Prime Minister asked various departments of the government what British terms should be in the late summer of 1916, the Foreign Office stated terms which they admitted could only be secured through Germany's defeat. The chief of the general staff argued that England should not even agree to an armistice until Germany promised to evacuate all occupied territory and surrender a portion of her fleet, and the same gentleman said in November that peace could only be considered by "cowards, cranks, and philosophers." The Allied reply to Wilson's overture, when it came on January 10, asked for the restoration of Belgium and Serbia with indemnities, the evacuation of

France, Russia, and Rumania, with reparations, and the "liberation" of all Slavs and Czechoslovaks, i.e., the suicide of the Austro-Hungarian Empire. "The war aims formulated by the Entente in camera," writes Fritz Fischer, "were not very much more modest than those of Germany."

No statesman could find common ground here. He would need the aid of internal upheavals and a large degree of luck besides. Wilson got neither in December, 1916. While he seems to have had in mind a settlement that today we would call fair, his ideas on the subject had no allure either for the Allies, who were led by men who believed their national existence required a broken Germany, or for the Central Powers, who held territory paid for in blood, which Wilson would surely confiscate if, as expected, he urged a peace along the lines of the status quo ante bellum.

War goals, of course, were not the real barrier, but a symbol of it. What prevented peace was the preference of the dominant groups in each bloc for a gamble on victory rather than submitting to the frustrations *and political risks* of compromise. In England, Asquith's government had never demonstrated the "weakness" of a real interest in going to the table with an undefeated Germany, and the accession of the Lloyd George government in early December if anything reinforced the British hard line. In Germany, Bethmann had formulated war aims in the late summer of 1916, which of course meant not that he polled the country or went to the universities to consult geographers and philosophers, but that he asked the Kaiser, the princes of the blood, admirals, and generals for their thoughtful suggestions as to what was the Fatherland's right, considering both her inherent virtue and her existing military advantages—and considering the political consequences to the ruling class if the war came to anything but a glorious end. The list of demands on the Allies that the chancellor somewhat reluctantly compiled adds new dimensions to the storied arrogance of the Teutonic mentality. Yet in both blocs the advice of the military was always to fight on, and while in normal times civilians could discount this, the war had swollen the military influence—who else would save the homeland?—to impressive proportions.

To be sure, there were in each bloc contrary pressures, groups, and individuals who urged a negotiated peace, but they were scattered and barred from power. In Germany, Bethmann's hints of a peace move in the fall of 1916 met with wide acclaim, especially from newspapers such as *Vorwarts,* organ of the Social Democratic Party, and a peace petition circulated by the socialists got nearly a million signatures. In England, the London *Nation* and the Manchester *Guardian* exerted their influence for compromise, portions of the Labour Party had similar tendencies, and the Cabinet itself contained some, including Lord Grey and Lord Lansdowne, who were at least open to the idea of a no-win peace.[4] But these were minority tendencies, and they were also at a disadvantage in that they bespoke the less satisfying human emotions—moderation, compromise, and a tiny bit of national self-doubt. Only a military disaster could have magnified their voices, and German arms were successful in the Balkans in the fall of 1916, while the Allies, bled by the Somme but no worse off on the ground than six months before, began to anticipate the submarine campaign that would bring American intervention.

Wilson's note had gone out on the eighteenth; after Christmas the replies came in, and they brought no pleasure to a peace-loving president, nor, one supposes, to the men in the filthy trenches. The Central Powers, on December 26, replied that their offer to talk had not included Wilson as mediator, and they declined to state war aims— which was taken to be a sign that their aims were shocking. Germany has been much criticized for this rebuff of Wilson. Arthur Link, Wilson's biographer, has argued that the president was by this time truly neutral and that Germany should have thrown herself upon his justice. But Link has had access to Wilson's papers. The Germans could only consult the past, and they found there little reason for trust. It is hard to see how one can expect a nation weary from three years of war, but with an advantage on the ground, to throw itself on the mercies of a man whose policies had so worked to the benefit of the Allies as to have staved off their almost certain defeat. At the same time that the president's countrymen made and sold the implements of war to Britain and France, Wilson curtailed the U-boat war to preserve the travel rights of a few tourists and businessmen. Wilson, the Germans knew, had never been neutral (they underestimated how hard it had been for him to enforce policies benefitting

4 Most outspoken opponents of the war were socialists: Ramsay Macdonald in Great Britain, Karl Kautsky and Karl Liebnecht in Germany, Fritz Adler in Austria. But occasionally one not only found a socialist leader hot for war to the end, but an aristocrat of unshakable social conservatism, like Lord Lansdowne, who openly questioned whether the war should be carried on much longer.

neither side, when one side commanded the sea); America had never acted impartially. They would not have been surprised at the now-famous note Wilson endorsed in the spring of 1916, which said in part: "Colonel House expressed the opinion that, if such a Conference met, it would secure peace on terms not unfavorable to the Allies; and, if it failed to secure peace, the U. S. would probably leave the Conference as a belligerent on the side of the Allies, if Germany was unreasonable." They would not have been startled had they learned that the Secretary of State in Wilson's "neutral" government wrote privately of Germany's "sinister purpose to dominate the world."

Perhaps Germany, expansionist as she was, would never have trusted a neutral. But that she should not have trusted Woodrow Wilson after more than two years of American neutrality was a fore-gone conclusion, and one for which Wilson himself was partly responsible. A few outbursts against England between May and De-cember were properly regarded as inexpensive gestures,[5] and altered nothing. It was not enough for Wilson to *be* truly neutral (as he seems to have been by December, 1916). He must provide the evidence, in policies as well as words, to reverse the deep impression he had made in all those months in which he headed a government of clearly pro-Allied sympathies. He did not do this—probably could not—but as a result Germany's suspicions remained and were both understandable and tragic. "I will not go to any Conference!" exploded the Kaiser when he read Wilson's December message. "Certainly not under his Chairmanship!" This in the same month that Wilson, speaking to House, said: "If Germany really wants peace she can get it, and get it soon, if she will but confide in me and let me have a chance."

To this line of argument some will answer that Wilson did what he could in the time he had between the *Sussex* Pledge and December—a time in which he also faced an election—and that the Germans, had they possessed any real desire for peace, could have apprized them-selves of his real mood. But while the Germans were admittedly stubborn, vain, brutal, and all of those German things that made them somewhat maladroit in diplomacy, they never possessed those conduits into official American circles that made British diplomatic judgment so flexible and successful from the beginning. A note from

---

5 Which is exactly what they were. The American Secretary of State wrote in the summer of 1916: "We must keep on exchanging notes [with England], because if we do not we will have to take radical measures."

Wilson came to the German government through Ambassador William Gerard, in whom Wilson (justifiably) placed little confidence, and it was for the German leaders to piece together what they could of this strange Presbyterian from cold print and their own skimpy intelligence reports. In Britain, Walter Hines Page carried notes to Whitehall to explain away their irritants and help compose an answer. In Washington, Colonel House, Lansing, and virtually the entire opinion-making establishment helped Wilson find the patience and insight to understand the plight of gallant England. With such friends, the Allied governments were not subject to the full extremes of mistrust as were the Central Powers, did not feel so out of communication and defensive.

A prime example—there are many—was Lansing's unauthorized activities following the president's note of December 18. The American appeal had come so close upon the German note that the Allies suspected collusion and were furious. But no less a figure than the Secretary of State relieved their minds. He called in the French ambassador Jusserand on December 20 to transmit assurances that the U. S. was firmly pro-Ally, and suggested that the Allies announce sweeping war aims (he sketched in a few, including a reformed and democratized Germany). He said the same things to British Ambassador Spring-Rice on December 22, urging London in effect to stiffen against Wilson's plans, scuttle peace talks, and await with confidence the inevitable German submarine campaign that would bring American intervention. Fortified with this news, which the ambassador at once telegraphed from Washington, the British government was not tempted to issue a peremptory refusal, which might have driven Wilson toward Germany, but at the same time was emboldened to make stiff demands, which fended off any peace talks. In a relaxed and leisurely way they prepared their January 10 reply, which conveyed terms so sweeping that a conference was out of the question, yet in language very friendly toward the U. S. The episode was one of many such occasions when the existence of special lines of communication between officials in Washington and London made Allied diplomacy proof against damaging extremes of ignorance and distrust. The severed German cable lines were symbolic of the lack of such lines of communication between Washington and the Central Powers, and this in part explains why Germany did not summon up the wisdom and the patience to entrust all her hopes to Woodrow Wilson in the winter of 1916–17, overruling the entreaties of her eager admirals, whose submarine fleet had now reached 103.

More was behind the failure of Wilson's last mediation attempt, of course, than poor communications or bad timing. War fed on sacrifices already made, blood already spilled, promises to allies of postwar spoils; peace meant sacrificing certain high and noble aims—glory, righteous vengeance, national security. Both hope and fear counseled another year of war. Hope transcended the glum facts of military stalemate, and hinted that one great springtime offensive would bring the victory that justified every sacrifice. But fear was at least as important, for it set the powerful elites of blood, land, and industry against talk of peace. The established classes sensed in their bones that a compromise peace was a strategem of the Left and would bring in its wake unsettlement, reform, revolution, the confiscation of property. They felt Bolshevism coming on. Count Westarp explained why the Conservative Party in Germany had shifted to annexationism and no-compromise after first seeing the war as defensive:

> The monarchist had to fear that the growth of radicalism, which is to be expected as a result of any war, would reach alarming proportions if the homecoming soldiers were to find as the reward for their heroism only an increased tax bill and were to become convinced that the government of the Kaiserreich had not understood how to profit from success in military operations.

In all countries, people of substance, whose governments had paid for the war by borrowing, counted upon the indemnities of victory to obviate a crushing postwar taxation, which would either bear heavily upon them, or radicalize the masses, or both. It should then be no surprise that the answer to Wilson's overture, both in diplomatic notes and in the language of the press and in windy speeches in the Reichstag and Parliament, was the language you expected from men who were not yet finished with war—talk of the righteousness of our cause, or the moral callousness of the American president who saw some justice on both sides, talk of the final and smashing victories over the enemies of humanity, hard, rigid, inflammatory talk, talk to stiffen the backs of the young men out in the mud and to underline the cowardice, the feminity, the treason of compromisers.

So the German reply of December 26 rebuffed Wilson's mediation and refused to state terms, and the Allied reply of January 10 stated terms Wilson found unreasonable. He pressed both sides to state their terms in private, where they might return to sanity. While he waited he composed and delivered before the Congress on January 22 the "Peace Without Victory" speech, in which he summarized the terms of a just and lasting peace. He thought it an important state paper, and indeed men in all countries saw in his address and his ideas a new opening out of the horror. But the interlude in which American mediation was even faintly possible ended on January 9, when, at Pless, the German government reached its decision for unrestricted submarine warfare. That door had closed. Europeans would continue to kill each other, and we were invited by both sides to leave our cash registers and pulpits and join them in the divine game.

1 February 1917 –2 April 1917

A different man might have asked for war at once, but Wilson hesitated even in breaking diplomatic relations. He was, of course, no pacifist; in two months he would ask for war. A different man might have waited forever. Even in the last weeks of American neutrality when all the big decisions had been made and there was little room, perhaps no room, to turn or reverse, a single man made a difference. Wilson was not entirely the plaything of fortune, unable to make the slightest personal contribution to history.

But granting the indeterminacy of those last days, one may say that any American president had at best one or two decisions he could make. Most courses were ruled out. Wilson's brief, vain effort of February to detach Austria from the war only underlined the absence of real, untried, promising alternatives. In this period we may see Wilson as waiting for public opinion to shift from indecision and mass behind belligerency. He waited while forces he could not see and certainly could not control—the track of torpedoes and darkened ships, the piling up of goods on American wharves, a sense of frustration among merchants and industrialists, the gradual dissipation of restraint under conditions of high tension—began to move America toward the trenches in France. But even if Wilson the politician waited for a clarification of public opinion, Wilson the intellectual grappled desperately with the issue, a pacifist intellectual with death at his back: "I am overwhelmed," he wrote a friend on 2 February, 1917; "my thought is under seas."

To say that he waited is not to say that he was idle. As February wore on it was apparent that American ships would not sail without protection, and pressure built up for some form of armed neutrality. This would mean convoying, or at the very least the arming of merchantmen with navy guns and perhaps navy crews. Wilson responded to this pressure on February 26, asking Congress to grant him authority to arm merchantmen. His resolve had presumably been stiffened by the receipt only two days before of the intercepted Zimmerman Note, in which Germany clarified the global nature of the European war by inviting Mexico to join her in the event of American belligerency. A small group of antiwar Senators filibustered until Congress adjourned on March 4, and Wilson, judging by their numbers that the public basically approved of the step, armed the ships by Executive Order on March 9.

Wilson had now played out his hand; he had no more plans. It was still his to decide whether the waiting would go on or whether he would take the only other remaining step—a declaration of war. And if he chose the latter, it was for him to decide on the timing of it and the words with which he would justify it. Sinkings, negligible in February, mounted in March: *Algonquin,* March 14; *City of Memphis, Illinois, Vigilencia,* March 18; *Healdton,* March 22; *Aztec,* April 1. Many scholars detect after the midlle of March a shift in public opinion that the president could not resist. It is certainly true that a wave of emotion swept through portions of the society, and feeling about the war intensified. Many newspapers editorialized about honor and patriotism. Uncommitted national figures, ranging from Governor Arthur Capper of Kansas to philosopher John Dewey, changed their positions in March and now asked for war. Six hundred Republicans met at the Union League Club in New York to demand intervention, and 12,000 people jammed into Madison Square Garden for a war rally on the twenty-second. Mass meetings were held in Philadelphia, Chicago, Boston, Denver, and other places. This and other evidence—sermons, speeches, diary entries, letters—suggest that many influential Americans either intensified their commitment to belligerency in these late March days, or became converted to it. Their patience had ebbed away; the waiting, the absence of national purpose when all the world seemed galvanized to heroism, began to take their toll of the hesitant and the uncommitted.

But we are not sure whether the desire to stay out of the war was not equally strong in this period. Pacifists also held mass meetings, and ran advertisements in national newspapers as late as March 29. And there were reports by contemporaries that the pressure for some sort of release from indecision was far from intolerable to average Americans out in the small towns and rural areas of Colorado, Wisconsin, or Georgia. There is no proof that the public demanded war. Most of it seems to have been satisfied to go on as it had.

But one really need not know how the people would have polled out on the question of war or peace in the last days of March, 1917. The pressure for action may not have been intolerable out in the Midwest or the Rockies. But it was felt to be intolerable in Washington, among men whose role it was to lead. Waiting, for public officials in the White House, the Congress, the State and War Departments, meant waiting for *themselves* to do something. And as they waited it must have seemed that the country had become ungovernable.[6] Among them, especially, opinion shifted in March. At the cabinet meeting on the nineteenth Wilson learned that the formerly divided cabinet was now united for war. On the twenty-first he called the Congress back into special session. When it met on the evening of April 2, he drove down in the rain with a cavalry escort and asked for a declaration of war upon Germany.

The galleries were jammed, and the atmosphere was electric. The president soberly reviewed the background to the crisis. The Chief Justice of the United States, much too old to go and fight, began to bang his hands in the middle of the long-awaited decisive sentence.

---

[6] There is evidence that much earlier Wilson had become deeply concerned about the divisiveness in the nation's political and emotional life, especially "hyphenate" disunity. He directed that the theme of the Democratic Convention at St. Louis in June, 1916, be "Americanism," and saw to it that the "Star-Spangled Banner" was frequently sung by the delegates. On his instructions William McCombs opened the convention with an address in which he tried to rouse the delegates' patriotism with sentences like "the chief tenet of faith [of the Democratic Party] is Americanism, and Americans are American." But the delegates stunned observers and brought tears to Bryan's eyes by demonstrating so wildly when Keynoter Martin H. Glynn stressed Wilson's peaceful intentions that Glynn was forced to depart from his text and extemporize for the delighted crowd upon the theme, "He kept us out of war." The incident has been taken to show the pacific mood of the country at that time; but Wilson's preparations for the convention demonstrate something equally important, that he was so concerned over the division and emotional tension in the country that he resorted to a bit of very uncharacteristic right-wing demagoguery about rallying 'round the flag in order to impose some control upon his party.

At the end of it, the chamber—excepting Senator LaFollette, we are told, and perhaps a few others—was on its feet, even on the chairs, yelling its appreciation. As Colonel House said later, "the tension was over and the die was cast"—and the feeling of relief was widespread. Wilson's secretary later remembered the president as saying: "My message today was a message of death for our young men. How strange it seemed to applaud that." They were not applauding that. They did not think of the deaths of young men when they thought of war, these representatives of the people. They thought of excitement, change, and travel, of an end to tension and ambiguity and humiliation, and of a great national coming-together after the bitter, partisan divisions that had almost paralyzed American political life.

Thoughts on the War Message

This desire to end the emotional and political division of the country was prominent among the factors leading Wilson to ask for war. Now, with the step taken, the war required unity for its prosecution. The wave of relief and enthusiasm that greeted his war message could not be expected to last beyond a few days. The articulate people who had never believed that the issues between Europeans were worth one American life would surely not be silenced by the Declaration of War by Congress. And their arguments might have a certain effect: we were not under attack, no official person had declared that our national security was in jeopardy, we would have to travel thousands of miles even to become involved in the war, and the war was sure to have its unpleasant costs, particularly in lives and money. To preserve a workable majority against such divisive thoughts would require that the war have a powerful, simple, emotionally appealing, and durable justification. Wilson may have asked for war, as a leading historian has said, because he had no other choice, but it would not do to attempt to prepare the nation for its exertions with such flimsy stuff. In April, 1917, and for the months ahead, the entry of the nation into the European war must have an explanation to enlist the energies and loyalties of a democratic people—simple, emotional, a tiny bit skeptical, deeply romantic. For this task it is impossible to imagine a more appropriate citizen than Woodrow Wilson. At calling men to sacrifice, at simplifying the complex, at extracting principle from secular confusion, no man of that generation was his equal. He understood from the start the need for public education of the most dramatic effectiveness (although he had some doubts of its side effects), and made his April 2 address the most impressive justification for American belligerency ever offered.

Wilson's war message, reprinted in this volume, repays close reading. His first and presumably chief reason for calling America to arms was to defend the rights of all mankind, now imperiled by German submarine warfare. The human rights under attack were broader than the right to travel safely on the seas even during a world war; they were the rights to peace and justice, of which the present German government had shown itself to be an implacable foe. The United States fought also for ends that were closely related to American self-interest and security, although Wilson did not state the matter quite in those terms—to defend the American form of government against authoritarianism (the Russian Revolution of March made this construction possible), to avoid those naval humiliations that would have eliminated the nation's status as a great power, and to construct a postwar "concert of free peoples as shall bring peace and safety to all nations."

When Wilson left the joint session to a deafening applause, when his old enemy Senator Lodge gripped his hand and thanked him for expressing the "'loftiest...sentiments of the American people," he must have known that the message was a superb success. He had provided the vocabulary for, and started in motion, that avalanche of "moist and numerous language," to borrow Mr. Dooley's phrase, which informed the American people why they must now become involved in a war that three years, and in some cases even days earlier, they had regarded with disgust. Editorial writers, preachers, stump speakers, teachers, and professors would see to it in the days ahead that the reasons we fought—simple, noble, overwhelming—were communicated throughout the country. The average draftee who was not a close reader of the *New York Times* or the *Congressional Record* now could be expected to understand why we were in the World War, and not to bother himself very much about it. But Wilson's success at framing convincing and communicable goals did as much as anything else to defeat those goals for which he had contended since foreign affairs began to claim so much of his attention in 1914.

It is hard in retrospect to approve either Wilson's timing or his reasoning in the fateful, difficult foreign policy decisions forced on him by the Great War in Europe.[7] He argued that the United States could no longer tolerate nonbelligerency because to submit to humiliations would be to permit the destruction of human rights and national prestige. If the national prestige was involved at all it was because he willed it so; neither law, economic necessity, nor tradition required a guarantee of rights of travel on armed belligerent vessels. As for the notion that human rights were somehow in jeopardy if Americans died on the high seas, the less said about that mystical idea the better for Wilson's reputation as an incisive thinker. Yet intelligent men have found reason to defend Wilson's decision to ask for intervention, not as the best of poor alternatives, but as a wise and proper step. In the view of the Realists, armed intervention was justified by a rational calculation of the national interest. America could not tolerate the domination of Europe by an undemocratic, expansionist Germany, and her vital interests now required armed intervention in a European war to secure the balance of power and construct an unprecedented union of nations for collective security. This view of international affairs was held as early as 1914 by men like Lewis Einstein and Walter Lippmann and has been adopted by most scholars since the 1940s. Some feel that Wilson stumbled accidentally onto the right course, others that despite his abstract language about principles, he

---

[7] It is *much* harder to defend the decisions of the German government throughout this period, and I hope it is clear that my inattention to this matter represents a deliberate decision to concentrate upon American policy and in no way suggests that in any discussion of human errors from 1914 on the government of Woodrow Wilson would require more space than others. The chief German blunder, aside from their share of responsibility for the outbreak of war in 1914, was probably in not taking a slightly more moderate course in January, 1917. While I have already argued that they could hardly have trusted Wilson, they might have resumed submarine warfare only on belligerent merchantmen and not upon American vessels and passenger liners. Wilson was ready to accept this despite his *Sussex* ultimatum, as the Germans learned when he made no reply to their January 10 announcement that belligerent merchantmen would now be sunk without warning. But they chose to go the whole way, miscalculating completely the impact of American intervention. A more limited submarine campaign would have delayed American intervention, and, their Eastern divisions freed by the Russian collapse in late 1917, the Germans would probably have forced the Allies to sue for peace. But they preferred to strike for total victory, trusting to American lethargy and their own submarine fleet to prevent effective American military intervention. At the end of the war they had sunk one American transport; two million men had come over to Europe safely.

intuitively understood that a German victory constituted a threat to American security and so conducted American foreign policy as to refuse to permit it. If he did not use phrases like "balance of power" and "American vital interests," it was because he faced a public of implacable naïveté and uninformed idealism, one which could only be motivated to the necessary sacrifices through the thrilling language of Protestant evangelism. But his drive to put himself and his country in a commanding position to mediate was strong from the beginning; it was one of the reasons he finally decided to intervene, and the sort of peace he wished to mediate did bear a close resemblance to the balance-of-power compromise the Realists approve.

Respected scholars have repeatedly made this argument for Wilson's intuitive realism, even though it requires some redefinition of his terminology and some careful scrutiny of the spaces between the lines. But if the president saw that our security was involved in the contest going on in Europe, as a few of his private remarks suggest, he made no effort to explain the matter to the American public. This may be credited to his own uncertainty rather than to political timidity. Wilson proved in the Brandeis appointment and later in the League fight that he was not afraid of political risks. But whether he was a slightly confused half-realist or a secret realist with exaggerated fears of the political risks involved in candor, Wilson spent the years from 1914 to 1917 talking about ideals, rights, and proper naval behavior. When he wrote state papers with his unrivaled eloquence, they were usually for the purpose of educating the Germans in their human and Christian responsibilities, not in educating his countrymen in the hard realities of modern geopolitics. When he asked for military preparedness, a logical step for one who wished his country to be in a position to influence events, he shaped a program of naval rearmament and left the army still puny—exactly what one would do who was in fact concerned with maritime rights rather than with European power dispositions. When he finally asked for intervention, he came across as a pure idealist on a mission of rescue for high, unassailable, but somehow precious ideals.

Guided by their president's words, which were repeated many times by pulpit and press, the boys went to beat the hell out of Germany for sinking our ships and for not being peace loving and democratic. Apparently the thrashing would be educational for the Germans, would produce great moral improvement among them, and would not only restore threatened human rights to their rightful place but would vindicate them forever. The attractiveness of this high enterprise, along with a general boredom, a habit of obedience, and perhaps above all an unrealistic expectation of what war would be like (Wilson himself thought the war would be over in six months and that our part in it would be primarily naval, and he was not alone)[8] was enough to call the nation to arms.

Of course, it is almost certain that he could not have persuaded the country to enter the war for realistic reasons. He could never have convinced an isolationist and parochial society to participate in history's most horrible war for such uninspiring goals as the restoration of the balance of power and the defense of England's security on the novel grounds that both had a close relation to our own *vital* interests. The number of Americans who thought in such terms was so small that the entire group could easily be locked into a White House bathroom. Many wished to declare war, but merely wishing a declaration of war on Germany did not make one a Realist. Even those around the president who favored war did not know until after April that the Allies were in grave danger of losing. They, too, in the days before April 2, had talked of principles and human rights. Wilson himself might have tried over the months from August, 1914, to create a realistic public understanding of the American stake in the war, but no sensible person argues that this would have been enough. Twenty years later another persuasive president tried, and never convinced a majority of his countrymen. But if an effort to achieve limited but attainable goals was ruled out by American tradition and the state of popular education, by what logic does one take the nation into war for goals that are unattainable and in fact hardly coherent, and whose only virtue has not to do with their connection to reality but their ability to move public opinion behind belligerency? Wilson got the country to act, but for the wrong reasons at the wrong time.

There were men, like Theodore Roosevelt, who thought that war

[8] The *American Banker* editorialized on 24 March, 1917 that our armed forces would "be entirely confined to the chasing of U-boats....Of course there can be no transportation of American troops to the scene of war across the sea." And *The Economist* on February 10 predicted that "it will be difficult to find points of contact." More realistic judgments were not nonexistent. The military had made plans for an expeditionary force, and Secretary Lansing in a diary entry of April 7 wrote: "Now to make ready our millions and send them overseas to bring victory to the cause of Liberty."

had no costs of any consequence, that fighting was in some way a beneficial experience for men and nations.[9] But Wilson was wiser than that. There is an apocryphal story, told by the journalist Frank Cobb, in which Wilson on the eve of the war message predicted that going into the war would cost the country most of the New Freedom gains and much of its internal tolerance and sanity. Although Cobb's story has recently been challenged, we know that Wilson reckoned the costs of war much more realistically than most contemporaries, especially the domestic costs. In addition, he knew that the language and ideas he must employ to create a large, enthusiastic majority out of the refractory isolationists and temporary pacifists who surrounded him would create a type of fervor that would probably make his goals unattainable. For Wilson, whatever his talk of moral absolutes and "force without stint or limit," went to Europe basically to effect a compromise. He remained more interested in diplomacy than in victory, and while he led the nation against the forces of darkness he was sure the guilt in Europe was not all on one side and insisted that the United States be designated an "associated power," not an ally. Three times in his war message he spoke of restraint, of the necessity to fight without passion or vindictiveness. But Americans listened to the Wilson they preferred: the moralist, not the conciliator. To get the nation into the war he had proclaimed war aims that made restrained action and limited involvement impossible and made reaction inevitable among a people who had not been dealt with candidly.

The disappointments he feared—but did not fear enough—came in full measure. Germany was beaten, but she did not learn the moral lessons Wilson intended. If human rights were better off for American entry, no man has yet found a way to measure the improvement. Nor did the American influence at Versailles create a lasting peace. Because we were there, the settlement was a bastard compromise, "fairer" than the one the Germans would have dictated if the United States had not entered, but by no means more conducive to the stability of Europe and the avoidance of the horrors of 1939–45. The democracies won the war, but their victory did not stem the slide of Western civilization into dictatorship and philosophic malaise.

These disappointments came to Wilson's international aspirations,

---

[9] Theodore Roosevelt loved war and is better described as an adolescent than as a realist. Marshall Joffre once said: "It costs from ten to fifteen thousand lives to train a major general." T.R. was eager to learn.

and there is no evidence that he foresaw the possibility of such defeats, although a number of hardened cynics were predicting them. Domestically, the costs of American involvement were far, far beyond even Wilson's relatively astute premonitions: 130,000 American lives lost in combat, 35,000 permanently disabled, approximately 500,000 influenza deaths in the U. S. in the winter of 1918–19 from a virus imported from the battlefields; an expenditure of $33.5 billion by 1919, to which may be added at least the $13 billion spent as of 1931 (according to economist John M. Clark) on veterans' pensions and interest on the war debt; 20 million person-years of labor diverted to war, or six months' work by every American; the 25 race riots of 1919; the stimulus to private indulgence and social irresponsibility; the decimation of the liberal center and the hobbling of the Left.

Such a brief sketch of the high costs and low yields of American participation in the war suggest an error in judgment. While Wilson had nothing like the influence over events that either he or his critics assumed, many doors of history hinged on his decisions. If it is too much to ask of any mortal political leader that, given the circumstances of spring, 1917, he choose division and national humiliation over unity and pride, it is not too much to ask for a different line of diplomacy reaching back to 1914, one that would not allow such restricted and self-defeating alternatives to hem him in.

It might be objected that a concentration on Wilson's decisions from 1914 forward ignores the historic trend toward a more active world role for the United States that commenced in the 1890s, and that this short-sighted perspective exaggerates his freedom. True, the United States in the twenty years before Wilson's Presidency had acquired an empire, intervened militarily in four countries where affairs had not gone to our liking and exerted diplomatic pressure in countless others, had built a modern navy, and had steadily expanded her international commercial contacts. But while this trend meant the inexorable approach of world power and involvement, it did not imply intervention in World War I. Our early military interventions had been limited in scope, had occurred in Latin America and the Far East, and had not been wildly popular.

Another argument with which I am not sympathetic holds that progressivism had an affinity for war. Progressives were activists, moralists, and had a strong sense of mission. They were therefore especially prone to foreign crusades, so the indictment runs. Those advancing this argument point to the fact that wars followed hard upon the reform eras of the 1890s, the Wilson years, the New Deal, the Fair Deal, the New Frontier. Further, they point to progressive Theodore Roosevelt's activist role in Panama and elsewhere, to Wilson's bellicose Mexican policy and his strong internationalism after World War I was over. A progressive President, a progressive country in 1914–1917—war was inevitable! But as plausible as these associations may appear, the case fails to convince. Close studies of progressive attitudes toward foreign policy consistently fail to detect a "progressive" position, whether activist, isolationist, or any other. Progressive T.R. wanted to intervene early, progressive Wilson tried for three years to stay out, and progressives LaFollette and Bryan fought intervention before 1917 and disapproved of it later. Reformers were of diverse minds on American foreign policy, and while some were quite jingoistic, the most opposition to the war came from the Left, liberal as well as radical.

Nonetheless, there is a tendency among modern students of Wilson to be so impressed with the long-term trend toward international involvement, and the supposed predisposition of the reform mind to crusades, not to mention the President's political and diplomatic difficulties, that Wilson's policies are presented as virtually inevitable. Sympathetic scholars point out that Wilson presided over often uncontrollable tides of passion and group interest and that he was forced many times to drift and wait, passive before forces he knew to be beyond his Constitutional and personal powers to shape. But he also acted decisively many times, channeling events within a reasonably wide belt of possibility. Where he had no alternatives or no reasonable ones, we cannot be revisionists. Where he had them we must make judgments, so long as they are tempered with a respect for historic forces which always dwarf men, and with sympathy for this brilliant, patriotic Christian who inherited such baffling dilemmas.

Perhaps no other president would have seen the importance of the early decisions regarding the British blockade and the Declaration of London. The way was politically clear for the administration to insist on the declaration, but most men would have weakened and let it go. No one expected a long war. But many of the decisions of the spring of 1915 bore Wilson's personal stamp. Demands on the belligerents could have been linked, and Germany could have been held to the same postwar accounting reserved for the Allies. Bryan requested a passenger ban at that time, and Wilson was not on principle opposed. Yet he declined to suggest one, insuring that the idea would come from Congress and require his opposition.

The loan decision is an interesting case. Charles Beard showed some years ago that Bryan himself flinched before the bankers' arguments. The country was in an economic recession in 1914, a recession that produced "the largest number of business failures in our country's history," according to *Bradstreet's Journal,* and that brought Andrew Carnegie to write Wilson on 23 November, 1914: "The present financial and industrial situations are very distressing. I have never known such conditions, such pressing calls upon debtors to pay. . . . " No one, from the Harvard Economics Department through the entire range of federal agencies, had any idea how to cope with it beyond maintaining a happy investment climate for the men who hired other men. We now know that recovery could have been achieved by having the government borrow funds from New York banks and reemploy people by a program of spending—on ships and tanks if it wished, but preferably on schools, hospitals, and housing. But this was advocated only by a few unbelievable socialists. The bankers showed Wilson a golden opportunity to put idle funds to work by simply *allowing* Europeans to borrow in New York and spend the money in this country. The pressure was enormous, and there were no real counterpressures and no constructive countersuggestions. Here was an apparently painless cure for America's economic troubles, and the enthusiasm for Allied loans and trade would certainly have broken Wilson politically had he blocked it only with arguments drawn from moral repugnance. *The New York Times* editorialized in early 1915:

> We have oversupplied ourselves with forces of production and they are idle in unusual proportion. . . . The Promise of the new year is that we shall accomplish a peaceful penetration of the world's markets to an extent we have never dreamed of. What others have shed blood to obtain through politics and force we shall obtain while bestowing our benevolence. . . . It is a new translation of the old beatitude, revised: blessed are the keepers of the peace for prosperity shall be within their homes and palaces.

Well might British ambassador Spring-Rice write to Grey in October: "When it became apparent that a loan was necessary, many secret forces began to act in its favour." It may now seem incredible that to achieve recovery the United States must ship to Europe both money and goods and call it a sharp bargain. But it made sense in a capitalistic order with only a rudimentary economic science, and there was literally no other plausible way in 1915 to get idle funds to work. The loan decision, while not inevitable, must be seen sympathetically in this light. Keynes' *General Theory* was twenty-one years away.

But if Wilson could hardly have been expected to maintain the ban against loans to good customers abroad, he might have eliminated munitions from the resulting trade. The Hitchcock bill of December, 1914, would have accomplished that, and there was ample precedent and political support for it. Embargoes on munitions were imposed by Denmark, Sweden, Italy, the Netherlands, Spain, and Norway. The United States itself had embargoed munitions to Mexico in 1913. A passenger ban might have easily been added in the spring of 1916, if not earlier. When the liner *Persia* was sunk on January 3, the principal Congressional reaction was anger that *American citizens had been aboard*. That month Wilson left for a speaking tour to gain support for preparedness and learned that the Congress accurately reflected the country's mood. A passenger ban was his for the asking; and while this would not have diminished the Allied trade, there would be no loss of American life to inflame the issue if Germany eventually resorted to unrestricted submarine warfare despite a ban on munitions, as she well might.

These two changes in policy taken together would have vastly altered the equation of forces. There were no other good alternatives of comparable importance, although Wilson passed up some minor opportunities for a more neutral course. The Lansing modus vivendi on armed ships could have been put into effect, but probably would not have made cruiser warfare the rule. Britain had been sending few armed ships to America anyway, and with Q-ships operating in British waters the submarines were still in danger on the surface. Yet the move would have been helpful. As for Wilson's mediation efforts, it is hard to fault his intentions or his persistence, except to wish that his general appeal had been issued earlier, and from a position of greater neutrality. But there was never much interest in a negotiated peace. Some small things he might have done. He might have fired Page and secured an ambassador to London who would not weaken protests against the blockade. He might, as some progressives urged, have dampened some enthusiasm in important quarters by declaring that, in the event of war, he would draft capital as well as men.

But the passenger ban and the munitions embargo were probably enough, and they were politically possible. Naval troubles with Germany would have arisen, but would have been manageable. With Wilson's rhetorical power and discipline of mind, the road to neutrality was diplomatically and politically passable.

Had Wilson acted along these lines the result would almost certainly have been a German victory, either in the form of a negotiated or a dictated peace. Hohenzollern Germany would dominate the continent —a nation adept in the industrial arts, astonishingly vigorous, nominally Christian, capitalistic, racially arrogant, militaristic, deep in its own internal struggle between the socialists and the entrenched and unimaginative conservatives of land and industry. At least the last years of the war and perhaps more, with their relentless butchery and crippling moral and political consequences, would have been averted. One is permitted to doubt the November, 1917 success of Lenin. Speculation could go on. It should also be noted that the education the American people supposedly received in their new international responsibilities would not have taken place, or at least not in the same way. In view of American foreign policy attitudes from 1919 through 1941, one contemplates the loss of this schooling with relative calm.

The allure of a different American diplomacy springs not from a blind aversion to warfare but from a reasoned conception of the nature of American security. Wilson was sure that our security lay in a respect for law, in the spread of parliamentary governments, in the prestige that comes to nations that do not tolerate the infringement of their rights, in a defeated Germany, in a just peace, and in a postwar league of nations. Much of this is silly, but some of it represents the deepest insight into modern international relations. His mistake lay not in his instincts, a compound of the profound and the harmless, so much as in his judgment of the circumstances. Given the circumstances —the uncontrollable passions of Europe and the ignorance that gripped his own great democracy—there was only one *sure* way to pursue American security, a familiar way, without staggering risks, and without death. It was by an intensification of that surge of internal reform to which he had already become committed: the purification of our own democracy, the diversion of more resources to the education and physical well-being of our people, the broadening of the sway of equality, the conservation of our resources, the humanizing of our hours and conditions of work, the enhancement of the efficiency of our industry, the beautification and ordering of our cities, the narrowing of the gap between the classes. But a decision was reached to interrupt this work for a different approach to national unity, a different approach to economic prosperity, a different approach to the respect of nations.

Ernest May has guessed that Wilson would have chosen differently if he had foreseen the casualties of the Argonne and Chateau-Thierry. In the last speech before his stroke, delivered at Pueblo, Colorado, on 25 September 1919, Wilson said, his face streaked with tears, "What of our pledges to the men that lie dead in France...? There seems to me to stand between us and the rejection or qualification of this treaty the serried ranks of those boys in khaki, not only those boys who came home, but those dear ghosts that still deploy upon the fields of France." We have seen much more of the twentieth century than Woodrow Wilson, and the doubts grow stronger.

part three

REFORM: 1917-1928

I.

Once the war intervened, conservatives were happy to predict that reform would be shelved. But their expectations were only half realized. Proving once and for all how different were the impulses making up progressivism, the war encouraged some reformers and withered the spirits of others.

To many progressives the goal of reform had been to generate a great secular revival, lifting men's thoughts above self to what was shared. Such reformers had occasionally appeared as radicals, dedicated to *removing* the inequalities that divided society. The war proved that they were glad to settle for an easier solution—getting men to *forget* those inequalities in a time of common danger. Unity was their end; justice had been a means to that end, but war served admirably. Wilson's Assistant Secretary of Agriculture Carl Vrooman, for example, a reformer of varied credentials, regarded the war bond drives of 1917–18 as the high point of progressivism. Progressives like Vrooman had been critics of capitalism because it fostered a spirit of competition and rivalry and division. The war provided a shortcut to the cooperative spirit they had sought through social reform, and they took it with enthusiasm. An editorial in the General Federation of Women's Clubs *Magazine* in June, 1917, expressed this sense that the war was the fulfillment of reform:

> We shall exchange our material thinking for something quite different, and we shall all be kin. We shall all be enfranchised, prohibition will prevail, many wrongs will be righted, vampires and grafters and slackers will be relegated to a class by themselves, stiff necks will limber up, hearts of stone will be changed to hearts of flesh, and little by little we shall begin to understand each other.

For others who did not so easily forget the substantive goals they pursued, the new federal responsibilities of the mobilization period brought unexpected opportunities. Multiplying federal agencies offered positions for those who had longed to offer their skills in the service of the public. For those in the Croly-Van Hise tradition of national planning, the war was a time when American industry could be directed by experts in search of productive efficiency, not entrepreneurs avid for profits. The War Industries Board was only the most prominent of the wartime agencies where such experts found fulfilling work. The few reformers who were interested in housing welcomed the first experience in public housing when the Department of Labor's U. S. Housing Corporation built dwellings to house six thousand families and seven thousand single men. It was a small but useful precedent.[1]

The war was also a brief but unforgettable experience for social workers, ministers, and other reformers who had long wished to direct

---

[1] Another federal agency mandated to oversee war workers' housing, the U.S. Shipping Board, preferred to lend money to corporations, and this produced about 16,000 more dwelling units. The total, obviously, is quite small, and the hopes that it might serve as a useful precedent to initiate postwar federal housing programs were shattered by the Congress in 1919 when it required that all federal housing and federally funded housing be sold (at bargain prices) and the entire experiment terminated. See Roy Lubove, "Homes and 'A Few Well-Placed Fruit Trees': An Object Lesson in Federal Housing," *Social Research,* 27 (Winter, 1960), 469–85.

Americans toward a more upright life. They found their chance in the establishment and management of training camps and recreation facilities for the army and the Red Cross. Progressives like Raymond B. Fosdick and the Boston social worker Robert Woods were able now with government backing to provide the sort of health and sanitation facilities, wholesome recreation, creative use of leisure time, and freedom from alcohol and loose women that they had yearned to bring to the urban working classes. As Woods put it:

> In no previous decade, certainly in no previous generation, would it have been possible that every nook and corner of our cities would have been under the close, responsible, friendly surveillance of men and women representing much that is best in our national life.... It (the mobilization) has been the occasion of a new and better order of things affecting the restraint of the liquor trade and of prostitution, and the promotion of ...old and new forms of health-giving community recreation.

Another prominent social worker, Edward T. Devine, described their new opportunities in more specific terms:

> Enthusiasm for social service is epidemic.... A luxuriant crop of new agencies is springing up. We scurry back and forth to the national capital; we stock offices with typewriters and new letter-heads; we telephone feverishly, regardless of expense, and resort to all the devices of efficient "publicity work".... It is all very exhilarating, stimulating, intoxicating.

If there is a bit of surprise at learning that a mature, urban American could become so stirred over such trifles, this reflects our ignorance. In view of the prewar resources of America's social welfare movement, Devine's excitement is entirely understandable. And whatever the initial reaction of the social workers at finding themselves so affluent, they adjusted their expectations quickly enough. After enumerating the new opportunities open to reformers in the wartime period of "true national collectivism," the busiest year of his life, Woods added: "Why should it not always be so? Why not continue in the years of peace this close, vast, wholesome organism of service, of fellowship, of constructive creative power?"

As the planners and social workers found employment for their talents, so the war created a climate that advanced other progressive goals that had seemed so distant. The Americanization movement had aimed at assimilating the immigrants who were coming in such indigestible numbers since about the turn of the century. Americanization bore all the marks of progressivism. It expressed a benevolent purpose, it took on the urgency of a crusade, it shared with the rest of progressivism the conviction that the powerful social forces that were reshaping America ought to be brought under control and that legislation was the way. Frances Kellor, a leading figure in the Americanization movement and appropriately enough a New Nationalism progressive, put it succinctly: "Nation building is to be in the future a deliberate formative process, not an accidental...arrangement." Accordingly, Miss Kellor's New York branch of the North American Civic League for Immigrants, allied in the effort with patriotic societies like the Daughters of the American Revolution, many of the settlements, the Young Men's Christian Association, and other groups, busied themselves with the staggering job of "educating" the immigrant in American behavior and principles. But all their efforts before 1917 had produced only uncoordinated city and state efforts at night classes in English or an occasional official "investigation" of conditions among the immigrant population. Americanization had not caught on with the public or their elected representatives, and private efforts were inadequate to the task.

The war brought the chance to involve the federal government in the Americanization struggle, and Miss Kellor, now head of the New York Committee for Immigrants, tirelessly pressed for the recognition of Americanization as a vital part of the war effort. Under her prodding, somnolent federal bureaus like the Bureau of Education and the Bureau of Naturalization took a new interest in the immigrant and his skills as worker and citizen. Social worker Josephine Roche joined the Committee on Public Information and guided a large amount of their propaganda toward immigrants. Interest in Americanization sprang up everywhere. Cities, patriotic groups, and industrialists like Henry Ford suddenly exerted themselves to accelerate and direct the melting-pot process—something they had been content to leave to chance in the past. The war in a few short months did what Frances Kellor's patient organizing efforts had failed to do in the years since T.R. first heard her reformer's plea in 1906. It brought to this sector of progressivism an undreamed-of public support.

Opportunities for other types of reform arose out of the mobilization, and they were not all lost. White women gained some forty thousand new jobs as they replaced men or moved into war industries, and the government formed the Committee on Women's Defense Work under Anna Howard Shaw to coordinate the woman's preparedness movement. The war provided the right climate for passage of the Constitutional amendment granting women federal suffrage, and the Nineteenth Amendment was ratified in 1920. Just earlier the Congress had finally yielded to the prohibitionists by passing the Eighteenth Amendment against the sale of alcoholic beverages, and in this case also the wartime need to conserve grain and preserve health offered reformers a decisive argument.

The war also produced among progressives a heightened determination to attack inequalities of wealth. One of the leading failures of the entire progressive movement had been its inability to appreciate and use the taxing power. This was especially true at the federal level, where the potentialities of taxation as a weapon of social policy were greatest. The federal revenue structure in 1914, after the reformers had done about all they seemed interested in doing in the area of taxation at the time of the Underwood Tariff battle, raised only $71 million of a total revenue of $734 million out of a graduated income tax. The rest, $663 million, was raised from customs duties, excises on liquor and tobacco, land sales, and the like, which meant that American federal tax burdens were carried by the consuming public. "The wealthy, obviously," writes Arthur S. Link, "enjoyed relative immunity from taxation."

It took the preparedness controversy of 1916 and its demands for new revenue to stimulate progressives to a heightened interest in one of their most promising and little-used weapons, taxation. In the spring of 1916, progressives in the Congress, led by North Carolina's Claude Kitchin and Wisconsin's Robert LaFollette, beat down an administration proposal to pay the cost of armament by a tax bearing predominantly upon lower and middle classes. Then these Congressional radicals, assisted by reform pressures outside the Congress such as the Association for an Equitable Federal Income Tax formed by John Dewey, Fred Howe, and others, pushed through a tax law in September that raised the surtax from 6 percent to 13 percent, doubled the tiny corporate tax, and added a small inheritance tax. In 1917 progressives again raised individual and corporate rates (to a maximum of 67 percent), increased estate taxes, and passed an excess profits tax. These efforts to insure that no one became a millionaire while young men died in France fell short of success. Huge profits were made from the war, but they would not have been taxed at all had no progressives made the effort, and each dollar taken from profits meant a dollar that would not have to be borrowed from the wealthy to finance the war and be repaid, plus interest, in the 1920s. Secretary of the Treasury William McAdoo finally raised about one dollar in three by taxation, which represented a failure to progressives like Amos Pinchot whose American Committee on War Finance had demanded pay-as-you-go (paying for the war entirely out of taxes, which meant virtually confiscating all higher incomes). But due to progressive efforts a tax program was enacted that was too radical for J. P. Morgan, Jr. and men of his class, who had preferred a rate of one to five. When the Bristol (Tennessee) *News Bureau* editorialized in 1918 that "war is a hothouse of income taxation," it spoke the truth only with reference to the ineffective tax efforts of prewar reformers.

II.

Yet while the war years brought new opportunities, which some progressives seized, we know that in the total story the war was fatal to the humanitarian, liberal component of reform. No historian has described this process in full detail, for it involves matters of mood and spirit as well as the traditional pull and haul of politics. The effect of war was, of course, uncomplicated in one area: to the peace movement it represented defeat and brought immediate dejection. A number of other reforms were simply shouldered aside by the preoccupations of wartime. The Federal Trade Commission, institutional embodiment of the anti-trust drive, had scarcely organized when the need for maximum wartime production forced it into a passive role. There were stirrings of the old New Freedom fervor after the war, but these were effectively scotched by the Court and by the 1925 appointment of that former lobbyist and genial friend of the corporation, William E. Humphrey, to the chairmanship. In another area, Wilson added one more defeat to the progressive conservation movement when, pressed by wartime concerns, he simply forgot to appoint the Waterways Commission, which conservationists had finally established by the Newlands Act of 1917 (the authority for the Commission was withdrawn in the Water Power Act of 1920). In still another, the war aborted the establishment of a government-owned armor plant proposed by Secretary of the Navy Josephus Daniels and mandated by Congress in the Naval Bill of August, 1916. Without American entry the government would have taken at least this step toward supplying a "yardstick" portion of its own defense tools, a small but interesting step away from the military-industrial complex of recent lament.

But the chief damage done by war to the progressive movement came not from the interruption of various prewar reform projects, for while war diverted energies from some causes it seemed to provide at least as many new outlets for the urge to social service as it directly or indirectly stifled. What hurt progressivism most were two products of the war: the perversion of the idea of a regulatory state as business groups came to dominate governmental policy, and the war-induced alteration of the reform mentality in the direction of ideas and impulses at once less confident and less generous.

Wilson himself, a man with as highly developed a sense of the dynamics of national opinion and political power as any of his generation, had anticipated that reactionary pressures would rise along with patriotism. Even if he did not speak prophetically along this line to Frank Cobb prior to the Declaration of War, others remembered similar predictions. "Every reform we have won," Secretary Daniels recalled Wilson saying before he made the decision for war, "will be lost if we go into this war. . . . War means autocracy. The people we have unhorsed will inevitably come into the control of the country, for we shall be dependent upon the steel, oil, and financial magnates. They will run the nation." And in they came: Wall Street's Bernard Baruch, B&O Railroad's Daniel Willard, International Harvester's Alexander Legge, Union Pacific's Robert Lovett, Cleveland industrialist Frank A. Scott, energetic, successful, patriotic capitalists who would man the new federal agencies such as the War Industries Board, the Food and Fuels Administration, the War Finance Corporation, the Railroad Administration, and who for two hectic years shared with the Congress the power to decide how the rewards and burdens of the wartime economy would be distributed. The well-being of any given American in 1919 was shaped by decisions made in Washington to a degree unprecedented in American history. The Congress determined who would be taxed and how; the financing activities of the Treasury and the Federal Reserve allocated the burdens of the second tax system, inflation, and the third tax system, interest rates on the federal debt; myriad agencies, led by the War Industries Board, wrote the cost-plus contracts, agreed upon prices (i.e., profits), allocated scarce resources among competing industries, and extended credit to stimulate expansion in uneconomic areas. The results, as Wilson and others had dimly foreseen, were reactionary. Despite efforts to tax away war profits, despite an unparalleled attention to the legitimate claims of labor (through the War Labor Board and labor representation on the War Industries Board), and despite some well-meaning attempts by Baruch and others to prevent profiteering, the wealthy seem generally to have managed to have the war paid for by somebody else. While the evidence is somewhat spotty, it appears that real wages went up imperceptibly if at all during the wartime boom, and working people put in longer hours and endured crowded living conditions to hold their own against inflation and taxation. For the great mass of salaried employees, the fiscal system worked out in Washington brought them, in George Soule's words, "unmitigated disaster:" the purchasing power of their pay dropped 22 percent between 1916 and 1919. Presumably it was just such people who, in a blind desire to punish those responsible for this injustice, supplied most of the energy for the postwar campaigns to eliminate aliens, radicals, and uppity blacks.

While these groups were permitted the morally bracing experience of sacrificing for their country, other groups were finding war nothing like the hell that Sherman had described. Farmers experienced a 25 percent gain in real income between 1915 and 1918, although it was a prosperity with only one or two more years to run. But the largest and most lasting benefits came to the larger capitalists. Corporate profits jumped to three times their prewar level in 1917, and even after the higher wartime taxes took effect it was estimated by John M. Clark that business profits were up 30 percent from 1913. A Federal Trade Commission inquiry into profiteering showed that in some sectors of the economy the war was literally golden. The profits of U. S. Steel went from a prewar average of $76 million to $478 million in 1917. In 1918 the profits of the largest ten steel mills ranged from 30 percent to 319 percent of invested capital, and a grateful management of Bethlehem Steel voted its top four officers a shared bonus of $2.1 million. After taxes in 1917, forty-eight lumber companies netted 17 percent of invested capital, oil companies averaged 21 percent, and twenty-four copper companies averaged 24 percent. The net earnings of national banks increased more in the 1914–19 period than in the preceding forty years. The number of taxpayers in the thirty to forty thousand dollars-a-year income bracket roughly tripled between 1914 and 1918, and at the war's end it was estimated that steep taxes had not prevented some forty-two thousand Americans from accumulating a million dollars or more.

Such figures reflect a secure grip upon government by the larger capitalists. The governmental machinery put together to organize war production was manned, with few exceptions, by men drawn from industry. There had been no alternative to this. When Bernard Baruch and the War Industries Board accepted the job of centralized control of the wartime economy they found themselves obliged to intervene in countless decisions about prices, wages, transportation and materiel priorities, and the only real source of talent in these complicated questions was the affected industries themselves. The universities of that day, the foundations, and the older governmental agencies could contribute only a handful of trained, experienced men. Newly appointed government officials with an industry background and point of view were naturally something less than implacable when bargaining with industry for terms that protected the interests of the public treasury and the labor force, especially since there was a war on and the army must be supplied. One result was high profits, but more important than this was the lesson absorbed by all those involved in the wartime cooperation between business and government. The uncertainties and tight profit margins of the competitive market could be replaced by the steady output and predictable, high profits of a system of government-sponsored planning. Nothing was lost save the worn-out doctrine of laissez-faire. The government proved sympathetic to industry's problems; it extracted no painful sacrifices in return for its gift of asylum from the hazards of competition and inadequate demand. The "entente" between big business and government that some scholars think they perceive in the administration of T.R. had indeed become a reality by 1918.

There are those—the younger Woodrow Wilson was among them— who have argued that such an outcome was inevitable, war or no war. A regulatory state in a capitalistic setting must wind up regulating in the interests of the largest and most powerful corporations. Thus progressivism, to the extent that it meant a regulatory state, has been seen as deeply conservative and involving no real reform at all. The relations of government and business during and after the war offer much support for such a view, but I think it mistaken. The enlarged powers of government in the prewar period were always potentially and sometimes actually out of the control of the large capitalistic interests. Even during the war, when government policy was most benign toward capital, the "entente" was uneasy and government officials could prove unreasonably stubborn in the defense of the public interest. Melvin Urofsky, in his very useful book, *Big Steel and the Wilson Administration* (1969), argues that the steel industry had its way on every important decision affecting its interests. But much that we know, and in fact much of Urofsky's evidence itself, points another way. At various times during the war the government threatened to take over plants, adopted revenue schedules designed to recapture up to 70 percent of excess profits, refused to drop the anti-trust suit against U. S. Steel instituted in 1911, and forced on the steel industry both an eight-hour day and promises to hold free shop elections and bargain with the resultant unions. No plants were actually commandeered, the revenue schedules were evaded by ingenious accounting procedures, the anti-trust suit was lost, and preoccupation with the League struggle undercut the administration's support of labor just at the crucial moment in the fall of 1919. But the President and stubborn New Freedom Democrats such as Josephus Daniels of the Navy Department, William McAdoo of the Treasury and Railroad Administration, Newton Baker in the War Department, and Felix Frankfurter, Secretary of the War Labor Policies Board, proved ideologically ill-adapted to an entente with big business. They were so unpredictable that leading businessmen wavered in their attachment to the idea of a post-war continuation of government planning and began to talk again of cutting government back to a minimal role and managing their economic problems through trade associations.

In the end the spirit of wartime cooperation did dominate the future. The dream of several government officials and dollar-a-year businessmen of an Industrial Board to continue government-industry cooperation into peacetime was shelved, but the regulatory powers of the progressive-era state—the ICC, FTC, Federal Reserve Board, Food and Drug Administration, Tariff Commission—were retained and did in fact prove friendly to capital in the 1920s. But it had not always been so. Wilson may have claimed too much when he said that the New Freedom had "unhorsed" the wealthy, but national progressivism had since 1902 managed to direct a significant proportion of the powers of the state toward the needs of groups other than the eastern corporate elite. Is it answered that the capitalists benefitted most from regulation? True enough, the benefits to large corporate interests seem to have outweighed the benefits to labor, small business, agriculture, and consumer, as of 1916. But the situation was fluid right up to the war (and even to some extent during the war, as government relations with the steel industry show), and the regulatory apparatus was capable of being used for predominantly public rather than predominantly private ends. There are many reasons why this was so, the chief among them being that the idea of the public interest as a distinct entity, overriding claims of property *and requiring frequent conflict with property,* was widely implanted in the heads of men —politicians, intellectuals, lawyers, even businessmen—who would shape public policy in the future.

But the decision to mobilize for war did turn out to be a decision to alter both the idea and the practice of federal economic regulation. Progressivism may have laid the egg of the regulatory state, and hatched it, but the formative wartime years were spent with foster parents from Wall Street. American industry did in fact work a miracle of production, and the natural result was a deep admiration and respect for Big Business and for the government-industry cooperation through which the miracle was arranged. The experience made a deep impression not only on the general public, but on the national elite of men who, as federal bureaucrats or as people flowing back and forth between private life and public service, would determine the nature of federal regulation in the future. To attain maximum wartime production, the federal bureaucracy, infused with industry-based personnel, put harmonious relations and uninterrupted production above stable and reasonable prices. It was a pivotal experience; the economy had never worked so well, and the cost was easily forgotten. The way of the future was the way of business-government cooperation. The 1920s, with their cozy government-industry relations, commenced when the dollar-a-year men entrained for Washington in the spring of 1917 to shoulder their patriotic duties.[2]

2 It took years for the reform mind to work its way free of the WIB experience. Even in the early days of the New Deal it was still thought that regulation and economic planning could best be accomplished through a cooperative, friendly process in which business helped to man the controls. Only in the late 1930s did men in government in significant numbers return to a more austere conception of federal regulation and make another start at realizing the promise of independent regulation in the public interest. Then war intervened again, production became paramount, and the regulatory tradition was warped a second time by military exigencies. Because of the Cold War we have never emerged from these conditions. In this century, war has aborted the regulatory experiment.

In addition to the advantages that it conferred on some of the traditional antagonists of reformers, the war undermined central progressive assumptions. A faith in the inherent goodness of The People underlay all the political alterations of the Direct Democracy component of progressivism, and a faith in man's rationality underlay the work of reformers who wished to substitute expertise and social control for drift. For those with the Jeffersonian confidence in the many, the sight of masses of men docilely and even in some cases with relish killing one another, and then throwing away the military victory by refusing to insist upon a just peace, suggested that the Jeffersonian view of man might be insufficiently pessimistic. And one could not help but be further discouraged by the news (revealed in *Army Mental Tests,* edited by C. S. Yoakum and R. S. Yerkes [1920]) that army mental tests showed some 30 percent of recruits to be illiterate, with forty-six thousand men in the first nine months of 1918 showing up for induction with a mental age of ten years or less. Such discoveries immobilized the pressures for Direct Democracy and worked havoc in any number of minds.

Those reformers in the Hamiltonian tradition who had all along been somewhat elitist could draw no more solace from the war period than the Jeffersonians. The pessimistic anthropology taught by the war stunned even the elitists, for a thorough skepticism about human nature undermined their faith even in the rationality of the experts. They were if anything more elitist after the war than before, but less sure where the elite was to be found and now reasonably certain that it would not be heeded.

And if loss of confidence in human rationality were not enough, the experiences of 1917–20 dealt a blow to progressive confidence in the state. Reformers had supposed that the state was benevolent, but Attorney General A. Mitchell Palmer, with the president's support, turned the power of government to the persecution of immigrants with European political views as well as native American radicals. Against a background of banned publications, arrests, and deportations under the Espionage Act of 1917, the Trading with the Enemy Act of 1917, the Sedition Act of 1918, and the Alien Act of 1918, veteran reformer Frederic C. Howe wrote in his autobiography: "I hated the new state that had arisen, hated its brutalities, its ignorance, its unpatriotic patriotism, that made profit from our sacrifices and used its power to suppress criticism of its acts." But if a liberal government could not be trusted, where were reformers to turn? Many became disoriented and entered a period of intellectual armistice, adopting the sort of cynicism which H. L. Mencken (whose cynicism, unlike that of most intellectuals, was not recent) expressed when he said: "If I am convinced of anything, it is that Doing Good is in bad taste."

The war thus revealed how much progressivism had rested upon certain vulnerable assumptions. It also demonstrated how the thrust and shape of the movement depended upon a very fragile mood. Progressive reform represented an intervention to project the values of the genial and neighborly nineteenth century into the twentieth, but the nineteenth century unfortunately offered a number of contradictory values to complicate the job of its defenders. It was little understood during the progressive era how vitally important was the mood of the time in determining which values would be uppermost, both as social goals and as guides to acceptable tactics. Some of these values were the generous values of Jefferson, Lincoln, and Theodore Parker, and in the sunny atmosphere of the prewar years these humane and liberal values were strong in the movement. But some of the values of the class from which progressivism was drawn were moralities of a different sort—the norms of the Anglo-Saxon Protestant New Englanders, ranging from sobriety and continence through an identification of "American" with white skins, northern European extraction, and small-town capitalism. The balance, as we see it in retrospect, was always a close one between the generous and the coercive impulses. In the tense, anxious war years with their bewildering changes, progressivism changed its mood and turned increasingly into a cultural counterattack against deviance from the traditional New England norms. The experiences of two progressive organizations document the ascendancy of the reactionary spirit that coincided with and was evidently caused by the war experience.

Nowhere do we see this line of struggle more clearly than in the Americanization movement. When Frances Kellor founded the New York branch of the North American Civic League for Immigrants in 1909, the league was financed by industrialists who were glad to contribute to an organization that would teach English, hygiene, and the rudiments of a patriotism that amounted largely to orderly behavior. Not scorning these goals, Miss Kellor from the first tried also to direct Americanization into areas such as factory safety legislation.

Thus the movement had a dual nature: one wing of the Americanization impulse sent industrial spies into the ranks of foreign-born workers or drilled law-and-order civics into them at night, and the other wing tolerated their language, religion, and habits and worked to improve their living and working conditions. The war ended the ambiguity. The conformist tendency became paramount and the permissive, humanitarian side almost vanished. Frances Kellor herself, in her book *Straight America* published in 1916, called for loyalty, discipline, and universal military service. The national crisis had tipped the delicate balance of this reform effort toward its hard, repressive aspect. To be Americanized after 1917 meant to be watched, to be forced to stop attending the local socialist club or workers' meetings designed to organize the shop. Americanization in wartime carried the early signs of the approaching red scare.

The same process may be seen at work inside the Southern Sociological Congress, a civic organization established in 1912 to improve social conditions in the South. At first the Congress had a strong social welfare and social gospel orientation, and its chief interests were in child welfare, public health and housing, adult dependency, recreation, temperance, and racial relations. Efforts along some of these lines—public health, for instance—benefitted the entire community, and while laborious they were not socially disturbing. But the Congress also took an advanced position on the treatment of the disadvantaged and on the question of race. It always had a strong evangelistic tone, but at first this sort of fervor was *social* gospel fervor, with the emphasis upon justice at least as much as upon morality.

The war caused a change of emphasis in the work of the Congress. In the convention of 1918 in Birmingham the new note was discernible. Clergy began to outnumber welfare workers, and the effort to improve the South was now seen by Congress speakers as less a matter of scientific study and social reform as a matter of spiritual inspiration. The Congress began to lose interest in changing conditions and take an interest in changing hearts. In the 1919 convention at Knoxville, the organization's historian tells us, "several speakers expressed concern over radical movements. Bolshevism was a product of atheism, they argued, and should be countered by 'genuine American patriotism.' " Women were advised to stay out of politics, to "give us happy homes and happy firesides and bolshevism cannot come in." In 1920 the nationalistic note was dominant, with Bishop Theodore D. Bratton telling the convention in Washington that the task of the Congress was to keep America American. The Congress had shifted entirely to the defensive. Five years later, with bolshevism put down in the United States, the Congress, its reform spirit thoroughly played out and domesticated, became the Home Betterment League.

III.

Transformations of this sort occurred across the range of progressive activities as the postwar atmosphere turned defensive and sour. Reactionary tendencies ultimately won out over desires to change the system so as to make it more democratic and more receptive to new impulses, and because they did, we see this rightward turn in American politics and social thought as the significant development in domestic affairs in the period 1918–20. But in these years just at the end of the war there was also a strong Left in the United States, ranging from the familiar progressive elements through a briefly invigorated Socialist Party and including, after 1919, two small communist parties. These "parties of movement," as Arno J. Mayer calls them, were in ferment and apparent growth both in Europe and America. Many contemporaries, observing the wave of strikes of 1918–19, thought the Left might be within months of a seizure of power. New York clothing workers went out in late 1918, followed by longshoremen; a general strike paralyzed Seattle in February; New England was swept by walkouts among telephone workers, railway labor, and even Boston policemen; and in September the great strike against U. S. Steel began. The Socialist Party itself experienced dramatic growth in 1917–18, polling 27 percent in the New York mayoralty election (a 500-percent increase over their showing in 1913), 34 percent in Chicago, and 44 percent in Dayton. In North Dakota, a number of ex-Socialists had organized the Non-Partisan League around the grievances of Dakota farmers, elected their own Governor, and were establishing state-owned enterprises from banks to grain elevators and flour mills. At least parts of the American public seemed to have been radicalized by the war,[3] and this included some intel-

---

[3] And by wartime inflation. With 1913 as a base year (index of 100), the cost of living was 104 in 1915, 131 in 1917, in 1918 was 159, in 1919 was 183, and in 1920 was 208 (calculated by A. Hansen, in Bureau of Labor Statistics, *Historical Statistics of the United States, 1789–1945* (1949), p. 235.

lectuals. Woodrow Wilson himself spoke of the need for a third party, and mused to a friend in 1918 that the world would probably be moving to the Left and that he would be going with it.

Thus both the Left and the Right were active, ambitious, and growing in strength just after the war, and there were abundant predictions of the success of each. In those months there was an air of expectancy, anxiety, chiliasm; opinion began to polarize, with both radicalism and reaction feeding on the reported successes of the other. We now know that the Right was much stronger and that the ferment of 1918–1919 would be rather decisively stifled. The triumph of the reactionary spirit was not engineered by some manipulative business elite, but was a national phenomenon expressing the ultimate decision of the great bulk of the American people that they would not tolerate any further disturbance or uncertainty, and were in no mood for idealism. The role of the Wilson administration in the postwar reaction, however, was far too cooperative. Different national leadership might have moderated, even if it could not entirely blunt, the swing to the Right. Wilson, preoccupied with the Versailles meetings and the fight to gain treaty ratification, allowed himself to make an almost complete default in the area of domestic leadership in 1919. He was in the country only ten days between December, 1918 and July, 1919, and in all of 1919 sent only three messages to Congress, none of them mentioning any specific reforms. Progressives needed and appealed for his leadership, but long before his stroke in September it was clear that Wilson would neither lead the Left nor actively combat the Right—except in the matter of the League of Nations. Despite progressive protest he terminated federal housing efforts and returned the railroads to private ownership; declined to help labor in its difficulties with steel management and secured injunctions against striking coal miners; and signed laws in the areas of water power, railroads, and merchant marine in 1920 that were more than generous to capital. In the area of civil liberties the administration could not even claim to have been the nonresisting accomplice of a conservative Congress. Attorney General A. Mitchell Palmer and Postmaster General Albert S. Burleson had enforced the wartime Espionage and Alien and Sedition Acts with excessive zeal, and Palmer ultimately put the Justice Department at the head of the Red Scare of 1919, with Wilson's consent.

It was a poor record for a progressive administration. Harding might as well have been in the White House from 1918 forward. Indeed, this might have been an improvement, since Harding freed Debs. But it is doubtful that the postwar triumph of reaction could have been entirely averted even had Wilson tried to chart a clear course to the Left. Liberals were shocked by the treaty when its unexpectedly harsh terms were revealed in June, 1919, and many were beginning to pull away not only from Wilson, who had talked them into the war and then failed to redeem their decision by bringing home a statesmanlike peace, but from idealistic exertions under any leadership. The broader public showed signs of moral fatigue as early as November, 1918, when the Republicans captured control of both houses of Congress. And although Attorney General Palmer's activities helped encourage the postwar politics of rigidity and fear, they were not only matched and exceeded, but also preceded, by grassroots repression and vigilantism directed against any ideas tainted with a critical edge. Beginning in the early days of 1919, the local groups who had been so vigilant against antiwar sentiment began to shift their attention to subversive political and economic ideas. From January, 1919, to May, 1920, the Republic was saved not just by a few FBI raids on immigrant political groups, but by local harassment of intellectually unconventional teachers, beatings administered to Socialists and Wobblies, and a few well-placed gunshots and hangings to emphasize the sincerity of popular feeling. It is not pleasant or particularly enlightening to repeat the details of the Red Scare of 1919–1920, especially the stimulus it gave to America's racial antagonisms. There were 25 large race riots in American cities in the summer of 1919, and more than 70 *reported* lynchings (whites lynching blacks; none of the other kind were reported, and one may be sure they would have been). The Red Scare was really a red-and-black-scare, aimed (if the word does not imply too much rationality) not only at political radicals but also at any Negroes, particularly the young males just back from France, who might have come into contact with the idea that their postwar existence would be any different from their existence before they put on a uniform or moved into war work in Detroit and Chicago. Any observer could have stated the principal reasons for such a constipated social climate: the Russian Revolution and the "threat" of international Marxism, the bombings and labor problems of 1919. But there would undoubtedly have been a red scare even without Leninism. Stanley Coben, in a perceptive article published in

1964, argues that the red scare was not so much aimed at Bolshevism as at the disturbing changes in values and behavior that everywhere undercut familiar things in postwar America. Undoubtedly the term "Bolshevism" denoted a number of sins. The bourgeois public broadened the term to include all forms of social criticism, and counterattacked to prevent the imminent onset of riot, expropriation, and free love. Bourgeois society, under the goad of the unrest of 1919, closed ranks against subversive ideas of all kinds, proscribing not only the really revolutionary sentiments of a few anarchists and Marxists but virtually all forms of social criticism.

So the atmosphere closed in by 1919, and the dreams of the socialists, the railroad nationalizers, the stray radicals hoping to convene a third party, all were shown to be the dreams of a small minority. The red scare, of course, was "over" by mid 1920; it required a degree of emotional excitation not far from that required for reform, and it was just such exertions the public was seeking to avoid. But the underlying doctrine of the anti-red crusade, that dissent in all its forms was revolutionary and intolerable, persisted in the 1920s in the stifling form of a credulous complacency. When the Right won the brief struggle of 1918–19, it won not just a year but a decade of dominance. The presidential politics of 1920 would mark the beginning of an extended reign of those forces committed against social criticism, against all forms of social change but the technological and commercial innovations of the private sector. The public, or most of it, continued until 1929 to find the economic order nearly perfect, and lived easily under the benevolent rule of the well-paid decision-makers in the worlds of industry, commerce, advertising, education, and religion. Such outbreaks of indignation and dissent as occurred were repeatedly put down by the political leadership of the established order. It was not a flourishing climate for social criticism, broad vision, or sustained attention to the public interest.

IV.

There was a time when historians left the story of progressivism here, fading Wilson and LaFollette out as Harding and all his hosts of conservatives reclaimed the country. While the stereotype of the conservative, complacent 1920s contains its truth, it needs to be emphasized that the eclipse of reform was never total. Ideas and projects distasteful to entrenched commercial groups continued to emanate from angry people, and if these efforts are forgotten simply because they were beaten back, we then exaggerate the placidity and consensus of the 1920s, and in addition are unprepared to understand 1929. Note the signs of insurgent activity with which the custodians of the ongoing social enterprise had to cope. In late 1919 Amos Pinchot, J. A. H. Hopkins, and other progressives organized the Committee of Forty-Eight to keep alive the prospects of political action, and the committee was the nucleus of a progressive coalition that met in Chicago in 1922. The majority of those at the Chicago meetings were representatives of the farmer-labor parties that had been springing up in states such as Minnesota, Iowa, Nebraska, and as far west as Washington, in angry response to the high unemployment and low farm prices of 1920–22. Out of two conferences in Chicago grew the Conference for Progressive Political Action, an assortment of old reformers, trade unionists, moderate socialists, and Non-Partisan Leaguers. What brought them together and held them together was a distaste for the conservatism of major party politics, and they had no difficulty persuading Bob LaFollette to run for president in 1924 on a Progressive Party ticket. LaFollette polled five million votes, a poor third, but his campaign was plagued by mistakes and difficulties, and that five million votes becomes an imposing sign of dissent when we understand it to be the hard core of a progressive vote that was in potential much larger. Had LaFollette not antagonized the Klan, had he not opposed America's participation in the war, had the progressive organization been more efficient, more states might have returned totals like those of California, where LaFollette received four times as many votes as the Democratic candidate, John W. Davis. Coolidge was easily elected, and the vote showed that most of the country was not only conservative but apathetic; only about 50 percent of registered voters bothered to vote. But under the apathy and conservatism of the majority ran an unmistakable current of protest.

This pressure for reform was felt in more places than presidential politics. The farm bloc in Congress secured passage of the Packers and Stockyards Act of 1921, the Grain Futures Act of 1922, several complicated farm credit arrangements enacted in 1921 and 1923, and the Cooperative Marketing Act of 1922. These legislative exertions did nothing to stem the slide of farm prices, but they were the only display of creative legislative power that spokesmen for what might be called underprivileged social groups were able to muster in the years of Republican dominance. Yet if insurgents did not have the strength to pursue their positive goals in the congressional atmosphere of the 1920s, they had considerable obstructive strength. In the Senate, George Norris was at the head of a list of reform-minded men full of irreverent language, dislike of large fortunes, distrust of large corporations, and sympathy for the underdog. Later generations have forgotten Frazier and Lemke from North Dakota, Shipstead and Johnson of Minnesota, Hiram Johnson of California, Brookhart of Iowa—have almost forgotten Norris and LaFollette. And with the exception of the latter two, the "Sons of the Wild Jackass" in the Senate *were* cranky, contentious, uninterested in sustained action, and effective in a negative way only on selected occasions. But they held the line against a few of the schemes of conservatives, such as the selling of government rights at Muscle Shoals, the appointment of John J. Parker to the Supreme Court, or a few of the more outrageous features of Andrew Mellon's tax plans. As Cedric Cowing reminds us in his *Populists, Plungers and Progressives,* these senatorial mavericks sustained a vigorous criticism throughout the 1920s and especially from January to October, 1929, of speculative excesses on the market and the timidity of the Federal Reserve Board in curbing the call loan market. They stand as a reminder that there were rebellious constituencies all over the country in the years of Harding, Coolidge, and Hoover.

Outside the government, voluntary associations in the social welfare and social service movements remained in existence and continued their struggles on behalf of labor legislation, social insurance, public housing, and adequate relief. Organizations like the National Consumers League, the Women's Trade Union League, and the group associated with *Survey* magazine refused to allow reduced budgets and public apathy to put an end to their efforts. The National Child Labor Committee helped push its Constitutional amendment through the Congress in 1924, and then lobbied it in the states. New organizations actually arose to join the old, such as the American Association for Old Age Security, founded in 1927 by Abraham Epstein. Fruition along these lines was delayed until the 1930s (and in some cases, such as those of adequate relief or national health insurance, did not come even then), but the 1920s were a time of at least theoretical advance toward some of the unattained goals of the progressive social welfare wing. A more successful reform campaign of the 1920s, in which some of the social service group also participated, was the effort to outlaw war. The peace forces of the progressive years regrouped after the war, and gained their pact against war in the Kellogg-Briand Treaty of 1928. In this battle at least the reformers had not only agitated and educated, but had won exactly what they wanted.

A review of the surviving reform activities thus produces no mean list. It is well to remember these pockets of resistance to the "let business alone" ethos lest we stereotype the 1920s, and, more important, lest we lose sight of the alternatives actually offered to the American public.

V.

Arthur Link wrote an article in 1959 in which he reviewed some of this evidence of dissent in the 1920s, and he nonetheless entitled the article "What Happened to Progressivism in the 1920s?" Economic reform in that period was almost totally frustrated, the scattered forces of reform in crippling disarray. A fairly widespread prosperity, a memory of the radical frights of 1919, a cycle of weariness and complacency, these constitute the chief causes of the weakness of progressivism in the 1920s, according to the classic external explanation. There is much to recommend such a line of argument; indeed, it is indispensable. But we know how much economic discontent there was, and no purely external explanation can account for the poor results attained by groups in revolt. Throughout the 1920s the forces of economic reform were frustrated by their inability—which went all the way back to the split of 1912—to concentrate sufficiently to capture one of the two major parties. This organizational problem was to a large extent a result of that factionalism and unruliness that had always characterized and hampered the reform forces. Their leadership problems in the 1920s were serious, with Wilson ill, Roosevelt gone, and LaFollette aging, but here again the problem was not new—they had never been able to unite behind one leader or one program. It was in the area of the reform program that the 1920s revealed inadequacies few had suspected. The progressives had largely run out of relevant ideas, Link argues, citing the stale formulas of the LaFollette platform and the helplessness of reformers in dealing with Secretary Mellon's tax cut proposals without benefit of a modern understanding of what public-sector spending could accomplish. Link and others have exaggerated the intellectual inadequacies of the reform universe (as distinct from individuals within it, who had plenty of inadequacies); while it would require a book to argue this conclusively, it is my impression that reform intellectuals and political leaders were in possession during the 1920s of a rather thorough understanding of the nature of poverty, the activities of antisocial groups in American economic life, and the principal steps necessary to seek humane adjustment. Undoubtedly they had an insufficient (almost nonexistent) understanding of the social uses of fiscal policy, but the New Dealers' conservatism in this area indicates that the concept was difficult to assimilate. Even given this undoubted intellectual inadequacy, the apparent obsolescence of the progressive mentality in the 1920s was as much a matter of will as of intellect.

This is not to directly disagree with critics like Randolph Bourne, Harold Stearns, or the historians David Noble and Eric Goldman who show that the pragmatic reform mind was so much more interested in action and technique than in goals and ultimate values that it did not function well in adversity. In the days when the entire nation was aroused, social evils seemed many but simple, their solution a matter of public enlightenment and applied intelligence, and the volunteer army of reform was large and enthusiastic. But once the bosses and slums did not vanish, public apathy began to silence the muckraking journals; the war crusade brought the hard knowledge that The People were ill-informed and irrational and the state preferred intellectual conformity to social service. Then the liberal mind was forced to rethink its task. This should not have been such a morale-shattering bit of work. The principal ideas of progressivism were sound enough: it was still true that private economic forces had made the cities close to intolerable, plundered the natural environment, and virtually eliminated (or perpetuated the lack of) real freedom from the lives of the great mass of Americans who had no capital and little education and therefore no real chances of spiritual and physical emancipation. And it was still true that intelligent, humane people who confronted such a social system knew what they must do: expose social maladjustments; denounce social drift; awaken a vision of a society made more just and more free through intelligent and democratic social control; amass and analyse social data; write; organize politically on all levels; revitalize public education; and above all, learn to use the state on a sustained basis.

All this had been known for years and had not lost its validity. Individual reformers certainly expected too much from simple exposure or the Australian ballot, and their resolve and ingenuity perhaps flagged when the world proved hard to remake. But despite its association with much that was fatuous, peripheral, and sometimes repressive, progressivism had identified America's social problems rather accurately, and had formulated and even experimented with many quite promising remedies. Reform faced political problems, since man was not what the reformers had thought. But in the universe of reform ideas there were priceless insights, which, had they been more widely adopted and implemented, would have made the way ahead much easier for the American nation. Such intellectual problems as remained were problems of technique that a normal amount of intelligence, flexibility, and inventiveness could solve. The malady of the reform mentality after the war was not so much bewilderment as discouragement. While the reformers' loss of effectiveness was naturally enough related to external circumstances, to the extent that it was internal it owed less to a poverty of suitable ideas than to the structure of the reform coalition and the nature of the reform calling.

To examine the surviving reformers in the 1920s is to gain a better sense of that mix of internal and external difficulties that so depleted reform ranks. Progressivism failed to hold the recruits it had attracted before the war, and it could ill afford to lose any reform-oriented person, least of all its chief intellectuals and politicians. The scores of reformers who dropped out of the movement after the war remind us not to overestimate the joys of their campaigns. Reform was tedious, hard, disappointing work. A few men established political careers through reform, but for most progressives there was little more in the game than sacrifice of time and energy for impalpable and transitory feelings of guilts eased and duties shouldered. Sacrifices such as they made were trifles when they were young and the movement so new that it was possible to believe that one or two elections would bring them home. But sacrifices and deferred personal lives seemed more burdensome as the 1920s wore on, with prospects for uplift and improvement now so dark. Whether or not a reformer any longer believed the thing could be done, he was usually ready for someone else to do it.

Accordingly, many reformers became ex-reformers and turned their hands to long-deferred private concerns. Those who had come from the professions into public service simply took up again the practice of law or medicine. Various business interests occupied those who had interrupted commercial careers. The reform journalists continued to write, but the shift away from public crusades was plainly outlined in their new themes. Muckrakers who had written of social evils now wrote innocuous romances, short stories for the *Saturday Evening Post,* or novels of the old West. History had a strong appeal for men who were disoriented and disappointed with the present. Samuel Hopkins Adams, for example, who had exposed the patent medicine industry in a series of articles for *Collier's,* wrote of the Erie Canal country of his youth, and Burton J. Hendrick began a history of the Confederacy. Some, like Ida Tarbell when she wrote a life of U. S. Steel's Judge Gary, eulogized men whom twenty years earlier they had stigmatized as Robber Barons. Of the muckrakers, historian Louis Filler found only two—Upton Sinclair and Ray Stannard Baker—who continued in the 1920s to write on contemporary social problems.

Lucrative law practices and pleasant little novels were not the only allurements that stripped the progressive movement of much of its intellectual talent. Brand Whitlock went to live abroad; Fred Howe to live in Nantucket; Carl Vrooman retired to his Illinois farm and the solace of religion; Charles R. Crane grew dates in Palm Springs or travelled in Europe; Raymond Robins became a grower and a banker in central Florida; Hutchins Hapgood grimly pursued the bohemian life in and around New York. But the effect of such new interests was the same—these reformers had laid down their burdens of duty and conscience and sought entirely private ends in the years that remained to them.

These defections thinned progressive ranks and exposed the environmental and internal difficulties that must have hampered even those who kept up what reformers called "the fight." In themselves, of course, defections do not explain the failure of reform in the 1920s since they are to be expected in some degree and would naturally have been replaced if the status quo continued to be abrasive among certain social groups. Since the status quo was well supplied with flaws and injustices in the 1920s, there were indeed recruits for the army of reform, even some for the idea of revolution. We wonder that there were not more, that the unemployed and the urban lower class and the blacks and the landless farmers did not join with those who *were* somewhat radicalized in the 1920s, the railway brotherhoods, Dakota farmers, middle-sized landowning farmers in the grain belts. Yet even when one counts out the old progressives who had resigned and the disadvantaged classes who were so strangely and pathetically docile, *still* we have the impression that the amount of discontent was considerable. What saved the day for the conservatives was not the success of the economy nor the happy loyalty of the citizenry but the fragmentation and disunity among the disinherited, the indignant, the apprehensive, the bored, and the morally sensitive. It was this disunity that allowed the decade to take on its misleading air of self-satisfaction.

Disunity among progressives derived from many factors, some not peculiar either to progressivism or to the 1920s. Any campaign to change institutions and practices is more prone to internal disagreements than the effort to defend them. Conservatives have always had that advantage. Woodrow Wilson had explained this to the young Franklin Roosevelt by likening the conservatives to a fist and the reformers to the extended, unjoined fingers of a hand. Another problem the reformers had faced since the beginning in the 1890s was the obtrusive individualism of Americans, which made coalition, organization, persistence and patience so difficult. The highest virtue among progressives—this was to some extent a generational trait— was "being true to my own ideals" or "a lonely fight against all the odds," the assumption that a man was never so right as when he stood alone and refused to compromise. This trait reared splendid individuals; it crippled political action. Progressives had always been plagued by it. And to make prospects for unity worse, there was the intense partisanship of American political life, which meant that reformers of essentially the same mind and purposes but of different parties would only under the rarest circumstances agree to ignore the party label of some otherwise useful person.

All of these potentially divisive factors were present when progressivism arose in the 1890s, and they hampered reformers over the years, although of course they were occasionally overcome. But the

1920s, fortunately for defenders of a status quo so flawed that it bred a mass of enemies, was a decade when the divisions among reformers were exaggerated into a chasm. The issue that divided them—the issue that dominated the decade—was the cultural antagonism between the urban and the rural ways of life.

That antagonism predated the 1920s, of course. Indeed, a large part of progressive reform had been an effort to insure that the standards of small-town, rural America would not be replaced by undesirable new habits imported from Europe, or spawned in the permissive, crowded, impersonal city. There was fervor in this, but in the hopeful atmosphere of the prewar period the attitudes of middle-class, white, farm, or small-town raised Americans (this included almost all the progressives) had not hardened into an obsession with the city's evils. Reformers, like everyone else, flocked to the city and took up residence there without hesitation, attracted by its opportunities and certain that its blemishes and bad habits could be corrected. Once there, reformers worried about the moral conditions of life, but they also worried about the physical conditions, about wealth, poverty, economic advantages, power. Agrarian and small-town reformers were rarely warm toward urban labor, but they took seriously their duty to "uplift" the laborer in both his physical and his moral life. As a result, coalitions could occasionally be effected between the urban working class and the rest of the progressive movement with its predominantly rural or small-town outlook. Their various goals might coincide on any number of material (as contrasted with moral) issues—locally, an improvement in city sanitation, or a shift in the tax burden from households to industry, or the humbling of a utility company; nationally, an antitrust law, a lowering of the tariff, a progressive income tax.

In the 1920s the chances of such coalitions plummeted. This was certainly not because material grievances had been removed. The urban and small-town middle class, true enough, had become less responsive to economic reform because of the increased flow of con-sumer goods that the non-agricultural middle classes enjoyed. But economic complaints were still widely felt by the urban labor force and a major part of rural America, especially the large staple crop areas. Persistent agricultural depression put rural people in the mood for insurgency, and the urban working class had not escaped its unsteady employment, its low wages, its exposure to industrial accident, its squalid housing. Inevitably and naturally, efforts to create a farmer-labor coalition were made many times in the 1920s because the logic of common interests and common enemies was so obvious. The most notable effort was the campaign of 1924, preceded by the farmer-labor parties formed in the upper Midwest.

Such efforts failed despite what appear in retrospect to have been promising circumstances. For just at this time when cultural differences between urban laborers and agrarians needed most to be ignored, they became the leading concern of the agrarians. As a result, most of the political energies of economically disadvantaged people were directed against other economically disadvantaged people.

It is not entirely clear why cultural antagonisms became strong enough in the 1920s to kill all chance of a coalition of rural and urban insurgents when roughly similar moral reforms before the war had not polarized the progressive movement. We know that urban areas continued to grow at the expense of the countryside, so that the census of 1920 showed more Americans lived in cities than on farms or in towns of less than 2,500. Young people drifting into the cities in 1900 seem to have had a sense that the old ways could be restored in these new cities, and that the dominance of the old New England culture was basically secure. Twenty years later they had a number of reasons to feel that the initiative had shifted to the vulgarization of morality, that time was running out and the utmost urgency was called for to halt the decline of a once proud, clean, white, Bible-reading, homogeneous society. Economic reform would have to wait until the more important matters of morals and behavior and ideas were dealt with.

The main outlines of the politics of cultural counterattack are well enough known. Defense of the Protestant-rural way of life required that alcoholic drinks be outlawed, that the flow of swarthy, Jewish immigrants be stopped, that the teaching of any biological theories that might undermine Scripture be terminated, that the public in general be alerted to the city-based moral deterioration that had resisted prewar progressive cleanups and now threatened to mongrelize the race, socialize the economy, and introduce in one intolerable package the practice of free love and the tyranny of the Pope. Given these priorities, the highlights of the public life of the 1920s may be reviewed without surprise: the quarantine from alien ideas and peoples accomplished by the red scare; the defeat of the League of Nations and the World Court; the Immigration Restriction Acts of 1921 and 1924; prohibition and its comic enforcement; the string of antievolution laws in southern and border states leading up to the trial at Dayton, Tennessee, which was a victory for the fundamentalists whatever the eastern press may have said; that most publicized and politicized of murder trials, the Sacco-Vanzetti case, which inflamed feelings for seven years (1920–27) and turned less on criminal evidence than on the anarchistic ideas and European identity of the accused; and the Ku Klux Klan. Above all one remembers in this connection yesterday's Mafia, the "Invisible Empire" of the Klan—reborn in Georgia in 1915, moribund until the fear-ridden atmosphere of 1920, mushrooming into a political force of some 2–4 million members, which made and broke politicians in Texas, Oregon, Oklahoma, Georgia, Alabama, Indiana, and Washington, D.C., tearing apart the Democratic Party in 1924 before subsiding toward the end of the 1920s in scandals, a returning prosperity, and disenchantment at its lack of constructive results.

The important effect of such crusades lay not in whether drink was really outlawed, Catholics-Jews-blacks permanently barred as political and sexual threats, or the Bible secured against all heresy, since in these, as all other reforms, legislation and aroused opinion proved inadequate to the task. What was significant about such political efforts was that they set potential allies at odds—ruralists and portions of the urban middle class whose cultural identification was rural, against the non-English ethnic component of the working class and urban intellectuals emancipated from Victorian standards. While one cannot be sure, it is at least possible that in the absence of such cultural agitations, with their drain on energy and their claim on analytical powers and political attention, a broad class alliance might have been formed, in portions of the country, if not nationally. Some rural people talked of industrial prices and profits, the tariff, the cost of credit, the existence of virtually untaxed fortunes—complaints that could have formed the core of an alliance with labor and stray progressives from the professions. But so long as most ruralists worried as much or more about the birth rate, drinking habits, and general unworthiness of the Dago, the Wop, and the Jew, the relative economic situation of the classes was sure to remain the same.

The spectacle of people on pinched incomes exerting their political talents against differently dressed people on pinched incomes must have given considerable pleasure to the masters of capital and their retainers, those who were not themselves, like Henry Ford, so unsophisticated as to be seriously involved in the holy war against city ways. Ford, of course, was deadly serious about the peril of the city, but had he been a political genius, which no one has ever suggested, he could not have devised a campaign better designed to shelter his wealth and prerogatives from his restless employees. Ethnocentric politics are conservative politics, as the southern ruling classes learned long ago. The summary of political life in the 1920s is brief enough: cultural conflict made it impossible for economic radicalism to mass.

Ironically, the illiberal crusades of the 1920s against urban lifestyles and heresies bear strong resemblances to the crusades of the prewar period. The 1920s were not so totally different from the decade before the world war, when citizens were aroused by Tom Johnson and T. R., leaders now departed. In both periods one has popular movements to restore the lost community, to cleanse, to uplift, to do good. We lack the solid evidence on the social composition of prewar and postwar social movements that would be necessary to announce that progressivism was carried on in the 1920s by the same social groups and classes, soured by the war experience and now putting the old methods to reactionary purposes. But in the absence of such evidence the similarities between the popular movements of 1912 and 1922 are striking enough to suggest to some historians that the 1920s ought to be thought of also as a progressive decade—but a progressivism with its illiberal side now having the upper hand.

Too much stress may be placed on continuities. Prewar reform may not be studied in the 1920s. Too much had changed, the ranks of the aroused had been depleted and refilled, the juxtaposition of issues was fundamentally altered. But the suspicion of a substantial continuity between prewar and postwar crusades has much to recommend it when one thinks particularly of rural and small-town rather than urban progressivism. Notice how the veterans of a certain type of reform often made the decision that the defense of the village way of life required a cultural rather than an economic emphasis: after the war we find old Tom Watson railing at Negroes and Jews, William Jennings Bryan putting down the Darwinian heresy, A. Mitchell Palmer straining every nerve to round up and export dangerous political ideas and their carriers. The case of Bryan is most instructive, for it shows how slight an alteration in stress and mood was required to adjust at least one variety of the progressive impulse for its postwar career. We remember Bryan's last years as a time of church services and revivals, and especially for the inept defense of the Fundamentalist reading of scripture at Dayton, Tennessee. This period has been pictured as an apostasy, but Lawrence Levine, in his fine book on Bryan, *Defender of the Faith,* makes two points about these last years that underline the consistency of Bryan's life. Bryan never forgot about, and certainly never changed his mind about, the economic injustices that he had been working against since the early 1890s. He labored to make the Democratic Platform of 1924 a progressive document and predicted that the leading election issues would be inequitable taxation, profiteering, agricultural distress, and governmental regulation of railroads and mines. His Dayton activities represented no total reorientation of values or effort; he was still for economic justice in the 1920s. But he had always stood for certain narrow moralities, and saw himself as fighting the same battle at Dayton in 1925 as he had fought when he made his convention speech in 1896, a fight to defend the integrity of rural America. He had always been an economic radical and a cultural reactionary. Rural progressivism had this same dual character. There was less of the first kind of progressivism in the 1920s because there was so much of the second.

VI.

How may progressivism be summarized, its various forms and extended history managed in the fewest generalizations? Historians must mediate between the untidy details of the movement and the desire of their readers for generalization. Scholars, as did contemporaries, strike out for two or three categories—more would be an intolerable mental burden—into which they may fit all the complex facts of an historical era such as this one. The oldest set of categories into which progressives have been put was one established by progressives themselves. It is the New Freedom–New Nationalism distinction, arising out of the political struggles of 1912. For all its flaws this is a useful division. A considerable number of reformers may be described as citizens who were primarily or even solely worried about large industrial and financial combinations, who wished them broken into competitive units, and who were uneasy with a powerful state whatever its motives.

And there were men of quite a different reform mind, who saw the combination movement as a natural feature of modern industrial life and were eager to control it through a vigorous government with both regulatory and welfare responsibilities. It is of no great importance that the labels do not entirely fit either Woodrow Wilson or Theodore Roosevelt, or that the parties they led under those labels were even more than the candidates' minds a mixture of creeds. Many progressives held views of the New Freedom or the New Nationalism variety with considerable tenacity, and whatever party they favored, the categories mark off and help us to speak about large areas of consistent attitudes and behavior. The New Freedom had reactionary tendencies, which became evident later on (T.R. and others perceived this at the time, calling it "rural toryism"), but it kept alive a healthy distrust of private economic power. The New Nationalism had affinities for a government that knew what was best and would put an end to the squabbling of groups, a government preferring unity to justice. In this respect it bore a few slight resemblances to the theories and practice later to be strutted about by Mussolini. But it understood industrial civilization better than the New Freedom, and it tried to teach the American mind to accept the necessity for constant management in the public interest by public officials.

These categories, as useful as they are, do not contain all the important styles among reformers. Another pair of typologies might be designated the moralists and the scientists. The moralists were those men and women who thought the answer to the "social problem" lay in a return to the values that had served the nineteenth century— honesty, abstinence, continence, individual effort, fiduciary integrity. They filled the prohibition ranks, tried to abolish prostitution, hounded men from office if they were stained with a bit of graft. Because they did all of these things with an air of righteousness (and because they did some of them at all) we do not remember the progressive moralists with nostalgia. Today we like neither their moral code nor the aggressive way in which they held it.

Quite in contrast were men who had rejected the Victorian code in their personal lives and had no thought of applying it to America's social problems. They preferred to apply science, or at the very least, rationality, rather than the Bible or tradition. Lincoln Steffens is perhaps best remembered (because of his *Autobiography*) for such attitudes, although he had little knowledge of science. He was uncomfortable with the upright reformers he encountered in his observation of American cities, dubious of the efficacy of mere honesty in office, and irresistibly drawn to the flexible, affable, wordly bosses who had a sense of humor he missed in the Goo Goos. To Steffens and men like him neither the moralistic reformer nor the political boss could bring America out of her crisis; the answer lay in science, in technically trained people, in "trained intelligence." If Steffens was the popularizer of a reform type uncomfortable with moral certitudes and full of confidence in the critical intelligence, John Dewey was its preeminent philosopher. This preference for science over received moral absolutes appealed to engineers, public health officials, economists, statisticians, architects, physicians, and even some businessmen, social types who had learned orderly and critical processes of thought and who were eager to bring their expertise to bear upon an unruly society in need of reorganization.

It is clear to us now that the reformers who were pragmatic and had a respect for science understood better the America of their time and the America in the making than did the moralists. They seemed to perceive the need for mental flexibility in a society so caught up in change, and they understood that progress would come only to the nation that trained and utilized its scientists and social scientists. They sensed that modern society required social control guided by a constant flow of data and that it could not proceed on the rigid truths of dated sermons. The saloon was not the prime menace to the well-being of Americans, nor was the political boss. An unregulated economy holds that honor, crashing on toward profits and blind to the social consequences. But while the scientific progressives were best equipped temperamentally and occasionally also intellectually to cope with modern problems, in retrospect we have been unable to commend them wholeheartedly.

In the first place, talk as they might about critical intelligence, technique, and urbane sophistication, most of them had not traveled very far from the fervid style that marked their entire generation. A scientist like Harvey Wiley might ground his crusade in figures and experimental data, but in ways he was as moralistic as the heavyset ladies of the WCTU. This was simply not a cool generation, and those in it who spoke admiringly of trained intelligence never managed to spring their own intelligences loose from service to some unexamined values. This inconsistency, however, is not what we chiefly regret in the scientific school. A consequence of their thought and activity seems to have been the impersonal, bureaucratic world that envelops us, crushing out spontaneity, disrupting community, and in general robbing us of some of the finer by-products of a premodern social order.

Every student may be allowed a third category, those reformers who had just the right vision and balance, who took from the moralists their passion for risky, worthy causes, and from the scientists their mental flexibility and their respect for technical expertise in the service of the public. But for anyone this is a small list, since so few men and women then or now avoided the excesses of dogmatism or manipulative urges. My own list includes Jane Addams and Lillian Wald, Benjamin Marsh, John B. Andrews, George Norris, Paul U. Kellogg, Judge Ben Lindsey, Mary White Ovington, and that "unwearied hoper," Florence Kelley.

VII.

One could go on noting these efforts at a taxonomy of progressive reform, but we are perhaps in a position to see the main outlines of what we wish to summarize. The progressive era was a compound of these elements: (1) attempts to impose order and modern procedures upon an archaic nineteenth-century society; (2) attempts to come to the aid of the casualties of industrialism—the ghetto dweller, the female factory laborer, the working child; and (3) attempts to impose nineteenth-century moral codes on a twentieth-century world. Each of these major objectives enlisted different social types, drew strength from different social classes, and more often than complementing each other, contradicted each other. Some overlap in leadership, and the usual confusion of legislative struggles and their inevitable blend of impulses and interest groups, have naturally blurred the outlines of these three types of reform effort. So also has the fog of self-justifying and generally sincere rhetoric. The common use of phrases such as *The People, Justice, restoration of American ideals,* helped obscure what was distinct about the components of progressivism. Yet even if these categories reflect the reality of what contemporaries saw as one undifferentiated movement for greater democracy, important and difficult tasks remain. How may these various objectives be ranked so that we understand with reasonable accuracy how that generation was apportioning its corrective energies? And what results were achieved in each area?

On the question of which objective predominated at the time, we have only impressions, uncorrected by any methodology capable of measuring the intensity of commitment of reformers in prewar America. The urge to submit social processes and governmental institutions to the discipline of technology and industrialism seems in retrospect to have been the most significant motivation of the period and one that met with the most far-reaching results. America at the beginning of this century was a modernizing society, shifting from agriculture to industry, from crude and small-scale industry to larger units, becoming daily more urbanized, technological, rationally and specially organized for specialized tasks. Efficiency, the hope of efficiency, and the sheer desire to expand meant that broad commercial interests would impinge upon narrow, local ones with mounting success. Ambitious entrepreneurs followed a vision of nationwide and predictable operations, and it was shared by experts who longed to manage large projects. Expanding enterprise confronted localized jurisdictions and habits, irresistibly pressing them toward subordination or obliteration. The bureaucratic habits of orderliness and regularity were prized, eccentricity and lack of planning discouraged. The initiative rested with the forces of centralization, integration of systems, rationalization, coordination, and efficiency, even though these were slowed by tradition and other impediments.

What has all this to do with reform? The rationalization of systems meant the internal reform of those large business enterprises that meant to participate in the future, and this required men with a respect for the methods of science, a passion for order, an expansionist psychology, and a sense of mission. Such men, and women, arose in business and the professions, and they may be called reformers as readily as we have used the word for public servants like Roosevelt, LaFollette, Pinchot. Samuel Haber's book *Efficiency and Uplift*, tells of the Taylor movement to bring efficiency to industry with stopwatches and efficiency studies, and the moral fervor and guiding principles of Taylorism mark it as a cousin to the well-known political aspects of progressivism. In the medical profession, the Flexner Report of 1910 should be equally recognizable as an event in reform history. The report exposed the chaotic manner of preparing and certifying physicians in the United States, and led to the rationalization of medical education through common standards and effective examination of aspirants. Another example from the private sector would be Seaman A. Knapp's pioneering efforts to establish demonstration farms and to educate adults in rural areas in the practices of scientific farming.

It was inevitable that this aggressive, modern spirit moving in the larger capitalist institutions and the professions would discover that it also had a calling to the reformation of public life. Indeed, the challenge here was even greater, since the world of business had forged ahead with modern methods and left public institutions stagnant and backward by contrast. Modern corporations were increasingly in command of their environments—gathering data, anticipating the future, eliminating uncertainty and waste. But the cities were fragmented, ignorant, leaderless, directionless. Roy Lubove's *Twentieth Century Pittsburgh* (1969) provides a good example of the shocking contrast between growing private order and public disorder. The steel industry was planned and poised for the future, while the city in which it sat was framented by class, ethnic, and residential divisions, unable to respond to its desperate problems. Not unnaturally, the coalition that emerged to attack the problems of Pittsburgh and other cities not only borrowed the methods of modern business, but enlisted the businessmen themselves. Those whose operations were citywide (or greater) wished a city government that answered to the data generated by experts rather than the haphazard appetites of a welter of wards with their local and parochial preoccupations and their tendency toward drift. For them, reform meant a strong, routinized government they could control or influence, with well-staffed regulatory agencies at all levels—public health, finance, police, public utilities, city planning, and the like. The ranks of urban reform were filled with people of lesser economic stake but a similar determination to have a modern, orderly city. They were often individuals of small-town background, lawyers, and other educated citizens ready for new professions, people who brought to the city the evangelical style of the Protestant countryside, which disguised urban progressivism with the rhetoric of moralism when its inner dynamic was really rationalization.

Men with similar outlook but with broader investments or professional horizons came to see the need for reform at the federal level—and reform meant new and enlarged functions performed by trained and properly oriented men. The regulatory measures at the federal level that form the best-known part of the progressive record—regulatory commissions in railroading, banking, special industries from meat-packing to pharmaceuticals, and a commission for all large industry[4]—were largely created by a special type of businessman and a special type of young professional. We have earlier reviewed the sources of regulatory statutes: disgruntled shippers demanded railroad regulation and enlightened owners and managers concurred; a coalition of noneastern bankers and small businessmen demanded banking reform and were joined in the idea if not all the details by the Wall Street financial leaders; meat-packers wanted a meat-packing inspection act; food processors and retail druggists pressed for a food and drug administration. And in all these struggles to reform business practices the pressure came not only from business interests but also from professional men, many already in the federal service, who had caught a glimpse of the public and personal advantages of bureaucratic control over the existing chaos.

This type of progressivism might occasionally talk of democracy, but it was elitist rather than democratic, efficiency-minded rather than justice-minded. Where it was successful, power was not diffused among The People but was concentrated in a knowledge-elite without whom no modern mayor or industrialist would dream of proceeding. While the opposition was fierce and often lumped this sort of reformer with the do-gooders who worried about the urban poor, poverty was no prime concern of theirs. They were out to end the diffusion of power and the randomness of social processes; they wished to vest social control in safe hands, and fewer hands.

Because of this conservative potential, and because they were in tune with the logic of industrialism, the exponents of efficiency and orderly procedures lost little momentum after the war. The effort to bring the advantages of centralized, bureaucratized government to the cities continued in the 1920s, with 303 cities turning to the commission-manager plan (only 31 cities had adopted the plan from 1905 to 1915). This was an innovation that centralized responsibility, with a few men elected on a citywide vote in place of the old unwieldy

---

[4] And the less well-known agencies established by the same pressures, whose functions were promotional rather than regulatory, such as the National Bureau of Standards (1901), the Bureau of the Census (1902), or the Bureau of Mines (1910).

council elected on a ward basis. Reformers promised that the result would be lower taxes even as services were strengthened and expanded. These changes had the strong support of most businessmen, who thought the old mayor and council system cumbersome and wasteful and deplored the strength (or at least, autonomy) it gave to working-class wards that would be underrepresented under a system of citywide elections.

The bulk of the postwar activity of this sort came at the state level, where a series of reform administrations wrote a reform history that has received insufficient attention. New York under Al Smith (1920–28), Pennsylvania under Gifford Pinchot (1924–28), California under Clement Young (1926–30), North Carolina under Cameron Morrison (1921–25), Alabama under Bibb Graves (1926–30), Louisiana under John W. Parker (1920–24), these and other states were the scenes of legislative activity and administrative reorganization that George Tindall has described as "business progressivism." Businessmen may have supported the new policies of the 1920s, since part of what was involved was a series of subsidies in the form of increased expenditure on transportation improvements and state agencies for promotion and research. But the central idea was not subsidies, but efficiency. By 1931 at least forty-one states had followed the lead of Indiana, which had in 1909 established an agency to coordinate other state agencies (in Indiana, the Department of Inspection and Supervision of Public Offices). In 1912 no state operated with a budget; by 1930, all but one had adopted that prerequisite to financial planning. No state in 1910 had a central purchasing agency; by 1930, thirty-five had centralized their purchasing. The 1920s in state government was a time of the integration and rationalization, as well as the expansion, of modern governmental bureaucracies.

After the war there were also continued efforts at the federal level to bring order to the economy through a scientific and technical bureaucracy. Federal government spending in 1930 was 350 percent greater than in 1915, and while much of this was war-related, the functions of government expanded yearly through the 1920s as bureaucrats and constituencies agreed to let fewer things alone in America. Spending on health and welfare did not keep pace with population increase, but the government became very active in the promotion and regulation of commerce and agriculture. The largest increases came in expenditures on transportation, the postal system, aid to shipping, the data-gathering functions of Bureau of Foreign and Domestic Commerce and the Bureau of Agricultural Economics. The Commerce Department under Herbert Hoover, an engineer who was impressed with the success of the War Industries Board at bringing rationality to sectors of industry (the WIB, for example, had standardized the shape of auto tires and bricks), became an agency with a mission—to foster efficiency and coordination in American business. Under Hoover's guidance (1920–28) the department gathered information on trade conditions, prices, and markets, and distributed it (free) to competing firms to allow them to eliminate wasteful competition. Agricultural economists like Mordekai Ezekiel and Louis Bean were doing the same things for farmers from their offices in the Department of Agriculture. The goal was predictability and control, the reduction of the bad guesses and wasteful duplications—in a word, the inefficiency—of American producing and selling. There were similar opportunities in the agencies involved in resource management for those bureaucrats who were ambitious to bring their expertise to bear upon decisions affecting irreplaceable natural resources. "Pinchot-type conservation did not deteriorate in the 1920s," historian Donald Swain tells us, "but expanded and matured" as agencies such as the Forest Service enlarged their operations.

The same thrust toward rationalization was apparent in the streamlined public administration at the federal level. The Budget and Accounting Act of 1921 carried out many of the recommendations of the Taft Commission on Economy and Efficiency (1911–13), most importantly establishing a Bureau of the Budget to coordinate not only federal spending plans but its bureaucratic procedures. Outside government one finds the same tendencies. City comptrollers, police and fire chiefs, state auditors, even mayors and governors organized in the 1920s, if they had not done so just before the war, and began to share information and standardize procedures. *World Convention Dates* for 1920 shows forty-five annual conventions of national organizations of public officials, and by 1930 the figure was ninety. President Hoover's Commission on Recent Social Trends reported that the 1920s had been a time of great change in American public administration, and the words the commission used over and over again were *centralization, simplification, supervision, research, efficiency.* There were no dramatic victories— this sort of reform rarely provided them. But the gains for social control progressivism were measurable and permanent.

Progressive speechmakers, our fathers who read the older textbooks, and our children now frowning their way through the social studies curriculum in junior high schools would all fail to reccognize the foregoing account as a description of the real core of the progressive movement. We see social control where older histories described liberation, we attribute reform measures to professional and commercial elites rather than the indignant rhetoricians of Congress, pulpit, and magazines, and we describe the goal as the rationalization and centralization, not the democratization, of American society. What jars most in all the new writing on progressivism, if one had been reared on more traditional accounts, is the discovery of businessmen swarming throughout the domain of reform, originating, shaping, modifying, and in general lobbying—unassimilable notion—for regulation. One may wonder what took us so long to discover them, and the answer seems to be a compound of the beguiling rhetoric of the reformers themselves, the advent of better sampling procedures, the intensification of monographic studies, and the congeniality of the discovery to the radicalized intellectuals of the 1960s. There is some reason to wonder if, under the latter influence, the younger historians are discovering too many of them. The most important task now is to try to learn the precise extent of the influence of commercial groups in the various sectors of that wave of deliberate social change we call progressivism. It is sufficiently clear that many of those working to impose rational processes upon the mass of individual liberties that made up the pretwentieth-century American economy and social order were in fact businessmen, and that the old Beard and Parrington theory that reform meant the common man was thrashing the predatory interests was no good at all in explaining progressivism—or what appeared to be the main or most significant part of progressivism. Two new theories have recently been offered to explain the emergence of a broad drive, at many levels across an entire nation, to achieve greater social control. Gabriel Kolko, in *The Triumph of Conservatism* (1965), and James Weinstein, in *The Corporate Ideal in the Liberal State, 1900–1918* (1968), see progressivism, at least at the federal level, as a businessman's drive to use the state to stabilize the large-scale capitalist system, which was threatened both by the uncertainties of vigorous competition and by a rising tide of political radicalism. These are brilliant, challenging books, but they are not entirely persuasive. Data formerly ignored are now being overemphasized.

Businessmen were reforming, but they were also being reformed. The scene is not at all tidy. A more convincing and conceptually much broader interpretive framework has been offered by Samuel P. Hays and by Robert Wiebe. In this view the nineteenth-century social structure, characterized by a local focus, small-scale operations, and personal, face-to-face relations (in Frederick Tonnies's encompassing term, *community,* or *Gemeinschaft*), was giving way at the turn of the century to a social order based on a cosmopolitan and national focus, large-scale operations, and impersonal, bureaucratic procedures (*society,* or *Gesellschaft*). Social groups who had a stake in hastening this transition—this would-be large businessmen and their professional allies in law, engineering, city planning, and the like—turned to the state to build a bureaucratic environment conducive of stability and congenial to greater social control. Their rhetoric obscured their real purposes, but this was not because they dissimulated but because in an exciting time when the young and enlightened were reordering society they turned to the only moving rhetoric they knew, the language of the Protestant Reformation, the Old Testament prophets, the Declaration of Independence, the great national vision of Lincoln. In any event they hardly understood the historic function they were performing. They were reformers, but in this view what was being reformed in the progressive years was not only or even primarily graft or poverty, but disorderly, inefficient, and unsystematic ways of doing things.

The conceptual scheme of Hays and Wiebe is an invaluable contribution to our understanding of the progressive era, preferable to the view of Kolko and Weinstein in that it accounts for the extensive role of business groups in various reform areas without ignoring the professionals, and without overemphasizing elements of conspiracy and naked self-interest. Wiebe's *The Search for Order* is the only systematic effort to place the diverse facts of the progressive era into this conceptual framework. The book clarifies so many things that one must make a decided effort to remember that in Wiebe's hands the community-society framework has not yet comfortably been made to contain all the data. Wiebe, intent on demonstrating the transcendent importance of the reformers who represented industrial and governmental rationalization, did not devote sufficient attention to the continuing counterattack of another set of reformers, the spokesmen of community.[5] But if this is a flaw, it is a flaw of proportion, not a flaw of his framework, which accommodates nicely the prohibitionists along with the apostles of scientific management. A more serious problem is the tendency of this framework to squeeze out the element of conscience in progressivism, i.e., the social welfare volunteers, the ladies of the settlements, the Social Gospel ministers and novelists, and every other contemporary whose Christian or Emersonian principles brought him, however briefly, into the orbit of progressive activism. Hence, in this study I have tried to devise categories that allow us to utilize the community-society concept, but that also provide a framework for understanding contradictory evidence. But that reform was to a great extent a drive to stabilize large-scale industrial society by centralization of decision-making and rationalization of social processes can no longer be seriously doubted.

Because the principal beneficiaries of this side of progressivism were the owners and managers of corporations and the experts who staffed the powerful new governmental and educational bureaucracies, progressivism is on its way, especially among younger scholars, to becoming a much resented social movement. It accelerated the demise of small, neighborly communities, about which we are nostalgic, and brought the domination of a bureaucratic, scientized, depersonalizing world, which feeds our bellies so well and our souls so badly. It talked of coercion and the imposition of restraints more effectively than it talked of freedom. It educated leading capitalists in how to use the state to prevent real change, and the mental lock-step and high profits of wartime America further revealed to them the conservative possibilities of large government.

But there were both liberating and radical possibilities in the urge to coordinate and plan for greater efficiency. In the minds of Croly and Veblen and T.R. himself efficiency led away from a profit standard toward standards of social usefulness, with efficiency only a way station. Engineers who harkened to Veblen, intellectuals who read Croly, were likely to find their minds permanently occupied by the

---

[5] Wiebe, of course, knew that they were operating contemporaneously with his apostles of order and modernity, but he discussed them at length only in his section on the 1890s. A brief treatment of the forces of community in the years between the wars may be found on pp. 172, and 179–80 of his book, a sensible and perceptive discussion but all too brief.

subversive idea that profit was not the point. Admittedly, neither the coordination and cooperative practices of the war nor the 1920s much resembled the radicals' social vision or followed their priorities. But the social control strain of progressive thought need not have been put to reactionary and repressive uses. Its leading thinkers sought freedom through order, not order for its own sake. They did not intend for the liberating possibilities of social discipline to be lost sight of. Croly sought to restrict certain economic liberties, but only because he knew there was no real freedom in a disorderly and uncontrolled economy. Margaret Sanger and the progressives of the eugenics movement proposed to submit the "right" to procreate to certain social controls; and while Adolf Hitler succeeded in putting such proposals under suspicion, Margaret Sanger was unquestionably right that real freedom in the future depended upon greater control over the production of human beings. The path that history actually took should not obscure the fact that the social control movement was at least in the beginning a liberal movement. Its leading theorists, people like Thorstein Veblen, Herbert Croly and John Dewey, assumed a basic conflict with the profit motive and saw in more cooperative forms of social organization a great step toward freedom. This legacy of progressive thought was reactivated in the 1930s as men like Adolf Berle and Rexford Tugwell took from that tradition their dream of an integrated economy run by social engineers responsible to the public. Ingrained individualism and jealous interest groups swept them aside as it had their progressive forerunners, but as the planet fills up with humanity the management of freedom will bring men back to the philosophers of social control.

VIII.

Another distinctive type of reformer was the social justice progressive. *Justice* was a word frequently used in progressive circles. Some defined justice as equal economic opportunity (equal access to resources and markets, not to jobs or housing), others as the right to exercise meaningful political power. But by *social* justice the progressives understood all those efforts to give assistance, usually but not always through an agency of the state, to groups that had for any reason fallen into an intolerable arrears in the "natural" social arrangements of modernizing America. Conservatives argued that what social justice progressives sought was neither just nor socially desirable; but whether it was justice or generosity, it was impossible to ignore. Had pressure for humanitarian legislation come only from directly affected groups it would have made little headway, for such groups were unorganized and apolitical. But support came from middle and upper classes—the professional altruists of the social work–social settlement movement, and their allies in law, journalism, and even politics. When these progressives were added to the groups who would be the beneficiaries and who happened to be organized or at least aroused—railway labor, retail clerks, seamen, certain groups of farmers—it became a coalition to be reckoned with. While a coalition of altruists[6] and beneficiaries was still not wealthy or numerically very strong, under fortunate circumstances it proved able to manipulate the political machinery with tangible effect.

Writers have been attracted to the social justice progressives, and for good reasons. On the whole these were attractive, humane people. But such writers have often implied that social justice was the central concern of the era, which it was not. Recently it has been implied by young scholars that the social justice component was either nonexistent or unimportant; but it was not that either. Compile a brief list of the men and women, the organizations, and the accomplishments of this effort, and the list has a familiar ring and a not inconsiderable bulk: Jane Addams, John B. Andrews, Roger Baldwin, Louis Brandeis, Paul Kellogg, Florence Kelley, Benjamin Marsh, Owen Lovejoy, Margaret Dreier Robins, Mary Simkhovitch, Graham Taylor, John A. Ryan, Stephen S. Wise, Lillian Wald; organizations so well known that their initials are enough, such as the NCL, WTUL, AALL, NCLC, NAACP, ACLU; institutions like Hull House, Greenwich House, University Settlement, Denison House, Chicago Commons, and all the Charities Organizations in the major cities; The Pittsburgh Survey of 1906; the Industrial Relations Commission Report of 1915; the New York Tenement Law of 1901; the child labor laws in the various states, and the long national campaign; thirty-nine maximum-hour laws for women by 1917, and fifteen

---

6 Their motivation was, of course, not quite this simple. Altruism was bred into these sons and daughters of the better families as a part of the code of their class; but it was abetted by a strong presentiment of doom to the middle classes if the proletariat should become so numerous and miserable as to turn to violence.

minimum wage laws for women by 1923; factory safety laws in most industrial states; workmen's compensation in forty-two states by 1920 —the list could easily be extended, but the outlines are clear.

Does such a list not sketch the outline of a kind of revolution, a shift from the heartless, devil-take-the-hindmost industrialism of the nineteenth century to a humanized, early version of the welfare state? Unfortunately, a close, skeptical look at the record does not sustain such optimism. Paper victories, though hard enough to win, had a way of melting away in the mazes of administration and judicial interpretation. Despite the child labor laws passed by the states after the founding of the National Child Labor Committee in 1904 (southern anti-child-labor groups had operated earlier) the census of 1910 showed more children at work than in 1900. State laws were notoriously weak, levying minimum penalties or none at all, providing for elaborate court review, excluding many industries, and—in nineteen of the thirty-one states passing child labor laws, providing no funds at all for even one inspector to enforce the law. Among other reasons for such inadequacies, state legislators complained that strict laws drove industry to relocate in friendlier states and argued that child labor regulation was properly a federal matter. When the NCLC overcame its Constitutional scruples and resorted to a federal law (the Keating-Owen law was passed in 1916 after Woodrow Wilson overcame *his* Constitutional scruples), it was declared unconstitutional in *Hammer* v. *Dagenhart* (1918). A differently phrased law of 1919 met the same fate, and the despairing reformers turned to a Constitutional amendment (passed finally by Congress in 1924) only to see it smothered in the tangle of state legislatures. A national ban on child labor came only in 1938 with the passage of the Fair Labor Standards Act, and it came then not so much because of four decades of agitation by reformers as because the most radical force of all, the dynamic American economy, had undermined the institution. State child labor and compulsory education laws had cut the proportion of working children from 18 percent in 1890 to 15 percent in 1910. The decline of the family farm and the farm labor force in general, along with the automation of the more repetitive jobs, brought a rapid postwar drop to a figure of 4 percent by 1930.

But victory over child labor, whatever the share of credit between reformers and impersonal economic forces, actually produced additional evidence of the superficiality of so many progressive remedies.

Even had the child labor reformers taken the children out of the mills, their home environments would have remained in many cases as brutalizing as the work environment. Industrial labor was hard on children, but the home lives of most such children were unrelieved by adequate recreational or educational opportunities. The child-labor reformers, like most progressives inclined toward simple, negative solutions, gave little thought to the total environment of the child. At the passage of the Fair Labor Standards Act, NCLC leader George Alger, ignoring the problem of school dropouts, delinquency, and the like, closed the books on their crusade with the remark that he "knew of no further legislation to suggest." The historian of child labor in New York State was forced to conclude that "child labor reform was purely surface in nature and failed to reach the basic problems of New York's youth," leaving them after the victory of 1938 worse off than when the reformers started thirty-five or forty years before.

The failure of child-labor reform was widely admitted and broke the hearts of many social justice progressives, as well it might. But it was not an atypical case. State labor legislation proved equally porous when it was enacted. Fifteen states passed minimum wage laws for women, but when the Supreme Court ruled the law for the District of Columbia unconstitutional in the *Adkins* case (1923), six of the state laws were nullified along with it. Yet while the *Adkins* case "killed all enforcement," as Elizabeth Brandeis wrote, the laws had never amounted to much in the first place. Of the fifteen laws only five were enforceable at all, the others being so badly drafted that they either failed to set up a minimum wage or established one beneath the prevailing minimum. Of the fifteen states willing to take even these shaky steps toward the protection of women workers, only two, Massachusetts and Wisconsin, were important industrial states. The others found the laws palatable because they had little industrial labor to regulate.

In the area of housing, it must be remembered that the legislative reforms that enhanced the record of progressives in cities like New York and Chicago built no new housing units but only purported to regulate the existing ones, or some of them. Leading housing reformer Lawrence Veiller was typical in his concentration on restrictive legislation to make existing tenements more livable; he explicitly rejected the idea of public housing. So long as such attitudes characterized progressive housing reformers, even had funds for tenement inspection and enforcement of restrictive laws been sufficient (which they never were), there would still have been no new units as the result of reformers' efforts, and no racial integration in the old ones.

The progressives' experience with housing reform well illustrates not only the intractability of modern social problems but also the occasional intellectual deficiencies that restricted the progressives from making much headway against the social evils they bravely attacked. Sweep away the slums with one clean legislative stroke, progressives like Veiller believed, and the cities will bustle with happy people. Their analysis in this instance was shallow and their remedy simplistic. Of course they were too optimistic and the law would be evaded; but even had the hallways been cleaned and lighted, the increased costs to tenement owners raised the whole question of who would build more urban housing, where would they build it, and how would it be designed? This was left to take care of itself. When the profit motive did not produce the right sort of housing for urban human beings, the New Dealers, feeling somewhat superior, took the next necessary step into public housing. They then learned how little both they and the progressives before them had known about what the "right" sort of housing was. People lived in neighborhoods, in a total environment; it was not enough to pile clean, well-lit apartments on top of one another in towers. We gave the slum-dwellers new buildings with modern elevators and kitchens, one New Dealer complained, "and they're still the same bunch of bastards they always were." The urban environment was not corrected to insure human happiness by the progressives—or by the New Dealers—not only because the scale of the job went far beyond both their awareness and their resources but also because they had no positive conception of what that environment ought to be. Yet it must be said for them that they at least launched the scientific study of housing and city planning, the ultimate source of better ideas than their own.

Social justice progressives are credited with bringing to America the idea and inaugurating in a modest way the practice of social insurance —the public assumption of responsibility to compensate victims of industrial accident, illness, old age, and unemployment. The unbearable private cost of industrial accidents generated a drive for workmen's compensation laws, pressed initially by "altruistic" organizations like the AALL and the NCL, which provided skilled lobbyists and careful studies based on the available data. Forty-three states had enacted workmen's compensation legislation by 1920. But we know from recent studies by Roy Lubove and James Weinstein that the workmen's compensation movement drew its main support from the employers, who preferred the predictable costs of such systems to the uncertainties of legal proceedings. The National Association of Manufacturers proved more important in the workmen's compensation drive than the tiny AALL. Businessmen adopted the workmen's compensation movement and saw to it that the system covered only about one-fourth of actual medical costs, and that (in most states) private insurance companies held and administered the funds rather than the government.

Whatever its defects, workmen's compensation was the only compulsory social insurance program operating in the United States before the 1930s. Conservatives often frightened themselves with the theory that any concession to reform would open the floodgates to socialism, but in practice the reverse was often the case. Roy Lubove writes: "Social insurance experts mistakenly assumed that the rapid spread of compensation legislation after 1911 would lead to other compulsory programs... (but) far from providing an entering wedge, it solidified the opposition of private interests to any further extension of social insurance." A small group of progressives began to agitate for health, old age, and unemployment insurance in 1915, calling health insurance "the next step." The step was likely to be a small one in any case, but the war killed whatever chance health insurance had, as opponents were able to condemn the idea as "Germanic." Absolutely nothing was accomplished along any of these lines at any level until the 1930s.

Thus, progressive social justice legislation brought very meager gains to the intended beneficiaries. The central statistical indicator that illuminates the social justice record is income distribution. Progressives were quite conscious that income redistribution was crucial to social reform, both as a matter of equity and to preserve the society from dangerous social extremes. Herbert Croly in his *The Promise of American Life* (1909), for example, argued that the decision to pursue "constructive national purpose" meant that "the American state will in effect be making itself responsible for a morally and socially desirable distribution of wealth." Many other reformers gave redistribution high priority. While the data on income and wealth leave much to be desired for the years before the 1930s, it appears that the distribu-

tion of income became, if anything, slightly *more* unequal over the
period from 1896 to 1929, the period when reformers thought themselves to be diminishing such inequalities both through taxation and
through regulatory laws that shifted more of the costs of production
onto the employer. Walter Spahr estimated in 1896 that 2 percent of
the people owned 50 to 60 percent of the wealth, but Willford I. King
in 1917 judged that the intervening years had seen "a marked concentration of income in the hands of the very rich." King's studies of
income distribution showed the top 5 percent of families receiving 28
percent of the national income in 1910, a slight increase (so far as he
could tell) over 1896; ten years later, in 1920, the war had apparently
caused some leveling, with the top 5 percent of families claiming 22
percent of the national income (according to Simon Kuznets); by
the mid 1930s, the share of the top 5 percent had risen to 29 percent.
Of course, income is much less concentrated than "static" wealth. King
found that in 1910 the top 1 percent of families claimed 15 percent
of the national income but 47 percent of the national wealth, a figure
roughly comparable to that for socially reactionary Prussia. All such
estimates are rough, and unquestionably underestimate the maldistribu-
tion, as they do not cover capital gains, gifts, and other forms of
untaxed compensation, which are substantial in the higher and negligible in the lower income brackets. The main outlines of income
distribution are clear: the first thirty years of this century saw a
gradually increasing concentration of income in the hands of the top
income tenth, generally at the expense of the middle- rather than the
lower-income receivers. "Reform" made no impact on this trend; only
the war interrupted it, and after the war the concentration commenced
again. Despite the lowering of the tariff in 1913, the pathbreaking
little income tax of the same year, and the other measures that the
wealthy claimed were tantamount to socialism, income distribution
at the very best remained about where it was when the fiddles of
reform tuned up in the 1890s.

While the actual results deriving from a few legislative victories
were often discouraging to social justice progressives, in some areas
of glaring inequality they achieved no victories at all, symbolic or
otherwise, because they never made the effort. Solicitous toward white
women and children, the social justice progressive was typically

uninterested in the plight of two groups in the most serious economic difficulties in those years (as now), the Negro and the rural poor.

To some extent these were overlapping categories, but most farm laborers and tenants were white, and they had a strong claim on the middle-class conscience if the degree of poverty established such a claim. But while progressives were often shocked by the state of life among the urban lower classes and addressed themselves to their improvement, they gave little time to the hidden agricultural lower class. There was a modest awakening to the problems of country life before the war, but the attention of men like the educational reformer Liberty Hyde Bailey or the founder of agricultural demonstration work, Seaman A. Knapp, was directed toward modernizing the middle-class, commercial farmer. Theodore Roosevelt's Country Life Commission studied the problems of rural life, but its report of 1909 neglected the landless farmer almost entirely. Considering the state of public and Congressional opinion, the flaws in their vision made little difference. Congress ignored even the slim recommendations of the Commission—better conservation, investigation of middleman profits, the banishment of the saloon, and similar measures of middle-class appeal. Progressivism came and went, leaving rural poverty untouched. Tenancy, the condition of 36 percent of American farmers in 1880, was up to 49 percent in 1920 and rising. Progressives, with very rare exceptions, were too busy to notice.

Also largely unnoticed was the Afro-American. The facts show that blacks were in a condition of sustained emergency. They were confined to the menial trades and the more brutal levels of agriculture, poorly paid, intellectually isolated, socially ostracized, and physically intimidated. The black illiteracy rate in the South approached 50 percent, as against a rate of 12 percent for whites. The life expectancy for blacks at birth was 32 years in 1900, while for whites it was 47. Blacks were harder hit by most diseases because their environment was harsher; yet they were also less likely to find or afford medical care. But, incredible enough, worse was yet to come. As the progressive era opened, the condition of blacks was in important respects deteriorating.

The last years of the nineteenth century produced a powerful tide of racism, more virulent and dangerous than had ever before marked American race relations. There had been earlier cycles of xenophobia that excited native Americans to abandon their uneasy tolerance and find ways to persecute alien peoples. But the nativism of the 1890s and after was not only more intense, but it now bore upon the blacks, who before had been somewhat protected by their status as chattel property. As the 1880s gave way to the 1890s one could notice the changing signs: rumors of the inundation of native Americans by hordes of unassimilable immigrants (these, in northern cities, included blacks), a torrent of speeches and books elaborating on the theme of white supremacy, talk of racial world conflict just ahead. To the Catholic and the Jew this spelled intolerance, suspicion, political and social discrimination. To the black it meant all these things, and also a degree of physical danger, which brought him in these years to the point Rayford Logan calls "the nadir of the Negro's status in American society."

C. Vann Woodward in *The Strange Career of Jim Crow* has described the legal expression of the new racism. A system of enforced segregation, unevenly developed before the 1890s, was perfected in the early progressive era, with the black everywhere confined to inferior civil rights and public facilities, or denied them altogether. The Negro had suffered economically perhaps more than any other group from the depression of the 1890s, but when prosperity returned the hurricane of racial intolerance made sure that the blacks would not fully participate in the recovery that other groups would experience. The agricultural black may have shared slightly in the rising farm prices after 1898, but the small black middle class was deliberately decimated. The rigid caste system of separate railroad cars and toilets was extended to jobs as well. The black began to disappear from trades he had formerly monopolized—tailoring, painting, smithing, carpentering. The depression initiated this downward pressure, and the intense nativist emotions after the turn of the century caused further displacement from reasonably attractive jobs. There were occasional pockets where blacks held out, such as coal mining, but for the most part they were the losers in a bitter struggle with whites for jobs that permitted an urban existence and something better than a marginal standard of life.

More dramatic than his economic difficulties was the increase in racial violence. Lynching in America had always had a strong class incidence—the rate was high among the poor and the transient—but it had been relatively color-blind before the 1890s. From 1882 to 1888 some 595 whites were lynched, and 440 blacks (this, of course, is a higher rate for blacks); by 1892 lynching was becoming racialized, with 169 blacks and 69 whites lynched that year. At the peak of the progressive period, 1906 to 1915, ten times as many blacks (620) as whites (61) were burned, beaten, or hanged to death. Inevitably the racial feelings behind these acts against individuals found occasion to shift to entire communities. Savage race riots broke out in New York and New Orleans in 1900, in Atlanta in 1906, in Springfield, Illinois in 1908. Between the reports of such incidents in the history of American race relations one could observe in the press and even in the best journals such as *Harpers, Scribner's,* and *Century,* the white mind at work reinforcing its racial stereotypes: the black man was subhuman, childlike, docile, comic, lazy, criminal, superstitious, oversexed, lying, and stupid, a nigger, a spade, a pickaninny, a coon. This view of the black, we now suspect, was more damaging to the black and his aspirations for the future than the economic deprivation and physical danger that burdened his body.

Surely this exploitation and suffering would not go unnoticed in the progressive era, when sentiment for the underdog ran high and the ideals of the Declaration of Independence were being revived. And in fact the conscience of the white community began to stir. A few journals, such as *The Independent, The Arena,* and *Charities,* spoke out editorially against lynching. *McClure's* displeased its southern readers by printing a mild denunciation of race relations by Carl Schurz in 1904, and a splendid series of articles in *The American Magazine* by Ray Stannard Baker gained further circulation when bound into the book *Following the Color Line* (1908). Baker's book was widely noticed, and, along with more detailed investigations such as Mary White Ovington's *Half a Man: The Status of the Negro in New York* (1911), Louis D. Bowen's *The Colored People of Chicago* (1913), and John Daniel's *In Freedom's Birthplace: A History of the Boston Negro* (1914), took at least the first, fact-gathering step toward intervention. Several Negro settlement houses were established, and one or two settlements mixed the black and white poor. The philanthropic urge was quickened in the progressive era generally, and some attention was paid to the educational needs of blacks in the establishment of the General Education Board by the Rockefeller Foundation in 1902, the Anna T. Jeanes Fund in 1905, the Julius Rosenwald Fund in 1913. And it was a group of white progressives and socialists, among them Miss Ovington, William English Walling, Charles Edward Russell,

Henry Moskowitz, and Oswald Garrison Villard, who took the organizational steps that led to the founding of the National Association for the Advancement of Colored People in 1909.

But these efforts do not add up to serious attention to the condition of blacks. The progressives had more pressing business than the welfare of the Negro, and the handful of reformers who concerned themselves with racial issues was unrepresentative and essentially ineffective. Progressivism at the local level discovered graft, captive political systems, inadequate public services; it never discovered the almost total lack of educational, medical, and eleemosynary institutions available to blacks. There were praiseworthy efforts in the South to abolish the infamous convict-lease system (six southern states had done so by 1917), but the southern jails and prison farms remained, as Frank Tannenbaum's *The Darker Phases of the South* reported in 1924, inhumanly brutal.[7] Race relations being what they were, the penal institutions of the South were the places where blacks had their most sustained, damaging contact with white power and where reform was both most urgent and least likely.

At the national level, progressivism disappointed the few articulate blacks and whites who heard the language of humanitarianism from presidential campaigners and misjudged the limits that would be set by the pervasive racism of the American public. Theodore Roosevelt showed an initial independence in the matter of black civil service appointees and dared to invite Booker T. Washington to dinner at the White House. But when there was criticism of his appointment and dining policies he not only abandoned them but further reassured his white critics by his handling of the Brownsville affair. The white citizens of Brownsville, Texas, had worked themselves into an ugly mood over the presence of black troops stationed at the edge of town, and a controverted shooting incident on the night of August 13, 1906, was at least partially and perhaps entirely their fault. But T.R. accepted the questionable evidence of black culpability and dishonorably discharged three companies of black infantry, thereby holding black soldiers to standards of docility, discipline, and collective guilt that

---

[7] The rest of the country also had a long way to go toward rational and humane penal institutions by the end of the progressive era. Social worker Homer Folks told the National Conference of Charities and Corrections in 1911 that while America might lead the world in the treatment of juvenile delinquents, "as to jails, the world leads us."

would have been unthinkable in the case of whites. After Brownsville, T.R. neither harmed nor helped the American black, and the Republican Party through 1912 continued to collect black votes and ignore the platform remnants of its Lincolnian heritage.

Despite the racial conservatism of the Democratic Party, Woodrow Wilson hinted strongly that blacks would be included among those aggrieved groups the New Freedom would help. But the humanitarian strain in Democratic progressivism was no match for its deep-seated racial attitudes. The Treasury and Post Office Departments segregated lunchrooms and bathrooms shortly after Wilson's cabinet took over, and, with Wilson refusing to intervene, black-held jobs dropped from 6 percent in 1913 to 5 percent in 1918. Despite repeated entreaties the president would not denounce lynching, never visited a black picnic or school. Booker T. Washington admitted in 1913 that he had "never seen the colored people so discouraged and bitter as they are at the present time." Wilson was personally no bigot, mixed with blacks when the occasion demanded it, and in fact had Washington to dinner at Princeton. But as President he would take absolutely no risks on the issue of race relations. Oswald Garrison Villard finally gained an interview with Wilson in October, 1913, and presented him with a plan for a national race commission to study the question. Wilson admitted that he would not endanger his program or administration by even that degree of involvement with the delicate racial issue: "I say it with shame and humiliation," he told Villard," but I have thought about this thing for twenty years and I see no way out. It will take a very big man to solve this thing."

Why had progressivism made such an infinitesimal difference in the racial attitudes and customs of Americans? The failure to place this issue higher on the agenda ought to be seen in historical perspective, or it will appear merely as a monumental and inexplicable display of callousness. At that time *all* white Americans were raised in an atmosphere of sustained racism. They were convinced of Negro inferiority and armed against reality by separate institutions and racial stereotypes. White Americans learned how to see (and not to see) the black from casual comments of parents and peers, from "Uncle Remus" stories, from novels such as the trilogy of Thomas Dixon, *The Leopard's Spots* (1902), *The Clansman* (1905), *The Traitor* (1907). A United States Senator (Benjamin Tillman, Dem., South Carolina) condemned Roosevelt's dinner with Booker T. Washington with the comment that "entertaining that nigger will necessitate our killing a thousand niggers in the South before they learn their place." To some that remark seemed proper; to the rest, understandable. Roosevelt himself thought blacks inferior and admitted the dinner was a mistake.

In such a climate, whites did not "think" about the black. Their notions were fixed; their armor against aberrant thoughts was impenetrable. Progressives were white Americans and their culture equipped them with these attitudes. And in those rare instances when an individual, through some combination of perhaps an abolitionist heritage and an unusual personal encounter with black refugees in the northern cities, broke free of the old attitudes and began to sympathize and seek reform, the state of public opinion made the race issue the most unpromising subject a reformer could raise.

But to credit their ineffectiveness on this issue to the racist climate of opinion is to miss an insight into the progressive mentality. The black was overlooked because the entire culture overlooked him, but he was overlooked by a reform movement that made a specialty of uncovering neglected social evils because that reform movement had built-in blinders when it came to the desperate troubles of society's lowest classes. Progressivism was a middle-class movement, and only in a few instances, such as the social welfare movement in New York City or the state movement in Oklahoma, did progressivism take up the grievances of really submerged people. Its faith in political democracy was in conflict with, and often overruled by, the instinctive elitism of the confident, educated people who were the backbone of reform. In the end progressivism was better at directing than at listening.

Progressivism was also associated with the rising group self-assertiveness and solidarity of the native white American. Reform was not only contemporaneous with nativism but seemed to have a symbiotic relationship with it. While there were reformers who were free of the fever of a Nordic mission, there was a tendency for people who became excited about progressive causes also to be excited about the duty of "the race" to preserve and extend its dominion. Recall the careers of Roosevelt, Albert Beveridge, William E. Borah, Hiram Johnson, or Woodrow Wilson, with their happy union of Nordic nationalism and progressivism. Reform required a bold, crusading, self-assertive temper and aggressive moral certainty. As subversive as it may have sounded to smug conservatives, reform did not encourage doubt or tolerance. Such qualities were dysfunctional in a war, which is the analogy the reformers most often drew upon in describing what they were doing. Reform drew its strength from the unquestioned moralities of the white Protestant American. From such an impulse the descendants of slaves could expect at best occasional paternalistic advice and charity, at worst the disfranchisement associated with southern progressivism and the harassments against Orientals common in Hiram Johnson's California.

These qualities of the reform mind help to explain its insensitivity to a social problem more serious, both in terms of fundamental human morality and of social efficiency, than the trusts, or political corruption, or child labor, or alcohol. White progressivism offered little aid to blacks. Yet the expectation that a time of idealism and social introspection would bring some breakthrough for the black American was not in error. Currents of thought found in white progressivism had their parallels among blacks. These were the years when Booker T. Washington's program of black self-effacement and industrial education began to lose its grip on the younger blacks, and men like W. E. B. DuBois and William Monroe Trotter revolted against white assumptions and social arrangements. Their speaking and writing expressed and encouraged a heightened group consciousness not unlike that which swept the white community. In the Niagra movement of 1905, and in the NAACP, this awakening of black professional and white-collar elites found organizational form. There were also several black organizations aimed, like their white counterparts, at rescuing the victims of urbanization—Victoria Earle Matthews's White Rose Industrial Organization founded in 1897 in New York, for example, or the Committee for Improving the Industrial Condition of Negroes in New York, founded by the black educator William Lewis Bulkley in 1906. Rejection of the status quo, the conviction that something could be done, organization, political pressure for state intervention, racial self-assertion, and the rhetoric of liberal humanitarianism—all these phenomena were found on a small scale among blacks at the same time that they appeared on a larger scale among whites.

We slight these beginnings because they were too little and too late. Yet from this distance it does in fact appear that a corner was turned in this period for this most exploited of America's oppressed groups. When real change in American race relations finally came, it would build upon the awakened conscience bequeathed by white progressivism, and the organization and self-discovery stimulated among blacks in this same era. If the social justice movement for blacks later took on a radical, even violent aspect, it was not because these early black reformers willed it so, but because the few hesitant steps of white progressives proved so ineffectual against the misery of blacks or the racial attitudes of the mass of whites.

So this problem was postponed. It was the progressive generation's most conspicuous failure, and yet, in view of the social realities in which they moved, their most understandable one. And it did not go entirely unnoticed. Walter Weyl, for example, wedged an important insight into his *The New Democracy* (1912) in one lapidary sentence: "The Negro problem is the mortal spot of the New Democracy."

IX.

Reform had a third major thrust, toward restoring the economic arrangements of small-scale capitalism and the social values of small-town America. To this cause rallied businessmen from the South and Midwest, and from small towns in all parts of the country where New England memories were strong. The most effective exponents of economic individualism were articulate young lawyers like George Record, William Borah, and Woodrow Wilson, who thought they were defending liberty rather than the interests of a dwindling entrepreneurial class. In its most intelligent forms, as in the thought of Louis D. Brandeis, this antitrust, and, at least covertly, antiurban school did have something to contribute to a dialogue about freedom and made a useful critique of the dominant tendencies toward centralization. In less intelligent hands its psychology was defensive and negative to a fault, and its social vision neither generous nor—since immigration was shut off so late—plausible.

The achievement of the economic individualists is hard to estimate, but the word *failure* suggests itself, despite its rough sound. The courts, the war, and a deep public ambivalence about economic concentration, all kept the progressive antitrust efforts from anything like a restoration of the conditions of nineteenth-century littleness. The worst fears of the economic individualists have come true: most Americans *have* slipped from self-employment to employee status. What is more, they seem to be adjusting to it. That was the main disaster these progressives feared, and they could not avert it. It is true that a few of their campaigns produced apparent victories. There was great vitality in the drive to break the stranglehold of eastern interests upon credit and transportation advantages, and some legislative successes were secured. But in the end small interests were usually outmaneuvered. The Federal Reserve Act set up a system of twelve decentralized districts so that New York could not dictate to Main Street or Market Street, but Wall Street actually emerged stronger than before, dominating the New York branch, which in turn dominated the system. The ICC gave southerners no satisfaction in their efforts to eliminate the long and short haul differentials in freight rates. Some have argued that the antitrust efforts of progressives at least humanized big business and taught it a sense of public responsibility, even if no real dissolution was achieved. Perhaps so. At least beginning in the 1920s, most corporations had sufficient concern for the public to hire public relations assistance.

This defensive component of progressivism had a cultural as well as an economic side. Its aim was a restoration of the nineteenth century community—classless, neighborly, hard at work, devout, morally disciplined. The threat came from the moral loosening of urban life, and from the sheer number and fecundity of the immigrant. The remedies they devised constitute a subcategory of the progressive uprising: exhortations to unity, the prohibition movement, the Americanization movement, the drive on prostitution, the eugenics movement. Return progressivism fought a reasonably successful rearguard action against the cultural challenge of urban America, but unfortunately it coerced an urban milieu that won out in the end, especially among the intellectuals. Since urbanized intellectuals write the histories, this sort of reform is treated with a conspicuous lack of sympathy. Some criticism is deserved. If the excess of progressivism identified with social control was to abandon under stress its democratic sympathies and to set an elite to dispensing national discipline, the excess of the school seeking to return to nineteenth-century values was to reduce reform to a drive for enforced conformity to a compromised moral code that was no longer held by a majority. What was valuable in that moral code has unfortunately not received its due, since the moral reformers were unable to make distinctions between lasting and outmoded virtues. Much can be said for small communities (including those found in large cities), for stable, small-family agriculture, and for "Victorian" virtues such as sobriety, self-discipline, and honesty—all, of course, in moderation. They were not much advanced by progressives, since they chose to identify the nineteenth-century moral inheritance with such obviously defunct ideas as the notion that drinking beer was an evil. We are in great need of some of the virtues of the premodern generation, but if we are to recover them we must ignore their public crusades and turn to biography, to the lives of splendid and untiring men and women like Louis Brandeis, Jane Addams, or the rabbi Stephen S. Wise.

Only a few perceptive contemporaries sensed that the goal of returning to nineteenth-century virtues was an odd bedfellow for the impulse to aid the underprivileged of the cities, or the impulse to enlarge the sway of trained intelligence in American life. Crusades to keep America a place where the Yankee culture was dominant were a part of progressivism by every test—chronology, fervor, middle class base, pressure for legislation, interlocking personnel with other reforms—but one. They were not liberal. At the core they expressed a reactionary spirit—hostile to change, suspicious of the cities, fearful of the future. They preferred faith and tradition to reason and were wedded to narrow racial, regional, and national loyalties just at the moment in history when basic forces urged broader perspectives. Some have been uneasy that the term *progressivism* has been arched to spread over illiberal social movements as well as those of a generous, tolerant, and rational cast. These irregularities should not drive us from the term. Parts of progressivism blended nicely with what later came to be known as liberalism, and parts did not. There is no need to define certain activities out of the movement simply because they contradicted other activities, reform values, or subsequent preoccupations. Internal contradictions existed at the time, but contemporary journalists, not blessed with the analytical and taxonomical skills of college professors, perceived the common elements in the uproar around them, and they were right to speak of a progressive movement. Prohibition, immigration restriction, and the antiprostitution drive were different in spirit—and usually attracted different types of reformers—from the scientific management effort, or conservation, or housing reform, but they were all middle-class, aroused, marching Americans, vintage 1910, and they shared a core of intellectual traits: they were activists, they had an unshakable confidence in intervention, they were equally optimistic that social practices could be changed by exhortation, scientific study, the police power of the state, or some combination. Abraham Flexner, writing in 1914, used the sort of language they used whether they were Social Gospelers, engineers, social workers, or young lawyers running for city council:

> Civilization has stripped for a life-and-death wrestle with tuberculosis, alcohol and other plagues. It is on the verge of a similar struggle with the crasser forms of commercialized vice. Sooner or later, it must fling down the gauntlet to the whole horrible thing. This will be the real contest—a contest that will tax the courage, the self-denial, the faith, the resources of humanity to their utmost.

Rhetorical similarities among the various sectors of reform went beyond an exhortative, crusading style. The word *efficiency* was a kind of litmus of reformism. All the renovators and innovators believed in efficiency, counted on its strong appeal to a generation impressed with the promise of science, and used it to justify the most diverse activities. The municipal Goo Goos wanted to make city government more efficient, not a difficult argument to follow, but we also find social worker Crystal Eastman justifying workmen's compensation on the grounds of efficiency, Louis Brandeis justifying railroad regulation and a complete social insurance system on the grounds of efficiency, Charles Edward Russell arguing that urban poverty was an inefficient use of human resources, and Irving Fisher appealing for prohibition on the grounds that it would so increase the national efficiency as to produce a 10–20 percent addition to the GNP. If nothing else tied together these various and occasionally contradictory crusades—and much else did—their common resort to the ideal of efficiency would be enough to suggest some sort of fundamental identity. Frederick W. Taylor, the father of scientific management (a synonym for efficiency), wrote in *The Principles of Scientific Management* (1911) that his principles "applied with equal force to all our social activities; to the management of our homes; the management of our farms; the management of the business of our tradesmen, . . . of our churches, our philanthropic institutions, our universities, and our governmental departments." His generation was in agreement. Each in his own way, the member of a civic voter's group, the city planner, the settlement worker, the prohibitionist, all had caught a common vision of a society happier because social engineers had brought an end to wastefulness and irrationality in all its various activities. So to a large extent they spoke a common tongue.

But the most compelling reason for spreading the word progressivism over somewhat contradictory social objectives is that one often finds some single reform or campaign that unites quite dissimilar values beyond any effort to factor them out. The most objectionable strain in Return progressivism was its racism, but it is possible to find even this harnessed with concern for some part of exploited and suffering humanity. Aileen Kraditor tells us, in *The Ideas of the Woman Suffrage Movement 1890–1920* (1965), how often anti-immigrant and anti-Negro sentiments appeared alongside the noble ideals of the Declaration of Independence in the inspirational literature of the movement. An equally good but less well-known example of a reform born of mixed impulses is the LaFollette Seaman's Act of 1915. The act improved the pay and working conditions of an historically exploited group and strengthened their hand in contractual arrangements with shipowners; it enlisted the support of progressive altruists who responded to Andrew Furseth's pleas for justice. But the act had strong southern support in the Congress because it was openly racist. In Jerold Auerbach's words, it was frankly designed "to drive Asiatics from American vessels" by eliminating the economic advantage in hiring orientals who either depressed "white" standards or drove occidentals from the merchant marine.

Another such combination appears in the drive against prostitution. It was often pressed by people who did not like sex, and who appear to modern eyes as not only prudish and coercive, but ethically misguided and probably no real friends of the American female. At the same time prostitution did involve exploitation and a threat to the public health, and the fight against it attracted nonprudish and thoroughly admirable people like Lillian Wald and Jane Addams who urged a scientific rather than a moralistic approach to the matter and who were primarily interested in the protection of virtually helpless individuals (females) from overpowering environmental pressures against their dignity and freedom. Some reformers spoke of the evils of prostitution and thought of how much they disliked not only the sex act but Jewish immigrant girls who were probably producing ethnically undesirable bastards; others spoke of the evils of prostitution and wished to stamp out disease and economic exploitation, not non-WASP breeding and nonconjugal love. Many reforms had this same schizophrenic composition, and virtually every campaign was laced with contradiction. Hiram Johnson's progressives in California found time and motivation to work on conservation, workmen's compensation, and laws excluding Japanese from landholding and citizenship. James K. Vardaman's progressive administration in Mississippi (1903–7) raised teacher's salaries, increased expenditures on mental and tuberculosis hospitals, attacked the convict-lease system, advocated the reduction of interest rates and higher taxes upon corporations, and at the same time cut appropriations for Negro education and set new lows in the rhetoric of bigotry. These and other progressive campaigns brought together impulses one might have thought incompatible until observing them in some dynamic blend. But the world of the progressive was confusing, and many emotions combined in their sense of social crisis. They sacrificed logic to action, and made reform a house of many mansions.

X.

Where in this scheme does one place the friends of political democracy? Most progressives of whatever type thought of themselves as advocating changes that were widely popular and would instantly prevail if the people were awakened by the written and spoken word. When this did not happen they suspected defective political machinery rather than the accuracy of their estimate of the state of public opinion. Blaming the political machinery for immobilizing their latent majority, they pressed for procedural reforms widening the suffrage and extending the popular influence. But the Direct Democracy aspects of reform do not constitute a distinct category, for they were usually not ends in themselves but means to other ends. The grant of federal suffrage to women was presented as a concession to the idea of individual worth, done because it was right for men to do so if they claimed to be democrats. But Alan P. Grimes shows, in *The Puritan Ethic and Woman Suffrage,* that in the western states where woman suffrage was strongest it drew strength not so much from egalitarian sentiment—there was some of that, mostly among women—as from the expectation that enfranchised women would further the drives to enact prohibition and immigration restriction laws. There were usually similar substantive hopes behind all the campaigns for procedural democratization. The Oregon reformer William S. U'Ren worked for years to democratize Oregon politics, but he was not primarily interested in Direct Democracy. "All the work we have done,

for Direct Legislation," he wrote late in life, "has been done with the
Single Tax in view." U'Ren was, in this respect at least, typical of
reformers interested in Direct Democracy measures. Progress depended
not merely on enlarging the political community, but on pursuing
certain ends with the newly acquired power. There was hardly a
distinct Direct Democracy component of progressivism since invigorated electoral procedures were almost invariably pressed as preliminary to and valued subsidiary to substantive changes. Jane Addams,
in an article "Why Women Should Vote" published in 1909, justified
their enfranchisement on the ground that they might then extend to
the entire city the cleanliness they maintained in their own homes.
Woman suffrage was a reform, but it was also a means to reform.

It is worth noting that disappointments in this area were the rule
rather than the exception. Enlarged electorates showed a stubborn
tendency to continue to vote for machine politicians (Boss Boise
Penrose, astonished that he was still in the Senate after the first
Pennsylvania election in which Senators ran before the people, was
supposed to have said, "give me the people every time"). The females
enfranchised in the Rocky Mountain states did in fact help the
prohibition forces, but the enfranchisement of women generally disappointed its supporters. As John Gordon Ross wrote in 1936: "After a
fair trial of 16 years, it seems just to appraise women's suffrage as one
of those reforms which, like the secret ballot, the corrupt-practices
acts, the popular election of senators, and the direct primary, promised
almost everything and accomplished almost nothing." And, much to
his disappointment, U'Ren and the single taxers in Oregon wore
themselves out on their procedural reforms only to find that the
broader electorate had as little interest in the single tax as the smaller
electorate of the late nineteenth-century.

The general ineffectiveness of Direct Democracy measures to accomplish the fine things promised by overexcited reformers has been
noticed many times, almost invariably with a touch of scorn that men
could believe such tripe about "the people." "A man that'd expict
to thrain lobsters to fly in a year is called a loonytic," said Mr.
Dooley, "but a man that thinks men can be tur-rned into angels be
an iliction is called a rayformer an' remains at large." It is hard to see
why observers of the progressive faith in democracy are so pleased at
discovering such gullibility; if the reformers were wrong, and it
appears that they were, the implications are not at all pleasant. Their
simple faith in the efficacy of drawing more and more people into

the voting booths reveals them—in view of the record—as hopeless innocents. But men who remark the proven invalidity of that faith are hardly realists if they do so smugly. We may know man better, after army intelligence tests, the analysis of dreams, pogroms, and a procession of regicides, but the last emotion this justifies is a sense of superiority.

XI.

Surveying this record of dreams of justice and promises of uplift in the moral and physical life of the people, and finding that it all came to so much less than the progressives had wanted, one wonders what meaning to draw from the gap. Some would say that capitalism was not substantially reformed because it cannot be, others because it need not be. Every person must decide whether such modest gains are the best a citizen can wish, or whether he prefers one of those twins who offer themselves as substitutes for reform—apathy and revolution. But a number of lesser inquiries are equally enlightening.

Notice the advantages held by the conservatives. The American character, individualistic, sanguine, and suspicious of the state, fought on the conservative side, resisting a movement that relied upon the irritations of criticism and the exertions of collective action. The holders of privileged positions were united by economic interest, by social outlook, and usually by intermarriage. The potential allies in any uprising were largely unorganized or at best poorly organized on the eve of the struggles of the progressive era. Of American workers, only 7 percent were in unions in 1904, and these were largely in the Gompers-led American Federation of Labor, emasculated politically by his doctrine that nothing could be expected from political action. Consumers were unorganized until Florence Kelley and others started the consumers' leagues in the late 1890s, but even after this their real power was negligible. The same is true of other social groups who might have joined any crusade to redistribute the good things of earth —Negroes, farmers,[8] and the more recent and less advantaged im-

---

[8] The Grange enrolled only 200,000 members in 1900, the Farmer's Union emerged in 1905 but shunned political activity, the Alliance movement was dead, and the politically powerful Farm Bureau Federation was not founded until after the war. The American Society of Equity (est. 1902) enrolled perhaps 150,000 farmers, largely in the wheat regions. Landless farmers were totally unorganized.

migrants. Of course the progressive era was the era of organization, and such gains as they made were made largely by organization, but it was slow work.

After men had been brought to see the necessity of organizing, either around their own interest or around a shared concern for the exploited and unfortunate, the job of actually redistributing advantages and burdens was staggering. It required endless patience, sustained pressure, and luck. An acceptable and talented leader had to be found, campaigns had to be pressed beyond the initial defeats and delays, public opinion had to be mobilized or at least neutralized, political and legislative machinery mastered, bureaucracies shouldered aside and new bureaucrats recruited, mistakes unraveled and the game begun again. As the months and years went by, both tedious and breathless, the Social Justice coalition tended to fragment, its components to return piece by piece to that apathetic impotence from which they had with such difficulty been aroused.

Even when some angry coalition forced its will through a legislative body, the courts could always be counted upon to defend property, and corporation counsel could always be counted upon to bring each reform enactment to judicial attention. Note the list of toppled regulatory, labor, or social insurance laws: in *E. C. Knight* (1895) it was learned that Congress had no control over manufacturing; in *Pollack* (1895), that Congress could not directly tax individuals; in *Lochner* (1905), that the legislature of New York could not set maximum hours for bakers; in *Hammer* v. *Dagenhart* (1918), that Congress could not outlaw child labor (although the Court had earlier decided that the memory of the Founders would not be outraged if Congress prohibited lotteries and the white slave trade; apparently property losses in the shady areas of capitalism were tolerable to the Constitution); in *Adkins* (1923) that Congress could not fix minimum wages for women who lived in the District of Columbia; and so on. When the Federal Trade Commission gave signs just after the war that it might construe broadly its mandate to investigate and indict practices in restraint of trade, the Court ruled the FTC findings of fact would not be accepted as prima facie evidence, but must pass through the filter of nine more reliable men than the commissioners. In all, American judges understood that their most sacred trust was to use the Constitution, with its wonderfully ambiguous language and varied precedent, to safeguard property rights. It must be said that they shouldered their responsibilities to civilization with that combination of determination and a passion for duty that has long marked the American patrician class. Wrote Chief Justice William Howard Taft as he held the conservative majority together in the 1920s: "I am older and slower and less acute and more confused. However, as long as things continue as they are, and I am able to answer in my place, I must stay on the Court in order to prevent the Bolsheviki from getting control. . . . The only hope we have of keeping a consistent declaration of Constitutional law is for us to live as long as we can."

The People, admittedly, *could* ultimately override the judiciary if they blocked the popular will; they *could* alter constitutions through the prescribed, laborious processes and bring the courts to heel. A number of progressives, among them Roosevelt in 1912, talked openly of the need for action against constitutional barriers and even against judges themselves. But constitutional alterations required the most sustained political effort, and curbing individual judges was an idea that made slow headway against the deep popular respect for the robe and the bench.

So conservatives—those who wanted wealth, economic and political authority, and social status to be held tomorrow and forever where they were held today—could throw up a formidable defense against meddling levelers. They were barricaded behind public and interest-group apathy, unrepresentative political systems, a conservative judiciary drawn from their class, conservative and intellectually stagnant universities, a genteel and irrelevant literature, a folklore that insisted that complete social mobility was a reality, and mass media owned by men who could be counted on (or if necessary forced by advertising cancellations) to mesmerize the public with trivia and either ignore or smear the radicals. It was a deep, complex maze through which few redistributionist proposals could pass at all, and none without crippling concessions. But this is to speak only of the defenses of conservatives. The progressive years saw them take the offensive, at first haltingly, and then with mounting success. Conservatives learned that their greatest advantage lay not in their defenses against government, but in their ability to manipulate it.

While the state had always been used by dominant groups to protect or extend their economic advantages, it is nonetheless true that the American ruling classes had not had a sustained and comprehensive resort to governmental power until the twentieth century. Admittedly there had always been a tariff, there had been railroad grants, and as the nation industrialized the upper classes saw to it that their government shouldered the task of repressing, through force or injunction, the restless laboring masses. Yet Barry Goldwater learned it to be a fact in 1964 that the dominant economic interests now demand a use of governmental power that is not sporadic and punitive but continuous and positive. The change did not come overnight, but we can state that if it did not exactly begin it at least accelerated sharply in the progressive era.

Prior to this century, those whom the industrial system (and the land) had made rich and comfortable used the state only infrequently, despised politics, counted upon conservative politicians to keep things quiet, and beat off the occasional inept attempts of radicals to actually use the state for other than police purposes. Basically the ruling classes were Sumnerians, or social Darwinists. They had no real vision of what the state might do for them beyond hiring policemen and judges and delivering the mail.

The progressive period was apparently a very educational period for them. Obviously, they learned that the state could be used against them, as waves of angry "little" businessmen from the South and West (shippers, commercial farmers, small bankers), as well as smaller waves of assorted do-gooders, assaulted the sleepy halls of legislatures and the Congress with coercive and confiscatory programs. The first impulse of the conservatives was to fight the very conception of the state as an active force in the economy, and because some of the less intelligent and imaginative among them still follow that impulse, it has come down to us that the business community has always been negatively oriented toward government. Actually, those few historians who have turned from the political life of intellectuals to the political life of American businessmen have found that a more positive con-. ception of the state took hold in certain sectors of the American upper class in the years before the war. The more sophisticated members of the upper classes overcame their doctrinaire Jeffersonian suspicion of state power and moved from obstruction to a position resembling that of the reformers—demanding sustained governmental intervention in the nation's economic life. There was no reason, they saw, why the regulatory agencies of the modernized state must serve the purposes of the radicals. In the words of such an enlightened conservative, Richard Olney, at the opening of the modern era:

The Commission (ICC), as its functions have now been limited by the courts, is, or can be made of great use to the railroads. It satisfied the popular clamor for governmental supervision of railroads at the same time that the supervision is almost entirely nominal. Further, the older such a commission gets to be, the more inclined it will be found to be to take the business and railroad view of things. It thus becomes a sort of barrier between the railroad corporations and the people and a sort of protection against hasty and crude legislation hostile to railroad interests.

Olney spoke for a small minority of businessmen in 1892, but his view made headway among men of his class. There was every reason for his confidence that a government of new and useful but potentially dangerous powers could be controlled by the owners of industry rather than the dispossessed. The only disadvantage of the entrenched classes was numerical inferiority. But they had instant access not only to legal talent for persuasive testimony before congressional committees but also to the sympathetic ear of politicians of a common ethnic and social background who respected wealth and breeding, sometimes despite themselves. If the politicians on infrequent occasions were pressed so hard by angry groups that a regulatory agency was set up under a law at least potentially dangerous, the corporations on the commanding heights still held numerous advantages. The agencies were kept on miserly appropriations and were never large enough for the research, field, and legal work required to survey a national economy. The FTC, in a rare mood, investigated the meat packing industry in 1919 on suspicion of fixing prices, and in that year the advertising budget of Swift and Co. was six times the total budget of the agency. But there was more to the matter than size. Governmental bureaucracies were composed of men who were cautious, basically conservative, and—largely because of the meager salaries the public was willing to pay—likely to be men who in intellect and energy were quite inferior to their legal and technical adversaries from industry. There is a revealing passage in Secretary of the Treasury William G. McAdoo's autobiography where McAdoo, whose $12,000 yearly salary was the highest in the American government excepting only the president's, set out to hire into the federal service the presidents of the railroads he had just seized (1918) in the wartime emergency. To men with salaries ranging upward from $100,000 yearly, government employment with its rewards ranging steeply down from $12,000 was a virtual disaster and an insult. McAdoo was embarrassed, and the government hired its railroad directors at $40,000–50,000, depending upon the region. Any contest between such men with their New York lawyers against the civil servants of the Interstate Commerce Commission was likely to be, as it had been since 1887, an unequal contest.

These advantages of the dominant interests were not necessarily permanent. Time brought changes that tended to make the governmental bureaucracy more independent—slightly larger appropriations for staff and research, the enhanced attractiveness of federal service to talented people, the gradual organization of more interest groups, the gradual improvement of public understanding of the stakes involved in public policy decisions. But these trends had not developed very far by the end of the progressive era. As a result, using government to reduce the economic advantage of those who *have* the economic advantage was uphill work. As the entrenched interests accepted the inevitability of enlarged government, they found themselves in a post position in the race for its favors.

XII.

This gloomy account derives largely from contemplation of the record of social justice progressivism. Progressive attempts to rationalize habits and institutions must be accounted partially successful and in the end irresistible. Progressive efforts to restore the moral consensus of the nineteenth century were moderately successful in the short run and served their therapeutic purpose. But while social justice progressivism was demonstrably the least successful component of reform, the preceding review of the advantages of conservatives in frustrating it gives us a perspective from which to estimate social justice accomplishments as a bit higher than nothing at all. Progressives of this sort had done a substantial damage to the conservative outworks, and although beaten back, their sappers' trenches were still at the wall for another day of siege.

Think of the advantages of conservatives that, while proving enough in the defense against social justice progressives, had been eliminated or weakened. For its defense the status quo counts heavily on abstract modes of thought—a legalistic constitutionalism, a fixation upon natural law or the divine order, and in the realm of education a curriculum firmly limited to the "classic," i.e., resolutely nonrelevant studies. But progressive thinkers riveted the attention of their era upon the current and the real. Realism was the most pervasive intellectual quality of the leading thought of their day, whether political theory, law, literature, or the arts. There is an obvious kinship between muckraking and oil paintings of ashcans and alleys, between social investigations like the Pittsburgh Survey or the Industrial Relations Commission of 1911, and short stories about denizens of saloons. That kinship resides in a common preference for the real, which to the progressive generation usually meant the hard and sordid side of existence, as against what William Dean Howells called "the smiling aspects of life." As perceptive conservatives suspected, such morbid and unswerving attention to social reality often led to the most subversive consequences. For the world to remain at rest, it is best that it not be thought about too much, certainly not studied with any rigor. This is not to ignore the importance of abstraction in reform thought itself. It is important that the progressives also served abstractions and that they were new ones—justice rather than the Constitution or property rights. But what gave progressive ideals an upper hand so often was the progressive mastery of the facts and relations of actual life. With these in hand their ideals—which were after all ancient ideals, but not heretofore much threat to the going arrangement of things—could no longer be domesticated to the primers of school children and the Sunday school lessons of victorian ladies. True, conservatives were able to block most of the agitation arising out of realist thought, but they were not able to exorcise realism itself, which went on working its corrosive way through the fabric of received ideas and habits.

Things-as-they-are were also protected at the turn of the century by the notion that freedom was a condition of being let alone, and especially let alone by the state, the form of power most suspected despite its relative puniness. Progressive intellectuals argued that freedom had a positive dimension and that the prerequisites for freedom included at the very least the presence of public institutions strong enough to intervene to secure economic opportunity. Some even went so far as to suggest that there was no freedom without good housing, health, and economic security in illness and old age. Such notions as these suggested that the way to freedom might lie in a measure of coercion—a complicated, paradoxical, troubling thought destined to grow in influence because it was increasingly true.

Equally disturbing was the redefinition of justice that certain progressive thinkers accomplished. Herbert Croly, for instance, went so far as to argue that merely seeing that all men started with the same political rights and the same economic opportunities (access to credit, markets, transportation, and inventions), as hard as they might be to achieve, would still constitute no guarantee of an even start. Even if equal access to profit-making opportunities were realized, only certain individuals could take advantage of it. "Those who have enjoyed the benefits of wealth and thorough education," Croly wrote in *The Promise of American Life,* "start with an advantage which can be overcome only by very exceptional men. . .; the average competitor without such benefits feels himself disqualified for the contest." The social environment from birth to age twenty-one had filtered out some who were deserving. If we may think of social justice for a moment as, among other things, careers open to talent, Croly saw that it would not be so cheaply bought as his contemporaries hoped. It would require some positive intervention to provide the sort of social environment in which no one of talent was stultified or deprived of the requisite stimulation. Croly did not see how radical such a thought might be. It was not only too radical for his time, but goes down hard in our own. It led to the conclusion that for careers to be truly open to talent there could be no real difference, around the nation and from class to class and race to race, in the factors that awaken and nurture talent from birth–nutrition, health care, exposure to intellectual and aesthetic stimulation, formal education, peer group aspirations. This suggests stunning alterations in our institutions and habits, and one can hardly claim the progressives had this fully in mind. Men such as Wilson aimed at justice only for young white males of good family, but there were men and women of his generation who saw that real justice would require more than he thought in the way of reforms and had in mind a broader range of social groups to whom it might reasonably be owed—to women, for example, and to recent immigrants. Yet if no one of that era followed the idea of social justice as far as it led, did not in any numbers and in any serious way extend it to Negroes and American Indians, for example, it is still to them we owe the reactivation—after a lapse of forty years and the death of men like Lincoln and Wendell Phillips—of one of the most disruptive, creative ideas of our time.

Another requirement of conservatism was that the existing legal and moral definitions of crime and good conduct remain unchallenged, since fortunes had been made and deviants had been jailed by men working on these assumptions. Some civic reformers thought it earthshaking to enforce rigorously the existing standards, punishing public officials for familiar crimes such as graft, and the outcry from threatened people encouraged the Goo Goo's image of himself as an advanced thinker. But what was really radical were ideas such as that popularized by E. A. Ross in *Sin and Society* (1907), that the modern age of social interdependence requires a new, social definition of sin. This meant less concentration on behavior affecting only oneself (drunkenness, reading pornography, lack of ambition), and identified as sinful any act that had deleterious social consequences (watering of stock or strip mining). Such a shift in values could not be accomplished in one generation no matter how many books were written, but it began to work its way into the leading minds, and today we see its growing influence. While some among us would still enforce the moral code of Anthony Comstock, many are coming to condemn more severely the man who drives "his" car with oily exhaust, operates "his" transistor radio on a bus, or carelessly lumbers "his" forest than we do the users of alcohol or hallucinogens or the committers of fornication.

Thought and practice in the realm of crime and punishment was vital to conservatives, whose lives had been built upon scrupulous moral rectitude in the familiar moral categories (in most cases), but whose fortunes had been built upon environmental pollution, exhaustion of resources, and health-breaking working conditions. And if it were not enough to suggest that the "best people" might in fact be criminals, some leading progressive thinkers were beginning to argue that the worst people were not at fault for their behavior. Reformer after reformer began by wishing to jail the municipal bosses. "Their motto," said Mr. Dooley, "was—'Arrest that man!'." These reformers ended up convinced that "the system" corrupted men and that it was neither humanly defensible nor socially efficacious to pillory the criminal. One sees Lincoln Steffens come to this in his autobiography, and Fred Howe in his *Confessions of a Reformer.* But the best example is surely California's crusading editor Fremont Older, who helped jail San Francisco's Boss Ruef; then, after reflecting upon the real sources of municipal corruption, Older worked as hard to get Ruef out of jail as he had to put him in. What was most significant in Older's action was not his sympathy for Ruef but the fact that he had shifted the blame from Ruef's character to the existing social arrangements.

These were some of the ideas let loose by progressive thinkers to discredit and disturb the status quo. The net effect of their thinking was to strengthen the social as against the private focus in American life. After the First World War the individualistic orientation reasserted itself, and the country (and many reformers) shrugged off such collectivist patterns of thought and action as had been foisted on it. As in the days when progressives began their uprising, the dominant current after the war was again toward those uncoordinated, egoistic strivings that had "built this country." But no postwar reaction could entirely erase the collectivized perspective. When the individualistic culture botched its best and in some ways its final opportunity, it would be somewhat easier to move toward collective solutions because of progressivism.

In rating the few intellectual steps toward collectivism as the most substantial accomplishment of progressivism, one would not wish to dismiss the institutional framework progressives erected. Through progressive reform there was established effective supervision of railroad rates, a central bank to begin mastering the art and science of monetary manipulation, innumerable well-staffed bureaus at all governmental levels where the public's interest in insurance funds, securities issues, sewage disposal, patent medicine, and public health might conceivably be protected. Progressivism revitalized the presidency. Progressivism spurred the organization of hundreds of interest groups, from architects to mayors to teachers, and even a few general interest groups for the few altruists and consumers who wished to work for broad public goals. These institutions and organizations are the scaffolding of a more rational, efficient, and possibly even a more liberal social order. We must not confuse this scaffolding with the actual achievement of such a social order, for it was far from that. But it was a beginning.

Impatient men in the troubled 1970s will not highly estimate this accomplishment—a few dangerous ideas, a few organizations, a few governmental agencies that might or might not serve their best implied ends. The study of progressivism does to some extent support the crushing judgment of some contemporaries, but those who incline to such a critical stance might gain a useful perspective by attempting to name the generation that accomplished more.

Fortunately for a movement with so much unfinished business, progressivism in all its forms would be given other chances. After

1929 the country would stand in especial need of the best qualities of those earlier reformers—an activist and hopeful spirit, a faith in human reason, a resourceful humanitarianism. It would need more than these qualities, but they were something, and they were vital. It would need above all their conviction that the forces loose in the "private" world must somehow be brought to public account, so that America could preserve her society in its precious, fragile inheritance: neighborliness, security, moral purpose, meaningful freedom.

No man better embodies all that was generous and sane in progressivism, along with much that was narrow and parochial, than William Jennings Bryan. Surely he spoke for progressivism at its best when, in 1912 with the movement at its apogee and another man selected to lead, he reaffirmed their commitment to an unwearying struggle for a better democracy with a ringing quotation from Byron:

> *The dead have been awakened—shall I sleep?*
> *The World's at war with Tyrants—shall I crouch?*
> *The Harvest's ripe and shall I pause to reap?*
> *I slumber not; the thorn is in my couch.*
> *Each day a trumpet soundeth in mine ear—*
> *It's echo in my heart.*

BIBLIOGRAPHIC ESSAY

A comprehensive essay citing the basic primary sources, syntheses, and monographs appropriate to the period discussed in this book would be as long as the book itself. This essay will identify those secondary sources that were most important in helping me make up my mind— or change it—on these matters. The top of the iceberg of primary materials— memoirs, manuscript collections, newspapers, diplomatic dispatches—are identified from time to time in the text and included among the accompanying documents. Many invaluable secondary sources will not even be cited, but the sort of reader who gets as far as this bibliographic essay will not need to be reminded of all the standard works. He will know this literature generally and wonder what material had a special weight in shaping this book. A few of my important debts to other historians are acknowledged below. The essay follows the text, and the source of direct quotations are identified sequentially. The search for the mood of turn-of-the-century America involves a research effort of some complexity, but it leads one to some absorbing books. Henry Adams' *The Education of Henry Adams* (Boston, 1918) was first privately printed in 1906. Among the recollections of life before the war, two of the most intelligent and literate are Dean Acheson, *Morning and Noon* (New York, 1965), and Henry Seidel Canby, *American Memoir: The Age of Confidence* (New York, 1947). Walter Lord, *The Good Years* (New York, 1960), is an impressionistic study where I found (pp. 2–3), among other things, the quotation from Reverend Hillis. Frederick Lewis Allen's *The Big Change* (New York, 1952) contains (p. 4) the quotation from Morgan's biographer. Other attempts to catch the mood of the period are Paul Angle, *Crossroads: 1913* (Chicago, 1963), Thomas Beer, *The Mauve Decade* (New York, 1926), and Albert Britt, *Turn of the Century* (New York, 1966). Journalist Mark Sullivan's *Our Times: The Turn of the Century,* Vol. 1 (New York, 1934), is a combination of history and recollection; his estimation of the mood in 1900, which I have partially quoted, is on p. 499. Van Wyck Brooks, *The Confident Years: 1885–1915* (New York, 1953) and Alfred Kazin, *On Native Grounds* (New York, 1942), are good studies of the literature of the era. Roderick Nash, "The American Cult of the Primitive," *American Quarterly* 18 (Fall, 1966), offers an important insight into the glorification of the primitive that characterized so much contemporary thought. A brilliant essay by John Higham, "The Reorientation of American Culture in the 1890s," in John Weiss (ed.), *The Origins of Modern Consciousness* (Detroit, 1965), describes the period as one of exuberance and rising vitality, with America largely free of the pessimism that laced European culture. Ray Ginger's *The Age of Excess* (New York, 1965) contains some powerfully evocative passages, although it has deficiencies as a sustained work of synthesis.

Urban history is a difficult genre, but two readable surveys appropriate for this period are Constance M. Green, *The Rise of Urban America* (New York, 1965) and Blake McKelvey, *The Urbanization of America: 1860–1915* (New Brunswick, 1963). Among the many urban biographies the best studies of the largest American cities are Constance M. Green, *Washington: Capital City, 1879–1950* (Princeton, 1963), Gilbert Osofsky, *Harlem: The Making of a Ghetto 1890–1930* (New York, 1966), Bessie L. Pierce, *A History of Chicago,* Vol. 3,

The Rise of a Modern City: 1871–1893 (New York, 1957), and Moses Rischin, *The Promised City: New York's Jews, 1870–1914* (Cambridge, Mass., 1962). The explosive growth of these and other cities created most of the social problems that occupied the progressive generation, but urbanization was a function of industrialization, another process that historians rarely describe with stylistic success. Thomas C. Cochran and William Miller, *The Age of Enterprise* (New York, 1942) and Edward C. Kirkland, *Industry Comes of Age: Business, Labor, and Public Policy 1860–1897* (New York, 1961) offer good descriptions of the economic developments that transformed American society.

On the question of what was bothering the progressives—from social problems to personal problems—one could cite the entire body of contemporary media, every autobiography, memoir, and diary. As for secondary literature, every volume in this bibliography contributes something, usually indirectly, to our understanding of the social crisis that produced progressivism. On the general fear of social disintegration, see Rowland T. Berthoff, "The American Social Order: A Conservative Hypothesis," *American Historical Review* 65 (April, 1960); Wallace D. Farnham, "The Weakened Spring of Government: A Study in 19th Century American History," *American Historical Review* 58 (April, 1963); James Willard Hurst, *Law and the Conditions of Freedom in the Nineteenth-Century United States* (Chicago, 1956); Mosei Ostrogorski, *Democracy and the Organization of Political Parties* (London, 1902), from which I have quoted (Vol. 2, p. 550); and Robert Wiebe, *The Search for Order 1877–1920* (New York, 1967). The quotation from Stephen J. Field is from his concurring opinion in the 1895 income tax case, *Pollock v. Farmers' Loan and Trust Co.*, 157 U.S. 607. The quotations from Henry Adams are from the *Education*, pp. 449 and 505.

Among the many factors accounting for the progressive uprising, perhaps none was more important than the Christian conscience. Charles H. Hopkins, *The Rise of the Social Gospel in American Protestantism, 1865–1915* (New Haven, 1940) and Henry May, *The Protestant Churches and Industrial America* (New York, 1949) are indispensable on reform sentiment within the churches, and indicate how deeply involved in reform were Christian ministers and laity. The importance of the Christian ethic is further illuminated in Carl N. Degler, *Out of Our Past* (New York, 1959), chapter 12, and Richard

Hofstadter, *The Age of Reform* (New York, 1955), chapter 5. The latter book is, among other things, the most extensive and stimulating discussion of the reformers' motivation. Any number of historians have joined the lively dispute over whether there was, as Hofstadter argued, a "status revolution." The most suggestive sociological evidence is presented in George E. Mowry, *The California Progressives* (Berkeley, 1951), chapter 4; Samuel P. Hays, "The 'Shame of the Cities' Revisited: The Case of Pittsburgh," in Herbert Shapiro (ed.), *The Muckrakers and American Society* (Boston, 1968); Eli D. Potts, "The Progressive Profile in Iowa," *Mid-America* 47 (October, 1965); Richard B. Sherman, "The Status Revolution and Massachusetts Progressive Leadership," *Political Science Quarterly* 78 (March, 1963); Jack Tager, "Progressives, Conservatives, and the Theory of the Status Revolution," *Mid-America* 48 (July, 1966); and Norman Wilensky, *Conservatives in the Progressive Era: The Taft Republicans of 1912* (Jacksonville, 1965).

Much, although not all, of this evidence indicates that conservatives as well as progressives came from the social classes Hofstadter (and Mowry) thought to be heavily progressive, and there have been some recent efforts to identify other social classes and groups as the principal sources of progressivism. J. Joseph Huthmacher made the first of several attempts to locate substantial reformism in the urban lower classes, in his "Urban Liberalism and the Age of Reform," *Mississippi Valley Historical Review,* 49 (September, 1962). More recently, the case for the participation of urban lower-class groups has been taken up by John D. Buenker; see his "The New Stock Politicians of 1912," *Journal of Illinois Historical Society,* 62 (Spring, 1969), and "Cleveland's New Stock Lawmakers and Progressive Reform," *Ohio History,* 25 (Spring, 1969). A contrasting and ultimately more convincing argument that municipal reformers, at least, were from the successful business classes, is made in Samuel P. Hays, "The Politics of Municipal Government in the Progressive Era," *Pacific Northwest Quarterly,* 60 (October, 1964). Also impressive is Robert Wiebe's association of reform with a "new middle class" of upward-mobile professionals, engineers, and businessmen, in *The Search for Order.* The literature on the social class of progressives is large and growing, and Hays's comprehensive summary of 1964 is now somewhat dated, as is my own bibliography on the subject, published in Otis L. Graham, Jr., *An Encore for Reform* (New York, 1967), pp. 229–30. The book that started this argument, Hofstadter's *The Age of Reform,* has had an impressive—and, of course, not always admiring—scholarly reception; see Otis L. Graham, Jr., (ed.), *From Roosevelt to Roosevelt: America, 1901–1941* (New York, 1971).

The quotation from Jane Addams is taken from her *Twenty Years at Hull House* (New York, 1910), p. 109. For an interesting use of the career of Jane Addams in the "status revolution" argument, see Staughton Lynd, "'Jane Addams and the Radical Impulse," *Commentary* 32 (July, 1961).

Conservative ideas at the end of the nineteenth century are ably discussed in Richard Hofstadter, *Social Darwinism in American Thought* (Boston, 1944), Robert G. McCloskey, *American Conservatism in the Age of Enterprise* (Cambridge, Mass., 1951), and Arnold M. Paul, *Conservative Crisis and the Rule of Law* (Ithaca, 1960). Reform thought has attracted a swarm of historians, some of the most perceptive being Henry Steele Commager, *The American Mind* (New Haven, 1950), Sidney Fine, *Laissez-Faire and the General Welfare State* (*Ann Arbor,* 1956), Morton D. White, *Social Thought in America* (New York, 1949), and Eric Goldman, *Rendezvous with Destiny* (New York, 1952), where I found the quotation from Justice Holmes (p. 105).

The best study of the settlement movement is Allen F. Davis, *Spearheads for Reform: The Social Settlements and the Progressive Movement 1890–1914* (New York, 1967). The centrality of the urge to functional organization was perceived by Hofstadter in *The Age of Reform,* and by Samuel P. Hays, *The Response to Industrialism 1885–1914* (Chicago, 1957). Two studies of engineers, Monte A. Calvert, *The Mechanical Engineer in America: 1830–1910* (Baltimore, 1967) and Edwin T. Layton, "The American Engineering Profession and the Idea of Social Responsibility," unpublished doctoral dissertation, University of California at Los Angeles, 1956, demonstrate that the progressive period was a spawning ground for professional organization, and that these organizations were not only chronologically but in spirit a part of the reform era. Lawrence Cremin has given us an invaluable book in *The Transformation of the School: Progressivism in American Education, 1876–1957* (New York, 1961), and the broader importance of public education to the progressive mind is examined in Rush Welter, *Popular Education and Democratic Thought in America* (New York, 1962).

There are many urban biographies, but only recently have we begun to have an adequate shelf of monographs on the progressive movement in the cities. Some of the more interesting studies are James Crooks, *Politics and Progress: The Rise of Urban Progressivism in Baltimore 1895–1911* (Baton Rouge, 1968), Melvin Holli, *Reform in Detroit: Hazen S. Pingree and Urban Politics* (New York, 1969), Arthur Mann, *Yankee Reformers in the Urban Era* (Cambridge, Mass., 1954), William D. Miller, *Memphis During the Progressive Era, 1900–1917* (Memphis, 1957), and Zane Miller, *Boss Cox's Cincinnati: Urban Politics in the Progressive Era* (New York, 1968). An interesting critical perspective on reform is found in Theodore Lowi, "Machine Politics—Old and New," *The Public Interest* 9 (Fall, 1967). Some of the more valuable state studies are Mowry's *The California Progressives,* Spencer Olin, *California's Prodigal Sons: Hiram Johnson and the Progressives 1911–1917* (Berkeley, 1968), Hoyt L. Warner, *Progressivism in Ohio, 1897–1917* (Columbus, Ohio, 1964), and the broader surveys of state politics in Russel B. Nye, *Midwestern Progressive Politics* (East Lansing, 1951) and C. Vann Woodward, *Origins of the New South 1877–1913* (Baton Rouge, 1951). I was also much enlightened by the treatment of middle-class reformers and their relations with urban labor in Irwin Yellowitz, *Labor and the Progressive Movement in New York State, 1897–1916* (Ithaca, 1965), and by a recent book on one of the more conservative state reform movements, Raymond Pulley, *Old Virginia Restored: An Interpretation of the Progressive Impulse 1870–1930* (Charlottesville, 1968). The sizable role of business groups is especially clear in California; see, for example, Olin's *California's Prodigal Sons,* and Gerald D. Nash, *State Government and Economic Development: A History of Admininistrative Policies in California, 1859–1933* (Berkeley, 1964). Roy Lubove, in "Workmen's Compensation and the Prerogatives of Voluntarism," *Labor History* 8 (Fall, 1967), and in *The Struggle for Social Security 1900–1935* (Cambridge, Mass., 1968) chapter 3, shows that businessmen were interested not only in the right kind of regulatory legislation but in some cases worked also for portions of the "social welfare legislation" agenda. The quotation above on p. 32 is from Lubove's article, p. 259.

There is a mountain of literature on national progressivism, and some of the best of it deals in one way or another with the career of Theodore Roosevelt. William H. Harbaugh, *Power and Responsibility:*

The Life and Times of Theodore Roosevelt (New York, 1961) and George E. Mowry, *The Era of Theodore Roosevelt: 1900–1912* (New York, 1958) are reasonably favorable to T.R. (both contain splendid bibliographies). More critical treatment may be found in Richard Hofstadter, *The American Political Tradition* (New York, 1948), chapter 9; Henry Pringle, *Theodore Roosevelt* (New York, 1931); John Blum, *The Republican Roosevelt* (Cambridge, Mass., 1954); Gabriel Kolko, *The Triumph of Conservatism: A Reinterpretation of American History, 1900–1916* (New York, 1963), chapters 3–5; and Samuel P. Hays, *Conservation and the Gospel of Efficiency: The Progressive Conservation Movement 1890–1920* (Cambridge, Mass., 1959), especially pp. 266–72. Contrasting accounts of the struggle over meat-packing legislation are given in John Braeman, "The Square Deal in Action," in John Braeman, Robert Bremner, and Everett Walters (eds.), *Change and Continuity in Twentieth-Century America* (Columbus, Ohio, 1964), and Kolko, *The Triumph of Conservatism*, chapter 4. On the Pure Food and Drug Act and its administration, see Oscar E. Anderson, *The Health of a Nation: Harvey Wiley and the Fight for Pure Food* (Chicago, 1958), a useful book that is flawed by the uncritical adoption of Wiley's view of who was for and against regulation; Thomas A. Bailey, "Congressional Opposition to Pure Food and Drug Legislation, 1879–1906," *American Journal of Sociology* 36 (July, 1930); the entire December, 1933 issue of *Law and Contemporary Problems,* especially the articles by C. C. Regier, "The Struggle for Pure Food and Drugs," and by L. T. Hayes and F. J. Ruff, "The Administration of the Federal Food and Drug Act." James Harvey Young has written two splendid and often hilarious books on food and drug adulteration and patent medicines in American history and the efforts to protect the consumer—*The Toadstool Millionaires: A Social History of Patent Medicines in America Before Federal Regulation* (Princeton, 1961), and *The Medical Messiahs: A Social History of Health Quackery in Twentieth-Century America* (Princeton, 1967). A gloomy view of the accomplishments of progressive efforts in this area will be visited upon anyone who reads Arthur Kallet and F. J. Schlink, *100,000,000 Guinea Pigs* (New York, 1932) or Ruth DeForest Lamb, *American Chamber of Horrors* (New York, 1936).

On railroad regulation under Roosevelt, see Blum, *The Republican Roosevelt,* Gabriel Kolko, *Railroads and Regulation* (Princeton, 1965), and William Z. Ripley, *Railroads: Rates and Regulation* (New York, 1912). By far the best book on progressive conservation is Samuel P. Hays, *Conservation and the Gospel of Efficiency*, and Hays's general interpretation is shared by James Penick, *Progressive Politics and Conservation: The Ballinger-Pinchot Affair* (Chicago, 1968). The People vs. The Interests interpretation may be found in an unconvincing form in Judson King, *The Conservation Fight: From Theodore Roosevelt to the Tennessee Valley Authority* (Washington, D.C., 1945), and more formidably in J. Leonard Bates, *The Origins of Teapot Dome: Progressives, Parties, and Petroleum, 1909–1921* (Urbana, Ill., 1963), and in Richard Lowitt, "A Neglected Aspect of the Progressive Movement: George W. Norris and Public Control of Hydro-Electric Power, 1913–1919," *The Historian* 27 (1965). A valuable survey with little interpretation is Elmo Richardson, *The Politics of Conservation: Crusaders and Controversies, 1897–1913* (Berkeley, 1962).

The indispensable source on Wilson is the multivolume biography by Arthur Link. Most important for the first administration are *Wilson: The New Freedom* (Princeton, 1965), Vol. 2 in the series, and Vol. 5, *Wilson: Campaigns for Progressivism and Peace* (Princeton, 1965). Arthur Walworth's *Woodrow Wilson* (New York, 1958) is uncritical but valuable as a detailed narrative. More critical treatment may be found in John Blum, *Woodrow Wilson and the Politics of Morality* (Boston, 1956), James Kerney, *The Political Education of Woodrow Wilson* (New York, 1926), and William Diamond, *The Economic Thought of Woodrow Wilson* (Baltimore, 1943). One ought not to ignore the view from the New Left, well stated in Martin J. Sklar, "Woodrow Wilson and the Political Economy of Modern United States Liberalism," *Studies on the Left* 1 (1960). On the Federal Reserve Act, in addition to Link, see Kolko, *The Triumph of Conservatism*, chapter 9, and J. Laurence Laughlin, *The Federal Reserve Act: Its Origin and Problems* (New York, 1933). On the trust issue, see James E. Anderson, *The Emergence of the Modern Regulatory State* (Washington, D.C., 1962), a clear if unoriginal survey, William Letwin, *Law and Economic Policy: The Evolution of the Sherman Anti-Trust Act* (New York, 1965), and Melvin Urofsky, "Wilson, Brandeis, and the Trust Issue, 1912–1914," *Mid-America* 49 (1967). New Freedom tax measures are reviewed in Sidney Ratner, *American Taxation* (New York, 1942). Alpheus T. Mason's Brandeis: *A Free*

Man's Life (New York, 1946) is a good biography of this very important ally and mentor of Wilson. A valuable article on the pressures behind Wilsonian policy is Richard Abrams, "Woodrow Wilson and the Southern Congressmen, 1913–1916," *Journal of Southern History* 22 (November, 1956).

Many good books have been written on the entire diplomatic record of the 1914–17 period. To my mind the best single volume is now Ernest R. May, *The World War and American Isolation* (Cambridge, Mass., 1959). Link's volumes 3 and 4, *Wilson: The Struggle for Neutrality, 1914–1915* (Princeton, 1960), and *Wilson: Confusions and Crises, 1915–1916* (Princeton, 1964), and volume 5, already cited, require a stronger word than invaluable. The most readable and plausible of the revisionist volumes are Charles C. Tansill, *America Goes to War* (New York, 1938), Walter Millis, *Road to War: America, 1914–1917* (Boston, 1935), and the otherwise sympathetic Ray Stannard Baker, *Woodrow Wilson: Life and Letters* (New York, 1927–39, 8 vols), especially volumes 5 and 6. Edwin Borchard and William P. Lage, *Neutrality for the United States* (New Haven, 1940), is more intemperate than most revisionist studies—and that requires a good deal of spleen—but contains a great deal of useful information on the difficult technical issues of neutrality. I found valuable information and invaluable correctives for the revisionist argument in Charles Seymour, *American Neutrality: 1914–1917* (New Haven, 1935), Daniel Smith, *Robert Lansing and American Neutrality: 1914–1917* (Berkeley, 1958), and Edward H. Buehrig, *Woodrow Wilson and the Balance of Power* (Bloomington, Ill., 1955). Paul Birdsall, in "Neutrality and Economic Pressures, 1914–1917," *Science and Society* 3 (Spring, 1939), provides an economic setting that clarifies a great deal, without utilizing any conspiracy theories.

For the policy-making process within Germany, and a firm grasp of German political pressures, see May, *The World War and American Isolation*, Karl E. Birnbaum, *Peace Moves and U-Boat Warfare* (Stockholm, 1958), and Arno J. Mayer, *Political Origins of the New Diplomacy, 1917–1918* (New Haven, 1959). Fritz Fischer's epochal book, *Germany's Aims in the First World War* (New York, 1967—a translation of *Griff nach der Weltmach*) was followed by a sizable critical literature. For the highlights of the argument, see Wolfgang J. Mommsen, "The Debate on German War Aims," in Walter Laquer and George L. Mosse, (eds.) *1914: The Coming of the First World*

War (New York, 1966). On the Allies, I found most useful Lord Beaverbrook, *Politicians and the War 1914–1916* (London, 1928), Viscount Grey of Fallodon, *Twenty-Five Years, 1892–1916* (London, 1925), Marion C. Siney, *The Allied Blockade of Germany, 1914–1916* (Ann Arbor, 1957), Gerda Crosby, *Disarmament and Peace in British Politics 1914–1919* (Cambridge, Mass., 1957), Kent Forster, *The Failures of Peace: The Search for a Negotiated Peace During the First World War* (Philadelphia, 1941), and Laurence W. Martin, *Peace Without Victory: Woodrow Wilson and the British Liberals* (New Haven, 1958). On Allied war aims, one must make do with A. J. P. Taylor, "The War Aims of the Allies in the First World War," in *Essays Presented to Sir Lewis Namier* (London, 1956), and Pierre Renouvin, "Les Buts de Guerre du Gouvernement Français (1914–1918)," *Revue Historique* (March, 1966).

Robert E. Osgood has nicely summarized the arguments that Wilson was primarily (and regrettably) an idealist, in *Ideals and Self-Interest in America's Foreign Relations* (Chicago, 1953). But the other side of the argument, that the president and his advisors had a firm grasp on reality and pursued the national interest as they saw it rather than the abstractions their language usually suggested, has recently gained authority with the publication of books like those of Buehrig, Link (see a brief statement of his view in "The Higher Realism of Woodrow Wilson," *Journal of Presbyterian History* 41 [March, 1963]), and May. A valuable summary of the argument for Wilson's realism is Daniel M. Smith, "National Interest and American Intervention, 1917: An Historiographical Appraisal," *Journal of American History* 53 (June, 1965). But Osgood's argument, especially as stated in "Woodrow Wilson, Collective Security, and the Lessons of History," *Confluence* (January, 1957), is still persuasive. The studies of Wilson's wartime and postwar diplomacy by Arno J. Mayer, *Politics and Diplomacy of Peacemaking* (Princeton, 1967), and N. Gordon Levin, *Woodrow Wilson and World Politics* (New York, 1968), depict Wilson, at least in the years after 1917, as a hard-headed American nationalist whose international commitments owed little to abstract and unrealizable ideals. In view of these apparently conflicting scholarly efforts, the surest ground seems to be that taken by Edward Buehrig in "Idealism and Statecraft," *Confluence* (October, 1956), where Wilson is presented as a man who mixed realism and idealism in a most unsettling way.

Useful monographs on some of the more important and difficult questions concerning the 1914–17 period are C.R.M.F. Cruttwell, *A History of the Great War* (London, 1936) and Cryril Falls, *The First World War* (New York, 1960) for military events; Ralph Nafziger, "The American Press and Public Opinion During World War I, 1914–1917," unpublished doctoral dissertation, University of Wisconsin, 1936, and Harold Syrett, "The Business Press and American Neutrality, 1914–1917," *Mississippi Valley Historical Review* 32 (September, 1945), on public opinion and the press; Samuel R. Spencer, *Decision for War: 1917* (Rindge, New Hampshire, 1953), for the tides of opinion in the weeks before intervention; Warren I. Cohen, *The American Revisionists and the Lessons of World War I* (Chicago, 1966), on revisionist historiography and its influence; and Charles Warren, "Troubles of a Neutral," *Foreign Affairs* (April, 1934), a lawyer's distillation of the lessons of the neutrality period as they might be (and virtually were) applied to prevent a second World War.

Historiographical surveys are numerous, the best recent ones being the article by Daniel M. Smith in *The Journal of American History*, Richard Leopold's "The Emergence of America as a World Power," in John Braeman, *et al.* (eds.) *Change and Continuity in Twentieth-Century America*, and Ernest R. May, *American Intervention: 1917 and 1941* (Washington, D.C., 1960). An admirable effort to sketch the costs of the war is John M. Clark, *The Costs of the World War to the American People* (New Haven, 1931), which may be supplemented by *The Annual Report of the Secretary of the Treasury: 1919* (Washington, D.C., 1920), for financial costs; Kevin McShane, "The 1918 Kansas City Influenza Epidemic," *Missouri Historical Review* 63 (October, 1968), for some of the noncombatant fatalities; and U. S. Senate Document 248, *Report of Federal Trade Commission Regarding Profiteering* (65th Cong., 2d sess., June 29, 1918), for one of the war's effects on the distribution of income.

The affinity of progressivism for an aggressive foreign policy was first suggested by Randolph Bourne and was given its best scholarly expression in William E. Leuchtenburg, "Progressivism and Imperialism: The Progressive Movement and American Foreign Policy, 1898–1916," *Mississippi Valley Historical Review*, 39 (December, 1952). A number of careful surveys of progressive opinion, especially in the Congress, have failed to substantiate this argument. The most important of these, by professors Allen, Sutton, and Bernstein and

Lieb, are summarized in John M. Cooper, Jr., "Progressivism and American Foreign Policy: A Reconsideration," *Mid-America,* 51 (October, 1969).

The Lansing quotation on p. 65 is from Robert Lansing, *War Memoirs of Robert Lansing, Secretary of State* (Indianapolis, 1935), p. 129. The quotation from Count Westarp on p. 81 is from May, *American Isolation,* p. 103. The quotations from *The American Banker* and *The Economist* on p. 89 are from the article by Harold Syrett, already cited. The quotation from Wilson on p. 82 is from Tansill, *America Goes to War,* p. 639. The Wilson quotation on p. 85 is from Walter Millis, *Road to War,* p. 443. The quotation from Andrew Carnegie on p. 93 is from Tansill, *America Goes to War,* p. 54. The *New York Times* quotation on p. 93 is from Millis, *Road to War,* p. 124. The quotation from Spring-Rice on p. 93 is from Millis, p. 115.

The domestic implications of the war, especially on the various segments of the prewar reform movement, are not yet thoroughly charted. Pioneering work has been done by Samuel Haber, *Efficiency and Uplift* (Chicago, 1964), Charles Hirschfeld, "Nationalist Progressivism and World War I," *Mid-America* 45 (July, 1963), Sidney Kaplan, "Social Engineers as Saviors: World War I and American Liberals," *Journal of the History of Ideas* (June, 1956), Walter Trattner, "Progressivism and World War I," *Mid-America* (July, 1962), and Allen F. Davis, "Welfare, Reform, and World War I," *American Quarterly* 19 (Fall, 1967). All of these articles emphasize the ways in which the war effort harmonized with certain strains in progressive thought and assisted certain reform efforts toward fruition, and all—especially the article by Kaplan—reveal how the war came to undermine the reform movement—intellectually, emotionally, politically. The latter development was confessed by a prointervention liberal, Herbert Croly, in his "Liberalism vs. the War," *New Republic* (8 December, 1920), and predicted in Randolph Bourne, *Untimely Papers* (New York, 1919). The conclusions of the Yoakum and Yerkes study, *Army Mental Tests,* are critically reviewed in Daniel J. Kevles, "Testing the Army's Intelligence: Psychologists and the Military in World War I," *Journal of American History* 55 (December, 1968).

A less pessimistic view of the war's impact may be found in George Mowry, "The First World War and American Democracy," in Jesse

D. Clarkson and Thomas C. Cochran (eds.), *War as a Social Institution* (New York, 1941). Other beneficial effects are outlined in Roy Lubove, "Homes and 'A Few Well-Placed Fruit Trees': An Object Lesson in Federal Housing," *Social Research* 27 (Winter, 1960), as well as in the pages of the *Proceedings of the National Conference of Social Work,* especially pp. 674–77 of the 1918 number of the *Proceedings,* where one finds a discussion entitled "The Future Prospects of Leading Wartime Efforts and Movements," and in the essay by Arthur J. Todd in the same number, entitled "New Social Data Growing Out of the War," pp. 683–86.

For evidence that there was great support for a conscription of wealth in April, 1917, see A. Russell Buchanan, "American Editors Examine American War Aims and Plans in April, 1917," *Pacific Historical Review* 9 (September, 1940). The history of the Left in the war period has not been written; for the Congressional Left, one may begin with Alex Arnet, *Claude Kitchin and the Wilson War Policies* (Boston, 1937), Seward Livermore, *Politics is Adjourned: Woodrow Wilson and the War Congresses, 1916–1918* (Middletown, Conn., 1966), the older survey by Frederic C. Paxson, *American Democracy and the World War* (Boston, 1936–45), and the relevant parts of Arno J. Mayer, *Political Origins of the New Diplomacy, 1917–1918* (New Haven, 1959). Scholars have recently developed a strong interest in the nature of business-government relations during the war. Without agreeing with them, I was particularly stimulated by James Weinstein's *The Corporate Ideal in the Liberal State, 1900–1918* (Boston, 1968), and Paul A. C. Koistinen, "The 'Industrial-Military Complex' in Historical Perspective: World War I," *Business History Review,* 41 (Winter, 1967). Melvin Urofsky describes the shaky entente between the steel industry, and especially U. S. Steel's Judge Gary, and the government, in *Big Steel and the Wilson Administration* (Columbus, Ohio, 1969).

The quotation from the *General Federation of Women's Clubs Magazine* on p. 98 is from William O'Neill, *Everyone Was Brave: The History of Social Feminism in America* (Chicago, 1969), p. 34. The quotations from social workers Woods and Devine on p. 99 are from Allen F. Davis, *Spearheads for Reform,* p. 222. The quotation from Robert Woods on p. 99 is from Robert Woods, "The Regimentation of the Free," *The Survey* 40 (6 July, 1918). The quotation from Frances Kellor on p. 100 is from John Higham,

Strangers in the Land (New Brunswick, 1955), p. 234. The quotation from Arthur Link on p. 101 is from Link, *Woodrow Wilson and the Progressive Era* (New York, 1954), pp. 192–93. The quotation from Josephus Daniels on p. 103 is from a letter to Ray Stannard Baker, in Baker, Woodrow Wilson: *Life and Letters,* Vol. 6, p. 506. Jerold Auerbach's "Woodrow Wilson's 'Prediction' to Frank Cobb: Words Historians Should Doubt Ever Got Spoken," *Journal of American History* 54 (December, 1967), convinced me that I can no longer quote this apocryphal story. In the exchange of letters between Wilson's biographer, Arthur S. Link, and Auerbach (see the *Journal of American History* 55 [June, 1968]), Link convinces me that Wilson uttered roughly similar prophecies if not this particular one, and Auerbach convinces me not only that Cobb's story ought to be retired, but that neither in this nor in any other 'prophecy' did Wilson show noticeable concern for the effect of the war on civil liberties. The quotation from Frederic Howe on p. 108 is from Howe, *The Confessions of a Reformer* (New York, 1925), p. 279. The quotation from Mencken on p. 109 is from Gerald Rabkin, *Drama and Commitment* (Indianapolis, 1964), p. 23. The quotation from the Southern Sociological Conference convention in 1919 at Knoxville is from E. Charles Chatfield, "The Southern Sociological Congress: Organization of Uplift," *Tennessee Historical Quarterly* (December, 1960).

The repressive atmosphere of 1919 is seen as largely the administration's fault in Harry N. Scheiber, *The Wilson Administration and Civil Liberties, 1917–1921* (Ithaca, 1960), and receives a more subtle explanation in Stanley Coben, "A Study in Nativism: The American Red Scare of 1919–20," *Political Science Quarterly* 79 (March, 1964); see also John Blum, "Nativism, Anti-Radicalism, and the Foreign Scare, 1917–1920," *Midwest Journal* 3 (1950–51). For a neglected side of the red scare, see William Tuttle, "Views of a Negro During 'The Red Summer of 1919,'" *Journal of Negro History* 51 (July, 1966). The legal issues are clarified in Zechariah Chafee, *Free Speech in the United States* (Cambridge, Mass., 1941). In *The Challenge to American Freedoms: World War I and the Rise of the American Civil Liberties Union* (Lexington, Ky., 1963), Donald D. Johnson describes the response of some intellectuals to the repression of the war period.

The best general analysis of the fate of reform in the 1920s is still Arthur S. Link, "What Happened to the Progressive Movement in the 1920s?" *American Historical Review* 64 (July, 1959). Richard

Hofstadter's *The Age of Reform,* pp. 282–301, contains insights that Link developed and that will probably be read with profit fifty years from now. Although many monographs have appeared since they were published, no one has yet written a better political history than William E. Leuchtenburg's *The Perils of Prosperity* (Chicago, 1958), or a more penetrating "social" history than Frederick Lewis Allen's *Only Yesterday* (New York, 1931).

Several studies reveal a persistence of progressive impulses in the 1920s. For the efficiency thrust, see George Tindall, "Business Progressivism: Southern Politics in the 1920s," *South Atlantic Quarterly* (Winter, 1963); James Weinstein, "Organized Business and the City Commission and Manager Movements," *Journal of Southern History* 28 (May, 1962), Donald Swain, *Federal Conservation Policy, 1921–1933* (Berkeley, 1963), and the contemporary view of Morris L. Cooke, "The Influence of Scientific Management on Government—Federal, State, and Municipal," *Bulletin of the Taylor Society* 9 (1924). An indispensable source in this connection is *Recent Social Trends in the United States* (New York: 1934). Attention is called to postwar social legislation in Elizabeth Brandeis, "Labor Legislation," in John R. Commons, *et al., History of Labor in the United States, 1896–1932,* Vol. 2 (New York, 1935), and Henry Seager, "Progress of Labor Legislation, 1900–1925," *American Labor Legislation Review* 20 (December, 1925). Both are forced to admit that the "gains" of the 1920s in such areas as state minimum wage or child labor legislation were very skimpy. Clarke Chambers' *Seedtime of Reform: Social Service and Social Action, 1918–1933* (Minneapolis, 1963), reinforces the impression of liberal discouragement, although the book was written to call attention to the survival of the social welfare wing of progressivism in the 1920s. The regulatory agencies established during the progressive era of course survived in the 1920s, but each in its turn was used by the interests it was designed to regulate or, if they had no work for it, was allowed to stagnate: see G. Cullum Davis, "The Transformation of the FTC, 1914–1929," *Mississippi Valley Historical Review* 49 (December, 1962), and E. Pendleton Herring, *Public Administration and the Public Interest* (New York, 1936). Another progressive reform turned to conservative uses is discussed in V. O. Key and Winston Crouch, *The Initiative and Referendum in California* (Berkeley, 1939).

The political activities of reform groups whose goals were primarily economic may be followed in Kenneth McKay, *The Progressive Move-*

ment of 1924 (New York, 1947), and James Shideler, "The Disintegration of the Progressive Party Movement of 1924," Historian (Spring, 1951), and James Weinstein, "Radicalism in the Midst of Normalcy," Journal of American History (March, 1966)—the latter discovering more discontent than is usually depicted, but nonetheless leaving intact the meager summary of results. David Burner's The Politics of Provincialism: The Democratic Party in Transition 1918–1932 (New York, 1968) is a very important study of the party, which somewhat by accident came to harbor the many conflicting impulses of modern reform. Burner's book, and Lawrence Levine, Defender of the Faith: William Jennings Bryan: The Last Decade 1915–1925 (New York, 1965), are superb introductions to the effect of cultural tensions on the politics of the 1920s.

Historians have from the beginning recognized that "efficiency" was one of the guiding ideas of the progressive movement, but most of the writing on this aspect of the reform impulse has come in the last few years. An early study was Benjamin P. DeWitt, The Progressive Movement (New York, 1915), chapter 15, "The Efficiency Movement." More recent books include Samuel P. Hays' volume on conservation, Raymond E. Callahan, Education and the Cult of Efficiency (Chicago, 1962), and Samuel Haber, Efficiency and Uplift: Scientific Management in the Progressive Era, 1890–1920 (Chicago, 1964). Efficiency invariably meant the application of scientific modes of thought to traditional processes, and it usually seemed to require centralization of authority under scientifically or at least technically minded people. The impact of this part of the progressive movement upon the size and functions of the federal government may be followed in A. Hunter Dupree, Science in the Federal Government: A History to 1940 (Cambridge, Mass., 1957), and in Arthur Johnson's shrewd analysis of T.R.'s approach to industrial problems, "Antitrust Policy in Transition, 1908: Ideal and Reality," Mississippi Valley Historical Review 48 (December, 1961). A good example of this sort of activity at the local level is the subject of James H. Cassedy's Charles V. Chapin and the Public Health Movement (Cambridge, 1962).

Men of conservative instincts and much to conserve often found it possible or even imperative to become progressives because of the emphasis placed on predictability and social control in some parts of the movement. Their influence, of course, increased the chances that reform would have a conservative outcome. Gabriel Kolko, in his The

Triumph of Conservatism, has gathered together all the evidence he could find (at the federal level) where this was the case. James Weinstein describes the conversion of some businessmen to a mild form of progressivism in his *The Corporate Ideal in the Liberal State: 1900–1918* (Boston, 1968). A pioneering study of businessmen as reformers is Marguerite Green, *The National Civic Federation and the American Labor Movement 1900–1925* (Washington, D.C., 1956). Robert Wiebe's *Businessmen and Reform* (Cambridge, Mass., 1962) does not have the clear thesis of the Kolko and Weinstein books, but it is more plausible. Wiebe finds businessmen favoring certain "reforms," hostile to others, and in general divided and uncertain when it came to utilizing the state.

Samuel P. Hays applied the "community-society" theory to turn of the century America in "Political Parties and the Community-Society Continuum," in W. N. Chambers and W. D. Burnham (eds.), *The American Party Systems* (New York, 1967). Robert Wiebe's *The Search for Order* is the first book-length synthesis for this period which utilizes this concept. The scholarly reception of this book, among others, is the subject of Otis L. Graham, Jr., *From Roosevelt to Roosevelt: 1901–1941* (New York, 1971).

The social justice impulse is the subject of Robert Bremner, *From the Depths: The Discovery of Poverty in the United States* (New York, 1956), Jeremy Felt, *Hostages of Fortune: Child Labor Reform in New York State* (Syracuse, 1965), Clarke Chambers, *Seedtime of Reform,* Allen F. Davis, *Spearheads for Reform,* Roy Lubove, *The Progressives and the Slums: Tenement House Reform in New York City, 1897–1917* (Pittsburgh, 1962), and Henry May, *The Protestant Churches and Industrial America* (New York, 1949). Two of the most consistent champions of the underdog in the progressive era and for years thereafter are the subject of Carl H. Voss, *Rabbi and Minister: The Friendship of Stephen S. Wise and John Haynes Holmes* (Cleveland, 1964). The quotation from George Alger on p. 141 is from Felt, *Hostages of Fortune,* p. 222. The New Dealer who complained of the inefficacy of housing reform, quoted on p. 142, was brought to my attention by John P. Dean, "The Myths of Housing Reform," *American Sociological Review* (1949), p. 106. The quotation from Roy Lubove on p. 143 is drawn from his *The Struggle for Social Security 1900–1935* (Cambridge, Mass., 1968), p. 45. The quotation on p. 143 is from Herbert Croly's *The Promise of American*

188

Life (New York, 1909), p. 23. The quotation on p. 144 is from Willford I. King, *The Wealth and Income of the People of the United
States* (New York, 1917), p. 231. Another valuable study of income
and its distribution is Simon Kuznets, *National Income: A Summary
of Findings* (New York, 1946).

On the attitude of reformers toward blacks, see Dewey Grantham,
Jr., "The Progressive Movement and the Negro," *South Atlantic
Quarterly* 54 (October, 1955), who finds little sensitivity to racial
injustice among reformers, and Gilbert Osofsky, "Progressivism and
the Negro: New York, 1900–1915," *American Quarterly* 16 (Summer,
1964), who shows that New York reformers in this area, as in many
others, were quite advanced for their time. Charles F. Kellogg's *The
NAACP: A History of the National Association for the Advancement
of Colored People, 1909–1920* (Baltimore, 1957), describes the organizational efforts of blacks. For something of the lives of blacks in this
period, see Rayford Logan, *The Negro in American Life and Thought:
The Nadir, 1877–1901* (New York, 1954). The best studies of the
two progressive presidents are Seth M. Scheiner, "President Theodore
Roosevelt and the Negro, 1901–1908," *Journal of Negro History* 47
(July, 1962), and Henry Blumenthal, "Woodrow Wilson and the
Race Question," *Journal of Negro History* 48 (January, 1963). Other
useful treatments of this problem are Allen F. Davis, *Spearheads for
Reform,* chapter 5; Louis Filler, *Crusaders for American Liberalism*
(New York, 1939), chapter 21; C. Vann Woodward, *The Origins of
the New South, 1877–1913* (Baton Rouge, 1951), chapters 12 and 13;
and a recent brief study by David Southern, *The Malignant Heritage:
Yankee Progressives and the Negro Question, 1901–1914* (Chicago,
1968). Two studies of the southern penal system are Jane Zimmerman,
"The Penal Reform Movement in the South During the Progressive
Era," *Journal of Southern History,* 17 (November, 1951), and Fletcher
M. Green, "Some Aspects of the Convict Lease System in the Southern
States," in Green (ed.), *Essays in Southern History* (Chapel Hill,
1949). The statement by Homer Folks quoted on p. 148 appeared in
National Conference of Charities and Corrections Proceedings (Fort
Wayne, 1911), p. 8. The remark by Wilson quoted on p. 149 was
called to my attention by Southern, *The Malignant Heritage,* on p. 78.
The comment of Walter Weyl on p. 152 is from Weyl, *The New
Democracy* (New York, 1912), p. 342.

Reformers who were primarily interested in defending the culture of the native white middle classes are the subject of James Timberlake's *Prohibition and the Progressive Movement: 1900–1925* (Cambridge, Mass., 1963), Joseph Gusfield, *Symbolic Crusade: Status Politics and the American Temperance Movement* (Urbana, Ill., 1963), and Norman H. Clark, *The Dry Years: Prohibition and Social Change in Washington* (Seattle, 1965). On the Klan, see the readable survey by David M. Chalmers, *Hooded Americanism: The History of the Ku Klux Klan* (New York, 1965), and the penetrating scholarly analysis of Charles C. Alexander, *The Ku Klux Klan in the Southwest* (Lexington, Ky., 1965). In Alexander's book, and to an ever greater extent in Kenneth T. Jackson, *The Ku Klux Klan in the City, 1915–1930* (New York, 1967), one sees that the Klan attracted many people who sought better schools and law enforcement and a stronger sense of community. The concentration on racial and religious persecution was a decision of the Klan leadership and obscured the similarities between the Klan and parts of prewar progressivism. On woman suffrage, in addition to Alan Grimes, see Eleanor Flexner's survey, *Century of Struggle: The Woman's Rights Movement in the United States* (Cambridge, Mass., 1959), and the thoughtful interpretation by Aileen Kraditor, *The Ideas of the Woman Suffrage Movement, 1890–1920* (New York, 1965).

The overlap between some forms of progressivism and turn-of-the-century nativism is illuminated in John Higham, *Strangers in the Land: Patterns of American Nativism 1860–1925* (New Brunswick, 1955), Roy Lubove, "The Progressives and the Prostitute," *The Historian* 24 (May, 1962), and in Egal Feldman, "Prostitution, The Alien Woman, and the Progressive Imagination: 1900–1915," *American Quarterly* (Summer, 1967). This article called my attention to the passage from Abraham Flexner's *Prostitution in Europe* (New York, 1914), p. 395, which is quoted on p. 155 above.

Crystal Eastman's argument for workmen's compensation is found in her book *Work-Accidents and the Law* (New York, 1910), a volume in the Pittsburgh survey. For Brandeis' argument that social insurance is mandated by the wastefulness and inefficiency of the present remorseless industrial system, as well as by human compassion, see his "Workingmen's Insurance—The Road to Social Efficiency," in *Proceedings of the National Conference of Charities and Corrections* (New York, 1911). Charles Edward Russell, in *The Uprising of the Masses* (New York, 1910), described poverty as social inefficiency.

Irving Fisher, in his "The Significance of the Anti-Alcohol Movement," *Proceedings of the National Conference on Social Welfare* (1919), summarized the reasons for prohibiting alcoholic beverages: "the ideals of work, the requirements of modern industrial competition, the findings of modern science, and the ideals of morality." Like most progressives, Fisher assumed that science, morality, and self-interest all directed the same reforms. All interests were ultimately harmonious. The quotation on p. 155 is from Frederick W. Taylor's *The Principles of Scientific Management* (New York, 1911), p. 8.

Some of the progressive campaigns that combined the social control, nativist, and social justice elements were woman suffrage, the La-Follette Seaman's Act, and the drive against prostitution. See Aileen Kraditor, *The Ideas of the Woman Suffrage Movement,* Jerold Auerbach, "Progressivism at Sea: The LaFollette Act of 1915," *Labor History* (Fall, 1961), and the article by Feldman on prostitution, cited above. A similar blend may be seen in the eugenics movement, which attracted many progressives: see Mark Haller, "Heredity in Progressive Thought," *Social Service Review* 37 (June, 1963). For an example of how the diverse strains of progressivism could combine in a political movement, see Albert D. Kirwan's study of Mississippi reform, *Revolt of the Rednecks: Mississippi Politics 1876–1925* (Lexington, Ky., 1951); for their combination in a single individual, see E. A. Ross, *Seventy Years of It* (New York, 1936), or Paul W. Glad, *The Trumpet Soundeth: William Jennings Bryan and His Democracy 1896–1912* (Lincoln, Neb., 1960). A very perceptive essay on the contradictions so often found in the progressive collective mentality is John Braeman's "Seven Progressives," *Business History Review* 35 (Winter, 1961). The remark by William S. U'Ren on p. 158 is taken from Earl Pomeroy's introduction to Lincoln Steffens, *The Upbuilders* (Seattle, 1968; originally published in 1909 by Doubleday, Page), p. xxxv. The quotation from John Gordon Ross on p. 158 is from Ross, "Ladies in Politics," *Forum* 95 (November, 1936). The Taft quotation on p. 161 is from Henry Pringle, *The Life and Times of William Howard Taft* (New York, 1939) Vol. 2, p. 967. The quotation from William Olney on p. 163 is from a letter to Charles E. Perkins, president of the Chicago, Burlington, and Quincy Railroad, dated sometime in 1892, and quoted in James R. Smith and Paul L. Murphy (eds.), *Liberty and Justice: A Historical Record of American Constitutional Development* (New York, 1958), pp. 292–293. William

McAdoo's autobiography is *Crowded Years: The Reminiscences of William Gibbs McAdoo* (New York, 1931). On the strain of realism in progressive thought, see Bremner, *From the Depths,* and Richard Hofstadter, "Charles Beard and the Constitution," *American Quarterly* (Fall, 1950). Those who enjoy the sayings of "Mr. Dooley" might begin with Louis Filler (ed.), *The World of Mr. Dooley* (New York, 1962).

Mrs. George Gould

Italian immigrant carrying home materials for the entire family to process at starvation pay, 1909

Courtesy of Brown Brothers, New York

Hester Street, New York City

Teddy Roosevelt

Courtesy of Brown Brothers, New York

Courtesy of Underwood & Underwood, New York

Woodrow Wilson speaking from observation platform of car, 1912

German troops on the attack at Villers-Bretonneaux, April 1, 1918.

Returning troops marching on Fifth Ave., New York City

U.S. Signal Corps. Courtesy of the National Archives

President Wilson and the Duke of Connaught being greeted by
children, Dover, England, 1919

A glimpse of the female ankle boarding trolley step entrances, 1908

DOCUMENTS

The documents included here have been chosen because, in addition to their intrinsic importance and influence upon contemporaries, they seem to me to present particularly well a leading progressive idea or conjunction of ideas. Thus, I have omitted books such as William Allen White's *The Old Order Changeth* or Jacob Riis' *How the Other Half Lived,* which embodied the progressive qualities of indignation, factual exposure, and optimism but which made no important intellectual contribution, and have included instead a selection from John Spargo's *The Bitter Cry of the Children,* which advanced a distinctly progressive idea about the relation of environment to justice.

Primary materials selected according to such tastes, it may be said, run the risk of presenting an unrepresentative picture of reform. One overlooks speeches heard by thousands, party platforms, bromidic but hugely popular reform novels, and a wide range of periodical literature because such items were banal and ephemeral; yet they bespoke the progressive mind in its typical forms. But the important ideas of the progressive generation were not all impounded in difficult books by Croly, Dewey, or Holmes. One can find expression that by form and occasion was clearly typical but that embodied some seminal idea or set of ideas in subtle, complex, and sometimes logic-defying combination. The primary materials reprinted here have the common touch because they were designed to persuade masses of voters, readers of popular magazines, fellow professionals, and citizens in large conventions and meetings. But they also display the progressive mind as it reached beyond emotions and formulas to achieve some penetrating insight into modern society, or as it combined several ideas in those breathtakingly implausible combinations that reveal for us as only primary materials can the *zeitgeist* of the era. Possibly the most interesting of such unlikely combinations, to our own generation at least, is the conjunction of racism with progressive idealism. Several selections blend such apparently irreconcilable sentiments. I chose them not to imply that the reformers were unusually racist for their day, since the muddle of evidence on this seems to suggest that most of them were typical of their day in their racial attitudes, and some were far better. The note of racism is deliberately included here because it was a part of their thought, and because an awareness of its pervasiveness helps us to understand the fate of reform in the 1920s.

For the period of diplomatic difficulties and war, 1914–18, I have reprinted documents that seem to demonstrate a peculiarly progressive way of looking at these questions. Thus, one will not find below the *Lusitania* or *Sussex* notes, but I have tried to present the evolving Wilsonian position, along with that of the liberal opposition. For the postwar years I have selected documents that reveal the reform mind as it groped for reorientation. The last five selections are assessments of the reform record by authorities with good but varying credentials.

I. REFORM: 1900-1916

1

JANE ADDAMS
The Subjective Necessity for Settlements

This essay by one of the most literate and interesting of all the reformers offers an invaluable insight into the psychological origins of the reform impulse. Jane Addams would be surprised to learn that careless readers of her essay (and of Richard Hofstadter's *The Age of Reform*), have thought the reformism of her generation grounded merely in boredom and guilt. A close reading of "The Subjective Necessity for Social Settlements" illuminates the interaction between undeniable social ills and individual psychology without distorting either. One also discovers a timeliness which few writers can claim. An affluent, educated, bored, and dispirited young person finds a healing purpose for her life in community service—and this was almost one hundred years ago.

The Ethical Culture Societies held a summer school at Plymouth, Massachusetts, in 1892, to which they invited several people representing the then new Settlement movement, that they might discuss with others the general theme of Philanthropy and Social Progress.

I venture to produce here parts of a lecture I delivered in Plymouth, both because I have found it impossible to formulate with the same freshness those early motives and strivings, and because, when published with other papers given that summer, it was received by the Settlement people themselves as a satisfactory statement. This paper is an attempt to analyze the motives which underlie a movement based, not only upon conviction, but upon genuine emotion, wherever educated

Reprinted with permission of The Macmillan Company from *Twenty Years at Hull House* by Jane Addams. Copyright 1910 by The Macmillan Company, renewed 1938 by James W. Linn. An earlier and slightly longer version of this essay appeared as "The Subjective Necessity for Social Settlements" in Jane Addams, *Philanthropy and Social Progress* (New York: Thomas Y. Crowell Company, 1893).

young people are seeking an outlet for that sentiment of universal brotherhood, which the best spirit of our times is forcing from an emotion into a motive. These young people accomplish little toward the solution of this social problem, and bear the brunt of being culti- vated into unnourished, oversensitive lives. They have been shut off from the common labor by which they live which is a great source of moral and physical health. They feel a fatal want of harmony between their theory and their lives, a lack of coördination between thought and action. I think it is hard for us to realize how seriously many of them are taking to the notion of human brotherhood, how eagerly they long to give tangible expression to the democratic ideal. These young men and women, longing to socialize their democracy, are animated by cer- tain hopes which may be thus loosely formulated; that if in a demo- cratic country nothing can be permanently achieved save through the masses of the people, it will be impossible to establish a higher political life than the people themselves crave; that it is difficult to see how the notion of a higher civic life can be fostered save through common intercourse; that the blessings which we associate with a life of refinement and cultivation can be made universal and must be made universal if they are to be permanent; that the good we secure for ourselves is precarious and uncertain, is floating in mid-air, until it is secured for all of us and incorporated into our common life. It is easier to state these hopes than to formulate the line of motives, which I believe to constitute the trend of the subjective pressure toward the Settlement. There is something primordial about these motives, but I am perhaps overbold in designating them as a great desire to share the race life. We all bear traces of the starvation struggle which for so long made up the life of the race. Our very organism holds memories and glimpses of that long life of our ancestors which still goes on among so many of our contemporaries. Nothing so deadens the sympathies and shrivels the power of enjoyment as the persistent keeping away from the great opportunities for helpfulness and a continual ignoring of the starvation struggle which makes up the life of at least half the race. To shut one's self away from that half of the race life is to shut one's self away from the most vital part of it; it is to live out but half the humanity to which we have been born heir and to use but half our faculties. We have all had longings for a fuller life which should include the use of these faculties. These longings are the physical complement of the "Intimations of Immortality," on which no ode has yet been written. To portray these would be the work of a poet, and it is hazardous for any but a poet to attempt it.

You may remember the forlorn feeling which occasionally seizes you when you arrive early in the morning a stranger in a great city: the stream of laboring people goes past you as you gaze through the plate-glass window of your hotel; you see hard workingmen lifting great burdens; you hear the driving and jostling of huge carts and your heart sinks with a sudden sense of futility. The door opens behind you and you turn to the man who brings you in your breakfast with a quick sense of human fellowship. You find yourself praying that you may never lose your hold on it all. A more poetic prayer would be that the great mother breasts of our common humanity, with its labor and suffering and its homely comforts, may never be withheld from you. You turn helplessly to the waiter and feel that it would be almost grotesque to claim from him the sympathy you crave because civilization has placed you apart, but you resent your position with a sudden sense of snobbery. Literature is full of portrayals of these glimpses: they come to shipwrecked men on rafts; they overcome the differences of an incongruous multitude when in the presence of a great danger or when moved by a common enthusiasm. They are not, however, confined to such moments, and if we were in the habit of telling them to each other, the recital would be as long as the tales of children are, when they sit down on the green grass and confide to each other how many times they have remembered that they lived once before. If these childish tales are the stirring of inherited impressions, just so surely is the other the striving of inherited powers.

"It is true that there is nothing after disease, indigence and a sense of guilt, so fatal to health and to life itself as the want of a proper outlet for active faculties." I have seen young girls suffer and grow sensibly lowered in vitality in the first years after they leave school. In our attempt then to give a girl pleasure and freedom from care we succeed, for the most part, in making her pitifully miserable. She finds "life" so different from what she expected it to be. She is besotted with innocent little ambitions, and does not understand this apparent waste of herself, this elaborate preparation, if no work is provided for her. There is a heritage of noble obligation which young people accept and long to perpetuate. The desire for action, the wish to right wrong and alleviate suffering haunts them daily. Society smiles at it indulgently instead of making it of value to itself. The wrong to them begins even farther back, when we restrain the first childish desires for "doing good" and tell them that they must wait until they are older and better fitted. We intimate that social obligation begins at a fixed date, forgetting that it begins with birth itself. We treat them as children who, with strong-growing limbs, are allowed to use their legs but not their arms, or whose legs are daily carefully exercised that after a while their arms may be put to high use. We do this in spite of the protest of the best educators, Locke and Pestalozzi. We are fortunate in the meantime if their unused members do not weaken and disappear. They do sometimes. There are a few girls who, by the time they are "educated," forget their old childish desires to help the world and to play with poor little girls "who haven't play things." Parents are often inconsistent: they deliberately expose their daughters to knowledge of the distress in the world; they send them to hear missionary addresses on famines in India and China; they accompany them to lectures on the suffering in Siberia; they agitate together over the forgotten region of East London. In addition to this, from babyhood the altruistic tendencies of these daughters are persistently cultivated. They are taught to be self-forgetting and self-sacrificing, to consider the good of the whole before the good of the ego. But when all this information and culture show results, when the daughter comes back from college and begins to recognize her social claim to the "submerged tenth," and to evince a disposition to fulfill it, the family claim is strenuously asserted; she is told that she is unjustified, ill-advised in her efforts. If she persists, the family too often are injured and unhappy unless the efforts are called missionary and the religious zeal of the family carry them over their sense of abuse. When this zeal does not exist, the result is perplexing. It is a curious violation of what we would fain believe a fundamental law—that the final return of the deed is upon the head of the doer. The deed is that of exclusiveness and caution, but the return, instead of falling upon the head of the exclusive and cautious, falls upon a young head full of generous and unselfish plans. The girl loses something vital out of her life to which she is entitled. She is restricted and unhappy; her elders, meanwhile, are unconscious of the situation and we have all the elements of a tragedy.

We have in America a fast-growing number of cultivated young people who have no recognized outlet for their active faculties. They hear constantly of the great social maladjustment, but no way is provided for them to change it, and their uselessness hangs about them heavily. Huxley declares that the sense of usefulness is the severest shock which the human system can sustain, and that if persistently sustained, it results in atrophy of function. These young people have had advantages of college, of European travel, and of economic study, but they are sustaining this shock of inaction. They have pet phrases, and they tell you that the things that make us all alike are stronger than the things that make us different. They say that all men are united by needs and sympathies far more permanent and radical than anything that temporarily divides them and sets them in opposition to each other. If they affect art, they say that the decay in artistic expression is due to the decay in ethics, that art when shut away from the human interests and from the great mass of humanity is self-destructive. They tell their elders with all the bitterness of youth that if they expect success from them in business or politics or in whatever lines their ambition for them has run, they must let them consult all of humanity; that they must let them find out what the people want and how they want it. It is only the stronger young people, however, who formulate this. Many of them dissipate their energies in so-called enjoyment. Others not content with that, go on studying and go back to college for their second degrees; not that they are especially fond of study, but because they want something definite to do, and their powers have been trained in the direction of mental accumulation. Many are buried beneath this mental accumulation which lowered vitality and discontent. Walter Besant says they have had the vision that Peter had when he saw the great sheet let down from heaven, wherein was neither clean nor unclean. He calls it the sense of humanity. It is not philanthropy nor benevolence, but a thing fuller and wider than either of these.

This young life, so sincere in its emotion and good phrase and yet so undirected, seems to me as pitiful as the other great mass of destitute lives. One is supplementary to the other, and some method of communication can surely be devised. Mr. Barnett, who urged the first Settlement—Toynbee Hall, in East London—recognized this need of outlet for the young men of Oxford and Cambridge, and hoped that the Settlement would supply the communication. It is easy to see why the Settlement movement originated in England, where the years of education are more constrained and definite than they are here, where class distinctions are more rigid. The necessity of it was greater there, but we are fast feeling the pressure of the need and meeting the necessity for Settlements in America. Our young people feel nervously the need of putting theory into action, and respond quickly to the Settlement form of activity.

Other motives which I believe make toward the Settlement are the result of a certain renaissance going forward in Christianity. The impulse to share the lives of the poor, the desire to make social service, irrespective of propaganda, express the spirit of Christ, is as old as Christianity itself. We have no proof from the records themselves that the early Roman Christians, who strained their simple art to the point of grotesqueness in their eagerness to record a "good news" on the walls of the catacombs, considered this good news a religion. Jesus had no set of truths labeled Religious. On the contrary, his doctrine was that all truth is one, that the appropriation of it is freedom. His teaching had no dogma to mark it off from truth and action in general. He himself called it a revelation—a life. These early Roman Christians received the Gospel message, a command to love all men, with a certain joyous simplicity. The image of the Good Shepherd is blithe and gay beyond the gentlest shepherd of Greek mythology; the hart no longer pants, but rushes to the water brooks. The Christians looked for the continuous revelation, but believed what Jesus said, that this revelation, to be retained and made manifest, must be put into terms of action; that action is the only medium man has for receiving and appropriating truth; that the doctrine must be known through the will.

That Christianity has to be revealed and embodied in the line of social progress is a corollary to the simple proposition that man's action is found in his social relationships in the way in which he connects with his fellows; that his motives for action are the zeal and affection with which he regards his fellows. By this simple process was created a deep enthusiasm for humanity, which regarded man as at once the organ and the object of revelation; and by this process came about the wonderful fellowship, the true democracy of the early Church, that so captivates the imagination. The early Christians were pre-eminently nonresistant. They believed in love as a cosmic force. There was no inconoclasm during the minor peace of the Church. They did not yet denounce nor tear down temples, nor preach the end of the world. They grew to a mighty number but it never occurred to them, either in their weakness or in their strength, to regard other men for an instant as their foes or as aliens. The spectacle of the Christians loving all men was the most astounding Rome had ever seen. They were eager to sacrifice themselves for the weak, for children, and for the aged; they identified themselves with slaves and did not avoid the plague; they longed to share the common lot that they might receive the constant revelation. It was a new treasure which the early Christians added to the sum of all treasures, a joy hitherto unknown in the world—the joy of finding the Christ which lieth in each man, but which no man can unfold save in fellowship. A happiness ranging from the heroic to the pastoral enveloped them. They were to possess a revelation as long as life had new meaning to unfold, new action to propose.

I believe that there is a distinct turning among many young men and women toward this simple acceptance of Christ's message. They resent the assumption that Christianity is a set of ideas which belong to the religious consciousness, whatever that may be. They insist that it cannot be proclaimed and instituted apart from the social life of the community and that it must seek a simple and natural expression in the social organism itself. The Settlement movement is only one manifestation of that wider humanitarian movement which throughout Christendom, but pre-eminently in England, is endeavoring to embody itself, not in a sect, but in society itself.

I believe that this turning, this renaissance of the early Christian humanitarianism, is going on in America, in Chicago, if you please, without leaders who write or philosophize, without much speaking, but with a bent to express in social service and in terms of action the spirit of Christ. Certain it is that spiritual force is found in the Settlement movement, and it is also true that this force must be evoked and must be called into play before the success of any Settlement is assured. There must be the overmastering belief that all that is noblest in life is common to men as men, in order to accentuate the likenesses and ignore the differences which are found among the people whom the Settlement constantly brings into juxtaposition. It may be true, as the Positivists insist, that the very religious fervor of man can be turned into love for his race, and his desire for a future life into content to live in the echo of his deeds; Paul's formula of seeking for the Christ which lieth in each man and founding our likenesses on him, seems a simpler formula to many of us.

In a thousand voices singing the Hallelujah Chorus in Handel's "Messiah," it is possible to distinguish the leading voices, but the differences of training and cultivation between them and the voices of the chorus, are lost in the unity of purpose and in the fact that they are all human voices lifted by a high motive. This is a weak illustration of what a Settlement attempts to do. It aims, in a measure, to develop whatever of social life its neighborhood may afford, to focus and give form to that life, to bring to bear upon it the results of cultivation and training; but it receives in exchange for the music of isolated voices the volume and strength of the chorus. It is quite impossible for me to say in what proportion or degree the subjective necessity which led to the opening of Hull-House combined the three trends: first, the desire to interpret democracy in social terms; secondly, the impulse beating at the very source of our lives, urging us to aid in the race progress; and, thirdly, the Christian movement toward humanitarianism. It is difficult to analyze a living thing; the analysis is at best imperfect. Many more motives may blend with the three trends; possibly the desire for a new form of social success due to the nicety of imagination, which refuses worldly pleasures unmixed with the joys of self-sacrifice; possibly a love of approbation, so vast that it is not content with the treble clapping of delicate hands, but wishes also to hear the brass notes from toughened palms, may mingle with these.

The Settlement, then, is an experimental effort to aid in the solution of the social and industrial problems which are engendered by the modern conditions of life in a great city. It insists that these problems are not confined to any one portion of a city. It is an attempt to relieve, at the same time, the overaccumulation at one end of society and the destitution at the other; but it assumes that this overaccumulation and destitution is most sorely felt in the things that pertain to social and educational privileges. From its very nature it can stand for no political or social propaganda. It must, in a sense, give the warm welcome of an inn to all such propaganda, if perchance one of them be found an angel. The one thing to be dreaded in the Settlement is that it lose its flexibility, its power of quick adaptation, its readiness to change its methods as its environment may demand. It must be open to conviction and must have a deep and abiding sense of tolerance. It must be hospitable and ready for experiment. It should demand from its residents a scientific patience in the accumulation of facts and the steady holding of their sympathies as one of the best instruments for that accumulation. It must be grounded in a philosophy whose foundation is on the solidarity of the human race, a philosophy which will not waver when the race happens to be represented by a drunken woman or an idiot boy. Its residents must be emptied of all conceit of opinion and all self-assertion, and ready to arouse and interpret the public opinion of their neighborhood. They must be content to live quietly side by side with their neighbors, until they grow into a sense of relationship and mutual interests. Their neighbors are held apart by differences of race and language which the residents can more easily overcome. They are bound to see the needs of their neighborhood as a whole, to furnish data for legislation, and to use their influence to secure it. In short, residents are pledged to devote themselves to the duties of good citizenship and to the arousing of the social energies which too largely lie dormant in every neighborhood given over to industrialism. They are bound to regard the entire life of their city as organic, to make an effort to unify it, and to protest against its overdifferentiation.

It is always easy to make all philosophy point one particular moral and all history adorn one particular tale; but I may be forgiven the reminder that the best speculative philosophy sets forth the solidarity of the human race; that the highest moralists have taught that without the advance and improvement of the whole, no man can hope for any lasting improvement in his own moral or material individual condition; and that the subjective necessity for Social Settlements is therefore identical with that necessity, which urges us on toward social and individual salvation.

2

ROBERT HUNTER

Poverty

Robert Hunter's book *Poverty* (1904) accomplished a number of things: it not only called attention to the existence of at least ten million Americans who lived in desperate poverty, but it went on to suggest that their economic condition was not "their fault," but was the result of a number of virtually irre-

Robert Hunter, *Poverty* (New York: Harper & Row, Publishers, 1965. Reprinted with permission of Harper & Row, Publishers; first edition, The Macmillan Company, 1904), pp. 320–28, 332–37, 338–40.

sistible social forces that converged upon certain Americans, in some cases from their very birth. His readers might have concluded even more forcefully than Hunter that poverty would be with us until there occurred massive social intervention against those causes, but this was a hard lesson to learn. In proof of this, note Michael Harrington's *The Other America* (1962), which discovered poverty again and drew much the same conclusions.

Having been drawn, about twelve years ago, to some interest in the problems of poverty, there happened to me the common experience of all those of like interests. The poor in the broader sense of that word were busily at work and trying rather to conceal than to make evidence of their poverty; while the beggars, vagrants, idlers, and dependents of all sorts were more or less always pressing forward their necessities. It was natural, therefore, for me to confuse the problem of poverty with that of pauperism and to take up with some enthusiasm the ideas which are a part of the propaganda of many useful charitable organizations. To the charitable workers these problems of vagrancy and pauperism seem possible of solution. Many reforms—among which wise giving, friendly visiting, workrooms, work-tests, model lodging-houses, rent-collecting, etc., are a few— were, in the early nineties, making rapid headway. They were, at that time, ranked first in importance in the category of organized movements for diminishing the evils of pauperism. Many committees were at work promoting these reforms, and in different cities I was able to help in their efforts. The result of their work was not discouraging, but in every instance they came hard up against one almost insurmountable obstacle. The pauper and the vagrant were not dissatisfied; they clamored for alms, but they did not wish to alter their way of living. Even those who possessed the capacity for industrial usefulness and who might have become self-supporting did not wish to go back again into the factories, mills, or mines. In fact, so far as one could see, they were as unwilling as the others to alter their ways of living. However miserable their lot seemed to those of us on the Committees, to them it seemed to be, on the whole, acceptable enough to bring a certain sort of content. However malarious and poisonous and undrained, they loved their valley of idleness and quiet; they hated the hill upon which they were constrained to toil; they shrank from its disappointments, its bruises, its weariness and bitterness, while its meanness and ugliness of life were but slightly less mean and ugly than their own. The children, bred into the ways of pauperism, nearly always took up the vices of their parents. They were pleasure-loving, and whatever was toilsome seemed abhorrent to them. The girls took the easier path; it appeared unquestionably more desirable to their childish standards, and for a time at least it gave them more of everything, for which most human beings seem to hunger,—finery, leisure, and a kind of pleasure. The men and boys liked vagrancy, and those who were not attracted to these ways settled down into a satis- fied, imperturbable pauperism. They lived in God only knows what misery. They ate when there were things to eat; they starved when there was lack of food. But, on the whole, although they swore and beat each other and got drunk, they were more contented than any other class I have happened to know. It took a long time to understand them. Our Committees were busy from morning until night in giving them opportunities to take up the fight again, and to become inde- pendent of relief. They always took what we gave them; they always promised to try; but as soon as we expected them to fulfil any promises, they gave up in despair, and either wept or looked ashamed, and took to misery and drink again,—almost, so it seemed to me at times, with a sense of relief.

But as long as one works with, or observes only, the dependent classes, the true, or at least what seems to me the true, explanation of this apparent satisfaction of vagrants and paupers remains in the dark. It was not until I had lived for several years among the toilers in a great industrial community that the reason for the content of the dependent classes became clear to me. In this community of workers several thousand human beings were struggling fiercely against want. Day after day, year after year, they toiled with mar- vellous persistency and perseverance. Obnoxious as the simile is, they worked from dawn until nightfall, or from sunset until dawn, like galley slaves under the sting of want and under the whip of hunger. On cold, rainy mornings, at the dusk of dawn, I have been awakened, two hours before my rising time, by the monotonous clatter of hob- nailed boots on the plank sidewalks, as the procession to the factory passed under my window. Heavy, brooding men, tired, anxious women, thinly dressed, unkempt little girls, and frail, joyless little lads passed along, half awake, not one uttering a word as they hurried to the great factory. From all directions thousands were entering the

various gates,—children of every nation of Europe. Hundreds of
others—obviously a hungrier, poorer lot than those entering the gates;
some were most ragged and almost shoeless, but all with eager faces—
waited in front of a closed gate until finally a great red-bearded man
came out and selected twenty-three of the strongest, best-looking of
the men. For these the gates were opened, and the others, with down-
cast eyes, marched off to seek employment elsewhere or to sit at
home, or in a saloon, or in a lodging-house, until the following morning, when they came wistfully again to some factory gate. In this
community, the saddest in which I have ever lived, fully fifty thousand
men, women, and children were all the time either in poverty or on
the verge of poverty. It would not be possible to describe how they
worked and starved and ached to rise out of it. They broke their
health down; the men acquired in this particular trade a painful and
disabling rheumatism, and consumption was very common. The girls
and boys followed in the paths of their parents. The wages were so
low that the men alone often could not support their families, and
mothers with babies toiled in order to add to the income. They gave
up all thought of joyful living, probably in the hope that by tremendous exertion they could overcome their poverty; but they gained
while at work only enough to keep their bodies alive. Theirs was a
sort of treadmill existence with no prospect of anything else in life
but more treadmill. When they were not given work in the mill, they
starved; and when they grew desperate, they came to my office and
asked for charity. Here was a mass of men whose ways of living were
violently opposed to those of the vagrant or the pauper. They were
distorting themselves in the struggle to be independent of charity and
to overcome poverty. That they hated charity must be taken without
question. The testimony of scores of men is proof of it, even if, indeed,
their very lives were not. But despite all their efforts they lived in
houses but little, if any, better than those of the paupers; they were
almost as poorly dressed; they were hardly better fed.

In other words, these men, women, and children were, to my mind,
struggling up the face of a barren precipice,—not unlike that up
which Dante toiled,—sometimes in hope, sometimes in despair, yet
bitterly determined; the abyss of vice, crime, pauperism, and vagrancy
was beneath them, a tiny ray of hope above them. Flitting before
them was the leopard, persistently trying to win them from their
almost hopeless task by charms of sensuality, debauch, and idleness.

The lion, predatory and brutal, threatened to devour them; the she-wolf (Greed), hungry for them, enriched herself by their labors. Some were won from their toil by sensual pleasures, some were torn from their footholds by economic disorders, others were too weak and hungry to keep up the fight, and still others were rendered incapable of further struggle by diseases resulting from the unnecessary evils of work or of living.

This may seem to many persons an overdrawn simile; so, at any rate, it would have seemed to me several years ago. But it is a true picture, and I am convinced a just simile of the conditions in which the mass of those workers live who are already defined as being in poverty. At any rate, two or three things seem clearer to me now, after arriving at the conclusion so well represented by Dante's picture. It is easier to understand the reason for the abhorrence which the pauper and the vagrant and the prostitute have for that terrible struggle with poverty, and only less easy is it to understand their apparent willingness to live on rubbish or alms. Furthermore, it is clear that the poverty which undermines the workers is the great and constantly active cause of the fixed states of degeneracy represented by the pauper, the vagrant, the inebriate, etc. In other words, when the working people, by reason of whatever misery poverty brings, once fall into the abyss, they so hate the life of their former struggles and disappointments and sorrows that almost no one, however well-intentioned or kindly, can induce them to take it up again. In the abyss they become merely breeders of children, who persist in the degeneration into which their fathers have fallen; and, like the tribe of Ishmael or the family of the Jukes, they have neither the willingness nor the capacity to respond to the efforts of those who would help, or force, them back again into the struggle.

However merciful and kind and valuable the works of the charitable and the efforts of those who would raise up again the pauper and the vagrant, they are not remedial. In so far as the work of the charitable is devoted to reclamation and not to prevention, it is a failure. Not that any one could wish that less were done in the direction of reclamation. The fact only is important that effort is less powerful there than in overcoming the forces which undermine the workers and those who are struggling against insurmountable difficulties. It is an almost hopeless task to regenerate the degenerate, especially when, if the latter are to succeed, they must be made to take up again the battle with those very destructive forces which are all the time undermining stronger, more capable, and more self-reliant men than they. The all-necessary work to be done is not so much to reclaim a class which social forces are ever active in producing, as it is to battle with the social or economic forces which are continuously producing recruits to that class. The forces producing the miseries of pauperism and vagrancy are many, but none are so important as those conditions of work and of living which are so unjust and degrading that men are driven by them into degeneracy. When the uncertainties, hardships, trials, sorrows, and miseries of a self-supporting existence become so painful that good, strong, self-reliant men and women are forced into pauperism, then there is but little use in trying to force the paupers and the vagrants back into the struggle. ...

Besides the complexity of the problem, there is still another, perhaps an even greater, obstacle firmly set in the past of constructive reform. And this is a political difficulty; namely, the anarchic principle of state rights which divides this country into two score and more small legislative areas. National problems of the character herein dealt with cannot therefore be treated in a national way, as they are in most countries abroad. Legislation concerning child labor, tuberculosis, tenements, factories, dangerous trades, sanitation, etc., must be of a variety of kinds, often warring with each other, throwing industrial advantages now to this state and now to that. The child-labor laws which have been won in the Northern states by years of vigorous agitation give an advantage to the parasitic industries of the South. It is even likely that the textile industry may move to the South partly at least in order to have the privilege of employing little children. Manufacturers threaten the state legislatures (more often to be sure, than they carry out the threat) that they will move into another state if any laws protecting the workmen are passed. There is perhaps a certain business justification for such protests, for, unquestionably, by reason of our legislative anarchy, a parasitic industry in one state may thrive while an industry in another state, shorn of its parasitic privileges by legislation, may remain at a standstill, if it does not actually lose its trade. For this reason social and industrial legislation is usually more difficult to obtain in America than in any other great industrial country. Our political machinery itself, therefore, seriously retards and perhaps renders impossible any national standard of education, of sanitation, of working or of living conditions, etc. It is probable that there can be no national solution of some of these more remedial of the problems of poverty.

Another obstacle stands in the way of justice. The selfish interests of capitalists and land-owners too often either prevent good legislation or vitiate, by their influence, its enforcement. One can understand the determined opposition of men to socialistic measures seriously changing or violating the so-called rights of property; but it is not so easy to understand opposition to measures which, while affecting property interests, do not destroy any rights which may be exercised without injury to another. When property rights become property wrongs by injuring others, especially when they cause the physical degeneration and the human misery represented in poverty, they may for a time, but will surely not always, stand in the way of remedial action. The sense of justice may for a time be so warped and distorted as to value property more than human life, but only for a time. The real cause of our present errors of judgment in this matter lies in the corruption of our political institutions. The business and propertied interests have bought the bosses of our political machinery, and at present our laws are made and enforced in the interest of the owners. When the shame of our cities is notorious; when state and national governments are in the hands of corrupt politicians, owned by corporate interests; when "the laws which should preserve and enforce all rights are made and enforced by dollars;" when "it is possible... with dollars to 'steer' the selection of the candidates of both the great parties for the highest office *in our Republic*, ...so that the people, as a matter of fact, must elect one of the 'steered' candidates;" when "it is possible to repeat the operation in the selection of candidates for the executive and legislative conduct and control of every state and municipality in the United States, and with a sufficient number of dollars to 'steer' the doings of the law-makers and law-enforcers of the national, state, and municipal governments of the people, and a sufficient proportion of the court decisions to make absolute any power created by such direction;" when the country is being daily betrayed by the "enemies of the republic,"—it seems utopian to appeal to these powers to do justice to their workers. This may seem a dark view to take of our political institutions, but, considering the great mass of evidence accumulated in the last few years, it is surely warranted. So far as the problem of poverty is concerned, we can perhaps hope for little in the way of justice or reform during the next few years. For, by the help of this corruption, reform is fought at three stages: in the legislature, in the courts, and at the time of its enforcement.

In consequence of this temporary perversion of our democratic institutions pessimism runs high. Professor Franklin H. Giddings, our most distinguished sociologist, says: "We are witnessing to-day, beyond question, the decay—perhaps not permanent, but at any rate the decay—of republican institutions. No man in his right mind can deny it." A president of one of our greatest universities prophesies that we shall have an emperor in the United States in twenty-five years. Charles Fourier may have been right when he prophesied one hundred years ago that "vast joint-stock companies, destined to monopolize and control all branches of industry, commerce, and finance, would establish an industrial or commercial feudalism that would control society by the power of capital, as did the old baronial or military feudalism by the power of the sword" and "by the monopoly of the land." Or again we may have Mr. Ghent's "benevolent feudalism." If this be the tendency of the times, the poverty of the ten million people of this country will receive scant attention. Indeed, poverty will become wider spread and grow more distressing. Even the moderate proposals for reform made in this book will, if viewed solely from the standpoint of their effect upon property, seem radical, and, in so far as they affect property interests, unjust. This is not mere speculation. I could mention a score of incidents connected with efforts to get child-labor or tenement-house legislation in Illinois and New York to prove that this is even now true. Progress on these reform lines has been so slow in the last decade as to seem almost no progress. Much of the best legislation has been won only after a bitter fight with the propertied interests; and legislation, once secured, simply cannot, in most cases, be enforced because the political machine is owned by the propertied classes. Furthermore, when any so-called reform administration does enforce the laws, the corporate interests lump their campaign donations and punish the reformers with ignominious defeat.

However, the difficulties which lie in the way of any progress along social reform lines are beside the purpose of this book. That purpose is largely satisfied when the problem is stated, and, in so far as possible, I have summarized it in the following sentences. There are probably in fairly prosperous years no less than 10,000,000 persons in poverty;

that is to say, underfed, underclothed, and poorly housed. Of these about 4,000,000 persons are public paupers. Over 2,000,000 working-men are unemployed from four to six months in the year. About 500,000 male immigrants arrive yearly and seek work in the very districts where unemployment is greatest. Nearly half of the families in the country are propertyless. Over 1,700,000 little children are forced to become wage-earners when they should still be in school. About 5,000,000 women find it necessary to work and about 2,000,000 are employed in factories, mills, etc. Probably no less than 1,000,000 workers are injured or killed each year while doing their work, and about 10,000,000 of the persons now living will, if the present ratio is kept up, die of the preventable disease, tuberculosis. . . .

To deal with these specific problems, I have elsewhere mentioned some reforms which seem to me preventive in their nature. They contemplate mainly such legislative action as may enforce upon the entire country certain minimum standards of working and of living conditions. They would make all tenements and factories sanitary; they would regulate the hours of work, especially for women and children; they would regulate and thoroughly supervise dangerous trades; they would institute all necessary measures to stamp out unnecessary disease and to prevent unnecessary death; they would prohibit entirely child labor; they would institute all necessary educational and recreational institutions to replace the social and educational losses of the home and the domestic workshop; they would perfect, as far as possible, legislation and institutions to make industry pay the necessary and legitimate cost of producing and maintaining efficient laborers; they would institute, on the lines of foreign experience, measures to compensate labor for enforced seasons of idleness, due to sickness, old age, lack of work, or other causes beyond the control of the workman; they would prevent parasitism on the part of either the consumer or the producer and charge up the full costs of labor in production to the beneficiary, instead of compelling the worker at certain times to enforce his demand for maintenance through the tax rate and by becoming a pauper; they would restrict the power of employer and of ship-owner to stimulate for purely selfish ends an excessive immigration, and in this way to beat down wages and to increase unemployment.

Reforms such as these are not ones which will destroy incentive, but rather they will increase incentive by more nearly equalizing opportunity. They will make propertied interests less predatory, and sensuality, by contrast with misery, less attractive to the poor. Or, in the terms of our simile, the greyhound—which Dante promised would one day come—will come to drive away the lion, the leopard, and the she-wolf. This does not mean that there is to be no struggle,—the mountain must still remain,—but rather that the life of the poorest toiler shall not be a hopeless thing from which many must turn in despair. In other words, the process of Justice is to lift stony barriers, against which the noblest beat their brains out, and from which the ignoble (but who shall say not more sensible?) turn away in despair. Let it be this, rather than a barren relief system, administered by those who must stand by, watching the struggle, lifting no hand to aid the toilers, but ever succoring those who flee and those who are bruised and beaten.

3

JOHN SPARGO
The Bitter Cry of the Children

This book, like Hunter's, was one of the classics of the progressive literature of exposure. One task of such books was to expose to middle-class view the suffering of invisible millions. Spargo did not limit himself to the ravages of factory labor alone, but examined the effects of economic deprivation on the nutrition, education, recreation, and family environment of millions of American children. The book had a powerful effect, and stimulated, among other things, the drive for a national child labor law. Like the best books of its type, it conveyed a message more disturbing than human suffering—that the sufferers were inno-cent, the victims of the social system. Spargo drew a radical conclusion: the answer was not charity for the casualties, but prevention, in the form of extensive social reconstruction.

The burden and blight of poverty fall most heavily upon the child. No more responsible for its poverty than for its birth, the helplessness and innocence of the victim add infinite horror to its suffering, for the centuries have not made tolerable the idea that the weakness or wrongdoing of its parents or others should be expiated by the suffering of the child. Poverty, the poverty of civilized man, which is everywhere coexistent with unbounded wealth and luxury, is always ugly, repellent, and terrible either to see or to experience; but when it assails the cradle it assumes its most hideous form. Underfed, or badly fed, neglected, badly housed, and improperly clad, the child of poverty is terribly handicapped at the very start; it has not an even chance to begin life with. While still in its cradle a yoke is laid upon its after years, and it is doomed either to die in infancy, or, worse still, to live and grow up puny, weak, both in body and in mind, inefficient and unfitted for the battle of life. And it is the consciousness of this, the knowledge that poverty in childhood blights the whole of life, which makes it the most appalling of all the phases of the poverty problem.

Biologically, the first years of life are supremely important. They are the foundation years; and just as the stability of a building must depend largely upon the skill and care with which its foundations are laid, so life and character depend in large measure upon the years of childhood and the care bestowed upon them. For millions of children the whole of life is conditioned by the first few years. The period of infancy is a time of extreme plasticity. Proper care and nutrition at this period of life are of vital importance, for the evils arising from neglect, insufficient food, or food that is unsuitable, can never be wholly remedied. "The problem of the child is the problem of the race," and more and more emphatically science declares that almost all the problems of physical, mental, and moral degeneracy originate with the child. The physician traces the weakness and disease of the adult to defective nutrition in early childhood; the penologist traces moral perversion to the same cause; the pedagogue finds the same explanation for his failures. Thanks to the many notable investigations made in recent years, especially in European countries, sociological science is being revolutionized. Hitherto we have not studied the great and pressing problems of pauperism and criminology from the child-end; we have concerned ourselves almost entirely with results while ignoring causes. The new spirit aims at prevention. . . .

According to the census of 1900, there were 25,000 boys under sixteen years of age employed in and around the mines and quarries of the United States. In the state of Pennsylvania alone,—the state which enslaves more children than any other,—there are thousands of little "breaker boys" employed, many of them not more than nine or ten years old. The law forbids the employment of children under fourteen, and the records of the mines generally show that the law is "obeyed." Yet in May, 1905, an investigation by the National Child Labor Committee showed that in one small borough of 7000 population, among the boys employed in breakers 35 were nine years old, 40 were ten, 45 were eleven, and 45 were twelve—over 150 boys illegally employed in one section of boy labor in one small town! During the anthracite coal strike of 1902, I attended the Labor Day demonstration at Pittston and witnessed the parade of another at Wilkesbarre. In each case there were hundreds of boys marching, all of them wearing their "working buttons," testifying to the fact that they were *bona fide* workers. Scores of them were less than ten years of age, others were eleven or twelve.

Work in the coal breakers is exceedingly hard and dangerous. Crouched over the chutes, the boys sit hour after hour, picking out the pieces of slate and other refuse from the coal as it rushes past to the washers. From the cramped position they have to assume, most of them become more or less deformed and bent-backed like old men. When a boy has been working for some time and begins to get round-shouldered, his fellows say that "He's got his boy to carry round wherever he goes." The coal is hard, and accidents to the hands, such as cut, broken, or crushed fingers, are common among the boys. Sometimes there is a worse accident: a terrified shriek is heard, and a boy is mangled and torn in the machinery, or disappears in the chute to be picked out later smothered and dead. Clouds of dust fill the breakers and are inhaled by the boys, laying the foundations for asthma and miners' consumption. I once stood in a breaker for half an hour and tried to do the work a twelve-year-old boy was doing day after day, for ten hours at a stretch, for sixty cents a day. The gloom of the breaker appalled me. Outside the sun shone brightly, the air was pellucid, and the birds sang in chorus with the trees and the rivers. Within the breaker there was blackness, clouds of deadly dust enfolded everything, the harsh, grinding roar of the machinery and the ceaseless rushing of coal through the chutes filled the ears. I tried to pick out the pieces of slate from the hurrying stream of coal, often missing them; my hands were bruised and cut in a few minutes; I was covered from head to foot with coal dust, and for many hours afterwards I was expectorating some of the small particles of anthracite I had swallowed.

I could not do that work and live, but there were boys of ten and twelve years of age doing it for fifty and sixty cents a day. . . .

Poverty and Death are grim companions. Wherever there is much poverty the death-rate is high and rises higher with every rise of the tide of want and misery. In London, Bethnal Green's death-rate is nearly double that of Belgravia; in Paris, the poverty-stricken district of Ménilmontant has a death-rate twice as high as that of the Elysée; in Chicago, the death-rate varies from about twelve per thousand in the wards where the well-to-do reside to thirty-seven per thousand in the tenement wards. The ill-developed bodies of the poor, underfed and overburdened with toil, have not the powers of resistance to disease possessed by the bodies of the more fortunate. As fire rages most fiercely and with greatest devastation among the ill-built, crowded tenements, so do the fierce flames of disease consume most readily the ill-built, fragile bodies which the tenements shelter. As we ascend the social scale the span of life lengthens and the death-rate gradually diminishes, the death-rate of the poorest class of workers being three and a half times as great as that of the well-to-do. It is estimated that among 10,000,000 persons of the latter class the annual deaths do not number more than 100,000, among the best paid of the working-class the number is not less than 150,000, while among the poorest workers the number is at least 350,000.

This difference in the death-rate of the various social classes is even more strongly marked in the case of infants. Mortality in the first year of life differs enormously according to the circumstances of the parents and the amount of intelligent care bestowed upon the infants. In Boston's "Back Bay" district the death-rate at all ages last year was 13.45 per thousand as compared with 18.45 in the Thirteenth Ward, which is a typical working-class district, and of the total number of deaths the percentage under one year was 9.44 in the former as against 25.21 in the latter. Wolf, in his classic studies based upon the vital statistics of Erfurt for a period of twenty years, found that for every 1000 children born in working-class families 505 died in the first year; among the middle classes 173, and among the higher classes only 89. Of every 1000 illegitimate children registered—almost entirely of the poorer classes—352 died before the end of the first year. Dr. Charles

R. Drysdale, Senior Physician of the Metropolitan Free Hospital, London, declared some years ago that the death-rate of infants among the rich was not more than 8 per cent, while among the very poor it was often as high as 40 per cent. Dr. Playfair says that 18 per cent of the children of the upper classes, 36 per cent of the tradesman class, and 55 per cent of those of the working-class die under the age of five years.

And yet the experts say that the baby of the tenement is born physically equal to the baby of the mansion. For countless years men have sung of the Democracy of Death, but it is only recently that science has brought us the more inspiring message of the Democracy of Birth. It is not only in the tomb that we are equal, where there is neither rich nor poor, bond nor free, but also in the womb of our mothers. At birth class distinctions are unknown. For long the hope-crushing thought of prenatal hunger, the thought that the mother's hunger was shared by the unborn child, and that poverty began its blighting work on the child even before its birth, held us in its thrall. The thought that past generations have innocently conspired against the well-being of the child of to-day, and that this generation in its turn conspires against the child of the future, is surcharged with the pessimism which mocks every ideal and stifles every hope born in the soul. Nothing more horrible ever cast its shadow over the hearts of those who would labor for the world's redemption from poverty than this spectre of prenatal privation and inherited debility. But science comes to dispel the gloom and bid us hope. Over and over again it was stated before the Inter-departmental Committee by the leading obstetrical authorities of the English medical profession that the proportion of children born healthy and strong is not greater among the rich than among the poor. The differences appear after birth. Wise, patient Mother Nature provides with each succeeding generation opportunity to overcome the evils of ages of ignorance and wrong, with each generation the world starts afresh and unhampered, physically, at least, by the dead past.

> *The world's great age begins anew,*
> *The golden years return.*

And herein lies the greatest hope of the race; we are not handicapped from the start; we can begin with the child of to-day to make certain a brighter and nobler to-morrow as though there had never been a yesterday of woe and wrong.

4

WALTER RAUSCHENBUSCH
The Social Gospel

It is hard to overestimate the influence of Christianity as one assesses the causes of the progressive uprising. Most Americans even then were not fervent, practicing Christians, and most clergymen did not find that their New Testament contained any grounds for criticism of the existing order. But men like Rauschenbusch, George Herron, Charles Sheldon, John A. Ryan, and the layman Richard T. Ely made a powerful case that Jesus would have been a reformer (or a socialist) if he came to America in the time of McKinley and Theodore Roosevelt. Their passionate sermons, essays, and novels swelled the ranks of reform with young men and women whose motivation was altruism, whose style was evangelical, and whose faith in moral suasion was boundless. A few, like Rauschenbusch, even rejected capitalism.

Our business life is the seat and source of our present troubles. So much ought to be plain to all who care to see. It is in commerce and industry that we encounter the great collective inhumanities that shame our Christian feeling, such as child labor and the bloody total of industrial accidents. Here we find the friction between great classes of men which makes whole communities hot with smoldering hate or sets them ablaze with lawlessness. To commerce and industry we are learning to trace the foul stream of sex prostitution, poverty, and political corruption. Just as an epidemic of typhoid fever would call for an analysis of the water supply, so these chronic conditions call for a moral analysis of the economic order and justify the presumption that it is fundamentally unchristian. Business men themselves concede that it is; some by calmly denying that Christian principles have anything to do with business; others by sadly confessing that Christianity ought to govern business, but that it would mean loss or ruin to put Christian ethics in practice.

Business life is the unregenerate section of our social order. If by

Walter Rauschenbusch, *Christianizing the Social Order* (New York: The Macmillan Company, 1912), pp. 156–57, 173–75, 177–79, 311–14, 14–15. Reprinted with permission.

some magic it could be plucked out of our total social life in all its raw selfishness, and isolated on an island, unmitigated by any other factors of our life, that island would immediately become the object of a great foreign mission crusade for all Christendom. Our argument, therefore, will now concentrate on this unredeemed portion of the social order.

Our first need is to analyze our economic system so that we may understand wherein and why it is fundamentally unchristian. Most of us have accepted our economic system as we accept our stomach, without understanding its workings. Nor is it easy to understand the moral essentials of this huge and complicated social machinery. We have no such historical perspective of it as our great-grandchildren will have when they study the Great Industrial Transition of the Twentieth Century in college. We are like a swimmer in a stormy sea. To negotiate the next wave is the great object of his concern, but whether that wave is part of a tidal current sweeping him toward shore or out to sea, his narrow horizon does not tell him. So amid the swift changes of our age we find it hard to distinguish between incidental troubles and the essential drifts of our economic system.

We stumble along untraveled trails when we attempt an analysis of our economic system from a Christian point of view. The collective intelligence of the Christian Church has not really come to any clearness about the fundamental moral relations involved in modern economic life. It instinctively condemns some of its worst excrescences, but even among its leaders many have no clear grasp of the moral nature and genius of our industrial and commercial world. We have been neglecting the Doctrine of Sin in our theology. We might look to Christian business men for an incisive comprehension of the moral conditions amid which they work, but most of them are so driven by business that they have no time to consider their situation broadly and with historical insight. They see keenly what is immediately necessary, but in the broader tendencies of their life a vast collective will bids them go, and they go. They are slaves of the lamp. Business imposes its point of view on them, just as the Catholic Church molds the ideas of the priests who labor in it. When "practical men" do theorize, they are often the dizziest theorizers of all. . . .

The reign of competition is a reign of fear. The rate of mortality for small business concerns is higher than infant mortality. If all the leaden weight of fear of all business men who watch a vanishing margin of profit through the year could be gathered up and set before us in some dramatic form, it would palsy our joy in life. Business panics merely render this chronic condition acute and make men high up who have been secure in prosperity feel the same sufferings which others have felt who went down before them. A reign of fear is never a reign of God. Fear makes children lie and business men cheat. In competition the worst man sets the pace, and good men follow because they are afraid. A capable mind with no bowels of mercy to hinder, who can wring the last ounce of strength from his men, and who puts women and children to work wherever men can be displaced, can outbid a morally sensitive man unless the latter has some counter-balancing advantage elsewhere. In a coöperating group the efficiency and courage of the best members of the team hold the rest up to their level; in commercial competition the greed and inhumanity of the worst infect the rest through the medium of fear. For this reason considerations of humanity have often had so little response from communities of business men composed largely of Christian persons. Individually they are kind-hearted men; but as members of a competitive social order they are driven by fear and forgetful of mercy. Workmen complain when their employers speed up the machinery, which compels them to keep up with its pace or be hurt. But their employers are also slaves of a huger machine, and many of them are seeking with laboring breath to keep up with a treadmill that will mangle them if they do not.

The objection will be raised that the instinct of competition is inherent in human life and that its free play is a necessary factor in the evolution of the race. That is quite true. Life would lose much of its zest and of its educational value if competition were eliminated from it. But there is no danger whatever that it will be. Young men will always compete for the love of woman (and sometimes that game is reversed); students will compete for educational honors; workmen will compete for leadership within their group; statesmen will compete for popularity and power. When the ablest are honored and promoted, it benefits all. A superior type is thereby placed in a conspicuous position, and the rest are more or less modeled after it. The unsuccessful competitors may suffer all the pangs of disappointed ambition, but they are not usually impoverished or disgraced. A college boy who fails to win a prize is not on that account reduced to high school rank. A workman who fails to be promoted to the position of foreman does not lose his old job. Such emulation advances some without ruining the rest. For that kind of competition an economic system founded wholly on cooperation would offer splendid chances, with more publicity and fame for the winners than is now offered in business life. . . .

For a century the doctrine of salvation by competition was the fundamental article in the working creed of the capitalistic nations. It was the "natural theology" of industry, and no political economy was orthodox that did not preach it. Governments felt it would be a sin to interfere while competitors were having a Donnybrooke Fair. In theory it is still in effect in our country. Business men are indignant when workingmen refuse to permit unrestrained competition among themselves. Government is supposed to punish combinations "in restraint of trade." But in practice competition is being hemmed in and tied up on all hands. None of the big leaders of business believe in it. If they do, their faith is even farther removed from their works than usually. The doctrine of competition was once historically useful because it helped to clear away an outgrown economic system and to substitute larger coöperating groups for the little groups of the handicraft system. But that work has been done, and to-day competition has itself become an antiquated method which ties us down to petty and inefficient forms of teamwork. The polliwog is through with its tail and gills, and is anxious to grow legs and lungs, and sit on a stone in the pride of its froghood. But legislators, lawyers, and old gentlemen generally are anxiously trying to coax back the vanishing tail. The only valid defense for the wastefulness and inefficiency of the competitive system is that it protects the consumer against the voracity of the monopolist. That end is wholly laudable, but we shall have to find more effective means of attaining it than moving back the clock-hands that destiny is driving forward.

Business is abandoning competition because it is inefficient, and larger and more powerful forms of association and teamwork are being wrought out. Christianity should help to end competition because it is immoral. Its murderous effect in England at the beginning of the capitalistic era is a matter of record. It has had much the same effect every time it invaded a new country or community. It is a short-sighted and suicidal policy. One nation after the other has had to hog-tie competition by government interference, inspection, and paternalism in the interests of safety and humanity. Competition as a principle is a denial of fraternity. In so far as it is allowed to do its unrestrained work, it establishes the law of tooth and nail, and brings back the age of savage warfare where every man's hand is against every man. It dechristianizes the social order. Whatever progress was achieved under the competitive system was secured, not by the competitive element in it, but by the fact that it allowed so large an application of the forces of association and teamwork. It behooves us to find forms of organization that will expand the present narrow areas of coöperation and make them nation wide. Men who are in the same line of work must be so organized that they can emulate while they cooperate. Commercial competition has developed in our commercial communities the lower instincts of selfishness, covetousness, and craft. A Christian social order must be such that it will develop and educate mutual interest and good will, and equip workmates with that sense of comradeship and solidarity to which they are entitled. . . .

Let us sum up the case of Christianity against Capitalism.

We saw that the distinctive characteristic of the capitalistic system is that the industrial outfit of society is owned and controlled by a limited group, while the mass of the industrial workers is without ownership or power over the system within which they work. A small group of great wealth and power is set over against a large group of propertyless men. Given this line-up, the rest follows with the inevitableness of a process in physics or chemistry.

Wherever the capitalist class remains in unorganized and small units, they will struggle for the prizes held out by modern industry. Capitalism in its youth threw off the restraints upon competition created by the older social order, and a fierce, free fight followed. Wherever the competitive principle is still in operation, it intensifies natural emulation by the size of the stakes it offers, enables the greedy and cunning to set the pace for the rest, makes men immoral by fear, and puts the selfish impulses in control. The charge of Christianity against competitive capitalism is that it is unfraternal, the opposite of coöperation and teamwork.

Capitalism gives the owners and managers of industry autocratic power over the workers. The dangers always inherent in the leadership of the strong are intensified by the fact that in capitalistic industry this power is unrestrained by democratic checks and fortified by almost absolute ownership of the means of production and life. Consequently the master class in large domains of industry have exacted excessive toil, and have paid wages that were neither a just return for the work done nor sufficient to support life normally. The working class is everywhere in a state of unrest and embitterment. By great sacrifices it has tried to organize in order to strengthen its position against these odds, but the master class has hampered or suppressed the organizations of labor. This line-up of two antagonistic classes is the historical continuation of the same line-up which we see in chattel slavery and feudal serfdom. In recent years the development of corporations has added a new difficulty by depersonalizing the master. The whole situation contradicts the spirit of American institutions. It is the last intrenchment of the despotic principle. It tempts the class in power to be satisfied with a semimorality in their treatment of the working class. It is not Christian.

The capitalist class serves society in the capacity of the middleman, and modern conditions make this function more important than ever before. But under the capitalistic organization this wholesome function is not under public control, and the relations created call out the selfish motives and leave the higher motives of human nature dormant. Under competition business readily drifts into the use of tricky methods, sells harmful or adulterated goods, and breaks down the moral self-restraint of the buyer. Under monopoly the middleman is able to practice extortion on the consumer. The kindly and friendly relations that abound in actual business life between the dealer and the consumer are due to the personal character of the parties and the ineradicable social nature of man, and are not created by the nature of business itself.

In all the operations of capitalistic industry and commerce the aim that controls and directs is not the purpose to supply human needs, but to make a profit for those who direct industry. This in itself is an irrational and unchristian adjustment of the social order, for it sets money up as the prime aim, and human life as something secondary, or as a means to secure money. The supremacy of Profit in Capitalism stamps it as a mammonistic organization with which Christianity can never be content. "Profit" commonly contains considerable elements of just reward for able work; it may contain nothing but that; but where it is large and dissociated from hard work, it is traceable to some kind of monopoly privilege and power,— either the power to withhold part of the earnings of the workers by the control of the means of production, or the ability to throw part of the expenses of business on the community, or the power to over-charge the public. In so far as profit is derived from these sources, it is tribute ‚collected by power from the helpless, a form of legalized graft, and a contradiction of Christian relations.

Thus our capitalistic commerce and industry lies alongside of the home, the school, the Church, and the democratized States as an unregenerate part of the social order, not based on freedom, love, and mutual service, as they are, but on autocracy, antagonism of interests, and exploitation. Such a verdict does not condemn the moral character of the men in business. On the contrary, it gives a remarkable value to every virtue they exhibit in business, for every act of honesty, justice, and kindness is a triumph over hostile condi-tions, a refusal of Christianity and humanity to be chilled by low temperature or scorched by the flame of high-pressure temptation. Our business life has been made endurable only by the high qualities of the men and women engaged in it. These personal qualities have been created by the home, the school, and the Church. The State has also made Business tolerable by pulling a few of the teeth and shortening the tether of greed. Thus moral forces generated outside of Capitalism have invaded its domain and supplied the moral qualities without which it would have collapsed. But capitalistic business in turn is invading the regenerate portions of the social order, paralyzing their activities, breaking down the respect for the higher values, desecrating the holy, and invading God's country. . . .

Immediately after the Methodist General Conference, in December, 1908, the Federal Council of the Churches of Christ in America was organized at Philadelphia, representing and uniting thirty-three Pro-testant denominations. This organization marked an epoch in the history of American Protestantism. But no other session created so profound an interest as that devoted to "Social Service." The report of the Commission was heard with tense feeling, which broke into prolonged and enthusiastic applause at the close. The Bill of Rights adopted by the Methodist Convention was presented with some changes and adopted without the slightest disposition to halt it at any point. The following declaration, therefore, has stood since 1908 as the common sense of the Protestant churches of America:—

"We deem it the duty of all Christian people to concern themselves directly which certain practical industrial problems. To us it seems that the churches must stand—

> For equal rights and complete justice for all men in all stations of life.
>
> For the right of all men to the opportunity for self-maintenance, a right ever to be wisely and strongly safeguarded against encroachments of every kind.
>
> For the right of workers to some protection against the hardships often resulting from the swift crises of industrial change.
>
> For the principle of conciliation and arbitration in industrial dissensions.
>
> For the protection of the worker from dangerous machinery, occupational disease, injuries, and mortality.
>
> For the abolition of child labor.
>
> For such regulations of the conditions of toil for women as shall safeguard the physical and moral health of the community.
>
> For the suppression of the 'sweating system.'
>
> For the gradual and reasonable reduction of the hours of labor to the lowest practicable point, and for that degree of leisure for all which is a condition of the highest human life.
>
> For a release from employment one day in seven.
>
> For a living wage as a minimum in every industry, and for the highest wage that each industry can afford.
>
> For the most equitable division of the products of industry that can ultimately be devised.
>
> For suitable provision for the old age of the workers and for those incapacitated by injury.
>
> For the abatement of poverty.

To the toilers of America and to those who by organized effort are seeking to lift the crushing burdens of the poor, and to reduce the hardships and uphold the dignity of labor, this Council sends the greeting of human brotherhood and the pledge of sympathy and of help in a cause which belongs to all who follow Christ."

5

EDWARD ALSWORTH ROSS

Sin and Society

Ross's important little book *Sin and Society*, read by Theodore Roosevelt among other people, tried to forward reform by updating the American ethical system. In the harsh survival situation of early America such sins as drunkenness and theft were serious in their social consequences, and when one man injured another it was usually a matter of physical assault. The rise of a complicated industrial society allowed some men to injure millions impersonally, and the old ethical focus upon individual behavior and personal violence allowed more important modern forms of antisocial activity to go undenounced and unimpeded. In undertaking to reorient the public morality Ross went to the very heart of the reform task. Since the American people have not yet successfully shifted from an individualistic to a collective ethic, *Sin and Society* has a freshness and relevance few books of that period can match, despite its somewhat dated, biblical style.

The sinful heart is ever the same, but sin changes its quality as society develops. Modern sin takes its character from the mutualism of our time. Under our present manner of living, how many of my vital interests I must intrust to others! Nowadays the water main is my well, the trolley car my carriage, the banker's safe my old stocking, the policeman's billy my fist. My own eyes and nose and judgment defer to the inspector of food, or drugs, or gas, or factories, or tenements, or insurance companies. I rely upon others to look after my drains, invest my savings, nurse my sick, and teach my children. I let the meat trust butcher my pig, the oil trust mould my candles, the sugar trust boil my sorghum, the coal trust chop my wood, the barb wire company split my rails.

But this spread-out manner of life lays snares for the weak and opens doors to the wicked. Interdependence puts us, as it were, at one another's mercy, and so ushers in a multitude of new forms of

Edward Alsworth Ross, *Sin and Society* (Boston: Houghton Mifflin Company, 1907), pp. 3–7, 9–11, 14–16, 29–30, 40–42, 46–48, 54–57, 97–101.

wrong-doing. The practice of mutualism has always worked this way. Most sin is preying, and every new social relation begets its cannibalism. No one will "make the ephah small" or "falsify the balances" until there is buying and selling, "withhold the pledge" until there is loaning, "keep back the hire of the laborers" until there is a wage system, "justify the wicked for a reward" until men submit their disputes to a judge. The rise of the state makes possible counterfeiting, smuggling, peculation, and treason. Commerce tempts the pirate, the forger, and the embezzler. Every new fiduciary relation is a fresh opportunity for breach of trust. To-day the factory system makes it possible to work children to death on the double-quick, speculative building gives the jerry-builder his chance, long-range investment spawns the get-rich-quick concern, and the trust movement opens the door to the bubble promoter.

The springs of the older sin seem to be drying up. Our forced-draught pace relieves us of the superabundance of energy that demands an explosive outlet. Spasms of violent feeling go with a sluggish habit of life, and are as out of place to-day as are the hard-drinking habits of our Saxon ancestors. We are too busy to give rein to spite. The stresses and lures of civilized life leave slender margin for the gratification of animosities. In quiet, side-tracked communities there is still much old-fashioned hatred, leading to personal clash, but elsewhere the cherishing of malice is felt to be an expensive luxury. Moreover, brutality, lust, and cruelty are on the wane. In this country, it is true, statistics show a widening torrent of bloody crime, but the cause is the weakening of law rather than an excess of bile. Other civilized peoples seem to be turning away from the sins of passion.

The darling sins that are blackening the face of our time are incidental to the ruthless pursuit of private ends, and hence quite "without prejudice." The victims are used or sacrificed not at all from personal ill-will, but because they can serve as pawns in somebody's little game. Like the wayfarers run down by the automobilist, they are offered up to the God of Speed. The essence of the wrongs that infest our articulated society is betrayal rather than aggression. Having perforce to build men of willow into a social fabric that calls for oak, we see on all hands monstrous treacheries,—adulterators, peculators, boodlers, grafters, violating the trust others have placed in them. The little finger of Chicane has come to be thicker than the loins of Violence.

The sinister opportunities presented in this webbed social life have been seized unhesitatingly, because such treasons have not yet become infamous. The man who picks pockets with a railway rebate, murders with an adulterant instead of a bludgeon, burglarizes with a "rake-off" instead of a jimmy, cheats with a company prospectus instead of a deck of cards, or scuttles his town instead of his ship, does not feel on his brow the brand of a malefactor. The shedder of blood, the oppressor of the widow and the fatherless, long ago became odious, but latter-day treacheries fly no skull-and-crossbones flag at the mast-head. The qualities which differentiate them from primitive sin and procure them such indulgence may be clearly defined. . . .

The stealings and slayings that lurk in the complexities of our social relations are not deeds of the dive, the dark alley, the lonely road, and the midnight hour. They require no nocturnal prowling with muffled step and bated breath, no weapon or offer of violence. Unlike the old-time villain, the latter-day malefactor does not wear a slouch hat and a comforter, breathe forth curses and an odor of gin, go about his nefarious work with clenched teeth and an evil scowl. In the supreme moment his lineaments are not distorted with rage, or lust, or malevolence. One misses the dramatic setting, the time-honored insignia of turpitude. Fagin and Bill Sykes and Simon Legree are vanishing types. Gamester, murderer, body-snatcher, and kidnapper may appeal to a Hogarth, but what challenge finds his pencil in the countenance of the boodler, the savings-bank wrecker, or the ballot-box stuffer? Among our criminals of greed, one begins to meet the "grand style" of the great criminals of ambition, Macbeth or Richard III. The modern high-power dealer of woe wears immacu-late linen, carries a silk hat and a lighted cigar, sins with a calm countenance and a serene soul, leagues or months from the evil he causes. Upon his gentlemanly presence the eventual blood and tears do not obtrude themselves. . . .

Because of the special qualities of the Newer Unrighteousness, because these devastating latter-day wrongs, being comely of look, do not advertise their vileness, and are without the ulcerous hag-visage of the primitive sins, it is possible for iniquity to flourish greatly, even while men are getting better. Briber and boodler and grafter are often "good men," judged by the old tests, and would have passed for virtuous in the American community of seventy years ago. Among the chiefest sinners are now enrolled men who are pure and kind-hearted, loving in their families, faithful to their friends, and generous to the needy.

One might suppose that an exasperated public would sternly castigate these modern sins. But the fact is, the very qualities that lull the conscience of the sinner blind the eyes of the onlookers. People are sentimental, and bastinado wrong-doing not according to its harmfulness, but according to the infamy that has come to attach to it. Undiscerning, they chastise with scorpions the old authentic sins, but spare the new. They do not see that boodling is treason, that blackmail is piracy, that embezzlement is theft, that speculation is gambling, that tax-dodging is larceny, that railroad discrimination is treachery, that the factory labor of children is slavery, that deleterious adulteration is murder. It has not come home to them that the fraudulent promoter "devours widows' houses," that the monopolist "grinds the faces of the poor," that mercenary editors and spellbinders "put bitter for sweet and sweet for bitter." The cloven hoof hides in patent leather; and to-day, as in Hosea's time, the people "are destroyed for lack of knowledge." The mob lynches the red-handed slayer, when it ought to keep a gallows Haman-high for the venal mine inspector, the seller of infected milk, the maintainer of a fire-trap theatre. The child-beater is forever blasted in reputation, but the exploiter of infant toil, or the concocter of a soothing syrup for the drugging of babies, stands a pillar of society. The petty shoplifter is more abhorred than the stealer of a franchise, and the wife-whipper is outcast long before the man who sends his over-insured ship to founder with its crew....

The grading of sinners according to badness of character goes on the assumption that the wickedest man is the most dangerous. This would be true if men were abreast in their opportunities to do harm. In that case the blackest villain would be the worst scourge of society. But the fact is that the patent ruffian is confined to the social basement, and enjoys few opportunities. He can assault or molest, to be sure; but he cannot betray. Nobody depends on him, so he cannot commit breach of trust,—that arch sin of our time. He does not hold in his hand the safety or welfare or money of the public. He is the clinker, not the live coal; vermin, not beast of prey. To-day the villain most in need of curbing is the respectable, exemplary, trusted personage who, strategically placed at the focus of a spider-web of fiduciary relations, is able from his office-chair to pick a thousand pockets, poison a thousand sick, pollute a thousand minds, or imperil a thousand lives. It is the great-scale, high-voltage sinner that needs the shackle. To strike harder at the petty pickpocket than at the prominent and unabashed person who in a large, impressive way sells out his constituents, his followers, his depositors, his stockholders, his policy-holders, his subscribers, or his customers is to "strain at a gnat and swallow a camel.". . .

The real weakness in the moral position of Americans is not their attitude toward the plain criminal, but their attitude toward the quasi-criminal. The shocking leniency of the public in judging conspicuous persons who have thriven by anti-social practices is not due, as many imagine, to sycophancy. Let a prominent man commit some offense in bad odor and the multitude flings its stones with a right good will. The social lynching of the self-made magnate who put away his faded, toil-worn wife for the sake of a soubrette, proves that the props of the morality have not rotted through. Sex righteousness continues to be thus stiffly upheld simply because man has not been inventing new ways of wronging woman. So long ago were sex sins recognized and branded that the public, feeling sure of itself, lays on with promptness and emphasis. The slowness of this same public in lashing other kinds of transgression betrays, not sycophancy or unthinking admiration of success, but perplexity. The prosperous evildoers that bask undisturbed in popular favor have been careful to shun—or seem to shun—the familiar types of wickedness. Overlooked in Bible and Prayer-book, their obliquities lack the brimstone smell. Surpass as their misdeeds may in meanness and cruelty, there has not yet been time enough to store up strong emotion about them; and so the sight of them does not let loose the flood of wrath and abhorrence that rushes down upon the long-attainted sins.

The immunity enjoyed by the perpetrator of new sins has brought into being a class for which we may coin the term criminaloid. . . .

Nation-wide is the zone of devastation of the adulterator, the rebater, the commercial free-booter, the fraud promoter, the humbug healer, the law-defying monopolist. State-wide is the burnt district of the corrupt legislator, the corporation-owned judge, the venal inspector, the bought bank examiner, the mercenary editor. But draw near the sinner and he whitens. If his fellow men are wronged clear to his doorstep he is criminal, not criminaloid. For the latter loses his sinister look, even takes on a benign aspect, as you come close. Within his home town, his ward, his circle, he is perhaps a good man, if judged by the simple old-time tests. Very likely he keeps his marriage vows, pays his debts, "mixes" well, stands by his friends, and has a contracted kind of public spirit. He is ready enough to rescue imperiled babies, protect maidens, or help poor widows. He is unevenly moral: oak in the family and clan virtues, but basswood in commercial and civic ethics. In some relations he is more sympathetic and generous than his critics; and he resents with genuine feeling the scorn of men who happen to have specialized in other virtues than those that appeal to him. Perhaps his point of honor is to give bribes but not to take them; perhaps it is to "stay bought" or not to sell out to both sides at once.

The type is exemplified by the St. Louis boodler, who, after accepting $25,000 to vote against a certain franchise, was offered a larger sum to vote for it. He did so, but returned the first bribe. He was asked on the witness-stand why he had returned it. "Because it wasn't mine!" he exclaimed, flushing with anger. "I hadn't earned it."

Seeing that the conventional sins are mostly close-range inflictions, whereas the long-range sins, being recent in type, have not yet been branded, the criminaloid receives from his community the credit of the close-in good he does, but not the shame of the remote evil he works.

Sometimes it is *time* instead of *space* that divides him from his victims. It is tomorrow's morrow that will suffer from the patent soothing-syrup, the factory toil of infants, the grabbing of public lands, the butchery of forests, and the smuggling in of coolies. In such a case the short-sighted many exonerate him; only the far-sighted few mark him for what he is. Or it may be a social interval that leaves him his illusion of innocence. Like Robin Hood, the criminaloid spares his own sort and finds his quarry on another social plane. The labor grafter, the political "striker," and the blackmailing society editor prey upward; the franchise grabber, the fiduciary thief, and the frenzied financier prey downward. In either case the sinner moves in an atmosphere of friendly approval and can still any smart of conscience with the balm of good fellowship and adulation. . . .

Our moral pace-setters strike at bad personal habits, but act as if there was something sacred about money-making; and, *seeing that the master iniquities of our time are connected with money-making,* they do not get into the big fight at all.

Because society develops, comes into new situations, runs into strange perils, finds old foes with new faces and enemies masquerading as friends, it is folly to train its guns ever on the same spot. Yesterday's battle-cries of conscience cannot thrill us, and so the battle-cries of to-day may have little meaning for our children's children. They, perhaps, will be worrying about the marriage of the tainted, or the two-child system. Every age has to reconnoitre its foes and mark where they are massing. Like a rudderless steamer on a river of savage Africa, society, caught in the current of evolution, dips, lurches, drifts, swings, exposing now port, now starboard, to the missiles of fresh enemies that present themselves in strange guise at every turn of the stream. . . .

The conclusion of the whole matter is this: —

Our social organization has developed to a stage where the old righteousness is not enough. We need an annual supplement to the Decalogue. The growth of credit institutions, the spread of fiduciary relations, the enmeshing of industry in law, the interlacing of government and business, the multiplication of boards and inspectors,— beneficent as they all are, they invite to sin. What gateways they open to greed! What fresh parasites they let in on us! How idle in our new situation to intone the old litanies! The reality of this close-knit life is not to be *seen* and *touched;* it must be *thought*. The sins it opens the door to are to be discerned by knitting the brows rather than by opening the eyes. It takes imagination to see that bogus medical diploma, lying advertisement, and fake testimonial are death-dealing instruments. It takes imagination to see that savings-bank wrecker, loan shark, and investment swindler, in taking livelihoods take lives. It takes imagination to see that the business of debauching voters, fixing juries, seducing law-makers, and corrupting public servants is like sawing through the props of crowded grand-stand. Whether we like it or not, we are in the organic phase, and the thickening perils that beset our path can be beheld only by the mind's eye.

The problem of security is therefore being silently transformed. Blind, instinctive reactions are no longer to be trusted. Social defense is coming to be a matter for the expert. The rearing of dikes against faithlessness and fraud calls for intelligent social engineering. If in this strait the public does not speedily become far shrewder in the grading and grilling of sinners, there is nothing for it but to turn over the defense of society to professionals.

6

FREDERICK W. TAYLOR
Scientific Management

The "efficiency craze" permeated nearly every corner of the reform era, as the next six selections will show. The ideal of efficiency spurred conservationists, social workers, food and drug purifiers, and reformers of city politics. It also raised up a band of men, usually engineers, whose reform energies were spent largely in the world of factories and corporations rather than in governments or slums, but they too were progressives.

The central figure in the cosmos of those who yearned for a more efficient America was undoubtedly Frederick W. Taylor. Taylor began his working life as a machinist, but his background was that of most progressives—scion of an old Pennsylvania Quaker family with deep roots in the antislavery tradition—and he carried into the factories the zeal for social harmony and human betterment that others of his generation turned toward political affairs. Scientific management, in its passion for facts, its assault upon traditional modes, its desire to assert control over haphazard processes, and its assumption of an identity of interests between capital and labor, was clearly in the mainstream of progressive thought. And like much of progressivism, it lent itself in the end more to the purposes of the large capitalists than to the social classes beneath them. This, we may be fairly sure, was never Taylor's intention.

Taylor began to articulate his ideas in 1895, when he read a paper before the American Society of Mechanical Engineers; he gave them final form in 1911 with the publication of *The Principles of Scientific Management*. The book was serialized by *The American Magazine* in the spring of 1911, and Ray Stannard Baker's introduction to those articles is reprinted in part below.

For three days last November I sat in the court room of the Interstate Commerce Commission at Washington, listening to one of the most remarkable cases ever presented before that distinguished body. On one side were ranged the powerful Eastern railroads, present in the persons of some half a hundred attorneys, and pleading permission from the Government to raise their rates; on the other side were the

Eastern shippers, disputing the demands of the railroads. Upon the issue hung vast commercial and financial interests.

The railroads pleaded that they must have more money from the people to meet the "increased cost of living," especially the wages of their employees. The shippers responded by boldly attacking the railroads at the point where they have always felt strongest—that of managerial efficiency. The shippers declared that the railroads were not efficiently managed, and that if they would "look within," they could save more money than they now demanded in increased rates.

To support this bold response Mr. Louis D. Brandeis, the shippers' attorney, placed on the stand eleven witnesses who told of a singular new system or method of securing a marvelous degree of efficiency in all manner of industrial operations. This new system, or philosophy, which they said, frankly, was revolutionary in its aims, they called Scientific Management.

Few of those present had ever even heard of Scientific Management or of Mr. Taylor, its originator, and the testimony, at first, awakened a clearly perceptible incredulity. Nor was such incredulity surprising; for it was asserted that Scientific Management would commonly double or treble the producing capacity of every workman in a given industry, it would raise wages, it would increase profits, it would go far toward solving the labor problem. It was even asserted with confidence by one witness, Mr. Emerson, that, if applied to the railroads, Scientific Management could be counted upon to save at least $1,000,000 a day.

To those who heard this testimony there seemed at first something almost magical about the new idea; but as one sober, hardheaded business man after another testified as to what had been actually accomplished in his plant, when it appeared that Scientific Management had been applied with extraordinary results to widely diversified industries, from steel plants to bleacheries and cotton mills, and including railroad repair shops, the spirit of incredulity changed to one of deep interest. Another factor in carrying conviction to the hearers was the extraordinary fervor and enthusiasm expressed by every man who testified. Theirs was the firm faith of apostles: it was a philosophy which worked, and they had the figures to show it.

"This," said Mr. Commissioner Lane to one of the witnesses, "has become a sort of substitute for religion with you."

"Yes, sir," responded Mr. Gilbreth.

Since then I suppose there have been thousands of articles and editorials written for the newspapers regarding Scientific Management, with every view advanced, from that of sarcastic unbelief to that of firm conviction.

Mr. Taylor himself was not present at the hearing, but he was constantly referred to as the originator of the system; and he has since become a man of whom the world wishes to know more. . . .

TAYLOR:

President Roosevelt, in his address to the Governors at the White House, prophetically remarked that "The conservation of our national resources is only preliminary to the larger question of national efficiency."

The whole country at once recognized the importance of conserving our material resources and a large movement has been started which will be effective in accomplishing this object. As yet, however, we have but vaguely appreciated the importance of "the larger question of increasing our national efficiency."

We can see our forests vanishing, our water-powers going to waste, our soil being carried by floods into the sea; and the end of our coal and our iron is in sight. But our larger wastes of human effort, which go on every day through such of our acts as are blundering, ill-directed, or inefficient, and which Mr. Roosevelt refers to as a lack of "national efficiency," are less visible, less tangible, and are but vaguely appreciated.

We can see and feel the waste of material things. Awkward, inefficient, or ill-directed movements of men, however, leave nothing visible or tangible behind them. Their appreciation calls for an act of memory, an effort of the imagination. And for this reason, even though our daily loss from this source is greater than from our waste of material things, the one has stirred us deeply, while the other has moved us but little.

As yet there has been no public agitation for "greater national efficiency," no meetings have been called to consider how this is to be brought about. And still there are signs that the need for greater efficiency is widely felt.

The search for better, for more competent men, from the presidents of our great companies down to our household servants, was never more vigorous than it is now. And more than ever before is the demand for competent men in excess of the supply.

What we are all looking for, however, is the ready-made, competent man; the man whom some one else has trained. It is only when we fully realize that our duty, as well as our opportunity, lies in systematically cooperating to train and to make this competent man, instead of in hunting for a man whom some one else has trained, that we shall be on the road to national efficiency.

In the past the prevailing idea has been well expressed in the saying that "Captains of industry are born, not made"; and the theory has been that if one could get the right man, methods could be safely left to him. In the future it will be appreciated that our leaders must be trained right as well as born right, and that no great man can (with the old system of personal management) hope to compete with a number of ordinary men who have been properly organized so as efficiently to cooperate.

In the past the man has been first; in the future the system must be first. This in no sense, however, implies that great men are not needed. On the contrary, the first object of any good system must be that of developing first-class men; and under systematic management the best man rises to the top more certainly and more rapidly than ever before.

This paper has been written:

First. To point out, through a series of simple illustrations, the great loss which the whole country is suffering through inefficiency in almost all of our daily acts.

Second. To try to convince the reader that the remedy for this inefficiency lies in systematic management, rather than in searching for some unusual or extraordinary man.

Third. To prove that the best management is a true science, resting upon clearly defined laws, rules, and principles, as a foundation. And further to show that the fundamental principles of scientific management are applicable to all kinds of human activities, from our simplest individual acts to the work of our great corporations, which call for the most elaborate cooperation. And, briefly, through a series of illustrations, to convince the reader that whenever these principles are correctly applied, results must follow which are truly astounding. . . .

The principal object of management should be to secure the maximum prosperity for the employer, coupled with the maximum prosperity for each employé.

The words "maximum prosperity" are used, in their broad sense, to mean not only large dividends for the company or owner, but the development of every branch of the business to its highest state of excellence, so that the prosperity may be permanent.

In the same way maximum prosperity for each employé means not only higher wages than are usually received by men of his class, but, of more importance still, it also means the development of each man to his state of maximum efficiency, so that he may be able to do, generally speaking, the highest grade of work for which his natural abilities fit him, and it further means giving him, when possible, this class of work to do.

It would seem to be so self-evident that maximum prosperity for the employer, coupled with maximum prosperity for the employé, ought to be the two leading objects of management, that even to state this fact should be unnecessary. And yet there is no question that, throughout the industrial world, a large part of the organization of employers, as well as employés, is for war rather than for peace, and that perhaps the majority on either side do not believe that it is possible so to arrange their mutual relations that their interests become identical.

The majority of these men believe that the fundamental interests of employés and employers are necessarily antagonistic. Scientific management, on the contrary, has for its very foundation the firm conviction that the true interests of the two are one and the same; that prosperity for the employer cannot exist through a long term of years unless it is accompanied by prosperity for the employé, and *vice versa;* and that it is possible to give the workman what he most wants—high wages—and the employer what he wants—a low labor cost—for his manufactures.

Why is it, then, in the face of the self-evident fact that maximum prosperity can exist only as the result of the determined effort of each workman to turn out each day his largest possible day's work, that the great majority of our men are deliberately doing just the opposite, and that even when the men have the best of intentions their work is in most cases far from efficient?

There are three causes for this condition, which may be briefly summarized as:

First. The fallacy, which has from time immemorial been almost universal among workmen, that a material increase in the output of each man or each machine in the trade would result in the end in throwing a large number of men out of work.

Second. The defective systems of management which are in common use, and which make it necessary for each workman to soldier, or work slowly.

Third. As to the third cause for slow work, considerable space will later in this paper be devoted to illustrating the great gain, both to employers and employés, which results from the substitution of scientific for rule-of-thumb methods in even the smallest details of the work of every trade. The enormous saving of time and therefore increase in the output which it is possible to effect through eliminating unnecessary motions and substituting fast for slow and inefficient motions for the men working in any of our trades can be fully realized only after one has personally seen the improvement which results from a thorough motion and time study, made by a competent man. . . .

This paper will show that the underlying philosophy of all of the old systems of management in common use makes it imperative that each workman shall be left with the final responsibility for doing his job practically as he thinks best, with comparatively little help and advice from the management. And it will also show that because of this isolation of workmen, it is in most cases impossible for the men working under these systems to do their work in accordance with the rules and laws of a science or art, even where one exists.

The writer asserts as a general principle (and he proposes to give illustrations tending to prove the fact later in this paper) that in almost all of the mechanic arts the science which underlies each act of each workman is so great and amounts to so much that the workman who is best suited to actually doing the work is incapable of fully understanding this science, without the guidance and help of those who are working with him or over him, either through lack of education or through insufficient mental capacity. In order that the work may be done in accordance with scientific laws, it is necessary that there shall be a far more equal division of the responsibility between the management and the workmen than exists under any of the ordinary types of management. Those in the management whose duty it is to develop this science should also guide and help the workman in working under it, and should assume a much larger share of the responsibility for results than under usual conditions is assumed by the management. . . .

The necessity for systematically teaching workmen how to work to the best advantage has been several times referred to. It seems desirable, therefore, to explain in rather more detail how this teaching is done. In the case of a machine-shop which is managed under the modern system, detailed written instructions as to the best way of doing each piece of work are prepared in advance, by men in the planning department. These instructions represent the combined work of several men in the planning room, each of whom has his own specialty, or function. One of them, for instance, is a specialist on the proper speeds and cutting tools to be used. He uses the slide-rules which have been above described as an aid, to guide him in obtaining proper speeds, etc. Another man analyzes the best and quickest motions to be made by the workman in setting the work up in the machine and removing it, etc. Still a third, through the time-study records which have been accumulated, makes out a timetable giving the proper speed for doing each element of the work. The directions of all of these men, however, are written on a single instruction card, or sheet.

These men of necessity spend most of their time in the planning department, because they must be close to the records and data which they continually use in their work, and because this work requires the use of a desk and freedom from interruption. Human nature is such, however, that many of the workmen, if left to themselves, would pay but little attention to their written instructions. It is necessary, therefore, to provide teachers (called functional foremen) to see that the workmen both understand and carry out these written instructions.

Under functional management, the old-fashioned single foreman is superseded by eight different men, each one of whom has his own special duties, and these men, acting as the agents for the planning department (see paragraph 234 to 245 of the paper entitled "Shop Management"), are the expert teachers, who are at all times in the shop, helping and directing the workmen. Being each one chosen for his knowledge and personal skill in his specialty, they are able not only to tell the workman what he should do, but in case of necessity they do the work themselves in the presence of the workman, so as to show him not only the best but also the quickest methods.

One of these teachers (called the inspector) sees to it that he understands the drawings and instructions for doing the work. He teaches him how to do work of the right quality; how to make it fine and exact where it should be fine, and rough and quick where accuracy is not required,—the one being just as important for success as the other. The second teacher (the gang boss) shows him how to set up the job in his machine, and teaches him to make all of his personal motions in the quickest and best way. The third (the speed boss) sees that the machine is run at the best speed and that the proper tool is used in the particular way which will enable the machine to finish its product in the shortest possible time. In addition to the assistance given by these teachers, the workman receives orders and help from four other men; from the "repair boss" as to the adjustment, cleanliness, and general care of his machine, belting, etc.; from the "time clerk," as to everything relating to his pay and to proper written reports and returns; from the "route clerk," as to the order in which he does his work and as to the movement of the work from one part of the shop to another; and, in case a workman gets into any trouble with any of his various bosses, the "disciplinarian" interviews him. . . .

Hundreds of people have already mistaken the mechanism of this system for its essence. Messrs. Gantt, Barth, and the writer have presented papers to the American Society of Mechanical Engineers on the subject of scientific management. In these papers the mechanism which is used has been described at some length. As elements of this mechanism may be cited:

Time study, with the implements and methods for properly making it.
Functional or divided foremanship and its superiority to the old-fashioned single foreman.
The standardization of all tools and implements used in the trades, and also of the acts or movements of workmen for each class of work.
The desirability of a planning room or department.
The "exception principle" in management.
The use of slide-rules and similar time-saving implements.
Instruction cards for the workman.
The task idea in management, accompanied by a large bonus for the successful performance of the task.
The "differential rate."
Mnemonic systems for classifying manufactured products as well as implements used in manufacturing.
A routing system.
Modern cost system, etc., etc.

These are, however, merely the elements or details of the mechanism of management. Scientific management, in its essence, consists of a certain philosophy, which results, as before stated, in a combination of the four great underlying principles of management:[1]

As one of the elements incident to this great gain in output, each workman has been systematically trained to his highest state of efficiency, and has been taught to do a higher class of work than he was able to do under the old types of management; and at the same time he has acquired a friendly mental attitude toward his employers and his whole working condition, whereas before a considerable part of his time was spent in criticism, suspicious watchfulness, and sometimes in open warfare. This direct gain to all of those working under the system is without doubt the most important single element in the whole problem.

Is not the realization of results such as these of far more importance than the solution of most of the problems which are now agitating both the English and American peoples? And is not the duty of those who are acquainted with these facts, to exert themselves to make the whole community realize this importance?

7

NATIONAL CONSERVATION CONGRESS
The Many Meanings of Conservation

The conservation movement was only one aspect of progressivism, but the conservation ideal was capable of uniting virtually all the reform causes of that period. To read through the *Proceedings* of the National Conservation Congresses is to meet the progressive movement in all its variety: scientists and others who wished to preserve dwindling resources from wasteful use; large business concerns eager to close off access to lumber and mineral reserves

---

[1] *First.* The development of a true science. *Second.* The scientific selection of the workman. *Third.* His scientific education and development. *Fourth.* Intimate friendly cooperation between the management and the men....

against fly-by-night competitors; social workers determined to extend the idea of conservation to human resources; ladies from patriotic and genealogical societies ardent to conserve the purity of "the race"; political figures and intellectuals who wanted an end to unbridled individualism. And all the qualities of the progressive collective mentality are in evidence in these volumes—social urgency, a sense of righteousness, the leaning toward cooperation, the faith in applied science and the state. Reprinted below are a few selections from speeches given to the First and Second National Conservation Congresses, where individuals as diverse as Theodore Roosevelt, a representative of the New York Manufacturer's Association, and an official of the Daughters of the American Revolution found common ground in the idea of conservation.

MR. GIFFORD PINCHOT, FORESTER,
UNITED STATES DEPARTMENT OF AGRICULTURE; CHAIRMAN,
NATIONAL CONSERVATION COMMISSION.

I think it is fair to say that the first idea of real foresight in connection with natural resources did arise in connection with the forest. From it sprang the movement which gathered impetus until it resulted in the great Convention of Governors at Washington something over a year ago. Then came the second official meeting of the National Conservation movement last December in Washington. Both these meetings, as Mr. Libby indicated, were in a certain sense official. Now comes the first gathering of citizens without official connection, brought together to handle this question as citizens of the United States are handling so many other questions, with the intention of expressing their judgment on what ought to be done, and contributing as powerfully as only such meetings can to the formation of public opinion. . . .

The first thing to say about conservation is that it stands for development. There has been a fundamental misconception that conservation meant nothing but the husbanding of resources for future generations. There could be no more serious mistake. Conservation does mean provision for the future, but it means also and first of all the recognition of the right of the present generation to the fullest necessary use of all the resources that this country is so abundantly blessed with. It means

---

Addresses and Proceedings of the First National Conservation Congress, 1909 (Washington, D.C., National Conservation Congress, 1910), pp. 70–76, 90–93, 167–78; *Proceedings of the Second National Conservation Congress, 1910* (Washington D.C., National Conservation Congress, 1911), pp. 82–83, 270–76.

the welfare of this generation and afterwards the welfare of the generations to follow.

The first principle of conservation is development, the use of the natural resources now existing on this continent for the benefit of the people of the people who live here now. There may be just as much waste in neglecting the development and use of certain natural resources as there is in their destruction by waste. We have a limited supply of coal, and only a limited supply. Whether it is to last for a hundred or a hundred and fifty or a thousand years, the coal is limited in amout and, except through geological changes which we can never see, there will never be any more if it than there is now. But coal is in a sense the vital essence of our civilization. If it can be preserved, if its life can be extended, if by preventing waste there can be more coal in this country when this generation is gone, after we have made every needed use of this source of power, then this country is just so much further ahead and the future so much the better off.

Conservation, then, stands emphatically for the use of substitutes for all the exhaustible natural resources, for the development and use of water power, and for the immediate development of water power as a substitute for coal. It stands for the immediate development of waterways under a broad and comprehensive plan as substitutes and assistants to the railroads. More coal and iron are required to move a ton of freight by rail than water, three to one.

In every case and in every direction the conservation movement has development for its first principle, and at the very beginning of its work. The development of our natural resources and the fullest use of them for the present generation is the first duty of this generation. So much for development.

In the second place conservation stands for the prevention of waste. There has come gradually—and most of us in this room today have seen nearly the whole of it—there has come gradually in this country an understanding that waste is not a good thing and that the attack on waste is a necessary and possible attack. I recall very well indeed how, in the early days of forest fires, they were considered simply and solely as acts of God, against which any opposition was hopeless and any attempt to control them not merely hopeless but childish. It was assumed that they came in the natural order of things as inevitably as seasons or the rising and setting of the sun. Today we understand that forest fires are wholly within the control of human agency.

These conservation ideas cover a wider field than the field of natural resources alone. Conservation means the greatest good to the greatest number for the longest time. One of its great contributions is that it has added to the worn and well-known phrase, "the greatest good to the greatest number," the additional words, "for the longest time," thus recognizing that this nation of ours is to endure and shall endure in the best possible condition for all its people.

Conservation advocates the use of foresight, prudence, thrift, and intelligence in dealing with public matters, for the same reasons and in the same way that we use foresight, prudence, thrift, and intelligence in dealing with our own affairs. It proclaims the right and duty of the people to act for the benefit of the people. Conservation demands the application of common sense to the common problems for the common good.

The principles of conservation thus described have a general application which is growing wider and wider every day. The development of resources and the prevention of waste and loss, the protection of the public interests by foresight, prudence, and the ordinary business and home-making virtues, all these apply to other things as well as to the conservation of resources. There is no interest of the people to which the principles of conservation do not apply.

The conservation point of view is valuable for education as well as in forestry; it applies to the body politic as well as to the earth and its minerals. A municipal franchise is as properly within its sphere as a franchise for water power. The same point of view governs in both. It applies as much to the subject of good roads as to waterways, and the training of our people in citizenship is as germane to it as to the productiveness of the earth. The application of common sense to any problem for the Nation's good will lead directly to national efficiency wherever applied. In other words, and that is the burden of what I have to say this morning, we are coming to see that it is the logical and inevitable outcome, that these principles, which arose in forestry, and have their bloom in the conservation of natural resources, will have their fruit in the increase and promotion of national efficiency along other lines of national life.

The outcome of conservation, the inevitable outcome, is national efficiency. In the great commercial struggle between nations which is eventually to determine the welfare of all, national efficiency will be the deciding factor. So from every point of view conservation is a good thing for the American people.

So we are coming in like manner to understand that the prevention of waste in all other directions is a simple matter of good business. The human race controls the earth it lives upon.

We are coming to be in a position more and more completely to say how much waste and destruction of natural resources is to be allowed to go on and where it is to stop. It is curious that the effort to stop waste, like the effort to stop forest fires, has often been considered as a matter controlled wholly by economic law. I think there could be no greater mistake. Forest fires were allowed to burn long after the people had means to stop them. The idea that men were helpless in the face of them held long after the time had passed when the means of control were fully within our reach. It was the old story that "as a man thinketh so is he;" we came to see that we could stop forest fires and we found the means at hand. When we came to see the control of logging in certain directions was profitable, we found it had long been possible. In all these matters of waste of natural resources, the education of the people to understand that they can stop these things comes before the actual stopping, and after the meant of stopping them have long been ready at our hands.

In addition to the principles of development and preservation of our resources, the length of the life of the exhaustible resources, the perpetuation and renewal of those which can be renewed and perpetuated, there is a third principle about which I want to say a word. I would say more about it except that the admirable paper of Mr. Teal yesterday set forth, as I could not hope to do, the third principle of conservation. It is this: the natural resources must be developed and preserved for the benefit of the many and not merely for the profit of a few. We are coming to understand in this country, as I have had occasion to say more than once, that public action for public benefit has a very much wider field and a much larger part to play than was the case when there were resources enough for everyone and before certain constitutional arrangements in this country of ours had given so tremendously strong a position to vested rights and property in general. President Hadley, of Yale, wrote an article in *The Independent* a year or more ago which has not attracted the attention it should. I hope it will be widely republished. The effect of it was that by reason of the fourteenth amendment to the Constitution, property rights in the United States occupy a stronger position than in any other country in the civilized world. I want to add that it becomes then a matter of multiplied importance, of a thousandfold importance, if you like, to see, when property rights once granted are so strongly entrenched, that they shall be granted only under such conditions as that the people shall get their fair share of the benefit which comes from the development of the country which belongs to us all. The time to do that is now. By so doing we shall avoid difficulties and conflicts which will surely arise if we allow vested rights to accrue outside the possibility of government and popular control.

Conservation of Child Life

MRS. J. ELLEN FOSTER,
CHAIRMAN, COMMITTEE ON CHILD LABOR;
NATIONAL SECRETARY,
DAUGHTERS OF THE AMERICAN REVOLUTION.

I wish to thank the gentlemen of the committee for their invitation to me to speak on this subject, the Conservation of Child Life. Strange that a woman should feel thankful for this, for have not we been accorded since the foundation of the world the guardianship of the children? But in these latter days there is rising a class of men—some of them old and a little stiff in keeping pace with the march of events and some of them young and a bit heady in their appreciation of sociological questions; these old men and these young men, men whom we have reared and nestled in our arms, sometimes say things we do not like. They talk about the decay of the motherly instinct. They tell what the old-fashioned women used to do, as if the new-fashioned woman did not do the same things. They say that our homes are in danger; that we do not care for our children; that we would rather make speeches on platforms and go to the polls and vote than take care of the little ones that have come to us through the Divine ordinance of marriage and our very hearts' life. These old men are dried up and have forgotten. These young men are not out of the period of adolescence. I am glad to be here. I care more about children than about forests and streams. Why do I care at all for forests and streams? Because of the children who are to be naked and bare and poor without them in the years to come unless you men of this great conservation work do well your work.

But please take comfort to your hearts, men and women; there is no trouble about the homes of America. I am associated with most of the forward movements advocated by women. I believe in all the movements that are asking for enlarged opportunities for women. And why do we ask it? Why do we want this and that and the other, and why are we getting this and that and the other? Washington is soon to make her tribute to the advance of women. Why is all this? It is because we want to take care of our children better, it is because we can serve the interests of the home better. The forces of nature since the foundation of the world have been on the side of the child with the mother; sometimes, and very largely, on the side of the child with the father, but always on the side of the child with the mother. Men and women, you utilize the force of gravitation but you don't make the force. God did that. You utilize women's love of a child, but you did not make it. God set us in families. So now we are all right; we will help you out. The lady who represents the conservation interests of the country as they are fostered and served by the Daughters of the American Revolution is Mrs. Bell Merril Draper, of Washington, D. C., chairman of the Conservation Committee. I chance to be speaking here today as her representative and also as chairman of the committee on Child Labor of this same great organization, the National Society of the Daughters of the American Revolution. We believe in all these forward movements because they are part of our inheritance; we are to the manner (sic) born; there is good blood in us, the blood of the Revolution, the blood of our fathers and mothers of the olden time who set the stakes of the constitution to which the first great speaker here has alluded. We are their children and want to save what they gave us. That is the basis of the membership of the National Society of the Daughters of the Revolution. That is who we are. Now, why have we formed this committee against child labor? Because just as surely as a big tree is worth more than a growing slip, so a man is worth more than a child. That is a wonderfully commercial way to state it, isn't it? It is not only that we love the child and want him for ourselves, but it is because we know he is worth more to the country, if he is allowed to grow up. He makes a better tree out of which to cut lumber to build a house or a church or a school if he is allowed to grow up to full stature and to develop himself fully. He cannot do that if he is put in a factory at a too early age. That is the economic side of the question. Of course you know the other side, the sentimental side, but you are hard-headed men, most of you. You deal in measurements of timber, measurements of water, as the great forces of nature, and we present our subject to you along the lines of your action. We say the boy is worth more by and by if he does not work in the factory now. And, gentlemen and ladies, the thing which is right morally, the thing which is right sentimentally is right economically. Oh, it is magnificent to get hold of a truth, a vital truth like this; you can tie to it and go anywhere with it.

Conservation and the Manufacturer

JAMES A. EMERY, REPRESENTING THE NEW YORK MANUFACTURERS' ASSOCIATION.

The American manufacturer, more than any other class, is interested in conserving all the great natural resources of this country and in everything that makes for industrial and commercial efficiency and the higher types of citizenship. He has been indirectly and directly criticized during the course of the discussions here, and in so far as some of the criticisms have a foundation in fact they are justified; but I speak for a great organization, perhaps the greatest organization in the world, which represents an investment of over five billion dollars in manufacturers and finds employment for three and a half millions of men, and which is extending its commercial supremacy not only through our own but through neighboring countries. Thanks to the sagacity and great ability and far-seeing commercial foresight of the distinguished gentleman on my right (the Hon. John Barrett), we are increasing our commercial and industrial relations with all the nations of the world.

The American manufacturer believes in conserving natural resources of soil, forest, and stream not only because he wants to draw upon them and to use them wisely and justly, but also because he desires to be protected against the enrichment of great single persons, either corporate or individual, that seek to control natural resources for their own gain and to the detriment and injury of those who suffer from extravagant and wasteful use. More than that he is a firm and determined believer in the conservation of child life in every form and in every place. He knows that when you keep the schools open you keep the jails closed; that he who preserves the child protects and makes more efficient the man. He is eager not only to protect and develop our natural resources in the present generation, but to preserve them for the future generations, and in that connection to conserve things moral and things educational with regard to our young men. Our chief competitors in foreign markets, with whom we most frequently jostle shoulders in the commercial world, are nations that are giving the greatest thought and concern, not only to protecting child life, but to providing it with practical instruments for future protection and support. Under our present school system, between six and seven million children annually enter our schools. A vast majority leave school between the ages of twelve and fourteen to enter on their struggle with the world, some from necessity, some from choice, some from the blindness, ignorance, or indifference of parents, some from the temptations of commercial life, the suggestion of rapid success; but are we today as a people preparing the American child to take up the responsibility of American manhood, not only from the moral but from the practical standpoint? With our much larger population and with far greater natural resources, we are doing far less in comparison with the great German Empire to prepare the vast army of growing boys to accept the responsibilities of manhood and to enter upon life prepared by training and education to take advantage of the opportunities of trade and commerce and to make for themselves a commanding place among mankind.

The manufacturer is interested in the great question of conservation because the great body to which I refer represents in its membership, in its growth, in its aspirations and ambitions the desires and hopes, moral and industrial, of the great middle class of the American people. It does not require in its membership the representatives of those vast monopolies that in a single grasp possess the wealth that kings had not in centuries past; it does not hold in its membership the very small that have not reached a leading place in the manufacturing world; but it stands in the great middle ground.

Situated between those two great combinations of capital and labor that excite our industrial interest, the American manufacturer strives to give force and effect to the great movement to conserve natural resources, because they lie at the foundation of all the great moral resources of the Nation, as the exercise of man's higher being depends upon the state of the stomach.

We are anxious that the conservation movement shall be understood. There has been a mistaken notion that conservation meant a miserly grasping and absolute prohibition of the use by the present generation of the natural resources which are essential to the development and maintenance of already existing commerce. But I know, and know from the expression of your own select representatives, from those who may be considered the fathers of conservation, that you advocate the development, the fullest and most generous use, without extravagance or waste, of all those benefits that come from our vast natural possessions, provided only that we shall not tresspass on our vast capital to our injury or the injury of the generations who must come after us.

There are those who will argue against conservation, because they desire to misunderstand it. There are those who will twist the logic of events to make it appear that every attempt to preserve the natural resources which the State holds as trustee for the people is an invasion of the rights of property. We must remember, moreover, that every man who has attempted to benefit his fellows and present large ideas for popular approval has had to meet criticism and determined opposition. There are those who find in the economies of conservation arguments against the very thing itself, against the safeguarding of natural resources by wise legislation in order that all and not merely a few may profit by their use. . . .

Let me say this final word, that the American manufacturer stands for conservation of morals. He believes in the physical conservation of the forces of this Nation in order to develop all that is best, strongest, and cleanest in citizenship. It is our great moral ideals that make us stand before the nations as the most original and striking nationality; we depend upon physical conditions that make the body clean and wholesome, and make the brain and heart great and strong, that we may have a firm grip, a clean conscience, a clear national vision, and thus obtain the benefits which these powers have always conferred through all the history of time. (Applause.)

The Waste of War

AUGUST F. KNUDSEN, REPRESENTING
THE GOVERNOR OF KOKANA, KANAI, HAWAII.

The waste of war is greatest of all. . . .

Has not the time arrived when we can put an end to this waste of material, waste of energy, waste of time, and waste of emotion? Shall we continue to spend forty-one per cent of our entire revenue for the maintenance of the army, navy, and fortifications, and an additional thirty-one per cent for the maintenance of the relics of a past war, leaving only twenty-eight per cent of the total revenue of this country for the government of the country and the performance of those works which we all recognize as being for the benefit of the nation at large— for the extension of such things, for instance, as the Postal Service, the Reclamation Service—the things that go to make life easier and better, therefore giving us a chance for culture and an higher civilization?

Think of it! Ten years ago a billion dollar Congress startled us, and now it is a billion dollar session, and 72 per cent of that is frittered away in non-production, in absolutely useless channels, or useful only if we first blind ourselves with the hallucination that we cannot maintain peace unless everyone is armed to the teeth.

The great cause of all this war between the nations and this war between individuals is the greed for wealth; and all conservation depends on self-restraint, which is the curbing of that greed for wealth. Individualism has so run riot today that the students of psychology, the students of men's minds and faculties, have discovered a new form of insanity, that of the "Exaggerated Ego," where the sense of egotism so blinds the individual that he places the privilege of the one as paramount over the rights of the many.

We cannot allow this to go on. Can we not see that that is a menace to our civilization?

Proceedings Second Conservation Congress

ADDRESS BY THEODORE ROOSEVELT

Mr. Chairman, and Governor; Governors, and fellow-guests; Men and Women of Minnesota: It is a very great pleasure to me to be here in Minnesota again, and especially to come here to speak on this particular subject of "National Efficiency." (Applause)

Minnesota is one of the States that almost always takes the lead in any great work (applause), and Minnesota has been one of the first to take hold of the Conservation policy in practical fashion; and she has done a great work and set an admirable example to the rest of us (applause)—a work representing a policy well set forth in your Governor's address yesterday—and I am glad that this Congress is held in such a State, where we can listen to such an address made by a Governor who had the right to make it. (Prolonged applause)

Much that I have to say on the general policy of Conservation will be but a repetition of what was so admirably said on this general policy by the President of the United States yesterday (great applause); and in particular all true friends of Conservation should be in heartiest agreement with the policy which the President laid down in connection with the coal, oil, and phosphate lands (applause), and I am glad to be able to say that at its last session Congress finally completed the work of separating the surface title to the land from the mineral beneath it. (Applause)

Now, my friends, America's reputation for efficiency stands deservedly high throughout the world. We are efficient probably to the full limits that are permitted by the methods hitherto used. The average American is an efficient man; he can do his business. It is recognized throughout the world that that is his type. There is great reason to be proud of our achievements, and yet no reason to think that we cannot excel our past (applause). Through a practically unrestrained individualism, we have reached a pitch of literally unexampled material prosperity. The sum of our prosperity in the aggregate leaves little to be desired, although the distribution of that prosperity, from the standpoint of justice and fair dealing, leaves a little more to be desired (laughter and applause). But we have not only allowed the individual a free hand, which was in the main right; we have also allowed great corporations to act as though they were individuals, and to exercise the rights of individuals, in addition to using the vast combined power of high organization and enormous wealth for their own advantage. This development of corporate action is doubtless in large part responsible for the gigantic development of our natural resources, but it is also true that it is in large part responsible for waste, destruction, and monopoly on an equally gigantic scale. (Applause)

The method of reckless and uncontrolled private use and waste has done for us all the good it can ever do, and it is time to put an end to it before it does the evil that it well may (applause). We have passed the time when heedless waste and destruction and arrogant monopoly are longer permissible (applause). Henceforth we must seek national efficiency by a new and a better way, by the way of the orderly development and use, coupled with the preservation, of our natural resources; by making the most of what we have for the benefit of all of us, instead of leaving the sources of material prosperity open to indiscriminate exploitation (applause). These are some of the reasons why it is wise that we should abandon the old point of view, and why Conservation has become a great moral issue, and become a patriotic duty. . . .

President BAKER—Ladies and Gentlemen: Can there be higher patriotism than in the efforts of this Congress to protect the rights of all? Conservation is true patriotism; and Mrs Matthew T. Scott, President-General of the National Society of Daughters of the American Revolution, will now address you on this subject. (Applause, the entire audience rising)

Mrs SCOTT—Mr President, Ladies and Gentlemen: In behalf of the National Society of Daughters of the American Revolution, I wish to make my grateful acknowledgments to the Executive Committee (through its President, Honorable Bernard N. Baker) for its courtesy in giving to Mrs Amos G. Draper, the able chairman of our D. A. R. Conservation Committee who has so splendidly inaugurated and developed this work, and to myself, the privilege and honor of taking part in these splendid exercises. In its last analysis the generic term "Conservation"—in its widest scope, and broadest sense—may be said to be the keynote and touchstone of our great D. A. R. organization. The finest brains and blood and nerve force of the land have been absorbed and found noble expression in various lines of work of the D. A. R. While the Daughters have turned their sympathetic attention to various material branches of Conservation work, we have not neglected the higher intellectual, ethical, and moral Conservation interests; we aim to help preserve the glorious heritage that has fallen to us of self-government, and hand down the birthright undiminished to those who come after us that the priceless boon of "government of the people by the people and for the people" perish not from the earth. (Applause)

It has been borne in upon me of late that there are two Conservation interests whose importance we have not fully recognized, and they are the conservation of true womanliness, and the conservation of the supremacy of the Anglo-Saxon race on this continent. As to the former, the President of the United States in a recent address at Washington before the annual Congress of the D. A. R., said that woman's place and sphere are on too high a plane to be even discussed. It is surely an inspiration to have the privilege before this splendid assemblage of representing the great patriotic movement, which under the banner of the D. A. R., marches steadily forward, with ever increasing numbers, enthusiasm, prestige, and practical power.

The Daughters of the American Revolution in distinctive and especial ways have lent their organized strength to various good causes, which may all be practically considered as Conservation interests: among other objects, to social uplift, to patriotic education in its widest scope, to placing bounds to the abuse of child labor, to playgrounds, to juvenile courts, to improvement of hygienic conditions in our great cities, to preservation of historic spots and records, to the safe and sane celebration of July Fourth; and to cooperation with the S. A. R. in their noble work for immigrants landing upon our shores and subsequently for these foreigners and their children in the effort to Americanize them and to innoculate them with ideals and principles known in this twentieth century as Americanism.

Much has been done also among the mountain whites of the South. Every mountaineer, child or adult, that in our work we help to educate toward intelligent citizenship—and many of these mountaineers are of Revolutionary ancestry—is a barrier raised against the anarchistic tendencies and the unrest of our great cities; is a guarantee for the supremacy of the Caucasian race in America. Read, if you can secure it, Mr Thomas Nelson Page's plea for the education of the Southern Mountain whites in his magnificent address delivered at Washington before the last Continental Congress! We are also preserving, all over this broad land, landmarks of history—sacred relics of a vanished age—which are object-lessons for our own youth and for the strangers who crowd our shores. Every monument we rear, every tablet we place, every statue we erect, every old fort or bastian, every Revolutionary relic or Revolutionary soldier's grave we honor, is a tribute to those to whom we owe the imperishable gifts of liberty, of independence, of the right to worship God in our own way. Every fountain or stone recording the trail of the pioneer, the priest, the trader, the soldier, or the devotion of the Revolutionary heroine, is a breath of incense wafted back to the immortals, an inspiration for "tangible immortality" for ourselves and those who come after us. (Applause)

The Conservation of our natural resources is a subject of intensely practical importance to the D. A. R. Representing as we do the motherhood of the Nation, we feel that it is for us to see that the children of this and future generations are not robbed of their God-given privileges. It is our high privilege and mission to see to it that the future shall be the uncankered fruit of the past. The ideal democracy solemnly dedicated by the Founders, we as their Daughters, declare shall not be forestalled. As women we cannot be silent and see the high ends at which they aimed made futile by the growth of a grovelling lust for material and commercial aggrandizement. This headlong haste for enormous gain, the total disregard of the future for the present moment, if not stopped will bring us to the condition of the Old World where the fertility and habitability of past ages have been destroyed forever. We feel that it is for us, who are not wholly absorbed in business, to preserve ideals that are higher than business—the outlook for the future, the common interests, and the betterment of all classes. The wasteful scrambling and greedy clutching at our natural treasures has made the present generation rich; but the mothers of the future must be warned by us lest they find that our boasted prosperity has been bought at the price of the suffering, of the poverty, and class war of our descendants. There is no lack of patriotic devotion in the country; but the mere thoughtlessness and inability or unwillingness of the commercial class to drop the interests of the moment long enough to realize how they are compromising the future—this hot haste and heedlessness, it is for us with our larger outlook to restrain.

Women have already preserved a large National forest in the Pennsylvania mountains; the women of Minnesota have to their credit the Minnesota National forests; it was the women of California who saved the immemorial groves of the Calaveras big trees. Our own work in behalf of the preservation of the Appalachian watersheds, in behalf of the preservation of historic sites, as well as the efforts being made by various women's organizations to preserve the natural beauty of the Palisades, of Niagara Falls, and of other precious scenic treasures of the Nation, are all steps in the right direction, are all preparation for the larger Conservation interests which the D. A. R. have begun actively to champion. It should be a second nature to women, with the spirit of motherhood and protecting care innate in them, to take an effective stand in the spirit of true patriotism—against the spirit of rank selfishness—the anti-social spirit of the man who declines to take into account any other interests than his own. (Applause)

There is another great world interest that is peculiarly our own as Daughters and descendants of the peace-loving patriots who took up arms a century and a half ago. They were not professional soldiers, but plain citizens hastily rallied together in often-wavering lines of defense of home and country. All the world wondered when at Lexington and

Concord, on the village green and at the wooden bridge, the embattled farmers stood across the line of march of the British regular army, and fired "the shot heard round the world." It is the opening decade of the twentieth century of the Christian era; it is time that brute force— the recourse of primitive, barbaric man—cease to be the last arbitrament between great nations calling themselves Christian and civilized, and that the Conservation of peace be established by international arbitration. (Applause)

Again, it is one of the glories of our great organization that we are first, last, and all the time, considering the child. Today in all civilized countries the child is leading the way. I am happy to be able to say that through the instrumentality of our chapters in different parts of the country, interest has been awakened in homeless and dependent children; organizations have been formed for children of foreign birth to teach them respect for the flag, and some things about our form of government. Many chapters provide instructive lectures in their own language for foreigners, who listen eagerly. Many chapters offer prize medals for the best essays on historical subjects—American history especially—and for memorizing our National songs. Nothing is more important than our organized work for the "Children of the American Revolution"—children of American birth and descent—unless it be our work for the "Children of the Republic" in teaching to be American citizens boys of foreign parentage who come to us with little idea of the difference between liberty and license. For patriotism consists as much in making good citizens as in saving the Nation from bad ones (applause). Every boy of foreign birth or extraction that we can help to transform into a thorough American through this magnificent branch of our work, every lad of foreign birth or extraction that we can help train to become a useful citizen and grow up into honorable manhood as a credit to his adopted land is an added asset to the ethical wealth of the country. Think for a moment what it means to help train these young foreigners in the plastic period of their life in the patriotic principles of their adopted country! A long stride has been taken in their patriotic and civic education, when through the exertions of noble women they have been given some idea of the great principles which are the basis of our form of government. . . .

As I said before, in the light of recent incidents and experiences, it has been borne in upon me that there are two great Conservation interests we have not yet sufficiently touched.

I plead, as the representative of a great National organization of the women of the land, for the Conservation of true womanliness, for the exalting, for the lifting up in special honor, of the Holy Grail of Womanhood. But not merely the cup whence flows the stream of human life, must we guard and cherish; we must look to the ingredients which are being cast into the cup. We must protect the fountain from pollution. We must not so eagerly invite all the sons of Shem, Ham, and Japhet, wherever they may have first seen the light, and under whatever traditions and influences and ideals foreign and antagonistic to ours they may have been reared, to trample the mud of millions of alien feet into our spring. We must conserve the sources of our race in the Anglo-Saxon line, Mother of Liberty and Self-government in the modern world. I would rather our coming census showed a lesser population and a greater homogeneity. Especially do I dread the clouding of the purity of the cup with color and character acquired under tropical suns, in the jungle, or in paradisian islands of the sea alternately basking in heavenlike beauty and serenity and devasted by earthquake and tornado and revolution. (Applause)

I come of the old Virginia stock (applause) which first passed over the Blue Ridge and possessed the great Middle West, just in time to prevent it from becoming Spanish or French or British. Some of the pioneers of Washington's times have stayed on right there, in that eagle's nest of pure Americans where Kentucky, Tennessee, and Virginia meet in the mountains against which Cornwallis' previously invincible raiding column—after devastating the Carolinas—dashed itself to pieces, wiped out by volunteer mountaineers in that wonderful battle of Kings Mountain which no general planned or even heard of until it was over. Personally, I would be willing to reduce our population-boast by many millions, had the remnant the unadulterated Americanism conserved to this day in these mountaineers' descendants! We may be destined to see our cup of liberty, which we have so generously proffered to the whole world, grow to the proportion of a grand mixing-bowl of races; but if so, will it not at least be wise to see that our own race dominate?

We, the mothers of this generation—ancestresses of future generations—have a right to insist upon the conserving not only of soil, forest, birds, minerals, fishes, waterways, in the interest of our future home-makers, but also upon the conserving of the supremacy of the Caucasian race in our land. This Conservation, second to none in pressing importance, may and should be insured in the best interests of all races concerned; and the sooner attention is turned upon it the better. (Great applause)

8

LOUIS D. BRANDEIS

Social Insurance and Social Efficiency

In the following essay the Boston lawyer (later U.S. Supreme Court Justice) Louis Brandeis grounds his case for social insurance in the idea of efficiency, i.e., that it is cheaper in the long run. As a lawyer who occasionally served corporations he knew that the promise of efficiency might soften the resistance of the cost-conscious American businessman, while an appeal to altruism would produce little result. This was a bold and pathbreaking article, for Brandeis was not only endorsing the full range of social insurance (workmen's compensation, which was implemented in some states in this period; and unemployment, health, and old age insurance, measures thought quite radical until the 1930s). In addition, he made one of the earliest and most powerful redefinitions of the concept of freedom. Both comprehensive social insurance and the incorporation of economic security into the idea of freedom were intellectual steps that most Americans were not ready to take until after the educative experience of the Great Depression.

Throughout the civilized world a developing sense of social responsibility has compelled the community to support in some manner its needy members whatsoever the cause of their inability to support themselves.

In granting this aid we are passing from sporadic, emotional charity to organized charities, and from mere relief to preventive measures. We have learned that financial dependence among the wage earner is due, in large part, to sickness, accident, invalidity, superannuation

Louis D. Brandeis, "Workingmen's Insurance—The Road to Social Efficiency," *Proceedings of the National Conference of Charities and Corrections, 1911* (Fort Wayne: Fort Wayne Printing Co., 1911), pp. 156–62.

or unemployment, or to premature death of the bread-winner of the family. Contingencies like these, referred to in the individual case as a misfortune, are now recognized as ordinary incidents of the lives of the wage-earners. And since our existing industrial system is converting an ever increasing percentage of the population into wage-earners, the need of providing indemnity against financial losses from such ordinary contingencies in the workingman's life has become apparent. So sickness and death benefits, and methods of compensation for accidents have been resorted to. But this partial workingmen's insurance has served mainly in making clear the need of a comprehensive system which shall extend protection also to the wage-earner in case of invalidity, superannuation or unemployment, and to the widows and orphans left helpless by the premature death of husband or father. In this movement to establish a comprehensive system of workingmen's insurance, Germany, Austria, France and latterly England have already advanced far.

An Essential of Democracy

The United States must follow on the same path; for the conditions which have led to the introduction of workingmen's insurance abroad are universal in their operation. Besides, the form and aims of our Government as well as the sense of social responsibility should lead us to action. American democracy rests upon the basis of the free citizen. We accord (to the men) universal suffrage. We urge strenuously upon every voter the duty of exercising this right. We insist that the voter should exercise it in the interest of others as well as of himself. We give thus to the citizen the rights of a free man. We impose upon him a duty that can be entrusted with safety only to free men. Politically the American workingman is free, so far as law can make him so. But is he really free? Can any man be really free who is constantly in danger of becoming dependent for mere subsistence upon somebody and something else than his own exertion and conduct? Men are not free while financially dependent upon the will of other individuals. Financial dependence is consistent with freedom only where claim to support rests upon right and not upon favor.

President Cleveland's epigram that it is the duty of the citizen to support the Government, not of the Government to support the citizen, is only qualifiedly true. Universal suffrage necessarily imposes upon the state the obligation of fitting its governors—the voters, for their task; and freedom of the individual is as much an essential condition of successful democracy as his education. If the government permits conditions to exist which made large classes of citizens financially dependent, the great evil of dependence should at least be minimized by the state's assuming, or causing to be assumed by others in some form, the burden incident to its own shortcomings.

A Part of the Daily Cost of Living

The cost of attaining freedom is usually high; and the cost of providing to the workingman, as an essential of freedom, a comprehensive and adequate system of insurance, will prove to be no exception to this general rule. But however large the cost, it should be fairly faced and courageously met. For the expense of securing indemnity against the financial losses attending accident, sickness, invalidity, premature death, superannuation, and unemployment, should be recognized as a part of the daily cost of living, like the more immediate demands for rent, for food, and for clothing. So far as it is a necessary charge, it should be met now as a current expense; instead of being allowed to accumulate as a debt with compound interest to plague us hereafter.

Few intelligent property owners omit to insure against fire. Everybody recognizes the fire insurance premium as a current expense. And yet the chance of loss by fire is very slight as compared with the chance of loss of earnings by sickness, accident or premature death. Every intelligent manufacturer makes in some form a regular charge for depreciation of machinery and plant. And yet the depreciation of man through invalidity and superannuation is no less certain, and frequently more severe, than the depreciation of machinery. Every intelligent manufacturer recognizes rent, interest and taxes as a current daily charge which continue although his plant is shut down or operates at less than full capacity. The manufacturer makes allowance for this in calculating the cost of production as an extra charge to be met from the earnings of active days. But the cost to the employer of carrying an unused plant is not as great relatively as the cost to the employee of carrying himself and family while unemployed. The manufacturer who fails to recognize fire insurance, depreciation, interest and taxes as current charges of the business, treads the path to bankruptcy. And that nation does the like which fails to recognize and provide against the economic, social and political conditions which impose upon the workingman so large a degree of financial dependence.

The High Cost of Adequate Insurance

What sum would be required annually to provide an adequate system of workingmen's insurance cannot be determined from existing data. The cost would obviously vary greatly in different occupations and different communities. An amount equal to ten per cent of current wages would go far towards relieving in many industries the distress now incident to sickness, accident, invalidity, premature death, superannuation and unemployment of the wage earner. But it is certain that the proceeds of even so large a charge as ten per cent of the average daily wage would, under present conditions, afford merely alleviation of and not indemnification for the losses now attendant upon those contingencies in the life of the workingman. The cost of providing complete indemnity would probably reach an amount equal to twenty-five per cent of the average daily wage. For the premiums requisite to secure indemnity from losses incident to sickness, accident, invalidity, premature death, or superannuation would probably aggregate fifteen per cent of the daily wage; while the average percentage required to indemnify for unemployment due to lack of work would probably rise above ten per cent.

The Huge Present Waste

This huge and apparently prohibitive expense should not, however, deter us from taking action now. It should on the contrary incite us to immediate and vigorous measures. Indeed it has in it elements of great encouragement. It will disclose how vast the waste incident to present social and industrial conditions is. And when the extent of that waste shall have been determined, and made clear to our people, a long step forward will have been taken on the road to improvement and resulting social economy.

Some idea of the possibilities of improvement in this connection are indicated by the following data:

Prof. Irving Fisher has compared the mortality record of the industrial life insurance companies which provide life insurance to the workingman in amounts of less than $500 on the weekly premium plan, with the mortality in the ordinary life insurance companies, in which the policies average $1,000 or more. The figures of deaths per year for each 1,000 persons insured are these:

INDUSTRIAL LIFE INSURANCE MORTALITY (METROPOLITAN LIFE EXPERIENCE)		ORDINARY LIFE INSURANCE MORTALITY (ENGLISH EXPERIENCE)
Age 20	10.5	7.3
25	14.1	7.8
35	17.2	9.3
55	35	21.7

The conditions under which that portion of our population lives and works who are insured in the ordinary life companies are far from ideal, and leave open a great opportunity for reduction of the death rate. But here we have an average death rate among the workingmen at their most productive age—25 to 35 years—which is nearly twice as great as the death rate among those engaged in other occupations. And this high death rate of the workingman is that of the average insured workingman, not the death rate of those engaged in extra hazardous trades.

Can there be any doubt that if this heavier mortality had to be adequately compensated for by the state, or the industries, and the insurance cost paid from current earnings, its causes would be adequately investigated, and the evil conditions of living and working which produce it would be remedied? Society and industry would find how much cheaper it is to conserve than to destroy.

The Economy of Humanity

How near at hand the remedy for high mortality lies is illustrated by the experience of the model factory village at Bourneville, near Birmingham. While the average death rate for all ages in England and Wales in the years 1902 to 1907 was 15.7, the death rate at Bourneville was 6.3; and yet the occupations of the inhabitants of Bourneville were fairly representative of the whole country. Over 50 per cent of the workers were factory hands; 36 per cent were mechanics, carpenters, brick layers and others of unclassified occupations, and about 13 per cent clerks and travelers.

Prof. Fisher concludes also that on the average every American is sick thirteen days in the year.

Possibilities of lengthening lives and avoiding sickness and invalidity, like the possibilities of preventing accidents, will be availed of when business as well as humanity demands it. . . .

Can there be any doubt that if every accident had to be carefully investigated and adequately compensated for, their number would be reduced to a half or a third.

Unnecessary Unemployment

And undoubtedly the paramount evil in the workingman's life,— irregularity of employment,—would yield in large measure to like treatment.

The New York Commission in its recent report on unemployment gives data from the Trade Unions showing "that organized workers lose on the average twenty per cent of their possible income through unemployment," and data from the charitable societies showing that "from 25 to 35 per cent of those who apply to them for relief every year have been brought to their destitute condition primarily through lack of work."

Some irregularity of employment is doubtless inevitable; but in the main irregularity is remediable. It has been overcome with great profit to both employer and employe in important businesses which have recognized the problem as one seriously demanding solution. Society and industry need only the necessary incentive to secure a great reduction in irregularity of employment. In the scientifically managed business irregularity tends to disappear. So far as it is irremediable it should be compensated for like the inevitable accident. . . .

Consider how great would be the incentive to humanize social and industrial conditions if the cost of inhuman conditions were not only made manifest, but had to be borne from day to day unless the inhuman conditions themselves were removed!

Mere description of the misery unnecessarily entailed by the inhuman conditions, mere statements of cost however clear and forceful, will fail to secure the removal of these inhuman conditions of industry and in the life of our people from which this misery springs. But if society and industry and the individual were made to pay from day to day the actual cost of the sickness, accident, invalidity, premature death or premature old age consequent upon excessive hours of labor or unhygienic conditions of work, of unnecessary risk, and of irregularity in employment, those evils would be rapidly reduced.

We need a comprehensive system of workingmen's insurance as an incentive to justice. We need it: "Lest we forget."

9

ANTI-SALOON LEAGUE
The Arguments Against Alcohol

Two speakers at the Sixteenth National Convention of the Anti-Saloon League of America, both clergymen, summarize the leading arguments against alcoholic beverages. Here again we find progressive concerns in a cluster—conservation, efficiency, opposition to "vice," and worries about the vigor of "the race."

Human Conservation

**BY REV. A. C. BANE, D.D.,
FINANCIAL SECRETARY OF
ANTI-SALOON LEAGUE OF AMERICA**

The greatest, noblest, bravest act ever performed for humanity's betterment, was when, just outside the gates of Jerusalem, Jesus died for man.

Had he died for his property, his liberty or his country, his sacrifice, however worthy, would have been forgotten by the modern historian; but the fact that he suffered and died for man makes his deed immortal. Love for mankind, devotion to human welfare, sacrifice for the people's good, these are the principles that will reflect that divine heart, and meet our modern social conditions.

Rev. A. C. Bane, "Human Conservation," *Proceedings of the Sixteenth National Convention of the Anti-Saloon League of America (1915)*, (Richmond, Ind. Anti-Saloon League, 1915), pp. 56–57; Rev. Wilbur F. Crafts, "The Five Fingers," *Proceedings*, pp. 244–47.

For several generations past the people of this nation and their public servants have made the dollar mark their coat of arms, they have followed gold, they have worshipped gold, they have served gold, and neglected human interests, and until recently most of our legislation has been in the interest of coin and commerce.

Cattle, sheep, hogs and horses, in the public marts of the nation, have been worth more than men. Stocks, bonds, houses, lands, crops and currency have had a higher value than boys and girls in the popular estimation. The government has been willing to furnish an expert to cure a hog of the cholera, a horse of the glanders, or a cow of tuberculosis, while permitting hundreds of human beings to die daily of neglect. But the time is rapidly approaching when we will think more of men and women than we do now of hogs; when we will cherish man as of superior value to mere things.

We are getting our eyes open to see Christ's value of humanity, as greater than that of all the material world, which estimate of value led the Eternal God to give up his life for man. This is evinced in the trend of all recent progressive legislation, which has been to protect human beings rather than dollars, and also in the many new organizations and efforts for the betterment of mankind.

SUPREME IMPORTANCE OF HUMAN WELFARE

In the consideration of every public question and problem of state craft, the query of supreme importance is, how does it affect the human weal, what influence will it have upon personal life and character?

There are numerous arguments that can be successfully used against the alcoholic liquor traffic.

We may argue against it that it debauches morals, wastes wealth, decreases efficiency, produces drunkards, and corrupts politics, but the overpowering argument against the traffic is, that it degenerates and destroys mankind.

There are many reasons that can be urged for its absolute Prohibition by legal enactment; we may urge its Prohibition on the ground that Prohibition will prevent crime, insanity and poverty; that it will save strength, health and wealth; that it will increase human efficiency, assure human safety and reduce taxation; but the supreme reason for the complete prohibition of the liquor traffic is found in the all inclusive statement: THE CONSERVATION OF HUMANITY. The present universal war on alcohol is a titanic struggle to save the human race.

We must realize that we are "our brothers' keeper," that we must "love our neighbor as ourself," that all legislation must have man's welfare in view. This vision is receiving modern consideration as never before; to save and conserve the whole man, in all his social relations, is the consummation for which the Christian world is now working.

Social sins, weaknesses, and imperfections; social waste, neglect and inequalities, are commanding public attention as never before. The people are studying the subject of poverty and wealth; the laboring man and woman and their safety, housing, recreations, and wages; the child and its welfare; motherhood; the social evil and all vice and crime; the home; personal health; efficiency; and good government. You cannot study these questions without facing the liquor traffic; you can see alcoholic liquor at every angle of these social problems; in fact the liquor traffic and habit will be found at the base of every social ill that curses humanity; John Barleycorn's face is reflected by every turn of the social mirror. The social ills of America and the world cannot be cured without abolishing the traffic in strong drink. We are almost ready to proclaim that Prohibition of the manufacture and sale of alcoholic liquors as the great "cure-all" for America's social woes.

The Five Fingers

**BY REV. WILBUR F. CRAFTS,
SUPERINTENDENT OF
INTERNATIONAL REFORM BUREAU,
WASHINGTON, D. C.**

And, now let me show to eye and ear the five fingers of the hand with which God is writing the doom of King Alcohol.

I. THE FINGER OF HYGIENE

...the strongest proof that alcoholic drinks injure health and shorten life is the testimony of life insurance.

The average length of life, as shown by experience of European insurance societies, indicates that the total abstainer at 20 years of age has expectation of 44 years of added life; average life 64 years.

The moderate drinker at 20 years of age has expectation of 31 years of added life; average life, 51 years.

The hard drinker at 20 years of age and after has expectation of 15 years of added life; average, 35 years; loss 29 years.

II. THE FINGER OF EFFICIENCY

Prof. G. Aschaffenberg's experiments, made on four printers on four consecutive days, shows the average loss of working ability due to alcohol to be about 9 per cent. Loss of working ability greatest in heaviest drinker; least in lightest drinker, but his work far short of expected.

The old argument for abstinence was that one who drinks may become a drunkard; the new argument is that only by abstinence can one reach the highest efficiency.

FOR EFFICIENCY AND SUCCESS, ABSTAIN.

III. THE FINGER OF HEREDITY

A man may be willing to fly the motto for himself: "A short life and a happy one," and risk both health and property for fuddle and fellowship, but not many who are fathers or mothers, or expect to be, will be indifferent when shown incontrovertible proofs that drinkers have fewer and weaker children than abstainers.

The investigation of 20 families by Prof. Demme, Bern, 1878–89, shows that in a total of 61 children of temperate families 50 were normal, 2 dwarfed and deformed, 2 backward, 2 with St. Vitus Dance, 5 died in infancy. But in a total of 57 children in 10 intemperate families, 10 were normal, 10 dwarfed and deformed, 7 idiotic, 5 epileptic, 25 died in infancy.

FOR THE SAKE OF THE CHILDREN, ABSTAIN.

IV. THE FINGER OF PATRIOTISM

In this connection we quote as of profound significance a statement of the Crown Prince of Sweden at the opening of the Good Templar Summer Festival, Hessellholm, 1910: "That nation which is first to free itself from the injuries effects of alcohol will thereby attain a marked advantage over other nations in the amicable, yet intensive, struggle for existence. I hope that our country will be the one which will first understand and secure this advantage."

In France also the patriotic argument is foremost. Long before the war, because France was a "dying nation," the government put up posters warning against tippling that falls short of drunkenness "for the future of the nation." Great Britain, too, takes up the patriotic argument, alarmed by the failure of 80 per cent of those who offered themselves for the Boer war to pass the examination.

The present war has made all open-minded men realize that patriotism calls for abstinence. The grandest achievement of the war is not some scene on the battlefield, but Russia's patriotic renunciation of intoxicants; and the meanest scene of the whole war is the refusal of the Anglican convocation at York to give up its clerical toddies even when Kitchener and the King led the way.

FOR THE SAKE OF OUR COUNTRY, ABSTAIN.

V. THE FINGER OF RACE DEGENERACY

Dr. J. H. Kellogg, of Battle Creek, pictures the decay of nations in a stereopticon lecture, by a series of six trees dying at the top. Bulgaria had the least dead wood, representing the fact that one person in every thousand in that country lives to pass the 100-year mark, and not a few live for half a century longer. The United States comes next, but with one centenarian in 25,000. Then the record grows worse and worse; Spain, 44,000; France, 190,000; England, 200,000; Germany, 700,000. It is not mere accident that the nation whose favorite drink is buttermilk stands at the head, while the nation which drinks eight times as much beer is the lowest in the line.

Alcohol is not alone responsible for race degeneracy. Sex abuses have done quite as much in the destruction of nations; and sins of ignorance and of willful indulgence in eating must take a share of the blame, and also tobacco and other habit-forming drugs that in less violent ways work with alcohol to undermine the health.

Sir Andrew Clark, physician to Queen Victoria, said that when he looked at the hospital wards, and saw that seven out of ten owed their diseases to alcohol, and when he thought of all the others evils wrought by drink he felt impelled to give up his profession, "To give up everything, and go forth upon a holy crusade, preaching to all men, 'Beware of this enemy of the race.' "

If we can not give up everything to do this grand and necessary work, surely we can give a little time, a little work, a little money, an earnest prayer, a few words, a good example, a temperance vote. FOR THE SAKE OF THE IMPERILED HUMAN RACE, ABSTAIN AND PROHIBIT.

10

NATIONAL AMERICAN WOMAN SUFFRAGE ASSOCIATION
Equality for Women

The volumes making up *The History of Woman Suffrage* (edited by several suffragettes, principally Elizabeth Cady Stanton, Susan B. Anthony, and Ida H. Harper), and in particular Volumes 4 (1883–1900) and 5 (1900–1920) are an indispensable source on the progressive movement. Reprinted below are various speeches given at conventions of the National American Woman Suffrage Association, and part of the Introduction to Volume 4, written by Susan B. Anthony and Ida H. Harper. They capture the seriousness and dedication that helped make this reform movement irresistible, and they also reveal how many diverse anxieties and hopes led these ladies to a single remedy.

National-American Convention of 1896

Miss Anthony closed with an earnest appeal that the committee would report in favor of a Sixteenth Amendment to the Constitution, thus enabling the women to carry their case to the Legislatures of the different States instead of to the masses of voters. She

Susan B. Anthony and Ida. H. Harper, eds., *The History of Woman Suffrage: 1883–1900*, Vol. 4 (Rochester: Charles Mann, 1902), pp. 268–69; Ida H. Harper, ed., *The History of Woman Suffrage: 1900–1920*, Vol. 5 (National American Woman Suffrage Association, 1922), pp. 82–83, 178–79, 352–53; Vol. 4, "Introduction," pp. xxii–xxiv, xxxiii.

then submitted for publication and distribution the address of Mrs. Stanton, which said in part:

> Could we resurrect from the archives of this Capitol all the petitions and speeches presented here by women for human freedom during this century, they would reach above this dome and make a more fitting pedestal for the Goddess of Liberty than the crowning point of an edifice beneath which the mother of the race has so long pleaded in vain for her natural right of self-government—a right her sons should have secured to her long ago of their own free will by statutes carved indelibly on the corner-stones of the Republic.. . . .
>
> As arguments have thus far proved unavailing, may not appeals to your feelings, to your moral sense, find the response so long withheld by your reason? Allow me, honorable gentlemen, to paint you a picture and bring within the compass of your vision at once the comparative position of two classes of citizens: The central object is a ballot box guarded by three inspectors of foreign birth. On the right is a multitude of coarse, ignorant beings, designated in our constitutions as male citizens—many of them fresh from the steerage of incoming steamers. There, too, are natives of the same type from the slums of our cities. Policemen are respectfully guiding them all to the ballot box. Those who can not stand, because of their frequent potations, are carefully supported on either side, each in turn depositing his vote, for what purpose he neither knows nor cares, except to get the promised bribe.
>
> On the left stand a group of intelligent, moral, highly-cultivated women, whose ancestors for generations have fought the battles of liberty and have made this country all it is to-day. These come from the schools and colleges as teachers and professors; from the press and pulpit as writers and preachers; from the courts and hospitals as lawyers and physicians; and from happy and respectable homes as honored mothers, wives and sisters. Knowing the needs of humanity subjectively in all the higher walks of life, and objectively in the world of work, in the charities, in the asylums and prisons, in the sanitary condition of our streets and public buildings, they are peculiarly fitted to write, speak and vote intelligently on all these questions of such vital, far-reaching consequence to the welfare of society. But the inspectors refuse their votes because they are not designated in the Constitution as "male" citizens, and the policemen drive them away.
>
> Sad and humiliated they retire to their respective abodes, followed by the jeers of those in authority. Imagine the feelings of these dignified women, returning to their daily round of duties, compelled to leave their interests, public and private, in the State and the home, to these ignorant masses. The most grievous result of war to the conquered is wearing a foreign yoke, yet this is the position of the daughters of the Puritans. . . .
>
> What a dark page the present political position of women will be for the future historian! In reading of the republics of Greece and

Rome and the grand utterances of their philosophers in pæans to liberty, we wonder that under such governments there should have been a class of citizens held in slavery. Our descendants will be still more surprised to know that our disfranchised citizens, our pariahs, our slaves, belonged to the most highly educated, moral, virtuous class in the nation, women of wealth and position who paid millions of taxes every year into the State and national treasuries; women who had given thousands to build colleges and churches and to encourage the sciences and arts. From the dawn of creation to this hour history affords no other instance of so large a class of such a character subordinated politically to the ignorant masses.

The National American Convention of 1903

The address of Miss Belle Kearney, Mississippi's famous orator, was a leading feature of the last evening's program—The South and Woman Suffrage . . . . The address closed as follows:

The enfranchisement of women would insure immediate and durable white supremacy, honestly attained, for upon unquestioned authority it is stated that in every southern State but one there are more educated women than all the illiterate voters, white and black, native and foreign, combined. As you probably know, of all the women in the South who can read and write, ten out of every eleven are white. When it comes to the proportion of property between the races, that of the white outweighs that of the black immeasurably. The South is slow to grasp the great fact that the enfranchisement of women would settle the race question in politics. The civilization of the North is threatened by the influx of foreigners with their imported customs; by the greed of monopolistic wealth and the unrest among the working classes; by the strength of the liquor traffic and encroachments upon religious belief. Some day the North will be compelled to look to the South for redemption from those evils on account of the purity of its Anglo-Saxon blood, the simplicity of its social and economic structure, the great advance in prohibitory law and the maintenance of the sanctity of its faith, which has been kept inviolate. Just as surely as the North will be forced to turn to the South for the nation's salvation, just so surely will the South be compelled to look to its Anglo-Saxon women as the medium through which to retain the supremacy of the white race over the African.

National American Convention of 1906

It was at this meeting that Miss Jane Addams of Hull House, Chicago, made the address on The Modern City and the

Municipal Franchise for Women, which was thenceforth a part of the standard suffrage literature. Quotations are wholly inadequate.

It has been well said that the modern city is a stronghold of industrialism quite as the feudal city was a stronghold of militarism, but the modern cities fear no enemies and rivals from without and their problems of government are solely internal. Affairs for the most part are going badly in these great new centres, in which the quickly-congregated population has not yet learned to arrange its affairs satisfactorily. Unsanitary housing, poisonous sewage, contaminated water, infant mortality, the spread of contagion, adulterated food, impure milk, smoke-laden air, ill-ventilated factories, dangerous occupations, juvenile crime, unwholesome crowding, prostitution and drunkenness are the enemies which the modern cities must face and overcome, would they survive. Logically their electorate should be made up of those who can bear a valiant part in this arduous contest, those who in the past have at least attempted to care for children, to clean houses, to prepare foods, to isolate the family from moral dangers; those who have traditionally taken care of that side of life which inevitably becomes the subject of municipal consideration and control as soon as the population is congested. To test the elector's fitness to deal with this situation by his ability to bear arms is absurd. These problems must be solved, if they are solved at all, not from the military point of view, not even from the industrial point of view, but from a third, which is rapidly developing in all the great cities of the world—the human-welfare point of view....

City housekeeping has failed partly because women, the traditional housekeepers, have not been consulted as to its multiform activities. The men have been carelessly indifferent to much of this civic housekeeping, as they have always been indifferent to the details of the household....The very multifariousness and complexity of a city government demand the help of minds accustomed to detail and variety of work, to a sense of obligation for the health and welfare of young children and to a responsibility for the cleanliness and comfort of other people. Because all these things have traditionally been in the hands of women, if they take no part in them now they are not only missing the education which the natural participation in civic life would bring to them but they are losing what they have always had.

National American Convention of 1912

Mrs. Jean Nelson Penfield, chairman of the Woman Suffrage Party of New York numbering 60,000 members, said in part:

The dominant thought in the world today is that of conservation; the tendency of the whole business world is toward economy. How to lessen the cost of production, how to improve the machinery of business so as to reduce friction—these are the questions that are being asked not only in the business world but in the affairs of state. No intelligent man in this scientific day would try to do anything by an indirect and wasteful method if he could accomplish his purpose by a direct and economic method. Even the bricklayer is taught how to handle his bricks so that the best results may be secured at the least possible expenditure of time and energy. Women alone seem to represent a great body of energy, vitality and talent which is unconserved, unutilized and recklessly wasted. If a man wants reforms he goes armed with a vote to the ballot box and even to the Legislature with that power of the vote behind him; but if women want these things they are asked to take the long, questionable, roundabout route of personal influence, of petition, of indirection. Women have accomplished a great deal in this way but it has required a long time.... Take, for instance, one class of work—the establishment of manual training, domestic science, open-air schools, school gardens and playgrounds—all once just "women's notions" but now established institutions. Women have to found and finance and demonstrate them before municipalities would have anything to do with them, but when city or State adopts these institutions the management is immediately and entirely taken out of the hands of women and placed in the hands of men....

Among thinking women there is a growing consciousness of being cut off, shut out from the civic life in which they have an equal stake with men. We ask you to recognize that the time is here for you to submit an amendment to the States for ratification which will give women the influence and power of the suffrage.

Aside from all political hostility, however, woman suffrage has to face a tremendous opposition from other sources. The attitude of a remonstrant is the natural one of the vast majority of people. Their first cry on coming into the world, if translated, would be, "I object." They are opposed on principle to every innovation, and the greatest of these is the enfranchisement of women. To grant woman an equality with man in the affairs of life is contrary to every tradition, every precedent, every inheritance, every instinct and every teaching. The acceptance of this idea is possible only to those of especially progressive tendencies and a strong sense of justice, and it is yet too soon to expect these from the majority. If it had been necessary to have the consent of the majority of the men in every State for women to enter the universities, to control their own property, to engage in the various professions and occupations, to speak from the public platform and to form great organizations, in not one would they be enjoying these privileges to-day. It is very probable that this would be equally true if they had depended upon the permission of a majority of women themselves. They are more conservative even than men, because of the narrowness and isolation of their lives, the subjection in which they always have been held, the severe punishment inflicted by society on those who dare step outside the prescribed sphere, and, stronger than all, perhaps, their religious tendencies through which it has been impressed upon them that their subordinate position was assigned by the Divine will and that to rebel against it is to defy the Creator. In all the generations, Church, State and society have combined to retard the development of women, with the inevitable result that those of every class are narrower, more bigoted and less progressive than the men of that class.

While the girls are crowding the colleges now until they threaten to exceed the number of boys, the demand for the higher education was made by the merest handful of women and granted by an equally small number of men, who, on the boards of trustees, were able to do so, but it would have been deferred for decades if it had depended on a popular vote of either men or women. The pioneers in the professions found their most trying opposition from other women, instigated by the men who did their thinking for them to believe that the whole sex was being disgraced. Married women almost universally were opposed to laws which would give them control of their property, being assured by their masculine advisers that this would deprive them of the love and protection of their husbands. Public sentiment was wholly opposed to these laws and no such objections ever have been made in Legislatures even to woman suffrage as were urged against allowing a wife to own property. The contest was won by the smallest fraction of women and a few strong, far-seeing men, the latter actuated not alone by a sentiment of justice but also by the desire of preventing husbands from squandering the property which fathers had accumulated and wished to secure to their daughters, and fortunate indeed was it that this action did not have to be ratified by the voters.

There are in the United States between three and four million women engaged in wage-earning occupations outside of domestic service. Would this be possible had they been obliged to have the duly recorded permission of a majority of all the men over twenty-one years old? If the question were submitted to the votes of these men to-day whether women should be allowed to continue in these employments and enter any and all others, would it be carried in the affirmative in a single State?

And yet this prejudiced, conservative and in a degree ignorant and vicious electorate possesses absolutely the power to withhold the suffrage from women. A large part of it is composed of foreign-born men, bringing from the Old World the most primitive ideas of the degraded position which properly belongs to woman. Another part is addicted to habits with which it never would give women the chance to interfere. Boys of twenty-one form another portion, fully imbued with a belief in woman's inferiority which only experience can eradicate. Men of the so-called working classes vote against it because they fear to add to the power of the so-called aristocracy. The latter oppose it because they think the suffrage already has been too widely extended and ought to be curtailed instead of expanded. The old fogies cast a negative ballot because they believe woman ought to be kept in her "sphere," and the strictly orthodox because it is not authorized by the Scriptures. A large body who are "almost persuaded," but have some lingering doubts as to the "expediency," satisfy their consciences for voting "no" by saying that the women of their family and acquaintance do not want it. Thus is the most valuable of human rights—the right of individual representation—made the football of Legislatures, the shuttlecock of voters, kicked and tossed like the veriest plaything in utter disregard of the vital fact that it is the one principle above all others on which the Government is founded. . . .

But have we not reason to hope, in this era of rapid fulfilment—when in all material things electricity is accomplishing in a day what required months under the old régime—that moral progress will keep pace? And that as much stronger as the electric power has shown itself than the coarse and heavy forces of the stone ard iron periods, so much superior will prove the *noblesse oblige* of the men and women of the present, achieving in a generation what was not possible to the narrow selfishness and ignorant prejudice of all the past ages?

A part of the magnificent plan to beautify Washington, the capital of the nation, is a colossal statue to American Womanhood. The design embodies a great arch of marble standing on a base in the form of an oval and broken by sweeps of steps. On either side are large bronze panels, bearing groups of figures. One of these will be a symbolic design showing the spirit of the people descending to lay offerings on woman's altar. Lofty pillars crowned by figures representing Victory, are to be placed at the approaches. Surmounting the arch will be the chief group of the composition, symbolizing Woman Glorified. She is rising from her throne to greet War and Peace, Literature and Art, Science and Industry, who approach to lay homage at her feet. Inside the arch is a memorial hall for recording the achievements of women.

How soon this symbol shall become reality and woman stand forth in all the glory of freedom to reach her highest stature, depends upon the use she makes of the opportunities already hers and the fraternal assistance she receives from man. Fearless of criticism, courageous in faith, let each take for a guide these inspiring words which it has been said the Puritan of old would utter if he could speak: "I was a radical in my day; be thou the same in thine! I turned my back upon the old tyrannies and heresies and struck for the new liberties and beliefs; my liberty and my belief are doubtless already tyranny and heresy to thine age; strike thou for the new!"

11

EDWARD M. HOUSE
Philip Dru, Administrator

Colonel Edward M. House, the Texan who became Woodrow Wilson's closest friend and an important adviser in foreign affairs, wrote a novel as a young man which was published in 1912 as *Philip Dru, Administrator.* It projected every progressive's guiding aspiration for himself, or his expectation of the new leadership coming forward, or both. Philip Dru, courageous, honest, and far-sighted (where earlier political figures had been corruptible and without national vision), rises to the presidency in a time of internal turmoil and external threat, and saves the nation by an unconquerable blend of efficiency, patriotism, strong leadership, dedication to the essentials of democratic politics, and a kindly defense of the downtrodden. In this otherwise undistinguished novel,

Edward M. House, *Philip Dru, Administrator* (New York: Ben Huebsch, 1912), pp. 56–59.

House uttered the reigning fantasy of his day—that all problems yielded to inspired leadership under true principles. In the selection below Dru sketches his social creed. As with so many reformers, he bases his argument on efficiency rather than some less reliable idea, such as justice.

After sifting the offers made him, Philip finally accepted two, one from a large New York daily that syndicated throughout the country, and one from a widely read magazine, to contribute a series of twelve articles. Both the newspaper and the magazine wished to dictate the subject matter about which he was to write, but he insisted upon the widest latitude. The sum paid, and to be paid, seemed to him out of proportion to the service rendered, but he failed to take into account the value of the advertising to those who had secured the use of his pen.

He accepted the offers not alone because he must needs do something for a livelihood, but largely for the good he thought he might do the cause to which he was enlisted. He determined to write upon social subjects only, though he knew that this would be a disappointment to his publishers. He wanted to write an article or two before he began his permanent work, for if he wrote successfully, he thought it would add to his influence. So he began immediately, and finished his first contribution to the syndicate newspapers in time for them to use it the following Sunday.

He told in a simple way, the story of the Turners. In conclusion he said the rich and the well-to-do were as a rule charitable enough when distress came to their doors, but the trouble was that they were unwilling to seek it out. They knew that it existed but they wanted to come in touch with it as little as possible.

They smothered their consciences with the thought that there were organized societies and other mediums through which all poverty was reached, and to these they gave. They knew that this was not literally true, but it served to make them think less badly of themselves.

In a direct and forceful manner, he pointed out that our civilization was fundamentally wrong inasmuch as among other things, it restricted efficiency; that if society were properly organized, there would be none who were not sufficiently clothed and fed; that the laws, habits and ethical training in vogue were alike responsible for the inequalities in opportunity and the consequent wide difference between the few

*and the many; that the result of such conditions was to render ineffi-
cient a large part of the population, the percentage differing in each
country in the ratio that education and enlightened and unselfish laws
bore to ignorance, bigotry and selfish laws.* But little progress, he said,
had been made in the early centuries for the reason that opportunity
had been confined to a few, and it was only recently that any considerable part of the world's population had been in a position to
become efficient; and mark the result. Therefore, he argued, as an
economical proposition, divorced from the realm of ethics, the far-
sighted statesmen of to-morrow, if not of to-day, will labor to the
end that every child born of woman may have an opportunity to
accomplish that for which it is best fitted. Their bodies will be
properly clothed and fed at the minimum amount of exertion, so that
life may mean something more than a mere struggle for existence.
Humanity as a whole will then be able to do its share towards the
conquest of the complex forces of nature, and there will be brought
about an intellectual and spiritual quickening that will make our
civilization of to-day seem as crude, as selfish and illogical as that
of the dark ages seem now to us.

Philip's article was widely read and was the subject of much comment, favorable and otherwise. There were the ever-ready few, who
want to re-make the world in a day, that objected to its moderation,
and there were his more numerous critics who hold that to those that
have, more should be given. These considered his doctrine dangerous
to the general welfare, meaning their own welfare. But upon the
greater number it made a profound impression, and it awakened many
a sleeping conscience as was shown by the hundreds of letters which
he received from all parts of the country. All this was a tremendous
encouragement to the young social worker, for the letters he received
showed him that he had a definite public to address, whom he might
lead if he could keep his medium for a time at least. Naturally, the
publishers of the newspaper and magazines for which he wrote understood this, but they also understood that it was usually possible to
control intractable writers after they had acquired a taste for publicity, and their attitude was for the time being one of general
enthusiasm and liberality tempered by such trivial attempts at control
as had already been made.

No sooner had he seen the first story in print than he began for-
mulating his ideas for a second.

12

THEODORE ROOSEVELT
Annual Message, 1908

The message to Congress of December 8, 1908, went farther in criticism of the existing social arrangements and in proposing reforms than any utterance of Roosevelt during his presidency. In it he spoke not only of control of corporations, but of the supervision of securities issuance, the abolition of child labor, the reform of taxation, and a national workmen's compensation law. He would not go much beyond these measures in 1912, although an angrier tone would make him appear in that campaign a much more radical figure than he had been as president. This section of Roosevelt's message presents his idea of the proper relation between large business enterprise and the state, a concept of extensive regulation of large, even monopolistic corporations by a vigorous national government. This concept, later the cornerstone of the New Nationalism, appealed to many progressives and businessmen who found the other progressive approach, a return to competition through antitrust action, to be negative and reactionary, a threat to the gains in efficiency and stability that industrial concentration was bringing. Roosevelt's statement on the matter in the 1908 message is probably a better source than his campaign speeches in 1912, since it is more cautious and more solicitous of the capitalistic ethic. Roosevelt in 1912 sounded a bit dangerous, and of course government regulation could indeed have threatened profits, but the statement of 1908 rings with a friendliness to business interests that accurately foretold the future of federal regulation.

Corporations

As regards the great corporations engaged in interstate business, and especially the railroad, I can only repeat what I have already again and again said in my messages to the Congress. I believe that under the interstate clause of the Constitution the United States has complete and paramount right to control all agencies of interstate commerce; and I believe that the National Government alone can exercise this right with wisdom and effectiveness so as both

---

Theodore Roosevelt, Annual Message of 1908, U. S. Congress, *Congressional Record*, Vol. 43, Part I, pp. 16–28 (8 December 1908).

to secure justice from, and to do justice to, the great corporations which are the most important factors in modern business. I believe that it is worse than folly to attempt to prohibit all combinations as is done by the Sherman antitrust law, because such a law can be enforced only imperfectly and unequally, and its enforcement works almost as much hardship as good. I strongly advocate that instead of an unwise effort to prohibit all combinations there shall be substituted a law which shall expressly permit combinations which are in the interest of the public, but shall at the same time give to some agency of the National Government full power of control and supervision over them. One of the chief features of this control should be securing entire publicity in all matters which the public has a right to know, and furthermore, the power, not by judicial but by executive action, to prevent or put a stop to every form of improper favoritism or other wrong-doing. . . .

It is hard to say whether most damage to the country at large would come from entire failure on the part of the public to supervise and control the actions of the great corporations, or from the exercise of the necessary governmental power in a way which would do injustice and wrong to the corporations. Both the preachers of an unrestricted individualism, and the preachers of an oppression which would deny to able men of business the just reward of their initiative and business sagacity, are advocating policies that would be fraught with the gravest harm to the whole country. To permit every lawless capitalist, every law-defying corporation, to take any action, no matter how iniquitous, in the effort to secure an improper profit and to build up privilege, would be ruinous to the Republic and would mark the abandonment of the effort to secure in the industrial world the spirit of democratic fair dealing. On the other hand, to attack these wrongs in that spirit of demagogy which can see wrong only when committed by the man of wealth, and is dumb and blind in the presence of wrong committed against men of property or by men of no property, is exactly as evil as corruptly to defend the wrong-doing of men of wealth. The war we wage must be waged against misconduct, against wrong-doing wherever it is found; and we must stand heartily for the rights of every decent man, whether he be a man of great wealth or a man who earns his livelihood as a wage-worker or a tiller of the soil.

It is to the interest of all of us that there should be a premium put upon individual initiative and individual capacity, and an ample reward for the great directing intelligences alone competent to manage the great business operations of to-day. It is well to keep in mind that exactly as the anarchist is the worst enemy of liberty and the reactionary the worst enemy of order, so the men who defend the rights of property have most to fear from the wrong-doers of great wealth, and the men who are championing popular rights have most to fear from the demagogues who in the name of popular rights would do wrong to and oppress honest business men, honest men of wealth; for the success of either type of wrong-doer necessarily invites a violent reaction against the cause the wrong-doer nominally upholds. In point of danger to the nation there is nothing to choose between on the one hand the corruptionist, the bribe-giver, the bribe-taker, the man who employs his great talent to swindle his fellow citizens on a large scale, and, on the other hand, the preacher of class hatred, the man who, whether from ignorance or from willingness to sacrifice his country to his ambition, persuades well-meaning but wrong-headed men to try to destroy the instruments upon which our prosperity mainly rests. Let each group of men beware of and guard against the shortcomings to which that group is itself most liable. Too often we see the business community in a spirit of unhealthy class consciousness deplore the effort to hold to account under the law the wealthy men who in their management of great corporations, whether railroads, street-railways, or other industrial enterprises, have behaved in a way that revolts the conscience of the plain, decent people. Such an attitude cannot be condemned too severely, for men of property should recognize that they jeopardize the rights of property when they fail heartily to join in the effort to do away with the abuses of wealth. On the other hand, those who advocate proper control on behalf of the public, through the State, of these great corporations, and of the wealth engaged on a giant scale in business operations, must ever keep in mind that unless they do scrupulous justice to the corporation, unless they permit ample profit, and cordially encourage capable men of business so long as they act with honesty, they are striking at the root of our national well being; for in the long run, under the mere pressure of material distress, the people as a whole would probably go back to the reign of an unrestricted individualism rather than submit to a control by the State so drastic and so foolish, conceived in a spirit of such unreasonable and narrow hostility to wealth, as to prevent business operations from being profitable, and therefore to bring ruin upon the entire business community, and ultimately upon the entire body of citizens.

The opposition to government control of these great corporations makes its most effective effort in the shape of an appeal to the old doctrine of States' rights. Of course there are many sincere men who now believe in unrestricted individualism in business, just as there were formerly many sincere men who believed in slavery—that is, in the unrestricted right of an individual to own another individual. These men do not by themselves have great weight, however. The effective fight against adequate government control and supervision of individual, and especially of corporate, wealth engaged in interstate business is chiefly done under cover; and especially under cover of an appeal to States' rights. It is not at all infrequent to read in the same speech a denunciation of predatory wealth fostered by special privilege and defiant of both the public welfare and law of the land, and a denunciation of centralization in the centralized and organized wealth. Of course the policy set forth in such twin denunciations amounts to absolutely nothing, for the first half is nullified by the second half. The chief reason, among the many sound and compelling reasons, that led to the formation of the National Government was the absolute need that the Union, and not the several States, should deal with interstate and foreign commerce; and the power to deal with interstate commerce was granted absolutely and plenarily to the central government and was exercised completely as regards the only instruments of interstate commerce known in those days—the waterways, the highroads, as well as the partnerships of individuals who then conducted all of what business there was. Interstate commerce is now chiefly conducted by railroads; and the great corporation has supplanted the mass of small partnerships or individuals. The proposal to make the National Government supreme over, and therefore to give it complete control over, the railroads and other instruments of interstate commerce is merely a proposal to carry out to the letter one of the prime purposes, if not the prime purpose, for which the Constitution was founded. It does not represent centralization. It represents merely the acknowledgment of the patent fact that centralization has already come in business. If this irresponsible outside business power is to be controlled in the interest of the general public it can only be controlled in one way—by giving adequate power of control to the one sovereignty capable of exercising such power—the National Government. Forty or fifty separate State governments cannot exercise that power over corporations doing business in most or all of them; first, because they absolutely lack the authority to deal with interstate business in any form; and second, because of the inevitable conflict of authority sure to arise in the effort to enforce different kinds of State regulation, often inconsistent with one another and sometimes oppressive in themselves. Such divided authority cannot regulate commerce with wisdom and effect. The central government is the only power which, without oppression, can nevertheless thoroughly and adequately control and supervise the large corporations. To abandon the effort for national control means to abandon the effort for all adequate control and yet to render likely continual bursts of action by States legislatures, which cannot achieve the purpose sought for, but which can do a great deal of damage to the corporation without conferring any real benefit on the public. . . .

Those who believe in efficient national control, on the other hand, do not in the least object to combinations; do not in the least object to concentration in business administration. On the contrary, they favor both, with the all-important proviso that there shall be such publicity about their workings, and such thoroughgoing control over them, as to insure their being in the interest, and not against the interest, of the general public. We do not object to the concentration of wealth and administration; but we do believe in the distribution of the wealth in profits to the real owners, and in securing to the public the full benefit of the concentrated administration. We believe that with concentration in administration there can come both the advantage of a larger ownership and of a more equitable distribution of profits, and at the same time a better service to the commonwealth. We believe that the administration should be for the benefit of the many; and that greed and rascality, practised on a large scale, should be punished as relentlessly as if practiced on a small scale.

We do not for a moment believe that the problem will be solved by any short and easy method. The solution will come only by pressing various concurrent remedies. Some of these remedies must lie outside the domain of all government. Some must lie outside the domain of the Federal Government. But there is legislation which the Federal Government alone can enact and which is absolutely vital in order to secure the attainment of our purpose. Many laws are needed. There should be regulation by the National Government of the great inter-state corporations, including a simple method of account-keeping, publicity, supervision of the issue of securities, abolition of rebates, and of special privileges. There should be short-time franchises for all corporations engaged in public business; including the corporations which get power from water rights. There should be national as well as State guardianship of mines and forests. The labor legislation herein-after referred to should concurrently be enacted into law.

To accomplish this, means of course a certain increase in the use of —not the creation of—power, by the central government. The power already exists; it does not have to be created; the only question is whether it shall be used or left idle—and meanwhile the corporations over which the power ought to be exercised will not remain idle. Let those who object to this increase in the use of the only power available, the national power, be frank, and admit openly that they propose to abandon any effort to control the great business corporations and to exercise supervision over the accumulation and distribution of wealth; for such supervision and control can only come through this particular kind of increase of power. We no more believe in that empiricism which demands absolutely unrestrained individualism than we do in that empiricism which clamors for a deadening socialism which would destroy all individual initiative and would run the country with a completeness that not even an unrestrained individualism itself could achieve. The danger to American democracy lies not in the least in the concentration of administrative power in responsible and accountable hands. It lies in having the power insufficiently concentrated, so that no one can be held responsible to the people for its use. Concentrated power is palpable, visible, responsible, easily reached, quickly held to account. Power scattered through many administrators, many legis-lators, many men who work behind and through legislators and admin-istrators, is impalpable, is unseen, is irresponsible, cannot be reached, cannot be held to account. Democracy is in peril wherever the admin-istration of political power is scattered among a variety of men who work in secret, whose very names are unknown to the common people. It is not in peril from any man who derives authority from the people, who exercises it in sight of the people, and who is from time to time compelled to give an account of its exercise to the people.

Labor

There are many matters affecting labor and the status of the wage-worker to which I should like to draw your attention, but an exhaustive discussion of the problem in all its aspects is not now necessary. This administration is nearing its end; and, moreover, under our form of government the solution of the problem depends upon the action of the States as much as upon the action of the nation. Nevertheless, there are certain considerations which I wish to set before you, because I hope that our people will more and more keep them in mind. A blind and ignorant resistance to every effort for the reform of abuses and for the readjustment of society to modern industrial conditions represents not true conservatism, but an incitement to the wildest radicalism; for wise radicalism and wise conservatism go hand in hand, one bent on progress, the other bent on seeing that no change is make unless in the right direction. I believe in a steady effort, or perhaps it would be more accurate to say in steady efforts in many different directions, to bring about a condition of affairs under which the men who work with hand or with brain, the laborers, the superintendents, the men who produce for the market and the men who find a market for the articles produced, shall own a far greater share than at present of the wealth they produce, and be enabled to invest it in the tools and instruments by which all work is carried on. As far as possible I hope to see a frank recognition of the advantages conferred by machinery, organization, and division of labor, accompanied by an effort to bring about a larger share in the ownership by wage-worker of railway, mill, and factory. In farming, this simply means that we wish to see the farmer own his own land; we do not wish to see the farms so large that they become the property of absentee landlords who farm them by tenants, nor yet so small that the farmer becomes like a European peasant. Again, the depositors in our savings-banks now number over one-tenth of our entire population. These are all capitalists, who through the savings-banks loan their money to the workers—that is, in many cases to themselves—to carry on their various industries. The more we increase their number, the more we introduce the principle of co-operation into our industry. Every increase in the number of small stockholders in corporations is a good thing, for the same reasons; and where the employees are the stockholders the result is particularly good. Very much of this movement must be outside of anying that can be accomplished by legislation; but legislation can do a good deal. Postal savings-banks will make it easy for the poorest to keep their savings in absolute safety. The regulation of the national highways must be such that they shall serve all people with equal justice. Corporate finances must be supervised so as to make it far safer than at present for the man of small means to invest his money in stocks. There must be prohibition of child labor, diminution of woman labor, shortening of hours of all mechanical labor; stock watering should be prohibited, and stock gambling so far as is possible discouraged. There should be a progressive inheritance tax on large fortunes. Industrial education should be encouraged. As far as possible we should lighten the burden of taxation on the small man. We should put a premium upon thrift, hard work, and business energy; but these qualities cease to be the main factors in accumulating a fortune long before that fortune reaches a point where it would be seriously affected by any inheritance tax such as I propose. It is eminently right that the nation should fix the terms upon which the great fortunes are inherited. They rarely do good and they often do harm to those who inherit them in their entirety.

13

WOODROW WILSON
The First Inaugural

Wilson's First Inaugural Address was delivered on March 4, 1913. The speech fuses virtually every theme of the progressive movement—rededication to old ideals, moral passion, a concern for the unfortunate, alarm at the waste of natural resources, the need for an activist government. It is an unsurpassable distillation of the progressive spirit.

My fellow citizens:

There has been a change of government. It began two years ago, when the House of Representatives became Democratic by a decisive

Woodrow Wilson, First Inaugural Address, U. S. Congress, *Congressional Record*, Vol. 50, Part I, pp. 2–3 (4 March 1913).

majority. It has now been completed. The Senate about to assemble will also be Democratic. The offices of President and Vice-President have been put into the hands of Democrats. What does the change mean? That is the question that is uppermost in our minds to-day. That is the question I am going to try to answer, in order, if I may, to interpret the occasion.

It means much more than the mere success of a party. The success of a party means little except when the Nation is using that party for a large and definite purpose. No one can mistake the purpose for which the Nation now seeks to use the Democratic Party. It seeks to use it to interpret a change in its own plans and point of view. Some old things with which we had grown familiar, and which had begun to creep into the very habit of our thought and of our lives, have altered their aspect as we have latterly looked critically upon them, with fresh, awakened eyes; have dropped their disguises and shown themselves alien and sinister. Some new things, as we look frankly upon them, willing to comprehend their real character, have come to assume the aspect of things long believed in and familiar, stuff of our own convictions. We have been refreshed by a new insight into our own life.

We see that in many things that life is very great. It is incomparably great in its material aspects, in its body of wealth, in the diversity and sweep of its energy, in the industries which have been conceived and built up by the genius of individual men and the limitless enterprise of groups of men. It is great, also, very great, in its moral force.

Nowhere else in the world have noble men and women exhibited in more striking forms the beauty and the energy of sympathy and helpfulness and counsel in their efforts to rectify wrong, alleviate suffering, and set the weak in the way of strength and hope. We have built up, moreover, a great system of government, which has stood through a long age as in many respects a model for those who seek to set liberty upon foundations that will endure against fortuitous change, against storm and accident. Our life contains every great thing, and contains it in rich abundance.

But the evil has come with the good, and much fine gold has been corroded. With riches has come inexcusable waste. We have squandered a great part of what we might have used, and have not stopped to conserve the exceeding bounty of nature, without which our genius for enterprise would have been worthless and impotent, scorning to be careful, shamefully prodigal as well as admirably efficient. We have been proud of our industrial achievements, but we have not hitherto stopped thoughtfully enough to count the human cost, the cost of lives snuffed out, of energies overtaxed and broken, the fearful physical and spiritual cost to the men and women and children upon whom the dead weight and burden of it all has fallen pitilessly the years through. The groans and agony of it all had not yet reached our ears, the solemn, moving undertone of our life, coming up out of the mines and factories and out of every home where the struggle had its intimate and familiar seat. With the great Government went many deep secret things which we too long delayed to look into and scrutinize with candid, fearless eyes. The great Government we loved has too often been made use of for private and selfish purposes, and those who used it had forgotten the people.

At last a vision has been vouchsafed us of our life as a whole. We see the bad with the good, the debased and decadent with the sound and vital. With this vision we approach new affairs. Our duty is to cleanse, to reconsider, to restore, to correct the evil without impairing the good, to purify and humanize every process of our common life without weakening or sentimentalizing it. There has been something crude and heartless and unfeeling in our haste to succeed and be great. Our thought has been "Let every man look out for himself, let every generation look out for itself," while we reared giant machinery which made it impossible that any but those who stood at the levers of control should have a chance to look out for themselves. We had not forgotten our morals. We remembered well enough that we had set up a policy which was meant to serve the humblest as well as the most powerful, with an eye single to the standards of justice and fair play, and remembered it with pride. But we were very heedless and in a hurry to be great.

We have come now to the sober second thought. The scales of heedlessness have fallen from our eyes. We have made up our minds to square every process of our national life again with the standards we so proudly set up at the beginning and have always carried at our hearts. Our work is a work of restoration.

We have itemized with some degree of particularity the things that ought to be altered and here are some of the chief items: A tariff which cuts us off from our proper part in the commerce of the world, violates the just principles of taxation, and makes the Government a facile instrument in the hands of private interests; a banking and currency system based upon the necessity of the Government to sell its bonds fifty years ago and perfectly adapted to concentrating cash and restricting credits; an industrial system which, take it on all its sides, financial as well as administrative, holds capital in leading strings, restricts the liberties and limits the opportunities of labor, and exploits without renewing or conserving the natural resources of the country; a body of agricultural activities never yet given the efficiency of great business undertakings or served as it should be through the instrumentality of science taken directly to the farm, or afforded the facilities of credit best suited to its practical needs; watercourses undeveloped, waste places unreclaimed, forests untended, fast disappearing without plan or prospect of renewal, unregarded waste heaps at every mine. We have studied as perhaps no other nation has the most effective means of production, but we have not studied cost or economy as we should either as organizers of industry, as statesmen, or as individuals.

Nor have we studied and perfected the means by which government may be put at the service of humanity, in safeguarding the health of the Nation, the health of its men and its women and its children, as well as their rights in the struggle for existence. This is no sentimental duty. The firm basis of government is justice, not pity. These are matters of justice. There can be no equality of opportunity, the first essential of justice in the body politic, if men and women and children be not shielded in their lives, their very vitality, from the consequences of great industrial and social processes which they can not alter, control, or singly cope with. Society must see to it that it does not itself crush or weaken or damage its own constituent parts. The first duty of law is to keep sound the society it serves. Sanitary laws, pure food laws, and laws determining conditions of labor which individuals are powerless to determine for themselves are intimate parts of the very business of justice and legal efficiency.

These are some of the things we ought to do, and not leave the others undone, the old-fashioned, never-to-be-neglected, fundamental safeguarding of property and of individual right. This is the high enterprise of the new day: To lift everything that concerns our life as a Nation to the light that shines from the hearthfire of every man's conscience and vision of the right. It is inconceivable that we should do this as partisans; it is inconceivable we should do it in ignorance of the facts as they are or in blind haste. We shall restore, not destroy. We shall deal with our economic system as it is and as it may be modified, not as it might be if we had a clean sheet of paper to write upon; and step by step we shall make it what it should be, in the spirit of those who question their own wisdom and seek counsel and knowledge, not shallow self-satisfaction or the excitement of excursions whither they can not tell. Justice, and only justice, shall always be our motto.

And yet it will be no cool process of mere science. The Nation has been deeply stirred, stirred by a solemn passion, stirred by the knowledge of wrong, of ideals lost, of government too often debauched and made an instrument of evil. The feelings with which we face this new age of right and opportunity sweep across our heartstrings like some air out of God's own presence, where justice and mercy are reconciled and the judge and the brother are one. We know our task to be no mere task of politics but a task which shall search us through and through, whether we be able to understand our time and the need of our people, whether we be indeed their spokesmen and interpreters, whether we have the pure heart to comprehend and the rectified will to choose our high course of action.

This is not a day of triumph; it is a day of dedication. Here muster, not the forces of party, but the forces of humanity. Men's hearts wait upon us; men's lives hang in the balance; men's hopes call upon us to say what we will do. Who shall live up to the great trust? Who dares fail to try? I summon all honest men, all patriotic, all forward-looking men, to my side. God helping me, I will not fail them, if they will but counsel and sustain me!

14

WOODROW WILSON
A Review of Accomplishments, 1916

In this speech accepting his renomination by the Democratic Party, delivered at Shadow Lawn, New Jersey, September 2, 1916, Wilson gave his view of the problems his first administration faced and the accomplishments it could claim. But the speech offers more than a partisan history of the most productive reform presidency since the Civil War. In it Wilson is at pains to demonstrate his concern that business thrive and expand, especially abroad. This side of progressivism is often overlooked, but it helps to explain, among other things, the gradual assumption of a larger global role under T.R. and Wilson. Santo Domingo, Haiti, Nicaragua, Mexico, and finally France—these American interventions came easily to reform administrations not only because progressives were activists, but also because they assumed the beneficence of capitalism and the backwardness of most of the world's peoples. Since some of the rhetoric of reform obscured these latter assumptions I have reprinted the Shadow Lawn speech and the speech to the Grain Dealers' Association (see Document No. 15). This concern to midwife an expanding business enterprise forms one bridge between the first and second Wilson administrations, between the campaigns at home and the campaigns abroad.

I cannot accept the leadership and responsibility which the National Democratic Convention has again, in such generous fashion, asked me to accept without first expressing my profound gratitude to the party for the trust it reposes in me after four years of fiery trial in the midst of affairs of unprecedented difficulty, and the keen sense of added responsibility with which this honour fills (I had almost said burdens) me as I think of the great issues of national life and policy involved in the present and immediate future conduct of our Government. I shall seek, as I have always sought, to justify the extraordinary confidence thus reposed in me by striving to purge my heart and purpose of every personal and of every misleading party motive and devoting every energy I have to the service of the nation as a whole, praying that I may continue to have the counsel and support of all forward-looking men at every turn of the difficult business.

For I do not doubt that the people of the United States will wish the Democratic Party to continue in control of the Government. They are not in the habit of rejecting those who have actually served them for those who are making doubtful and conjectural promises of service. Least of all are they likely to substitute those who promised to render them particular services and proved false to that promise for those who have actually rendered those very services.

Boasting is always an empty business, which pleases nobody but the

---

Woodrow Wilson, speech at Shadow Lawn, New Jersey, September 2, 1916, from Ray Stannard Baker and William E. Dodd, eds., *The New Democracy: The Public Papers of Woodrow Wilson*, Vol. 2 (New York: Harper & Row, Publishers, 1926), pp. 275–80. Reprinted by permission.

boaster, and I have no disposition to boast of what the Democratic Party has accomplished. It has merely done its duty. It has merely fulfilled its explicit promises. But there can be no violation of good taste in calling attention to the manner in which those promises have been carried out or in adverting to the interesting fact that many of the things accomplished were what the opposition party had again and again promised to do but had left undone. Indeed that is manifestly part of the business of this year of reckoning and assessment. There is no means of judging the future except by assessing the past. Constructive action must be weighed against destructive comment and reaction. The Democrats either have or have not understood the varied interests of the country. The test is contained in the record.

What is that record? What were the Democrats called into power to do? What things had long waited to be done, and how did the Democrats do them? It is a record of extraordinary length and variety, rich in elements of many kinds, but consistent in principle throughout and susceptible of brief recital.

The Republican party was put out of power because of failure, practical failure and moral failure; because it had served special interests and not the country at large; because, under the leadership of its preferred and established guides, of those who still make its choices, it had lost touch with the thoughts and the needs of the Nation and was living in a past age and under a fixed illusion, the illusion of greatness. It had framed tariff laws based upon a fear of foreign trade, a fundamental doubt as to American skill, enterprise, and capacity, and a very tender regard for the profitable privileges of those who had gained control of domestic markets and domestic credits; and yet had enacted antitrust laws which hampered the very things they meant to foster, which were stiff and inelastic, and in part unintelligible. It had permitted the country throughout the long period of its control to stagger from one financial crisis to another under the operation of a national banking law of its own framing which made stringency and panic certain and the control of the larger business operations of the country by the bankers of a few reserve centers inevitable; had made as if it meant to reform the law but had faint-heartedly failed in the attempt, because it could not bring itself to do the one thing necessary to make the reform genuine and effectual, namely, back up the control of small groups of bankers. It had been oblivious, or indifferent, to the fact that the farmers,

upon whom the country depends for its food and in the last analysis
for its prosperity, were without standing in the matter of commercial
credit, without the protection of standards in their market transactions, and without systematic knowledge of the markets themselves;
that the labourers of the country, the great army of men who man
the industries it was professing to father and promote, carried their
labour as a mere commodity to market, were subject to restraint by
novel and drastic process in the courts, were without assurance of
compensation for industrial accidents, without federal assistance in
accommodating labour disputes, and without national aid or advice
in finding the places and the industries in which their labour was most
needed. The country had no national system of road construction and
development. Little intelligent attention was paid to the army, and
not enough to the navy. The other republics of America distrusted
us, because they found that we thought first of the profits of American
investors and only as an afterthought of impartial justice and helpful
friendship. Its policy was provincial in all things; its purposes were
out of harmony with the temper and purpose of the people and the
timely development of the nation's interests.

So things stood when the Democratic Party came into power. How
do they stand now? Alike in the domestic field and in the wide field
of the commerce of the world, American business and life and industry have been set free to move as they never moved before.

The tariff has been revised, not on the principle of repelling foreign
trade, but upon the principle of encouraging it, upon something like
a footing of equality with our own in respect of the terms of competition, and a Tariff Board has been created whose function it will
be to keep the relations of American with foreign business and industry
under constant observation, for the guidance alike of our business
men and of our Congress. American energies are now directed towards
the markets of the world.

The laws against trusts have been clarified by definition, with a
view to making it plain that they were not directed against big
business but only against unfair business and the pretense of competition where there was none; and a Trade Commission has been created
with powers of guidance and accommodation which have relieved
business men of unfounded fears and set them upon the road of
hopeful and confident enterprise.

By the Federal Reserve Act the supply of currency at the disposal of active business has been rendered elastic, taking its volume, not from a fixed body of investment securities, but from the liquid assets of daily trade; and these assets are assessed and accepted, not by distant groups of bankers in control of unavailable reserves, but by bankers at the many centers of local exchange who are in touch with local conditions everywhere.

Effective measures have been taken for the re-creation of an American merchant marine and the revival of the American carrying trade indispensable to our emancipation from the control which foreigners have so long exercised over the opportunities, the routes, and the methods ot our commerce with other countries.

The Interstate Commerce Commission has been reorganized to enable it to perform its great and important functions more promptly and more efficiently. We have created, extended and improved the service of the parcels post.

So much we have done for business. What other party has understood the task so well or executed it so intelligently and energetically? What other party has attempted it at all? The Republican leaders, apparently, know of no means of assisting business but "protection." How to stimulate it and put it upon a new footing of energy and enterprise they have not suggested.

For the farmers of the country we have virtually created commercial credit, by means of the Federal Reserve Act and the Rural Credits Act. They now have the standing of other business men in the money market. We have successfully regulated speculation in "futures" and established standards in the marketing of grains. By an intelligent Warehouse Act we have assisted to make the standard crops available as never before both for systematic marketing and as a security for loans from the banks. We have greatly added to the work of neighborhood demonstration on the farm itself of improved methods of cultivation, and, through the intelligent extension of the functions of the Department of Agriculture, have made it possible for the farmer to learn systematically where his best markets are and how to get at them.

The workingmen of America have been given a veritable emancipation, by the legal recognition of a man's labour as part of his life, and not a mere marketable commodity; by exempting labour organizations from processes of the courts which treated their members like fractional parts of mobs and not like accessible and responsible individuals; by releasing our seamen from involuntary servitude; by making adequate provision for compensation for industrial accidents; by providing suitable machinery for mediation and conciliation in industrial disputes; and by putting the Federal Department of Labor at the disposal of the workingman when in search of work.

We have effected the emancipation of the children of the country by releasing them from hurtful labour. We have instituted a system of national aid in the building of highroads such as the country has been feeling after for a century. We have sought to equalize taxation by means of an equitable income tax. We have taken the steps that ought to have been taken at the outset to open up the resources of Alaska. We have provided for national defense upon a scale never before seriously proposed upon the responsibility of an entire political party. We have driven the tariff lobby from cover and obliged it to substitute solid argument for private influence.

This extraordinary recital must sound like a platform, a list of sanguine promises; but it is not. It is a record of promises made four years ago and now actually redeemed in constructive legislation.

These things must profoundly disturb the thoughts and confound the plans of those who have made themselves believe that the Democratic Party neither understood nor was ready to assist the business of the country in the great enterprises which it is its evident and inevitable destiny to undertake and carry through. The breaking up of the lobby must especially disconcert them; for it was through the lobby that they sought and were sure they had found the heart of things. The game of privilege can be played successfully by no other means.

This record must equally astonish those who feared that the Democratic Party had not opened its heart to comprehend the demands of social justice. We have in four years come very near to carrying out the platform of the Progressive Party as well as our own; for we also are progressives. . . .

15

WOODROW WILSON

Speech to the Grain Dealers' Association, 1916

This campaign speech by the president, given on September 25, 1916, is one of his fullest statements on what American businessmen could expect from modern, progressive governments. Wilson's assumptions that unlimited American economic expansion would be entirely beneficent and that only an expanding export trade (nobody thought much about the import side) could protect the domestic economy from collapse were assumptions shared by virtually everyone in his day, conservative or progressive. Only the socialists dissented. But while wilson's progressive philosophy was in itself no more congenial to economic expansionism than the views of his conservative contemporaries, it had behind it great quantities of energy and idealism. Thus, progressives often pioneered in more adventurous foreign policies.

. . . What I have come to say to you to-day, I would wish to say in an atmosphere from which all the vapors of passions have been cleared away, for I want to speak to you about the business situation of the world, so far as America is concerned. I am not going to take the liberty of discussing that business situation from the special point of view of your association, because I know that I would be bringing coals to Newcastle. I know that I am speaking to men who understand the relation of the grain business to the business of the world very much better than I do; and I know that it is true that, except under very unusual circumstances such as have existed in the immediate past, the export of grain from this country has been a diminishing part of our foreign commerce rather than an increasing part; that the increase of our own population—the decrease in proportion to that increase, of our production of grains—has been rendering the question of foreign markets less important, though still very important, than it was in past generations, so far as the dealing in grain is concerned. I also remember, however, that we have only begun in this country the process by which the full production of our agricul-

Ray Stannard Baker and William E. Dodd, eds., *The New Democracy*, Vol. 2, pp. 311–23. Reprinted by permission.

tural acreage is to be obtained. The agricultural acreage of this country ought to produce twice what it is now producing, and under the stimulation and instruction which have recently been characteristic of agricultural development I think we can confidently predict that within, let us say, a couple of decades, the agricultural production of this country will be something like double, whereas, there is no likelihood that the population of this country will be doubled within the same period. You can look forward, therefore, it seems to me, with some degree of confidence to an increasing, and perhaps a rapidly increasing, volume of the products in which you deal.

But, as I have said, I have not come to discuss that. I have come to discuss the general relation of the United States to the business of the world in the decades immediately ahead of us. We have swung out, my fellow citizens, into a new business era in America. I suppose that there is no man connected with your association who does not remember the time when the whole emphasis of American business discussion was laid upon the domestic market. I need not remind you how recently it has happened that our attention has been extended to the markets of the world; much less recently, I need not say, in the matters with which you are concerned than in the other export interests of the country. But it happened that American production, not only in the agricultural field and in mining and in all the natural products of the earth, but also in manufacture, increased in recent years to such a volume that American business burst its jacket. It could not any longer be taken care of within the field of the domestic markets; and when that began to disclose itself as the situation, we also became aware that American business men had not studied foreign markets, that they did not know the commerce of the world, and that they did not have the ships in which to take their proportionate part in the carrying trade of the world; that our merchant marine had sunk to a negligible amount, and that it had sunk to its lowest at the very time when the tide of our exports began to grow in most formidable volume.

One of the most interesting circumstances of our business history is this: The banking laws of the United States—I mean the Federal banking laws—did not put the national banks in a position to do foreign exchange under favorable conditions, and it was actually true that private banks, and sometimes branch banks drawn out of other countries, notably out of Canada, were established at our chief ports to do what American bankers ought to have done. It was as if America was not only unaccustomed to touching all the nerves of the world's business, but was disinclined to touch them, and had not prepared the instrumentality by which it might take part in the great commerce of the round globe. Only in very recent years have we been even studying the problem of providing ourselves with the instrumentalities.

Not until the recent legislation of Congress known as the Federal reserve act were the Federal banks of this country given the proper equipment through which they could assist American commerce not only in our own country but in any part of the world where they chose to set up branch institutions. British banks had been serving British merchants all over the world, German banks had been serving German merchants all over the world, and no national bank of the United States had been serving American merchants any where in the world except in the United States. We had, as it were, deliberately refrained from playing our part in the field in which we prided ourselves that we were most ambitious and most expert, the field of manufacture and of commerce. All that is past, and the scene has been changed by the events of the last two years, almost suddenly, and with a completeness that almost daunts the planning mind. Not only when this war is over, but now, America has her place in the world and must take her place in the world of finance and commerce upon a scale that she never dreamed of before.

My dream is that she will take her place in that great field in a new spirit which the world has never seen before; not the spirit of those who would exclude others, but the spirit of those who would excel others. I want to see America pitted against the world, not in selfishness, but in brains.

The first thing that brains have to feed upon is knowledge, and when I hear men proposing to deal with the business problems of the United States in the future as we dealt with them in the past I do not have to inquire any further whether they are equipped with knowledge. I dismiss them from the reckoning, because I know that the facts are going to dominate, and they know nothing about these facts. And the most that we can supply ourselves with just now is, not the detailed program of policy, but the instrumentalities of gaining thorough knowledge of what we are about. Every man of us must for some time to come be "from Missouri!" We must want to know what the facts are, and when we know what the facts are, we shall know what the policy ought to be.

What instrumentalities have we provided ourselves with in order that we may be equipped with knowledge? There has been an instrumentality in operation for four or five years of which, strangely enough, American business men have only slowly become aware. Some four or five years ago the Congress established, in connection with the department which was then the Department of Commerce and Labor (now the Department of Commerce) a Bureau of Foreign and Domestic Commerce, and one of the advantages which the American Government has derived from that bureau is that it has been able to hire brains for much less than the brains were worth. It is in a way a national discredit to us, my fellow citizens, that we are paying studious men, capable of understanding anything and of conducting any business, just about one-third of what they could command in the field of business; and it is one of the admirable circumstances of American life that they are proud to serve the Government on a pittance. There are such men in the Bureau of Foreign and Domestic Commerce. They have been studying the foreign commerce of this country as it was never studied before, and have been making reports so comprehensive and so thorough that they compare to their great advantage with the reports of any similar bureau of any other government in the world. . . .

And then, in addition to that, there was recently created the Federal Trade Commission. It is hard to describe the functions of that commission; all I can say is that it has transformed the Government of the United States from being an antagonist of business into being a friend of business. A few years ago American business men—I think you will corroborate this statement—took up their morning paper with some degree of nervousness to see what the Government was doing to them. I ask you if you take up the morning paper now with any degree of nervousness? And I ask you if you have not found, those of you who have dealt with it all, the Federal Trade Commission to be put there to show you the way in which the Government can help you and not the way in which the Government can hinder you?

But that is not the matter that I am most interested in. It has always been a fiction—I don't know who invented it or why he invented it—that there was a contest between the law and business.

There has always been a contest in every government between the law and bad business, and I do not want to see that contest softened in any way; but there has never been any contest between men who intended the right thing and the men who administered the law. But what I want to speak about is this: One of the functions of the Federal Trade Commission is to inquire with the fullest powers ever conferred upon a similar commission in this country into all the circumstances of American business for the purpose of doing for American business exactly what the Department of Agriculture has so long and with increasing efficiency done for the farmer, inform the American business man of every element, big and little, with which it is his duty to deal. Here are created searching eyes of inquiry to do the very thing that it was imperatively necessary and immediately necessary that the country should do—look upon the field of business and know what was going on!

And then, in the third place, you know that we have just now done what it was common sense to do about the tariff. We have not put this into words, but I do not hesitate to put it into words: We have admitted that on the one side and on the other we were talking theories and managing policies without a sufficient knowledge of the facts upon which we were acting, and, therefore, we have established what is intended to be a non-partisan Tariff Commission to study the conditions with which legislation has to deal in the matter of the relations of American with foreign business transactions. Another eye created to see the facts! And I am hopeful that I can find the men who will see the facts and state them, no matter whose opinion those facts contradict. For an opinion ought always to have a profound respect for a fact, and when you once get the facts opinions that are antagonistic to those facts are necessarily defeated. I have never found a really courageous man who was afraid to put his opinion to the test of facts, or a morally sincere man who was not ready to surrender to the facts when they were contrary to his opinion. The Tariff Commission is going to look for the facts no matter who is hurt. We are creating one after another the instrumentalities of knowledge, so that the business men of this country shall know what the field of the world's business is and deal with that field upon that knowledge.

Then, when the knowledge is obtained, what are we going to do? One of the things that interests me most about an association of this sort is that the intention of it is that the members should share a common body of information, and that they should concert among themselves those operations of business which are beneficial to all of them; that, instead of a large number of dealers in grain acting separately and each fighting for his own hand, you are willing to come together and study the problem as if you were partners and brothers and co-operators in this field of business. That has been going on in every occupation in the United States of any consequence. Even the men that do the advertising have been getting together, and they have made this startling and fundamental discovery, that the only way to advertise successfully is to tell the truth. There are many reasons for that. One of the chief reasons is that when you get found out it is worse for you than it was before; but the great reason, the sober reason, is that business must be founded on the truth, and you men get together in order to create a clearing house for the truth about your business.

Very well, that is a picture in small of what we must do in the large. We must co-operate in the whole field of business, the Government with the merchant, the merchant with his employee, the whole body of producers with the whole body of consumers, to see that the right things are produced in the right volume and find the right purchasers at the right place, and that, all working together, we realize that nothing can be for the individual benefit which is not for the common benefit.

You know that there was introduced in the House of Representatives recently a bill, commonly called the Webb bill, for the purpose of stating it as the policy of the law of the United States that nothing in the anti-trust laws now existing should be interpreted to interfere with the proper sort of co-operation among exporters. The foreign field is not like the domestic field. The foreign field is full of combinations meant to be exclusive. The anti-trust laws of the United States are intended to prevent any kind of combination in the United States which shall be exclusive of new enterprises within the United States, any combination which shall set up monopoly in America; but the export business is a very big business, a very complicated business, a very expensive business, and it ought to be possible, and it will be possible and legal, for men engaged in exporting to get together and manage it in groups, so that they can manage it at an advantage instead of at a disadvantage as compared with foreign rivals—not for the purpose of exclusive and monopolistic combination, but for the purpose of co-operation, and there is a very wide difference there. I for myself despise monopoly, and I have an enthusiasm for co-operation. By co-operation I mean working along with anybody who is willing to work along with you under definite understandings and arrangements which will constitute a sound business program. There can be no jealousy of that, and if there had been time, I can say with confidence that this bill, which passed the House of Representatives, would have passed the Senate of the United States also. So that any obstacle that ingenious lawyers may find in the anti-trust laws will be removed. . . .

And then there must be co-operation, not only between the Government and the business men, but between business men. Shippers must coöperate, and they ought to be studying right now how to coöperate. There are a great many gentlemen in other countries who can show them how! They ought to look forward, particularly, to caring for this matter, that they have vehicles in which to carry their goods. We must address ourselves immediately and as rapidly as possible to the re-creation of a great American merchant marine. . . .

And it is absolutely necessary now to make good our new connections. Our new connections are with the great and rich Republics to the south of us. For the first time in my recollection they are beginning to trust and believe in us and want us, and one of my chief concerns has been to see that nothing was done that did not show friendship and good faith on our part. You know that it used to be the case that if you wanted to travel comfortably in your own person from New York to a South American port, you had to go by way of England or else stow yourself away in some uncomfortable fashion in a ship that took almost as long to go straight, and within whose bowels you got in such a temper before you got there that you did did not care whether she got there or not. The great interesting geographical fact to me is that by the opening of the Panama Canal there is a straight line south from New York through the canal to the western coast of South America, which hitherto has been one of the most remote coasts in the world so far as we were concerned. The west coast of South America is now nearer to us than the eastern coast of South America ever was, though we have the open Atlantic upon which to approach the east coast. Here is the loom all ready upon which to spread the threads which can be worked into a fabric of friendship and wealth such as we have never known before! The real wealth of foreign relationships, my fellow citizens, whether they be the relationships of trade or any other kind of intercourse, the real wealth of those relationships is the wealth of mutual confidence and understanding. If we do not understand them and they do not understand us, we cannot trade with them, much less be their friends, and it is only by weaving these intimate threads of connection that we shall be able to establish that fundamental thing, that psychological, spiritual nexus which is, after all, the real warp and woof of trade itself. We have got to have the knowledge, we have got to have the co-operation, and then back of all that has got to lie what America has in abundance and only has to release, that is to say, the self-reliant enterprise.

There is only one thing I have ever been ashamed of in America, and that was the timidity and fearfulness of Americans in the presence of foreign competitors. I have dwelt among Americans all my life and am an intense absorbent of the atmosphere of America, and I know by personal experience that there are as effective brains in America as anywhere in the world. An American afraid to pit American business men against any competitors anywhere! Enterprise, the shrewdness which Americans have shown, the knowledge of business which they have shown, all these things are going to make for that peaceful and honorable conquest of foreign markets which is our reasonable ambition.

America has stood in the years past for that sort of political understanding among men which would let every man feel that his rights were the same as those of another and as good as those of another, and the mission of America in the field of the world's commerce is to be the same: that when an American comes into that competition he comes without any arms that would enable him to conquer by force, but only with those peaceful influences of intelligence, a desire to serve, a knowledge of what he is about, before which everything softens and yields, and renders itself subject. That is the mission of America, and my interest, so far as my small part in American affairs is concerned, is to lend every bit of intelligence I have to this interesting, this vital, this all-important matter of releasing the intelligence of America for the service of mankind.

II. WAR: 1914-1918

16

WILLIAM JENNINGS BRYAN AND WOODROW WILSON

Policy Disagreements in the Lusitania *Crisis*

The following exchange of notes reveals the divergence of Wilson and his first Secretary of State on the vital issues of principle and national security raised by the naval war as it developed in the Atlantic in 1915. The *Falaba* sinking on March 28, 1915, which resulted in the death of an American citizen, first put the hard issue of neutral rights to the Wilson circle of advisers. The sinking of another British liner, the *Lusitania,* on May 7, required a policy decision. Bryan, as the letters reveal, would take fewer risks than Wilson, as he feared war more than potential damage to neutral rights. Despite the complexities of opinion on this issue, Bryan spoke for the bulk of the Left. When he found the president resistant to his arguments and himself isolated in the Cabinet, Bryan resigned. Wilson accepted his resignation on June 6, and the firm "second *Lusitania* note" went to Germany on the 9th.

The Secretary of State to President Wilson

WASHINGTON, *April 23, 1915.*

MY DEAR MR. PRESIDENT: In a note to you this afternoon I stated that Mr. Lansing would take your instructions to Old Point Comfort and prepare a tentative draft of note in the Thrasher case, during his stay there.

As I have not been able to reach the same conclusion to which you have arrived in this case I feel it my duty to set forth the situation as I see it. The note which you propose will, I fear, very much

Papers Relating to the Foreign Relations of the United States: The Lansing Papers, 1914–1920 (Washington: Government Printing Office, 1939), Vol. I, pp. 378–80, 411, 422–26, 437–38.

inflame the already hostile feeling against us in Germany, not entirely because of our protest against Germany's action in this case, but in part because of its contrast with our attitude toward the Allies. If we oppose the use of the submarine against merchantmen we will lay down a law for ourselves as well as for Germany. If we admit the right of the submarine to attack Merchantmen but condemn their particular act or class of act as inhuman we will be embarrassed by the fact that we have not protested against Great Britain's defense of the right to prevent foods reaching non-combatant enemies.

We suggested the admission of food and the abandonment of torpedo attacks upon Merchant vessels. Germany seemed willing to negotiate but Great Britain refused to consider the proposition. I fear that denunciation of one and silence as to the other will be construed by some as partiality. You do not make allowance for the fact that we were notified of the intended use of the submarine, or for the fact that the deceased knowingly took the risk of travelling on an enemy ship. I cannot see that he is differently situated from those who by remaining in a belligerent country assume risk of injury. Our people, will, I believe, be slow to admit the right of a citizen to involve his country in war when by exercising ordinary care he could have avoided danger.

The fact that we have not contested Great Britain's assertion of the right to use our flag has still further aggravated Germany and we cannot overlook the fact that the sale of arms and ammunition, while it could not be forbidden under neutrality, has worked so entirely for the benefit of one side as to give to Germany—not justification but an excuse for charging that we are favoring the Allies. I have mentioned these things to show the atmosphere through which the Thrasher note will be received by Germany.

Believing that such a note as you propose is, under the conditions that now exist, likely to bring on a crisis, I venture to suggest an alternative, namely, an appeal to the nations at war to consider terms of peace. We cannot justify waiting until both sides, or even one side, asks for mediation. As a neutral we cannot have in mind the wishes of one side more than the wishes of the other side. The neutral nations have both rights and we are the neutral nation looked to give expression to those.

Nearly nine months have passed since the war began, and after the expenditure of over ten billion dollars and the sacrifice of several millions of the flower of Europe the war is a draw. Surely the most sanguinary ought to be satisfied with the slaughter. I submit that it is this nation's duty to make, not a secret but a public appeal for the acceptance of mediation. All the neutral nations would support the appeal—several have suggested it. Our own interests justify it—we may be drawn into the conflict if it continues. Our obligation to the neutral nations demand it. Our friendship to the nations at war requires it. They cannot reason calmly and neither side is in a position to ask for mediation. As the well-wisher of all we should act; as the leader in the peace propaganda we should act; as the greatest christian nation we should act—we cannot avoid the responsibility. The loss of one American, who might have avoided death, is as nothing compared with the tens of thousands who are dying daily in this "causeless war." Is it not better to try to bring peace for the benefit of the whole world than to risk the provoking of war on account of one man? We cannot foresee the result of such an appeal as you can make, but if it is right to do it, there ought not to be lacking the faith to try. You have such an opportunity as has not come to any man before. I most earnestly urge you to make the appeal.

With assurances [etc.]

W. J. BRYAN

President Wilson to the Secretary of State

WASHINGTON, *April 28, 1915.*

MY DEAR MR. SECRETARY: I have thought a great deal about the contents of the letter you wrote me (the letter written in your own hand)about the Thrasher case. It of course made a deep impression on me.

As I told you yesterday at Cabinet, I am not at all confident that we are on the right track in considering such a note as I outlined for Mr. Lansing to work on. I am not sure that my outline really expressed what I would myself say in the note, for, after all, the character of a note is chiefly in the way the thing is said and the points developed. Perhaps it is not necessary to make formal representations in the matter at all.

What I have been thinking about most is your alternative proposition, that we publicly call upon the belligerents to end the war.

I wish I could see it as you do. But in view of what House writes

me I cannot. It is known to every government concerned that we
believe the war should be ended and that we speak for all neutral
nations in that wish. It is known to them that we are seeking to help
and that anything they want to say to one another which they are
too proud or too prudent to say directly and officially they can say
privately through us. They are at present most appreciative and
cordial,—ready to accept help when they can accept it. We know
their minds and we know their difficulties. They are dependent upon
their own public opinion (even Germany) and we know what that
opinion is. To insist now would be futile and would probably be
offensive. We would lose such influence as we have for peace.

I am afraid, Mr. Secretary, that there is much in this that will
seem to you disputable; but I can only state my conviction in the
matter, and God knows I have searched my mind and conscience both
to get the best, the nearest approach to wisdom, there is in them.

With warmest regard and appreciation,

Faithfully yours,

WOODROW WILSON

President Wilson to the Secretary of State

WASHINGTON, *20 May, 1915*

MY DEAR MR. SECRETARY: The proposed note to Great Britain,
drawn by Mr. Lansing, reached me in New York, and I shall at the
earliest possible moment go over it and work it into what seems to
me its best expression.

But the more I think about this matter the clearer it becomes to me
that we ought not to send this note, or any other on this subject,
to Great Britain, until we have the reply of the Imperial German
Government to our note to it, because we cannot afford even to seem
to be trying to make it easier for Germany to accede to our demands
by turning in similar fashion to England concerning matters which
we have already told Germany are none of her business. It would
be so evident a case of uneasiness and hedging that I think it would
weaken our whole position fatally.

There is no reason to feel that our note to Germany is being looked
upon by them as unfriendly; and it is right that we should oblige
them to consider our rights upon the seas so far as they are concerned
without regard to anything we mean to say or do in the case of
England.

In every such decision I feel very keenly the force of your counter judgment and cannot claim that I feel cock sure of the rightness of my own conclusions; but I can only follow what grows more and more clear to me the more I think the matter out.

Faithfully Yours,

W. W.

The Secretary of State to President Wilson

WASHINGTON, *June 3, 1915, morning.*

MY DEAR MR. PRESIDENT:

... In dealing with the *Lusitania,* it is, in my judgment, necessary to bear in mind that our only concern is with the protection of our people. We have not felt called upon to express an opinion on submarine warfare when other vessels not bearing Americans have been sunk. Whatever views we may have as to the moral character of the means employed by the belligerents, we do not feel it our duty to express opinions merely for the purpose of announcing our views. We could, of course, contribute something towards the formation of public opinion against the belligerent which employs methods which we might denounce and in favor of the belligerent which was the victim of the methods so denounced, but even the most biased among our citizens would hardly feel justified in asking us to make [*take?*] any position merely for the purpose of helping one side or the other.

It seems to me that, having stated our position without equivocation, we are not only justified but compelled by duty to do what we can to prevent our citizens incurring unnecessary risks. The precedents for this are abundant. Take the case of a riot for instance, the authorities are not absolved from the duty of enforcing order and of punishing those guilty of violence, but as a matter of precaution, they restrain citizens from the exercise of their rights in order to prevent injuries that might otherwise be inflicted unintentionally. The bystander is always in danger when there is shooting upon the street and no government would feel justified in refusing to warn noncombatants away from the dangerous place, merely because the citizens ordinarily have the right to go upon the streets.

For the same reason we advised all American citizens to leave Mexico, not because they did not have a right to stay there, but because we thought it unwise for them to incur the risks involved in staying. We went to the expense of bringing out those who were not able to pay their own way. We did not refuse to give such protection as was possible to those who remained, but we warned them of the extraordinary danger involved in remaining. It seems to me that we cannot well justify a failure to warn American citizens against going into the danger zone on foreign ships—especially on ships which, by carrying ammunition, invite extraordinary risks. It is not sufficient to say that, according to international law, American citizens have a right to go anywhere and that the Government's protection will follow them no matter what risks they take. If the authorities of a city are justified in warning people off the streets of the city in which they reside, surely a nation is justified in warning its citizens off of the water highways which belong to no nation alone, but to all the nations in common.

The German Government pleads as one reason for the attack upon the *Lusitania* that it was carrying 5,400 cases of ammunition "destined for the destruction of brave German soldiers, etc." This ammunition was valued at about $150,000. We have clearly stated the Government's position in regard to the rights of Americans and if it is thought desirable, this right can be restated in language specifically asserting that according to this Government's view of international law, citizens have a right to travel with contraband and that their rights cannot be violated merely because the vessel carries contraband. Still it is not only consistent, but, in my judgment, a matter of imperative duty to not [only] warn our citizens against the exercise of this time [*right?*], but to do whatever lies in our power to prevent the incurring of such risks. Would it not be advisable to reverse the rule by which passenger ships are permitted to carry ammunition? The law says that no ship shall carry gun powder without a license. This has been interpreted by a department order not to apply to gun powder contained in small ammunition. If that order was involved [*invoked?*] and it was interpreted to exclude all ammunition, it would add to the security of passengers.

I believe that Germany is looking for a way out and that, having stated our position unequivocally on the subject of the use of submarines against merchantmen, we would be justified in taking all the precaution possible to prevent our citizens taking risks. If—not for the benefit of Germany but for the benefit of our own people—we announce that passenger ships will not hereafter be allowed to carry ammunition, I think Germany would be very likely to say that no passenger ship would be attacked if assurances were given that it did not

carry ammunition. This we could do without invoking any new legislation. In my judgment, you would be justified in going even further
and saying that Congress would be asked for legislation authorizing the
refusal of clearance to passenger ships carrying contraband. If such a
rule was adopted, contraband would be carried on ships without pas-
sengers and thus the safety of passenger ships would be assured. But
even if you do not feel justified in going so far as to advise the legislation suggested, forbidding the carrying of contraband on passenger
ships, I believe the order in regard to ammunition would have a powerful influence upon Germany just at this time, and I feel sure that it
would be approved in this country. A person would have to be very
much biased in favor of the Allies to insist that ammunition intended
for one of the belligerents should be safe-guarded in transit by the
lives of American citizens or, for that matter, by the lives of citizens of
any country.

I hope you will pardon the length of this note but I am sincerely
anxious to render you any service I can in the solution of the difficult
problem presented by the *Lusitania* disaster. I recognize, of course,
that the responsibility rests upon you and that in the final decision
your judgment and your conscience are the only guides upon which
you are justified in relying. Those of us who have been honored by
being selected as advisors are in duty bound to give you, when desired,
the benefit of our judgment and conscience, but none of your associates
realize more fully than I that we can only assist insofar as the reason[s]
which support our conclusions appeal to you. I know of no other way
of discharging the duty of an advisor than to outline the course that I
would pursue if the responsibility for action were upon me. The ear-
nestness with which I have spoken in the discussion of these questions
measures the depth of my solicitude and the sincerity of my desire that
your decisions may, by safeguarding our country's welfare, redound
to your own personal credit and to the advantage of our party. With
assurances [etc.]

W. J. BRYAN

The Secretary of State to President Wilson

WASHINGTON, June 5, 1915.

MY DEAR MR. PRESIDENT: The fact that the note to Germany has not yet been completed encourages me to trespass upon your time for a moment to present again three matters which, to my mind, are necessary to insure us against war with Germany—

> First, A reference to the plan embodied in our thirty treaties—the principle of which has been accepted by Germany. Her mention of arbitration opens the way and makes the suggestion easy, if it does not in fact compel the suggestion. It will ensure a peaceful settlement of this controversy. And we can not forget that this peace plan for investigation in all cases was endorsed by the Senate and is now in force with Great Britain, France, and Russia.
>
> Second, Steps to prevent passenger ships from carrying ammunition. This is referred to by Germany. Action ought, in my judgment, to be taken before the reply is sent.
>
> Third, Before we send another note to Germany I think we should make a renewed protest to Great Britain against interference with our trade with neutrals. These three propositions have been under consideration before. The first was decided upon—that is the idea was to be given to the public and communicated to Germany, but you were dissuaded by some thing that you heard. The second is thought by the Attorney General to be possible—and even if it could not be accomplished as a matter of fact the same end could be reached almost as well by advice such as was given to Americans in Mexico. The third suggestion was about to be carried out but you were dissuaded by a message from Mr. House.

I beg to renew the suggestions most urgently believing as I do, that without them the note as you outlined it at cabinet meeting would be likely to cause a rupture of diplomatic relations and this might rush us into war in spite of anything we could do. If the initiative were with us I would not fear war, for I am sure you do not want it, but when the note is sent it is Germany's next move—if the note causes her to act in an unfriendly way it may cause conditions here that will increase the difficulties of our position. This may be our last chance to speak for peace, for it will be much harder to propose investigation after some unfriendly act than *now*.

Pardon me for presenting these suggestions so earnestly but I am sure that the sober judgment of the people will not sustain any word or act that provokes war—they will support you if war comes but they will do all in their power to prevent war, and I fully share their desire and purpose in this respect.

With assurances [etc.]

W. J. Bryan

President Wilson to the Secretary of State

WASHINGTON, *5 June, 1915.*

MY DEAR MR. SECRETARY: I hope that you realize how hard it goes with me to differ with you in judgment about such grave matters as we are now handling. You always have such weight of reason, as well as such high motives, behind what you urge that it is with deep misgiving that I turn from what you press upon me.

I am inclined to think that we ought to take steps, as you suggest, to prevent our citizens from travelling on ships carrying munitions of war, and I shall seek to find the legal way to do it. I fear that, whatever it may be best to do about that, it is clearly impossible to act before the new note goes to Germany.

I am sorry to say that, study as I may the way to do it without hopelessly weakening our protest, I cannot find a way to embody in our note the principle of long discussion of a very simple state of facts; and I think that our object with England can be gained better by not sending a note in connection with this one than by sending it; and, after all, it is our object and the relief of our trade that we wish to accomplish.

I recast the note last night. I hope you will think a little better of it.

I would be very much obliged if you would go over it for substance, making any suggestions that may occur to you, and that you will ask Mr. Lansing to go over it for form and validity of statement and claim.

With the warmest regard, and with a very solemn and by no means self-confident sense of deep responsibility.

Cordially and faithfully yours,

WOODROW WILSON

17

Letter to Senator Stone, February 25, 1916

This letter amazed some of Wilson's contemporaries, who had no idea the president had hardened himself against German submarine warfare to this extent. It triggered a Congressional revolt that smouldered through the armed neutrality controversy and never really subsided. But Wilson's arguments became those of the majority.

To Senator Stone, Chairman of the
Committee on Foreign Relations

THE WHITE HOUSE
WASHINGTON, *February 24, 1916.*

MY DEAR SENATOR: I very warmly appreciate your kind and frank letter of to-day, and feel that it calls for an equally frank reply.

You are right in assuming that I shall do everything in my power to keep the United States out of war. I think the country will feel no uneasiness about my course in that respect. Through many anxious months I have striven for that object, amidst difficulties more manifold than can have been apparent upon the surface, and so far I have succeeded. I do not doubt that I shall continue to succeed. The course which the Central European powers have announced their intention of following in the future with regard to undersea warfare seems for the moment to threaten insuperable obstacles, but its apparent meaning is so manifestly inconsistent with explicit assurances recently given us by those powers with regard to their treatment of merchant vessels on the high seas, that I must believe that explanations will presently ensue which will put a different aspect upon it. We have had no reason to question their good faith or their fidelity to their promises in the past, and I for one feel confident that we shall have none in the future.

Foreign Relations: 1916 Supplement, pp. 177–78.

But in any event our duty is clear. No nation, no group of nations, has the right while war is in progress to alter or disregard the principles which all nations have agreed upon in mitigation of the horrors and sufferings of war; and if the clear rights of American citizens should ever unhappily be abridged or denied by any such action, we should, it seems to me, have in honor no choice as to what our own course should be.

For my own part, I cannot consent to any abridgment of the rights of American citizens in any respect. The honor and self-respect of the nation is involved. We covet peace, and shall preserve it at any cost but the loss of honor. To forbid our people to exercise their rights for fear we might be called upon to vindicate them would be a deep humiliation indeed. It would be an implicit, all but an explicit, acquiescence in the violation of the rights of mankind everywhere, and of whatever nation or allegiance. It would be a deliberate abdication of our hitherto proud position as spokesmen, even amidst the turmoils of war, for the law and the right. It would make everything this Government has attempted, and everything that it has achieved during this terrible struggle of nations meaningless and futile.

It is important to reflect that if in this instance we allowed expediency to take the place of principle, the door would inevitably be opened to still further concessions. Once accept a single abatement of right, and many other humiliations would certainly follow, and the whole fine fabric of international law might crumble under our hands piece by piece. What we are contending for in this matter is of the very essence of the things that have made America a sovereign nation. She cannot yield then without conceding her own impotency as a nation, and making virtual surrender of her independent position among the nations of the world.

I am speaking, my dear Senator, in deep solemnity, without heat, with a clear consciousness of the high responsibilities of my office, and as your sincere and devoted friend. If we should unhappily differ, we shall differ as friends; but where issues so momentous as these are involved we must, just because we are friends, speak our minds without reservation.

Faithfully yours,

Woodrow Wilson

18

WOODROW WILSON
'Peace Without Victory' Speech, January 22, 1917

In light of the circumstances as we now know them, this speech was entirely futile and of no importance to the course of events in those early days of 1917. But the speech established the guiding principles of what the world would come to know as Wilsonianism, an approach to foreign relations that came to have an strong appeal to liberal and left groups and parties in every country. Thus while it failed to affect the immediate maneuvers of statesmen the speech accomplished Wilson's other purpose—it released an idea of enormous power into a world desperate for something better than the worship of force that had put it into the murderous trenches.

GENTLEMEN OF THE SENATE: On the 18th of December last I addressed an identic note to the governments of the nations now at war requesting them to state, more definitely than they had yet been stated by either group of belligerents, the terms upon which they would deem it possible to make peace. I spoke on behalf of humanity and of the rights of all neutral nations like our own, many of whose most vital interests the war puts in constant jeopardy. The Central powers united in a reply which stated merely that they were ready to meet their antagonists in conference to discuss terms of peace. The Entente powers have replied much more definitely and have stated, in general terms, indeed, but with sufficient definiteness to imply details, the arrangements, guarantees, and acts of reparation which they deem to be the indispensable conditions of a satisfactory settlement. We are that much nearer a definite discussion of the peace which shall end the present war. We are that much nearer the discussion of the international concert which must thereafter hold the world at peace. In every discussion of the peace that must end this war it is taken for granted that peace must be followed by some definite concert of power which will make it virtually impossible

Foreign Relations: 1917 Supplement, pp. 24–29.

that any such catastrophe should ever overwhelm us again. Every lover of mankind, every sane and thoughtful man, must take that for granted.

I have sought this opportunity to address you because I thought that I owed it to you, as the council associated with me in the final determination of our international obligations, to disclose to you without reserve the thought and purpose that have been taking form in my mind in regard to the duty of our Government in the days to come when it will be necessary to lay afresh and upon a new plan the foundations of peace among the nations.

It is inconceivable that the people of the United States should play no part in that great enterprise. To take part in such a service will be the opportunity for which they have sought to prepare themselves by the very principles and purposes of their polity and the approved practices of their Government ever since the days when they set up a new nation in the high and honourable hope that it might in all that it was and did show mankind the way to liberty. They can not in honour withhold the service to which they are now about to be challenged. They do not wish to withhold it. But they owe it to themselves and to the other nations of the world to state the conditions under which they will feel free to render it.

That service is nothing less than this, to add their authority and their power to the authority and force of other nations to guarantee peace and justice throughout the world. Such a settlement cannot now be long postponed. It is right that before it comes this Government should frankly formulate the conditions upon which it would feel justified in asking our people to approve its formal and solemn adherence to a league for peace. I am here to attempt to state those conditions.

The present war must first be ended; but we owe it to candour and to a just regard for the opinion of mankind to say that, so far as our participation in guarantees of future peace is concerned, it makes a great deal of difference in what way and upon what terms it is ended. The treaties and agreements which bring it to an end must embody terms which will create a peace that is worth guaranteeing and preserving, a peace that will win the approval of mankind, not merely a peace that will serve the several interests and immediate aims of the nation engaged. We shall have no voice in determining what those terms shall be, but we shall, I feel sure, have a voice in determining whether they shall be made lasting or not by the guarantees of a universal covenant; and our judgment upon what is fundamental and essential as a condition precedent to permanency should be spoken now, not afterwards when it may be too late.

No covenant of cooperative peace that does not include the peoples of the New World can suffice to keep the future safe against war; and yet there is only one sort of peace that the peoples of America could join in guaranteeing. The elements of that peace must be elements that engage the confidence and satisfy the principles of the American governments, elements consistent with their political faith and with the practical convictions which the peoples of America have once for all embraced and undertaken to defend.

I do not mean to say that any American government would throw any obstacle in the way of any terms of peace the governments now at war might agree upon, or seek to upset them when made, whatever they might be. I only take it for granted that mere terms of peace between the belligerents will not satisfy even the belligerents themselves. Mere agreements may not make peace secure. It will be absolutely necessary that a force be created as a guarantor of the permanency of the settlement so much greater than the force of any nation now engaged or any alliance hitherto formed or projected that no nation, no probable combination of nations, could face or withstand it. If the peace presently to be made is to endure, it must be a peace made secure by the organized major force of mankind.

The terms of the immediate peace agreed upon will determine whether it is a peace for which such a guarantee can be secured. The question upon which the whole future peace and policy of the world depends is this: Is the present war a struggle for a just and secure peace, or only for a new balance of power? If it be only a struggle for a new balance of power, who will guarantee, who can guarantee, the stable equilibrium of the new arrangement? Only a tranquil Europe can be a stable Europe. There must be, not a balance of power, but a community of power; not organized rivalries, but an organized common peace.

Fortunately we have received very explicit assurances on this point. The statesmen of both of the groups of nations now arrayed against one another have said, in terms that could not be misinterpreted, that it was no part of the purpose they had in mind to crush their antagonists. But the implications of these assurances may not be equally clear to all—may not be the same on both sides of the water. I think it will be serviceable if I attempt to set forth what we understand them to be.

They imply, first of all, that it must be a peace without victory. It is not pleasant to say this. I beg that I may be permitted to put my own interpretation upon it and that it may be understood that no other interpretation was in my thought. I am seeking only to face realities and to face them without soft concealments. Victory would mean peace forced upon the loser, a victor's terms imposed upon the vanquished. It would be accepted in humiliation, under duress, at an intolerable sacrifice, and would leave a sting, a resentment, a bitter memory upon which terms of peace would rest, not permanently, but only as upon quicksand. Only a peace between equals can last, only a peace the very principle of which is equality and a common participation in a common benefit. The right state of mind, the right feeling between nations, is as necessary for a lasting peace as is the just settlement of vexed questions of territory or of racial and national allegiance.

The equality of nations upon which peace must be founded if it is to last must be an equality of rights; the guarantees exchanged must neither recognize nor imply a difference between big nations and small, between those that are powerful and those that are weak. Right must be based upon the common strength, not upon the individual strength, of the nations upon whose concert peace will depend. Equality of territory or of resources there of course cannot be; nor any other sort of equality not gained in the ordinary peaceful and legitimate development of the peoples themselves. But no one asks or expects anything more than an equality of rights. Mankind is looking now for freedom of life, not for equipoises of power.

And there is a deeper thing involved than even equality of right among organized nations. No peace can last, or ought to last, which does not recognize and accept the principle that governments derive all their just powers from the consent of the governed, and that no right anywhere exists to hand peoples about from sovereignty to sovereignty as if they were property. I take it for granted, for instance, if I may venture upon a single example, that statesmen everywhere are agreed that there should be a united, independent, and autonomous Poland, and that henceforth inviolable security of life, of worship, and of industrial and social development should be guaranteed to all peoples who have lived hitherto under the power of governments devoted to a faith and purpose hostile to their own.

I speak of this, not because of any desire to exalt an abstract political principle which has always been held very dear by those who have sought to build up liberty in America, but for the same reason that I have spoken of the other conditions of peace which seem to me clearly indispensable—because I wish frankly to uncover realities. Any peace which does not recognize and accept this principle will inevitably be upset. It will not rest upon the affections or the convictions of mankind. The ferment of spirit of whole populations will fight subtly and constantly against it, and all the world will sympathize. The world can be at peace only if its life is stable, and there can be no stability where the will is in rebellion, where there is not tranquility of spirit and a sense of justice, of freedom, and of right.

So far as practicable, moreover, every great people now struggling towards a full development of its resources and of its powers should be assured a direct outlet to the great highways of the sea. Where this can not be done by the cession of territory, it can no doubt be done by the neutralization of direct rights of way under the general guarantee which will assure the peace itself. With a right comity of arrangement no nation need be shut away from free access to the open paths of the world's commerce.

And the paths of the sea must alike in law and in fact be free. The freedom of the seas is the *sine qua non* of peace, equality, and cooperation. No doubt a somewhat radical reconsideration of many of the rules of international practice hitherto thought to be established may be necessary in order to make the seas indeed free and common in practically all circumstances for the use of mankind, but the motive for such changes is convincing and compelling. There can be no trust or intimacy between the peoples of the world without them. The free, constant, unthreatened intercourse of nations is an essential part of the process of peace and of development. It need not be difficult either to define or to secure the freedom of the seas if the governments of the world sincerely desire to come to an agreement concerning it.

It is a problem closely connected with the limitation of naval armaments and the cooperation of the navies of the world in keeping the seas at once free and safe, and the question of limiting naval armaments opens the wider and perhaps more difficult question of

the limitation of armies and of all programmes of military preparation. Difficult and delicate as these questions are, they must be faced
with the utmost candour and decided in a spirit of real accommodation if peace is to come with healing in its wings, and come to stay.
Peace cannot be had without concession and sacrifice. There can be
no sense of safety and equality among the nations if great preponder-
ating armaments are henceforth to continue here and there to be
built up and maintained. The statesmen of the world must plan for
peace and nations must adjust and accommodate their policy to it as
they have planned for war and made ready for pitiless contest and
rivalry. The question of armaments, whether on land or sea, is the
most immediately and intensely practical question connected with
the future fortunes of nations and of mankind.

I have spoken upon these great matters without reserve and with
the utmost explicitness because it has seemed to me to be necessary if
the world's yearning desire for peace was anywhere to find free voice
and utterance. Perhaps I am the only person in high authority
amongst all the peoples of the world who is at liberty to speak and
hold nothing back. I am speaking as an individual, and yet I am
speaking also, of course, as the responsible head of a great government, and I feel confident that I have said what the people of the
United States would wish me to say. May I not add that I hope and
believe that I am in effect speaking for liberals and friends of
humanity in every nation and of every programme of liberty? I would
fain believe that I am speaking for the silent mass of mankind everywhere who have as yet had no place or opportunity to speak their
real hearts out concerning the death and ruin they see to have come
already upon the persons and the homes they hold most dear.

And in holding out the expectation that the people and Government of the United States will join the other civilized nations of the
world in guaranteeing the permanence of peace upon such terms as
I have named I speak with the greater boldness and confidence
because it is clear to every man who can think that there is in this
promise no breach in either our traditions or our policy as a nation,
but a fulfilment, rather, of all that we have professed or striven for.

I am proposing, as it were, that the nations should with one accord
adopt the doctrine of President Monroe as the doctrine of the world:
that no nation should seek to extend its polity over any other nation
or people, but that every people should be left free to determine its

own polity, its own way of development, unhindered, unthreatened, unafraid, the little along with the great and powerful.

I am proposing that all nations henceforth avoid entangling alliances which would draw them into competitions of power, catch them in a net of intrigue and selfish rivalry, and disturb their own affairs with influences intruded from without. There is no entangling alliance in a concert of power. When all unite to act in the same sense and with the same purpose, all act in the common interest and are free to live their own lives under a common protection.

I am proposing government by the consent of the governed; that freedom of the seas which in international conference after conference representatives of the United States have urged with the eloquence of those who are the convinced disciples of liberty; and that moderation of armaments which makes of armies and navies a power for order merely, not an instrument of aggression or of selfish violence.

These are American principles, American policies. We could stand for no others. And they are also the principles and policies of forward-looking men and women everywhere, of every modern nation, of every enlightened community. They are the principles of mankind and must prevail.

19

WOODROW WILSON
The War Message, April 2, 1917

Few men who heard Wilson begin his address knew for certain that he would ask for war, and this suspense, along with Wilson's stirring eloquence, made the evening one of the most dramatic in the public affairs of the American people. But while contemporaries listened intently for the final decision, all the rhetoric that went with it bears close study. Hardly less important than the decision for war were the reasons for it.

Senate Document, 65th Cong., 1st sess. X, pp. 3–8.

GENTLEMEN OF THE CONGRESS:

I have called the Congress into extraordinary session because there are serious, very serious, choices of policy to be made, and made immediately, which it was neither right nor constitutionally permissible that I should assume the responsibility of making.

On the third of February last I officially laid before you the extraordinary announcement of the Imperial German Government that on and after the first day of February it was its purpose to put aside all restraints of law or of humanity and use its submarines to sink every vessel that sought to approach either the ports of Great Britain and Ireland or the western coasts of Europe or any of the ports controlled by the enemies of Germany within the Mediterranean. That had seemed to be the object of the German submarine warfare earlier in the war, but since April of last year the Imperial Government had somewhat restrained the commanders of its undersea craft in conformity with its promise then given to us that passenger boats should not be sunk and that due warning would be given to all other vessels which its submarines might seek to destroy, when no resistance was offered or escape attempted, and care taken that their crews were given at least a fair chance to save their lives in their open boats. The precautions taken were meagre and haphazard enough, as was proved in distressing instance after instance in the progress of the cruel and unmanly business, but a certain degree of restraint was observed. The new policy has swept every restriction aside. Vessels of every kind, whatever their flag, their character, their cargo, their destination, their errand, have been ruthlessly sent to the bottom without warning and without thought of help or mercy for those on board, the vessels of friendly neutrals along with those of belligerents. Even hospital ships and ships carrying relief to the sorely bereaved and stricken people of Belgium, though the latter were provided with safe conduct through the proscribed areas by the German Government itself and were distinguished by unmistakable marks of identity, have been sunk with the same reckless lack of compassion or of principle.

I was for a little while unable to believe that such things would in fact be done by any government that had hitherto subscribed to the humane practices of civilized nations. International law had its origin in the attempt to set up some law which would be respected and observed upon the seas, where no nation had right of dominion and where lay the free highways of the world. By painful stage after stage has that law been built up, with meagre enough results, indeed, after all was accomplished that could be accomplished, but always with a clear view, at least, of what the heart and conscience of mankind demanded. This minimum of right the German Government has swept aside under the plea of retaliation and necessity and because it had no weapons which it could use at sea except these which it is impossible to employ as it is employing them without throwing to the winds all scruples of humanity or of respect for the understandings that were supposed to underlie the intercourse of the world. I am not now thinking of the loss of property involved, immense and serious as that is, but only of the wanton and wholesale destruction of the lives of non-combatants, men, women, and children, engaged in pursuits which have always, even in the darkest periods of modern history, been deemed innocent and legitimate. Property can be paid for; the lives of peaceful and innocent people cannot be. The present German submarine warfare against commerce is a warfare against mankind.

It is a war against all nations. American ships have been sunk, American lives taken, in ways which it has stirred us very deeply to learn of, but the ships and people of other neutral and friendly nations have been sunk and overwhelmed in the waters in the same way. There has been no discrimination. The challenge is to all mankind. Each nation must decide for itself how it will meet it. The choice we make for ourselves must be made with a moderation of counsel and a temperateness of judgment befitting our character and our motives as a nation. We must put excited feeling away. Our motive will not be revenge or the victorious assertion of the physical might of the nation, but only the vindication of right, of human right, of which we are only a single champion.

When I addressed the Congress on the twenty-sixth of February last I thought that it would suffice to assert our neutral rights with arms, our right to use the seas against unlawful interference, our right to keep our people safe against unlawful violence. But armed neutrality, it now appears, is impracticable. Because submarines are in effect outlaws when used as the German submarines have been used against merchant shipping, it is impossible to defend ships against their attacks as the law of nations has assumed that merchantmen would defend themselves against privateers or cruisers, visible craft giving chase upon the open sea. It is common prudence in such circumstances, grim necessity indeed, to endeavour to destroy them before they have shown their own intention. They must be dealt with upon sight, if dealt with at all. The German Government denies the right of neutrals to use arms at all within the areas of the sea which it has proscribed, even in the defense of rights which no modern publicist has ever before questioned their right to defend. The intimation is conveyed that the armed guards which we have placed on our merchant ships will be treated as beyond the pale of law and subject to be dealt with as pirates would be. Armed neutrality is ineffectual enough at best; in such circumstances and in the face of such pretensions it is worse than ineffectual; it is likely only to produce what it was meant to prevent; it is practically certain to draw us into the war without either the rights or the effectiveness of belligerents. There is one choice we cannot make, we are incapable of making: we will not choose the path of submission and suffer the most sacred rights of our nation and our people to be ignored or violated. The wrongs against which we now array ourselves are no common wrongs: they cut to the very roots of human life.

With a profound sense of the solemn and even tragical character of the step I am taking and of the grave responsibilities which it involves, but in unhesitating obedience to what I deem my constitutional duty, I advise that the Congress declare the recent course of the Imperial German Government to be in fact nothing less than war against the government and people of the United States; that it formally accept the status of belligerent which has thus been thrust upon it; and that it take immediate steps not only to put the country in a more thorough state of defense but also to exert all its power and employ all its resources to bring the Government of the German Empire to terms and end the war. . . .

While we do these things, these deeply momentous things, let us be very clear, and make very clear to all the world what our motives and our objects are. My own thought has not been driven from its habitual and normal course by the unhappy events of the last two months, and I do not believe that the thought of the nation has been altered or clouded by them. I have exactly the same things in mind now that I had in mind when I addressed the Senate on the twenty-second of January last; the same that I had in mind when I addressed the Congress on the third of February and on the twenty-sixth of February. Our object now, as then, is to vindicate the principles of peace and justice in the life of the world as against selfish and autocratic power and to set up amongst the really free and self-governed peoples of the world such a concert of purpose and of action as will henceforth ensure the observance of those principles. Neutrality is no longer feasible or desirable where the peace of the world is involved and the freedom of its peoples, and the menace to that peace and freedom lies in the existence of autocratic governments backed by organized force which is controlled wholly by their will, not by the will of their people. We have seen the last of neutrality in such circumstances. We are at the beginning of an age in which it will be insisted that the same standards of conduct and responsibility for wrong done shall be observed among nations and their governments that are observed among the individual citizens of civilized states.

We have no quarrel with the German people. We have no feeling toward them but one of sympathy and friendship. It was not upon their impulse that their government acted in entering this war. It was not with their previous knowledge or approval. It was a war determined upon as wars used to be determined upon in the old, unhappy days when peoples were nowhere consulted by their rulers and wars were provoked and waged in the interest of dynasties or of little groups of ambitious men who were accustomed to use their fellow men as pawns and tools. . . .

We are accepting this challenge of hostile purpose because we know that in such a government, following such methods, we can never have a friend; and that in the presence of its organized power, always lying in wait to accomplish we know not what purpose, there can be no assured security for the democratic governments of the world. We are now about to accept gauge of battle with this natural foe to liberty and shall, if necessary, spend the whole force of the nation to check and nullify its pretensions and its power. We are glad, now that we see the facts with no veil of false pretense about them, to fight thus for the ultimate peace of the world and for the liberation of its peoples, the German peoples included: for the rights of nations great and small and the privilege of men everywhere to choose their way of life and of obedience. The world must be made safe for democracy. Its peace must be planted upon the tested foundations of political liberty. We have no selfish ends to serve. We desire no conquest, no dominion. We seek no indemnities for ourselves, no material compensation for the sacrifices we shall freely make. We are but one of the champions of the rights of mankind. We shall be satisfied when those rights have been made as secure as the faith and the freedom of nations can make them.

Just because we fight without rancour and without selfish object, seeking nothing for ourselves but what we shall wish to share with all free peoples, we shall, I feel confident, conduct our operations as belligerents without passion and ourselves observe with proud punctilio the principles of right and of fair play we profess to be fighting for.

I have said nothing of the governments allied with the Imperial Government of Germany because they have not made war upon us or challenged us to defend our right and our honour. The Austro-Hungarian Government has, indeed, avowed its unqualified endorsement and acceptance of the reckless and lawless submarine warfare adopted now without disguise by the Imperial German Government, and it has therefore not been possible for this Government to receive Count Tarnowski, the Ambassador recently accredited to this Government by the Imperial and Royal Government of Austria-Hungary; but that Government has not actually engaged in warfare against citizens of the United States on the seas, and I take the liberty, for the present at least, of postponing a discussion of our relations with the authorities at Vienna. We enter this war only where we are clearly forced into it because there are no other means of defending our rights.

It will be all the easier for us to conduct ourselves as belligerents in a high spirit of right and fairness because we act without animus, not in enmity towards a people or with the desire to bring any injury or disadvantage upon them, but only in armed opposition to an irresponsible government which has thrown aside all considerations of humanity and of right and is running amuck. We are, let me say again, the sincere friends of the German people, and shall desire nothing so much as the early reestablishment of intimate relations of mutual advantage between us,—however hard it may be for them, for the time being, to believe that this is spoken from our hearts. We have borne with their present government through all these bitter months because of that friendship,—exercising a patience and forbearance which would otherwise have been impossible. We shall, happily, still have an opportunity to prove that friendship in our daily attitude and actions towards the millions of men and women of German birth and native sympathy who live amongst us and share our life, and we shall be proud to prove it towards all who are in fact loyal to their neighbours and to the Government in the hour of test. They are, most of them, as true and loyal Americans as if they had never known any other fealty or allegiance. They will be prompt to stand with us in rebuking and restraining the few who may be of a different mind and purpose. If there should be disloyalty, it will be dealt with with a firm hand of stern repression; but, if it lifts its head at all, it will lift it only here and there and without countenance except from a lawless and malignant few.

It is a distressing and oppressive duty, Gentlemen of the Congress, which I have performed in thus addressing you. There are, it may be, many months of fiery trial and sacrifice ahead of us. It is a fearful thing to lead this great peaceful people into war, into the most terrible and disastrous of all wars, civilization itself seeming to be in the balance. But the right is more precious than peace, and we shall fight for the things which we have always carried nearest our hearts,— for democracy, for the right of those who submit to authority to have a voice in their own governments, for the rights and liberties of small nations, for a universal dominion of right by such a concert of free peoples as shall bring peace and safety to all nations and make the world itself at last free. To such a task we can dedicate our lives and our fortunes, everything that we are and everything that we have, with the pride of those who know that the day has come when America is privileged to spend her blood and her might for the principles that gave her birth and happines and the peace which she has treasured. God helping her, she can do no other.

20

RANDOLPH BOURNE
The War and the Intellectuals

Randolph Bourne in 1917 was a young intellectual who had joined the staff of *Seven Arts* magazine after studying literature at Columbia and writing two books on progressive education. Too young and too radical to be

called a progressive, Bourne nonetheless identified with the social reform movement before the war. In a famous series of essays bound together as *Untimely
Papers,* Bourne, angry at progressive support for American intervention, made one
of the most penetrating critiques of the reform mind offered by a contemporary.
Readers of Noam Chomsky's *The New American Mandarins* (1968) will recognize in that attack on intellectuals and the Vietnam war the rejection of liberal
pragmatism made by Bourne some fifty years ago. Yet I wish to credit Bourne
with more than an early expression of a seminal idea. Virtually every line of the
essay "Twilight of the Idols" is as brilliantly revealing today as it was in October,
1917. Few writers select subjects of such permanent significance or illuminate
them with such success.

The case of the intellectuals seems, therefore, only very speciously
rational. They could have used their energy to force a just peace or
at least to devise other means than war for carrying through American
policy. They could have used their intellectual energy to ensure that
our participation in the war meant the international order which
they wish. Intellect was not so used. It was used to lead an apathetic
nation into an irresponsible war, without guarantees from those
belligerents whose cause we were saving. The American intellectual,
therefore, has been rational neither in his hindsight nor his foresight.
To explain him we must look beneath the intellectual reasons to the
emotional disposition. It is not so much what they thought as how
they felt that explains our intellectual class. Allowing for colonial
sympathy, there was still the personal shock in a world-war which
outraged all our preconceived notions of the way the world was
tending. It reduced to rubbish most of the humanitarian internationalism and democratic nationalism which had been the emotional thread
of our intellectuals' life. We have suddenly to make a new orientation.
There were mental conflicts. Our latent colonialism strove with our
longing for American unity. Our desire for peace strove with our
desire for national responsibility in the world. That first lofty and
remote and not altogether unsound feeling of our spiritual isolation
from the conflict could not last. There was the itch to be in the great
experience which the rest of the world was having. Numbers of intelligent people who had never been stirred by the horrors of capitalistic
peace at home were shaken out of their slumber by the horrors of

---

Randolph Bourne, *Untimely Papers* (New York: Ben Huebsch, 1919), pp.
35–45, 122–39.

war in Belgium. Never having felt responsibility for labor wars and oppressed masses and excluded races at home, they had a large fund of idle emotional capital to invest in the oppressed nationalities and ravaged villages of Europe. Hearts that had felt only ugly contempt for democratic strivings at home beat in tune with the struggle for freedom abroad. All this was natural, but it tended to over-emphasize our responsibility. And it threw our thinking out of gear. The task of making our own country detailedly fit for peace was abandoned in favor of a feverish concern for the management of the war, advice to the fighting governments on all matters, military, social and political, and a gradual working up of the conviction that we were ordained as a nation to lead all erring brothers towards the light of liberty and democracy. The failure of the American intellectual class to erect a creative attitude toward the war can be explained by these sterile mental conflicts which the shock to our ideals sent raging through us.

Mental conflicts end either in a new and higher synthesis or adjustment, or else in a reversion to more primitive ideas which have been outgrown but to which we drop when jolted out of our attained position. The war caused in America a recrudescence of nebulous ideals which a younger generation was fast outgrowing because it had passed the wistful stage and was discovering concrete ways of getting them incarnated in actual institutions. The shock of the war threw us back from this pragmatic work into an emotional bath of these old ideals.

The primitive idea to which they regressed became almost insensibly translated into a craving for action. War was seen as the crowning relief of their indecision. At last action, irresponsibility, the end of anxious and torturing attempts to reconcile peace-ideals with the drag of the world towards Hell. An end to the pain of trying to adjust the facts to what they ought to be! Let us consecrate the facts as ideal! Let us join the greased slide towards war! The momentum increased. Hesitations, ironies, consciences, considerations,—all were drowned in the elemental blare of doing something aggressive, colossal. The new-found Sabbath "peacefulness of being at war"! The thankfullness with which so many intellectuals lay down and floated with the current betrays the hesitation and suspense through which they had been. The American university is a brisk and happy place these days. Simple, unquestioning action has superseded the knots of thought. The thinker dances with reality. . . .

The intellectuals whom the crisis has crystallized into an acceptance of war have put themselves into a terrifyingly strategic position. It is only on the craft, in the stream, they say, that one has any chance of controlling the current forces for liberal purposes. If we obstruct, we surrender all power for influence. If we responsibly approve, we then retain our power for guiding. We will be listened to as responsible thinkers, while those who obstructed the coming of war have committed intellectual suicide and shall be cast into outer darkness. Criticism by the ruling powers will only be accepted from those intellectuals who are in sympathy with the general tendency of the war. Well, it is true that they may guide, but if their stream leads to disaster and the frustration of national life, is their guiding any more than a preference whether they shall go over the right-hand or the left-hand side of the precipice? Meanwhile, however, there is comfort on board. Be with us, they call, or be negligible, irrelevant. Dissenters are already excommunicated. Irreconcilable radicals, wringing their hands among the débris, become the most despicable and impotent of men. There seems no choice for the intellectual but to join the mass of acceptance. But again the terrible dilemma arises,—either support what is going on, in which case you count for nothing because you are swallowed in the mass and great incalculable forces bear you on; or remain aloof, passively resistant, in which case you count for nothing because you are outside the machinery of reality.

Is there no place left, then, for the intellectual who cannot yet crystallize, who does not dread suspense, and is not yet drugged with fatigue? The American intellectuals, in their preoccupation with reality, seem to have forgotten that the real enemy is War rather than imperial Germany. There is work to be done to prevent this war of ours from passing into popular mythology as a holy crusade. What shall we do with leaders who tell us that we go to war in moral spotlessness, or who make "democracy" synonymous with a republican form of government? There is work to be done in still shouting that all the revolutionary byproducts will not justify the war, or make war anything else than the most noxious complex of all the evils that afflict men. . . .

How could the pragmatist mind accept war without more violent protest, without a greater wrench? Either Professor Dewey and his friends felt that the forces were too strong for them, that the war had to be, and it was better to take it up intelligently than to drift blindly in; or else they really expected a gallant war, conducted with jealous regard for democratic values at home and a captivating vision of international democracy as the end of all the toil and pain. If their motive was the first, they would seem to have reduced the scope of possible control of events to the vanishing point. If the war is too strong for you to prevent, how is it going to be weak enough for you to control and mold to your liberal purposes? And if their motive was to shape the war firmly for good, they seem to have seriously miscalculated the fierce urgencies of it. Are they to be content, as the materialization of their hopes, with a doubtful League of Nations and the suppression of the I. W. W.? Yet the numbing power of the war situation seems to have kept them from realizing what has happened to their philosophy. The betrayal of their first hopes has certainly not discouraged them. But neither has it roused them to a more energetic expression of the forces through which they intend to realize them. I search Professor Dewey's articles in vain for clews as to the specific working-out of our democratic desires, either nationally or internationally, either in the present or in the reconstruction after the war. No programme is suggested, nor is there feeling for present vague popular movements and revolts. Rather are the latter chided, for their own vagueness and impracticalities. Similarly, with the other prophets of instrumentalism who accompany Dewey into the war, democracy remains an unanalyzed term, useful as a call to battle, but not an intellectual tool, turning up fresh sod for the changing future. Is it the political democracy of a plutocratic America that we are fighting for, or is it the social democracy of the new Russia? Which do our rulers really fear more, the menace of Imperial Germany, or the liberating influence of a socialist Russia. In the application of their philosophy to politics, our pragmatists are sliding over this crucial question of ends. Dewey says our ends must be intelligently international rather than chauvinistic. But this gets us little distance along our way.

In this difficult time the light that has been in liberals and radicals has become darkness. If radicals spend their time holding conventions to attest their loyalty and stamp out the "enemies within," they do not spend it in breaking intellectual paths, or giving us shining ideas to which we can attach our faith and conscience. The spiritual apathy from which the more naïve of us suffer, and which the others are so busy fighting, arises largely from sheer default of a clear vision that would melt it away. Let the motley crew of ex-socialists, and labor radicals, and liberals and pragmatist philosophers, who have united for the prosecution of the war, present a coherent and convincing democratic programme, and they will no longer be confronted with the skepticism of the conscientious and the impossibilist. But when the emphasis is on technical organization, rather than organization of ideas, on strategy rather than desires, one begins to suspect that no programme is presented because they have none to present. This burrowing into war-technique hides the void where a democratic philosophy should be. Our intellectuals consort with war-boards in order to keep their minds off the question of what the slow masses of the people are really desiring, or toward what the best hope of the country really drives. Similarly the blaze of patriotism on the part of the radicals serves the purpose of concealing the feebleness of their intellectual light.

Is the answer that clear formulation of democratic ends must be postponed until victory in the war is attained? But to make this answer is to surrender the entire case. For the support of the war by radicals, realists, pragmatists, is due—or so they say—to the fact that the war is not only saving the cause of democracy, but is immensely accelerating its progress. Well, what are those gains? How are they to be conserved? What do they lead to? How can we further them? Into what large idea of society do they group? To ignore these questions, and think only of the war-technique and its accompanying devotions, is to undermine the foundations of these people's own faith.

A policy of "win the war first" must be, for the radical, a policy of intellectual suicide. Their support of the war throws upon them the responsibility of showing inch by inch the democratic gains, and of laying out a charter of specific hopes. Otherwise they confess that they are impotent and that the war is submerging their expectations, or that they are not genuinely imaginative and offer little promise for future leadership.

It may seem unfair to group Professor Dewey with Mr. Spargo and Mr. Gompers, Mr. A. M. Simons, and the Vigilantes. I do so only because in their acceptance of the war, they are all living out that popular American "instrumental" philosophy which Professor Dewey has formulated in such convincing and fascinating terms. On an infinitely more intelligent plane, he is yet one with them in his confidence that the war is motivated by democratic ends and is being made to serve them. A high mood of confidence and self-righteousness moves them all, a keen sense of control over events that makes them eligible to discipleship under Professor Dewey's philosophy. They are all hostile to impossibilism, to apathy, to any attitude that is not a cheerful and brisk setting to work to use the emergency to consolidate the gains of democracy. Not, Is it being used? but, Let us make a flutter about using it! This unanimity of mood puts the resenter of war out of the arena. But he can still seek to explain why this philosophy which has no place for the inexorable should have adjusted itself so easily to the inexorable of war, and why, although a philosophy of the creative intelligence in using means toward ends, it should show itself so singularly impoverished in its present supply of democratic values.

What is the matter with the philosophy? One has a sense of having come to a sudden, short stop at the end of an intellectual era. In the crisis, this philosophy of intelligent control just does not measure up to our needs. What is the root of this inadequacy that is felt so keenly by our restless minds? Van Wyck Brooks has pointed out searchingly the lack of poetic vision in our pragmatist "awakeners." Is there something in these realistic attitudes that works actually against poetic vision, against concern for the quality of life as above machinery of life? Apparently there is. The war has revealed a younger intelligentsia, trained up in the pragmatic dispensation, immensely ready for the executive ordering of events, pitifully unprepared for the intellectual interpretation or the idealistic focusing of ends. The young men in Belgium, the officers' training corps, the young men being sucked into the councils at Washington and into war-organization everywhere, have among them a definite element, upon whom Dewey, as veteran philosopher, might well bestow a papal blessing. They have absorbed the secret of scientific method as applied to political administration. They are liberal, enlightened, aware. They are touched with creative intelligence toward the solution of political and industrial problems. They are a wholly new force in American life, the product of the swing in the colleges from a training that emphasized classical studies to one that emphasized political and economic values. Practically all this element, one would say, is lined up in service of the war-technique. There seems to have been a peculiar congeniality between the war and these men. It is as if the war and they had been waiting for each other. One wonders what scope they would have had for their intelligence without it. Probably most of them would have gone into industry and devoted themselves to sane reorganization schemes. What is significant is that it is the technical side of the war that appeals to them, not the interpretative or political side. The formulation of values and ideals, the production of articulate and suggestive thinking, had not, in their education, kept pace, to any extent whatever, with their technical aptitude. . . .

It is true, Dewey calls for a more attentive formulation of war-purposes and ideas, but he calls largely to deaf ears. His disciples have learned all too literally the instrumental attitude toward life, and, being immensely intelligent and energetic, they are making themselves efficient instruments of the war-technique, accepting with little question the ends as announced from above. That those ends are largely negative does not concern them, because they have never learned not to subordinate idea to technique. Their education has not given them a coherent system of large ideas, or a feeling for democratic goals. They have, in short, no clear philosophy of life except that of intelligent service, the admirable adaptation of means to ends. They are vague as to what kind of a society they want, or what kind of society America needs, but they are equipped with all the administrative attitudes and talents necessary to attain it.

To those of us who have taken Dewey's philosophy almost as our American religion, it never occurred that values could be subordinated to technique. We were instrumentalists, but we had our private utopias so clearly before our minds that the means fell always into its place as contributory. And Dewey, of course, always meant his philosophy, when taken as a philosophy of life, to start with values. But there was always that unhappy ambiguity in his doctrine as to just how values were created, and it became easier and easier to assume that just any growth was justified and almost any activity valuable so long as it achieved ends. The American, in living out this philosophy, has habitually confused results with product, and been content with getting somewhere without asking too closely whether it was the desirable place to get. It is now becoming plain that unless you start with the vividest kind of poetic vision, your instrumentalism is likely to land you just where it has landed this younger intelligentsia which is so happily and busily engaged in the national enterprise of war. You must have your vision and you must have your technique. The practical effect of Dewey's philosophy has evidently been to develop the sense of the latter at the expense of the former. Though he himself would develop them together, even in him there seems to be a flagging of values, under the influence of war. *The New Republic* honorably clamors for the Allies to subordinate military strategy to political ends, technique to democratic values. But war always undermines values. It is the outstanding lesson of the whole war that statesmen cannot be trusted to get this perspective right, that their only motto is, first to win and then grab what they can. The struggle against this statesmanlike animus must be a losing one as long as we have not very clear and very determined and very revolutionary democratic ideas and programmes to challenge them with. The trouble with our situation is not only that values have been generally ignored in favor of technique, but that those who have struggled to keep values foremost, have been too bloodless and too nearsighted in their vision. The defect of any philosophy of "adaptation" or "adjustment," even when it means adjustment to changing, living experience, is that there is no provision for thought or experience getting beyond itself. If your ideal is to be adjustment to your situation, in radiant cooperation with reality, then your success is likely to be just that and no more. You never transcend anything. . . .

We are in the war because an American Government practiced a philosophy of adjustment, and an instrumentalism for minor ends, instead of creating new values and setting at once a large standard to which the nations might repair. An intellectual attitude of mere adjustment, of mere use of the creative intelligence to make your progress, must end in caution, regression, and a virtual failure to effect even that change which you so clear-sightedly and desirously see. This is the root of our dissatisfaction with much of the current political and social realism that is preached to us. It has everything good and wise except the obstreperous vision that would drive and draw all men into it.

The working-out of this American philosophy in our intellectual life then has meant an exaggerated emphasis on the mechanics of life at the expense of the quality of living. We suffer from a real shortage of spiritual values. A philosophy that worked when we were trying to get that material foundation for American life in which more impassioned living could flourish no longer works when we are faced with inexorable disaster and the hysterias of the mob. The note of complacency which we detect in the current expressions of this philosophy has a bad taste. The congruous note for the situation would seem to be, on the contrary, that of robust' desperation—a desperation that shall rage and struggle until new values come out of the travail, and we see some glimmering of our democratic way. In the creation of these new values, we may expect the old philosophy, the old radicalism, to be helpless. It has found a perfectly definite level, and there is no reason to think that it will not remain there. Its flowering appears in the technical organization of the war by an earnest group of young liberals, who direct their course by an opportunist programme of State-socialism at home and a league of benevolently imperialistic nations abroad. At their best they can give us a government by prudent, enlightened college men instead of by politicians. At their best, they can abolish war by making everybody a partner in the booty of exploitation. That is all, and it is technically admirable. Only there is nothing in the outlook that touches in any way the happiness of the individual, the vivifying of the personality, the comprehension of social forces, the flair of art,—in other words, the quality of life. Our intellectuals have failed us as value-creators, even as value-emphasizers. The allure of the martial in war has passed only to be succeeded by the allure of the technical. The allure of fresh and true ideas, of free speculation, of artistic vigor, of cultural styles, of intelligence suffused by feeling, and feeling given fiber and outline by intelligence, has not come, and can hardly come, we see now, while our reigning philosophy is an instrumental one.

Whence can come this allure? Only from those who are thorough malcontents. Irritation at things as they are, disgust at the continual frustrations and aridities of American life, deep dissatisfaction with self and with the groups that give themselves forth as hopeful,—out of such moods there might be hammered new values. The malcontents would be men and women who could not stomach the war, or the reactionary idealism that has followed in its train. They are quite through with the professional critics and classicists who, have let cultural values die through their own personal ineptitude. Yet these malcontents have no intention of being cultural vandals, only to slay. They are not barbarians, but seek the vital and the sincere everywhere. All they want is a new orientation of the spirit that shall be modern, an orientation to accompany that technical orientation which is fast coming, and which the war accelerates. They will be harsh and often bad-tempered, and they will feel that the break-up of things is no time for mellowness. They will have a taste for spiritual adventure, and for sinister imaginative excursions. It will not be Puritanism so much as complacency that they will fight. A tang, a bitterness, an intellectual fiber, a verve, they will look for in literature, and their most virulent enemies will be those unaccountable radicals who are still morally servile, and are now trying to suppress all free speculation in the interests of nationalism. Something more mocking, more irreverent, they will constantly want. They will take institutions very lightly, indeed will never fail to be surprised at the seriousness with which good radicals take the stated offices and systems. Their own contempt will be scarcely veiled, and they will be glad if they can tease, provoke, irritate thought on any subject. These malcontents will be more or less of the American tribe of talent who used either to go immediately to Europe, or starved submissively at home. But these people will neither go to Europe, nor starve submissively. They are too much entangled emotionally in the possibilities of American life to leave it, and they have no desire whatever to starve. So they are likely to go ahead beating their heads at the wall until they are either bloody or light appears. They will give offense to their elders who cannot see what all the concern is about, and they will hurt the more middle-aged sense of adventure upon which the better integrated minds of the younger generation will have compromised. Optimism is often compensatory, and the optimistic mood in American thought may mean merely that American life is too terrible to face. A more skeptical, malicious, desperate, ironical mood may actually be the sign of more vivid and more stirring life fermenting in America to-day. It may be a sign of hope. That thirst for more of the intellectual "war and laughter" that we find Nietzsche calling us to may bring us satisfactions that optimism-haunted philosophies could never bring. Malcontentedness may be the beginning of promise. That is why I evoked the spirit of William James, with its gay passion for ideas, and its freedom of speculation, when I felt the slightly pedestrian gait into which the war had brought pragmatism. It is the creative desire more than the creative intelligence that we shall need if we are ever to fly.

21

GEORGE RECORD
Letter to Woodrow Wilson, March 31, 1919

George Record, a New Jersey progressive who had known Wilson
in his days as governor, wrote to the president in the spring of 1919 in an attempt
to convince him to take a more vigorous position as a domestic reformer. Record
was not alone in his feeling that progressivism must move Left after the war.
Without a revived liberal reform movement, addressing itself especially to economic issues, Record and others knew that either the socialists or the reactionaries
would offer leadership—something progressivism had been designed to prevent
from the beginning.

I pay you the compliment [wrote Record to Wilson] of believing
that you are big and broad enough to welcome frank speech from
those who, like myself, are personally your friends and well wishers,
and who are sincerely devoted to improving the living and working
conditions of mankind. If I speak plainly, therefore, I know you will
take no offense.

As conditions are now, your political fortunes are at a low ebb,
your prestige impaired, and your party demoralized.

What is the reason for this condition? There are many minor reasons, and one big one. I deal with the big one.

In my judgment nothing that you have done as President, and
nothing that you are proposing in the League of Nations idea, will
give you a place in history as a great man, because at the end of your
term you will have rendered no great and lasting service that will lift
you above the average of our Presidents, and you have ignored the
great issue which is slowly coming to the front, the question of economic democracy, abolition of privilege, and securing to men the
full fruits of their labor or service.

There is no glory, because there is little service, in standing as you
have for the principles of political democracy. Political democracy
is a good thing and a step in evolution, but the men who will stand

James Kerney, *The Political Education of Woodrow Wilson* (New York:
Appleton-Century-Crofts, 1926), pp. 438–46.

high in history for services rendered to political democracy are those who rendered their services when it was dangerous to do so. Our fathers who established this Republic, as Franklin said, had to hang together or they would hang separately. In those days to stand for political democracy or any substantial application of it, was at the risk of life. To stand for political democracy in these days is like standing for the Ten Commandments,—it is a worthy thing to do, but there is nothing heroic or great about it.

No serious attempt is made to remove the existing obstacles to political democracy in this country; viz., the two legislative chambers of state and national government, the state and national constitutions, and the power of courts to set aside laws, which on all important matters prevent or delay the majority from writing their will into law, and give us therefore most of the time a government by the minority. A conspicuous example of this fact is the recent decision by the Supreme Court (by a vote of 5 to 4) declaring unconstitutional the Act of Congress forbidding that relic of barbarism, the employment of little children in mills. If there is any wickeder practice prevailing in any state, civilized or barbaric, than our practice of stunting the bodies and ruining the lives of our little children in our industrial slave pens, I do not know what it is. The ancients had a saying that when injury is done to little children, the throne of the Almighty rocks from side to side.

In the next place, it is apparent from one hundred and thirty years of the application of the principle of political democracy, that it is not the solution that our fathers fondly hoped that it would be of the problem of social inequality. They thought by abolishing the nobility and titles and hereditary privileges, that the question was solved. For nearly a century the enormous extent of our territory, which enabled us to give land free to all comers, covered up the fact that by establishing political democracy we had not rid ourselves of privilege. Industrial conditions in this country, it is now plain, are approximating the conditions of the old country, mainly because the natural resources of the country have passed into the hands of comparatively few owners. The percentage of our people who own their own farms or their own homes in villages and cities is growing smaller every decade, as evidenced by our census reports. The poverty in our great cities has become appalling, particularly in the winter season. While the cheers of street multitudes abroad are ringing in your ears, the teachers of New York City have shocked the public by revelations of the fearful privations inflicted upon the children of the poor, and the great milk trust is exposed, as it has often before, in its monopoly of this necessary of life.

Thousands upon thousands of the operatives in our great industries are working long hours at monotonous toil for a wage which only provides barely sufficient food, clothing and wretched shelter to keep them in working condition, which have been the essential conditions of slavery in every age of the world. In bad times the wage does not provide even this, because the employer can get new workmen when the old ones are unable to stand the conditions any longer. At the same time, wealth has piled up in the hands of a few of our people at a rate and in quantities unexampled in human history. Steadily the trusts are controlling the essential businesses of the country. They were never so strong nor so powerful. Your own Federal Trade Commission has pointed out exactly how five meat firms are not only swindling the public annually out of enormous sums, but are daily violating the law and maintaining a monopoly in food products, than which no more odious crime against humanity can be conceived. These powerful criminals go unwhipt by the law, while our courts send to prison for long terms poor, weak socialists, who have been driven to intemperate speech by the contemplation of the monstrous injustice involved in the immunity of these wealthy criminals, and other similar iniquities of our social and industrial system.

These illustrations show that there is present in our Republic a grave and menacing problem. It is steadily pressing upon public attention, as slavery did in the years between 1830 and 1860. If you fail to attempt to solve this problem, you will stand in history in my judgment exactly as the leaders of the Whig and Democratic parties stood when they turned their backs upon the rising question of slavery.

The issue of political democracy has passed. The issue is now one of industrial or economic democracy.

The League of Nations idea will not help your position, either now or in history, because, like all your other policies, it does not go to the root of the problem. Wars are caused by privilege. Every modern state is governed by the privileged, that is, by those who control industry by owning railroads, lands, mines, banks, and credit. These men thus obtain enormous and unearned capital, for which there is no use in the country where it is produced, because the poverty of the workers limits the home market. Those who control this surplus capital must seek new countries and new people to exploit, and this clash of selfish interests leads to war. The cure for war is the reign of justice, i.e., the abolition of privilege, in each of the great nations. I do not believe that you can set up machinery which will maintain justice in international relations among governments which deny justice to their own people. If the League works, it will be when and to the extent that justice is established within the countries which are parties to the League. Indeed, it is entirely possible, if not probable, that such a league established by the present governments of the Allies, if it has any real power, is very likely to be used as an international bulwark of privilege. That danger looms large after you pass off the scene. The people here cannot be aroused to an active interest in the League idea. They favor the general principle, but do not understand the details. They believe that the dreadful wastage of the war, and the destruction of German, Austrian, Russian and Turkish autocracy, will insure peace for at least a generation, which gives ample time for building up international treaties or machinery designed to substitute arbitration for war as a method of settling international differences. Whatever form the League takes, the whole subject disappears as a pressing issue upon the ratification of the treaty of peace.

I do not criticize your going abroad to fight for the League of Nations in the peace treaty; on the contrary I heartily approve of it. Something will come out of it which will mark an advance towards permanent peace. But my point is that you ought not to neglect the bigger domestic questions. If you are going to ride the storm, you have got to be big enough to handle the whole problem. . . .

The one real, big thing in the world today it the socialist experiments in government in Russia, Austria, and Germany. You cannot fight this idea by ignoring it, or by denouncing its advocates, or putting them in jail. Nor can we deny the socialist statement that our system of political democracy has permitted the steady development of social injustice in the form of privilege. The only way to meet this menace of socialism, if menace it is, is by offering a better program for the removal of injustice in our industrial and social relations.

This is the political situation here as I see it now. It is likely to grow worse. You have thrown on the present Democratic Congress the responsibility for finding a workable solution of the great domestic problems of the day. They will fail to work out any adequate solution, which will further impair your prestige and that of your party. In the meantime, men and women are being discharged from factories in every part of the United States, and we are in for hard times, if not for a panic. . . .

You have the capacity of mind and the opportunity to be one of the greatest men who have yet appeared in history. In fact, my main criticism of your whole public career is that you have been devoting talents of the very highest order to second rate tasks. You should now undertake a job worthy of your great abilities. You should become the real leader of the radical forces in America, and present to the country a constructive program of fundamental reform, which shall be an alternative to the program presented by the socialists, and the Bolsheviki, and then fight for it. . . .

This program will gather around you at once, as if by magic, the forces of intelligent and orderly radicalism who have been looking in vain to you for leadership, and are now in a state of profound discouragement. In all human probability in one year, with a dozen carefully prepared speeches delivered in different parts of this country, you could so educate the public that you could force this radical program into the platform of the Democratic party. . . .

If you are defeated in this attempt, you will go down with colors flying, and when the ideas triumph, as they inevitably must, your place in history, and consequently your service, would be recognized as that of a truly great man.

22

WOODROW WILSON
Message to Congress, May 20, 1919

Record's letter, and other similar appeals, did not fall on entirely barren ground. Wilson in 1919 seemed personally convinced that the nation needed to move to the Left, and this message cabled from France even appropriated Record's suggestion that the president espouse "economic democracy." While Record was vague as to exactly what economic democracy meant,

Wilson was vaguer still, and he further de-radicalized his discussion of the matter by adding that the details of a more democratic industrial order were to be left to the cooperative efforts of labor and management. This was hardly the leadership Record appealed for, but Wilson, tied up with the peace negotiations and in ill health, would take no more initiatives toward domestic reform. Even had his attention not been diverted by foreign policy questions and his weariness not been mounting, there is real question if Wilson's progressive philosophy would have permitted him to formulate and fight for a program sufficiently radical to steal the thunder of the socialists. As it turned out, the American government rode out the postwar unrest with a more negative policy fashioned by A. Mitchell Palmer, state governors, judges, and a few local mobs.

I deeply regret my inability to be present at the opening of the extraordinary session of the Congress. It still seems to be my duty to take part in the counsels of the Peace Conference and contribute what I can to the solution of the innumerable questions to whose settlement it has had to address itself: for they are questions which affect the peace of the whole world and from them, therefore, the United States cannot stand apart. I deemed it my duty to call the Congress together at this time because it was not wise to postpone longer the provisions which must be made for the support of the government. Many of the appropriations which are absolutely necessary for the maintenance of the government and the fulfillment of its varied obligations for the fiscal year 1919–1920 have not yet been made; the end of the present fiscal year is at hand; and action upon these appropriations can no longer be prudently delayed. It is necessary, therefore, that I should immediately call your attention to this critical need. It is hardly necessary for me to urge that it may receive your prompt attention.

I shall take the liberty of addressing you on my return on the subjects which have most engrossed our attention and the attention of the world during these last anxious months, since the armistice of last November was signed, the international settlements which must form the subject matter of the present treaties of peace and of our national action in the immediate future. It would be premature to discuss them or to express a judgment about them before they are brought to their complete formulation by the agreements which are now being sought at the table of the Conference. I shall hope to lay them before you in their many aspects so soon as arrangements have been reached.

I hesitate to venture any opinion or press any recommendation with regard to domestic legislation while absent from the United States and out of daily touch with intimate sources of information and counsel. I am conscious that I need, after so long an absence from Washington, to seek the advice of those who remained in constant contact with domestic problems and who have known them close at hand from day to day; and I trust that it will very soon be possible for me to do so. But there are several questions pressing for consideration to which I feel that I may, and indeed must, even now direct your attention, if only in general terms. In speaking of them I shall, I dare say, be doing little more than speak your own thoughts. I hope that I shall speak your own judgment also.

The question which stands at the front of all others in every country amidst the present great awakening is the question of labor; and perhaps I can speak of it with as great advantage while engrossed in the consideration of interests which affect all countries alike as I could at home and amidst the interests which naturally most affect my thought, because they are the interests of our own people.

By the question of labor I do not mean the question of efficient industrial production, the question of how labor is to be obtained and made effective in the great process of sustaining populations and winning success amidst commercial and industrial rivalries. I mean that much greater and more vital question, how are the men and women who do the daily labor of th world to obtain progressive improvement in the conditions of their labor, to made happier, and to be served better by the communities and the industries which their labor sustains and advances? How are they to be given their right advantage as citizens and human beings?

We cannot go any further in our present direction. We have already gone too far. We cannot live our right as a nation or achieve our proper success as an industrial community if capital and labor are to continue to be antagonistic instead of being partners. If they are to continue to distrust one another and contrive how they can get the better of one another. Or, what perhaps amounts to the same thing, calculate by what form and degree of coercion they can manage to extort on the one hand work enough to make enterprise profitable, on the other justice and fair treatment enough to make life tolerable. That bad road has turned out a blind alley. It is no thoroughfare to real prosperity. We must find another, leading in another direction and to a very different destination. It must lead not merely to accommodation but also to a genuine coöperation and partnership based upon a real community of interest and participation in control.

There is now in fact a real community of interest between capital and labor, but it has never been made evident in action. It can be made operative and manifest only in a new organization of industry. The genius of our business men and the sound practical sense of our workers can certainly work such a partnership out when once they realize exactly what it is that they seek and sincerely adopt a common purpose with regard to it.

Labor legislation lies, of course, chiefly with the states; but the new spirit and method of organization which must be effected are not to be brought about by legislation so much as by the common counsel and voluntary coöperation of capitalist, manager, and workman. Legislation can go only a very little way in commanding what shall be done. The organization of industry is a matter of corporate and individual initiative and of practical business arrangement. Those who really desire a new relationship between capital and labor can readily find a way to bring it about: and perhaps Federal legislation can help more than state legislation could.

The object of all reform in this essential matter must be the genuine democratization of industry, based upon a full recognition of the right of those who work, in whatever rank, to participate in some organic way in every decision which directly affects their welfare or the part they are to play in industry. Some positive legislation is practicable. The Congress has already shown the way to one reform which should be worldwide, by establishing the eight-hour day as the standard day in every field of labor over which it can exercise control. It has sought to find the way to prevent child labor, and will, I hope and believe, presently find it. It has served the whole country by leading the way in developing the means of preserving and safeguarding life and health in dangerous industries. It can now help in the difficult task of giving a new form and spirit to industrial organization by coördinating the several agencies of conciliation and adjustment which have been brought into existence by the difficulties and mistaken policies of the present management of industry, and by setting up and developing new Federal agencies of advice and information which may serve as a clearing-house for the best experiments and the best thought on this great matter, upon which every thinking man must be aware that the future development of society directly depends. Agencies of international counsel and suggestion are presently to be created in connection with the League of Nations in this very field; but it is national action and the enlightened policy of individuals, corporations, and societies within each nation that must bring about the actual reforms. The members of the committees on labor in the two houses will hardly need suggestions from me as to what means they shall seek to make the Federal Government the agent of the whole Nation in pointing out and, if need be, guiding the process of reorganization and reform. . . .

Will you not permit me, turning from these matters, to speak once more and very earnestly of the proposed amendment to the Constitution which would extend the suffrage to women and which passed the House of Representatives at the last session of the Congress? It seems to me that every consideration of justice and of public advantage calls for the immediate adoption of that amendment and its submission forthwith to the legislatures of the several states. Throughout all the world this long-delayed extension of the suffrage is looked for; in the United States, longer, I believe, than anywhere else, the necessity for it, and the immense advantage of it to the national life, has been urged and debated, by women and men who saw the need for it and urged the policy of it when it required steadfast courage to be so much beforehand with the common conviction; and I, for one, covet for our country the distinction of being among the first to act in a great reform.

The telegraph and telephone lines will of course be returned to their owners so soon as the retransfer can be effected without administrative confusion, so soon, that is, as the change can be made with least possible inconvenience to the public and to the owners themselves. The railroads will be handed over to their owners at the end of the calendar year; if I were in immediate contact with the administrative questions which must govern the retransfer of the telegraph and telephone lines, I could name the exact date for their return also. Until I am in direct contact with the practical questions involved I can only suggest that in the case of the telegraphs and telephones, as in the case of the railways, it is clearly desirable in the public interest that some legislation should be considered which may tend to make of these indispensable instrumentalities of our modern life a uniform coördinated system which will afford those who use them as complete and certain means of communication with all parts of the country as has so long been afforded by the postal system of the Government, and at rates as uniform and intelligible. Expert advice is, of course, available in this very practical matter, and the public interest is manifest. Neither the telegraph nor the telephone service of the country can be said to be in any sense a national system. There are many confusions and inconsistencies of rates. The scientific means by which communication by such instrumentalities could be rendered more thorough and satisfactory has not been made full use of. An exhaustive study of the whole question of electrical communication and of the means by which the central authorlty of the Nation can be used to unify and improve it, if, undertaken, by the appropriate committees of the Congress, would certainly result, indirectly even if not directly, in a great public benefit. . . .

I sincerely trust that I shall very soon be at my post in Washington again to report upon the matters which made my presence at the peace table apparently imperative, and to put myself at the service of the Congress in every matter of administration or counsel that may seem to demand executive action or advice.

23

PROGRESSIVE PARTY OF 1924
Platform

Many historians have dismissed this platform as a body of tired progressive ideas pushed forward by some old men who did not recognize the obsolescence of their reformist philosophy in the new postwar world. To be told their proposals were timid, obsolete and irrelevant would have astonished the Progressives, since the press easily convinced most of the public that they were dangerous radicals. Those who argue that the platform reveals the bankruptcy of the reform mind in the 1920s have presumably not noticed how much of the New Deal is foreshadowed in its proposals—including, if one reads closely, an ancestor of F.D.R.'s Court Plan of 1937.

Kirk H. Porter and Donald B. Johnson, eds., *National Party Platforms* (Urbana: University of Illinois, 1966), pp. 252–55. Reprinted with permission.

The great issue before the American people today is the control of government and industry by private monopoly.

For a generation the people have struggled patiently, in the face of repeated betrayals by successive administrations, to free themselves from this intolerable power which has been undermining representative government.

Through control of government, monopoly has steadily extended its absolute dominion to every basic industry.

In violation of law, monopoly has crushed competition, stifled private initiative and independent enterprise, and without fear of punishment now exacts extortionate profits upon every necessity of life consumed by the public.

The equality of opportunity proclaimed by the Declaration of Independence and asserted and defended by Jefferson and Lincoln as the heritage of every American citizen has been displaced by special privilege for the few, wrested from the government of the many.

Fundamental Rights in Danger

That tyrannical power which the American people denied to a king, they will no longer endure from the monopoly system. The people know they cannot yield to any group the control of the economic life of the nation and preserve their liberties. They know monopoly has its representatives in the halls of Congress, on the Federal bench, and in the executive departments; that these servile agents barter away the nation's natural resources, nullify acts of Congress by judicial veto and administrative favor, invade the people's rights by unlawful arrests and unconstitutional searches and seizures, direct our foreign policy in the interests of predatory wealth, and make wars and conscript the sons of the common people to fight them.

The usurpation in recent years by the federal courts of the power to nullify laws duly enacted by the legislative branch of the goverment is a plain violation of the Constitution. . . .

Distress of American Farmers

The present condition of Amercan agriculture constitutes an emergency of the gravest character. The Department of Commerce report shows that during 1923 there was a steady and marked increase in dividends paid by the great industrial corporations. The same is true of the steam and electric railways and practically all other large corporations. On the other hand, the Secretary of Agriculture reports that in the fifteen principal wheat growing states more than 108,000 farmers since 1920 have lost farms through foreclosure or bankruptcy; that more than 122,000 have surrendered their property without legal proceedings, and that nearly 375,000 have retained possession of their property only through the leniency of their creditors, making a total of more than 600,000 or 26 percent of all farmers who have virtually been bankrupted since 1920 in these fifteen states alone.

Almost unlimited prosperity for the great corporations and ruin and bankruptcy for agriculture is the direct and logical result of the policies and legislation which deflated the farmer while extending almost unlimited credit to the great corporations; which protected with exorbitant tariffs the industrial magnates, but depressed the prices of the farmer's products by financial juggling while greatly increasing the cost of what he must buy; which guaranteed excessive freight rates to the railroads and put a premium on wasteful management while saddling an unwarranted burden on to the backs of the American farmer; which permitted gambling in the products of the farm by grain speculators to the great detriment of the farmer and to the great profit of the grain gambler.

A Covenant with the People

Awakened by the dangers which menace their freedom and prosperity the American people still retain the right and courage to exercise their sovereign control over their government. In order to destroy the economic and political power of monopoly, which has come between the people and their government, we pledge ourselves to the following principles and policies:

The House Cleaning

1. We pledge a complete housecleaning in the Department of Justice, the Department of the Interior, and the other executive departments. We demand that the power of the Federal Government be used to crush private monopoly, not to foster it.

Natural Resources

2. We pledge recovery of the navy's oil reserves and all other parts of the public domain which have fraudulently or illegally leased, or otherwise wrongfully transferred, to the control of private interests; vigorous prosecution of all public officials, private citizens and corporations that participated in these transactions; complete revision of the water-power act, the general leasing act, and all other legislation relating to the public domain. We favor public ownership of the nation's water power and the creation and development of a national super-water-power system, including Muscle Shoals, to supply at actual cost light and power for the people and nitrate for the farmers, and strict public control and permanent conservation of all the nation's resources, including coal, iron and other ores, oil and timber lands, in the interest of the people.

Railroads

3. We favor repeal of the Esch-Cummins railroad law and the fixing of railroad rates upon the basis of actual, prudent investment and cost of service. . . .

Tax Reduction

4. We favor reduction of Federal taxes upon individual incomes and legitimate business, limiting tax exactions strictly to the requirements of the government administered with rigid economy, particularly by the curtailment of the eight hundred million dollars now annually expended for the army and navy in preparation for future wars; by the recovery of the hundreds of millions of dollars stolen from the Treasury through fraudulent war contracts and the corrupt leasing of the public resources; and by diligent action to collect the accumulated interest upon the eleven billion dollars owing us by foreign governments.

We denounce the Mellon tax plan as a device to relieve multi-millionaires at the expense of other tax payers, and favor a taxation policy providing for immediate reductions upon moderate incomes, large increases in the inheritance tax rates upon large estates to prevent the indefinite accumulation by inheritance of great fortunes in a few hands; taxes upon excess profits to penalize profiteering, and complete publicity, under proper safeguards, of all Federal tax returns.

The Courts

5. We favor submitting to the people for their considerate judgment, a constitutional amendment providing that Congress may by enacting a statute make it effective over a judicial veto.

We favor such amendment to the constitution as may be necessary to provide for the election of all Federal Judges, without party designation, for fixed terms not exceeding ten years, by direct vote of the people.

The Farmers

6. We favor drastic reduction of the exorbitant duties on manufactures provided in the Fordney-McCumber tariff legislation, the prohibiting of gambling by speculators and profiteers in agricultural products; the reconstruction of the Federal Reserve and Federal Farm Loan Systems, so as to eliminate control by usurers, speculators and international financiers, and to make the credit of the nation available upon fair terms to all and without discrimination to business men, farmers, and home-builders. We advocate the calling of a special session of Congress to pass legislation for the relief of American agriculture. We favor such further legislation as may be needful or helpful in promoting and protecting co-operative enterprises. We demand that the Interstate Commerce Commission proceed forthwith to reduce by an approximation to pre-war levels the present freight rates on agricultural products, including live stock, and upon the materials required upon American farms for agricultural purposes.

Labor

7. We favor abolition of the use of injunctions in labor disputes and declare for complete protection of the right of farmers and industrial workers to organize, bargain collectively through representa-

tives of their own choosing, and conduct without hindrance cooperative enterprises.

We favor prompt ratification of the Child Labor amendment, and subsequent enactment of a Federal law to protect children in industry. . . .

Peace on Earth

12. We denounce the mercenary system of foreign policy under recent administrations in the interests of financial imperialists, oil monopolies and international bankers, which has at times degraded our State Department from its high service as a strong and kindly intermediary of defenseless governments to a trading outpost for those interests and concession-seekers engaged in the exploitations of weaker nations, as contrary to the will of the American people, destructive of domestic development and provocative of war. We favor an active foreign policy to bring about a revision of the Versailles treaty in accordance with the terms of the armistice, and to promote firm treaty agreements with all nations to outlaw wars, abolish conscription, drastically reduce land, air and naval armaments, and guarantee public referendum on peace and war.

24

GRACE ABBOTT

The Child and the State—the 1920s

This remarkable book, published in the year of the first permanent and effective federal prohibition of child labor (Fair Labor Standards Act, 1938), surveyed the entire experience of the humanitarian effort to protect the child from economic exploitation. The portions of the book reprinted below report on surveys of working conditions for children in the postwar period. The evidence revealed a huge gap in the 1920s between the letter of the law—most states had passed some form of child labor regulation in the progressive period—and the industrial facts of life, a situation that was duplicated in many areas where reformers had won legislative victories.

Ohio—The Ohio child labor law of 1913 set a new standard in child labor legislation. It established a minimum working age of 15 years for boys and of 16 years for girls and an educational minimum which required completion of the sixth grade for boys and the seventh grade for girls. It prohibited the employment of boys under 16 and of girls between 16 and 18 more than 8 hours a day, 48 hours a week, or 6 days a week, or between 6 P.M. and 7 A.M.; the employment of boys between 16 and 18 after 10 P.M. was also prohibited. A preliminary examination to establish physical fitness was required before a child could get a work permit; and these permits the law required must be secured and kept on file by the employer for boys of 15 and for girls between 16 and 18 years of age. The Ohio statutory standards were therefore much higher than the standards set by the United States child labor act of September 1, 1916, or than those adopted by the War Labor Policies Board.

Ohio inspections made by the Child Labor Division during June, July, and August, 1918, were confined to the glass and pottery industries along the Ohio River from the East Liverpool district to Wheeling and west to Columbus and Cincinnati, one of the most important centers for these industries in the United States.

The glass factories in this district were manufacturing bottles, food containers, tumblers, and other tableware, druggist glass, magnifying glasses, automobile lenses, lantern and lighting globes, and art glass for churches and public buildings.

The Ohio pottery district is one of the oldest and most important in the United States. China tableware, stoneware jars and cooking utensils, electrical and chemical porcelains, vases and art potteries, heavy sanitary ware, floor and wall tiles are all produced in potteries which vary much in size, number of employees, and general conditions.

In 81 of the 95 plants inspected, violations of the State child labor

---

laws were found. As the State standards were higher than the Federal, there were fewer violations of Federal standards; still, in 62 establishments (65 per cent of the entire number inspected) there were violations of the Federal age and hour standards. The youngest child found at work was 8 years old, another was 9, 2 children were 10, 12 were 11 years old, 12 were 12, and 71 were 13 years old, making a total of 99 children under 14 employed in violation of the Federal age standard. The State standard was further violated by the employment of 173 boys and girls 14 years old and 55 girls 15 years old, making a total of 327 found at work who were below the minimum age limit fixed by the Ohio State law.

The proof of age required by the State statute gave the legal basis for a good certificating system. But the investigations made by the Child Labor Division in the summer of 1918 showed that in the cities and towns visited the certificating law was violated and ignored in practice, and no attempt was made to use it to prevent the employment of children in occupations where they were exposed to lead poisoning or dust hazards. . . .

CHILD LABORERS TODAY, AS DEPICTED IN THE NEW YORK WORLD
1924, BY HENRY F. PRINGLE, STAFF CORRESPONDENT
AND BY THE EDITOR [PAMPHLET]

Mississippi, since she has spent ten times as much during 1923 for her cattle as for the enforcement of her child labor laws, must plead guilty to sanctioning such violations as may occur in the Gulf Coast canneries and elsewhere.

Her laws are bad enough and would hardly protect the children of the State even if adequate machinery to see that they are obeyed were in operation. But the two factors—non-enforcement and poor laws— are demanding their price. Mississippi leads all the States in the union today, with 25.5 per cent. of her children between ten and fifteen years old at work. She is far down on the illiteracy scale, with 9.3 per cent. of her children of the same age group unable to read or write.

Mississippi, boastful of her natural resources, virtually encourages the exploitation of her future generation. Her compulsory school laws are as bad as her child labor laws. The cost of all this, speaking in terms other than that of dollars and cents considered by her Legislature, is a growing body of children who are being defrauded of education, bound to a particular industry as soon as they are able to earn a pittance, and suffering in health because of the intolerable living conditions in many of the industrial communities.

A. B. Hobbs who makes his headquarters at the State Capitol at Jackson, is the solitary factory inspector for the entire State. Mr. Hobbs said that with the present appropriation of but $5,500 for his work it was impossible to enforce the child labor laws. He declared he was greatly in favor of the enactment of a Federal amendment so the children would be protected despite the neglect of the State Legislature. A total of $5,500 to protect the children in industry! Mississippi can afford $50,000 for the prevention of stock diseases! Such was the sum appropriated for the protection of cattle in 1923. . . .

Manufacturers' Journals Denounce the Amendment

IT IS RUSSIAN IN ORIGIN

"WHAT THE CHILD LABOR AMENDMENT MEANS," MANUFACTURERS' RECORD (BALTIMORE, MD.), SEPTEMBER 4, 1924

Because the Child Labor Amendment in reality is not legislation in the interest of children but legislation which would mean the destruction of manhood and womanhood through the destruction of the boys and girls of the country, the *Manufacturers' Record* has been giving much attention to the discussion of the subject, and will continue to do so. . . .

This proposed amendment is fathered by Socialists, Communists and Bolshevists. They are the active workers in its favor. They look forward to its adoption as giving them the power to nationalize the children of the land and bring about in this country the exact conditions which prevail in Russia. These people are the active workers back of this undertaking, but many patriotic men and women without at all realizing the seriousness of this proposion, thinking only of it as an effort to lessen child labor in factories, are giving countenance to it.

If adopted, this amendment would be the greatest thing ever done in America in behalf of the activities of Hell. It would make millions of young people under 18 years of age idlers in brain and body, and thus make them the devil's best workshop. It would destroy the initiative and self-reliance and manhood and womanhood of all the coming generations.

A solemn responsibility to this country and to all future generations rests upon every man and woman who understands this situation to fight, and fight unceasingly, to make the facts known to their acquaintances everywhere. Aggressive work is needed. It would be worse than folly for people who realize the danger of this situation to rest content under the belief that the Amendment cannot become a part of our Constitution. The only thing that can prevent its adoption will be active, untiring work on the part of every man and woman who appreciates its destructive power and who wants to save the young people of all future generations from moral and physical decay under the domination of the devil himself.

IT WILL GIVE EMPLOYMENT TO GOVERNMENT PARASITES

"HIGH COST OF GOVERNMENT," MANUFACTURERS NEWS (CHICAGO, ILL.), OCTOBER 3, 1925, P. 12

Office holding parasites want to prohibit work by all minors under 18. Why? So they can put to work several thousand inspectors to see that the youth of the land are properly idle. Too much sociology. Too much bureaucracy. Too many payrollers. Too many drones in the hive. . . .

REUBEN DAGENHART IN 1923

"HOW SHARPER THAN A SERPENT'S TOOTH IT IS TO HAVE A THANKLESS CHILD"—KING LEAR. FROM AN ARTICLE BY LOWELL MELLETT, OF THE SCRIPPS-HOWARD NEWSPAPER SERVICE, PUBLISHED IN LABOR, NOVEMBER 17, 1923

This is the story of an ungrateful child. The story of a lad for whom all the machinery of the American judiciary was turned to preserve his constitutional rights and who, after six years, has not yet brought himself to give thanks.

The boy is Reuben Dagenhart, of Charlotte, N.C.

Six years ago, Federal Judge James E. Boyd, of the western North Carolina district, interposed the majesty of the law in Reuben's behalf. Some months later Chief Justice White and Justices Day, Van Devanter, McReynolds and Pitney did the same. They declared— and they made it stick—that the Congress of the United States could not take away from young Reuben Dagenhart his "constitutional" right to work more hours every day than a boy of 14 ought to work.

There may be another ungrateful boy in the picture—John Dagenhart. John, aged 12, had his constitutional rights defended by the same courts to the extent that he was allowed to go on working in a cotton mill at an age when no boy should work at all in a cotton mill. But two days' roving through the cotton mill towns around Charlotte last week failed to find John, and readers will have to be content with the story of Reuben. This leaves out, also, the story of Roland H. Dagenhart, father of the boys, whose constitutional right to put them to work in the mills and to receive their wages each Saturday was upheld by the same upright judges. . . .

And should not the Dagenhart boys be grateful for that?

Well, Reuben isn't.

I found him at his home in Charlotte. He is about the size of the office boy—weighs 105 pounds, he told me. But he is a married man with a child. He is 20 years old.

"What benefit," I asked him, "did you get out of the suit which you won in the United States Supreme Court?"

"You mean the suit the Fidelity Manufacturing Company won? (It was the Fidelity Company for which the Dagenharts were working.) I don't see that I got any benefit. I guess I'd been a lot better off if they hadn't won it.

'Look at me! A hundred and five pounds, a grown man and no education. I may be mistaken, but I think the years I've put in the cotton mills have stunted my growth. They kept me from getting any schooling. I had to stop school after the third grade and now I need the education I didn't get."

"How was your growth stunted?"

"I don't know—the dust and the lint, maybe. But from 12 years old on, I was working 12 hours a day—from 6 in the morning till 7 at night, with time out for meals. And sometimes I worked nights besides. Lifting a hundred pounds and I only weighed 65 pounds myself."

He explained that he and his sister worked together, "on section," spinning. They each made about a dollar a day, though later he worked up to where he could make $2. His father made $15 a week and infant John, at the time the suit was brought, was making close to $1 a day.

"Just what did you and John get out of that suit, then?" was asked.

"Why, we got some automobile rides when them big lawyers from the North was down here. Oh, yes, and they bought both of us a coca-cola! That's all we got out of it."

"What did you tell the judge when you were in court?"

"Oh, John and me never was in court! Just Paw was there. John and me was just little kids in short pants. I guess we wouldn't have looked like much in court. We were working in the mill while the case was going on. But Paw went up to Washington."

Reuben hasn't been to school, but his mind has not been idle.

"It would have been a good thing for all the kids in this state if that law they passed had been kept. Of course, they do better now than they used to. You don't see so many babies working in the factories, but you see a lot of them that ought to be going to school."

"What about John? Is he satisfied with the way things turned out?"

"I don't know. Prob'ly not. He's much bigger than me and he's got flat feet."

"How about your father?"

"Oh, he's satisfied, I guess. But I know one thing. I ain't going to let them put my kid sister in the mill, like he's thinking of doing! She's only 15 and she's crippled and I bet I stop that!"

III. REFORM: 1917-1928

25

FREDERIC C. HOWE

Confessions of a Reformer

Fred Howe's autobiography is one of the great books of the progressive movement because he spoke the mind of so many reformers as they passed from youthful conservatism into reform, and through its various stages to a final summing-up that was usually tinged with some frustration and disappointment. Reformers summed up their experience differently, of course, and some saw no need to modify attitudes adopted years ago in the morning of the movement. But many, including Howe, came out after the war with the feeling that they, and all of progressivism, had been guilty of some mental errors they would not repeat. The retrospective passage reprinted below reveals Howe as one of those progressives who might be said to have moved slightly Left of progressivism; but, again like many others, there are strong hints that nothing very radical was contemplated either at the beginning or the end of his admirable career.

The one thing I had clung to all these years was a belief in my class convinced by facts. It was mind that would save the world, the mind of my class aroused from indifference, from money-making, from party loyalty and coming out into the clear light of reason. I now began to see that men were not concerned over the truth. It did not interest them when economic interests were at stake. The mind was as closed to facts as a safety-deposit vault. There was a sign outside: "Do not enter here."

Aside from a few young men, I could not remember a person of prominence in the ten years' war in Cleveland who had been converted from his class by intellectual appeals. It had been a war of classes. . . .

I had built my life first around conventional morality, then about the mind. Conventional morals did not prevent men from making war, from corrupting the state, from destroying democracy. There were as many different kinds of morals as there were groups that held them. And the morals men held were in some way shaped by the things they wanted, by their economic interest, by the class in which they worked and lived. There was a group morality for the small town, for the university man, for the banker and the business man, for the lawyer and the doctor, for the politician and grafter, for the men who stood behind the politicians and profited from their grafting. And conventional morality seemed to find no difficulty in justifying these differing codes even to the extent of bringing on a cataclysmic war that had all but destroyed humanity.

Frederic C. Howe, *The Confessions of a Reformer* (New York: Charles Scribner's Sons, 1925, Quadrangle Books, Inc., 1967), pp. 322–25. Reprinted with permission.

And the mind had failed as completely as morals. Men did not think when social problems were involved. They did not use the mind. It refused to work against economic interest. This was so obviously true that I wondered it had not been stated. The mind worked with wonderful precision in the production of wealth, in the making of machines, in the realm of science, in all those fields where men were achieving their own lives and instincts. But when logic, evidence, convincing facts pointed one way and individual or class interest pointed another the mind closed itself to reason and refused to function. The world had not been saved by morality. Apparently it had little to hope for from the human mind.

But I made one reconciling discovery: my dreams—the things I wanted—were still alive under the ruins of most of what I had thought. I had wanted, since Johns Hopkins, to change things. Freedom seemed to me the law of life, and the single tax the most nearly perfect expression of it that had been given to the world. I would have accepted a lot of evil to get free trade, to end private ownership of the railways, to bring in the single tax. I had had no liking for Socialism; did not want to see struggle, initiative banished from the world. I liked these things and wanted rather to see them released, wanted every one to enter the race on equal terms, with no favoritism, no handicap; no advantages due to birth or ownership. I wanted a world of equal opportunity.

I wanted, too, an orderly world—a world that had the distinction that aristocracy gave; all of the personal distinction of individualism, and all of the wealth that human ingenuity could create, dispensed as its creators desired. I had no fear of great wealth, provided it was the creation of man, of his brain no less than his hands. I had no fear of freedom; rather liked it, but I wanted the freedom to be open to all, wanted the color, the variety, the waste of a world that produced in abundance and spent as abundantly as it produced.

I still wanted all this. But I had been wrong about the way to get it. My own class did not want such a world. And there was but one other class—the workers—those who produced wealth by hand or brain. Would labor want to end this universal war, would labor want a universal peace, would labor want the kind of world I had long wanted, a world of equal opportunity, a world in which the wealth created would be enjoyed by those that created it? It seemed to me that labor would want these things. Labor could not serve privilege, as privilege could only be enjoyed by the few. By necessity labor would serve freedom, democracy, equal opportunity for all.

My faith in the "goodness" of my class died hard, but its death did not leave me insolvent. My ideals were still undimmed; I had found a class whose interests ran hand in hand with the things I desired. And once the blinders were off, it seemed that my distrust of people not of my own class had little foundation. There were new leaders with vision and confidence. The movement seemed historically inevitable. Political power had been in continuous drift from the few to the many for a hundred years; first from the king to the nobility, then from the nobility to the landed aristocracy; from the landed aristocracy the drift continued to the commercial classes. The next step was the last and it could not be stopped. Labor had to make its own fight, it had to use its own power; the place for the liberal was in labor's ranks.

At fifty I saw myself as I saw the political state. I had lost the illusions I had spent a lifetime in hoarding. I had lost illusions of myself. Much of my intellectual capital had flown. Drafts on my mind came back indorsed: "No funds." But I was still not bankrupt. The new truth that a free world would only come through labor was forced on me. I did not seek it; did not welcome it. But it crowded into mind and demanded tenancy as the old occupants gave notice to leave.

26 ———————————————————————

THE SURVEY
"Where Are the Pre-War Radicals?"

The publication of Howe's autobiography in 1925 suggested to the editors of *The Survey* a symposium of surviving reformers on the question of the results and prospects of the progressive movement. The result was an illuminating collection of short retrospective pieces from reformers of varied credentials. Their disagreements over what the movement had been about, where it had gone wrong, and what if anything remained to be done make it easier to understand why this generation made somewhat fewer changes in the world than they had expected.

An intelligent answer requires us to recall at the outset that many of the things about which Mr. Howe was radical have been accomplished. American municipal government, which was a disgrace twenty-five years ago, is now both more honest and more efficient. The principle of municipal home rule has been adopted into state constitutions. Many cities have made and re-made their own charters and a series of informing experiments has been made in municipal institutions, so that city government is freer from bossism, more responsive to popular control and more efficient than it used to be. With these changes has come the full acceptance of the program of municipal activity for which radicals used to contend—better public schools, parks, bath houses and public control of public utility monopolies.

In the second place, we must admit that some of the things radicals contended for have been tried and found of less value in practice than they promised in theory. Among these are the initiative and referendum, the recall, the non-partisan primary, the commission form of government and proportional representation. That some of these have proved useful is clear, but their absolute importance is plainly less than was once supposed.

In the third place, when the great national test came after the World War, the radicals developed a wholly unsuspected lack of capacity to cooperate. When the war was over, real liberal cooperation would have captured the future for the world, but every radical liberal, apparently, had his own theory or his own grievance, and the conservative reaction marched through the liberal ranks, which were broken into fragments by their own dissensions.

In the fourth place, after the immeasurable destruction of the World War, a destruction alike of physical property and faith in human institutions, the stricken and terrified world demanded a respite. Instead of more destruction of things and faith, it wanted a chance to build again on its shattered foundation. Most of the radicals of the older day have responded to the call for constructive effort.

"Where Are the Pre-War Radicals," *The Survey* 55 (February 1, 1926), 556-66.

Lastly the experience of the Russian people under a degrading despotism, with radicals in the saddle, has tempered the welcome of radical ideas in other parts of the world.

None of the foregoing means that there is less room in the world or less need in the world for liberalism. Liberalism is a state of mind and not a creed. A liberal uses his fellow men for their benefit and not for his own. He judges political purposes by their effect on the common good and he has in his mind's eye, as the ultimate object of his concern, "the forgotten man," remote, obscure and inaudible in high places. Liberalism of this quality is imperishable and it has many brave services yet to perform for the American people.

NEWTON D. BAKER

Newton D. Baker, Tom Johnson's left hand in his long drawn municipal ownership fight in Cleveland, his successor as mayor of the city, and Woodrow Wilson's Secretary of War. Since then president of the Cleveland Chamber of Commerce.

I can answer "Here" to your roll-call of the "pre-war radicals." If I was indeed a radical then, I am still a radical, and no hopeless radical either, for my belief in certain great fundamentals of human relationship has not changed. I believed then that the basis of all advance in civilization was human understanding and human sympathy. I believe it still more vitally now. I am therefore more radical, not less.

Where I was mistaken as a "pre-war radical" was in thinking that what I wanted could be had by adopting certain easy devices of social inventions—otherwise, by shortcuts. What I have gained since is the knowledge that though the thing is true the time appointed is long. There are no miracles in progress; there is only the plodding but beautiful adventure of inquiry and education. Civilization does not come by control but by self-control. We cannot make the hurrah of elections and the enactment of laws take the place of personal conviction.

I deny being a "disillusioned radical"; but rather a deeper radical in the very sense of the word "root." We must go down deep where men live and try first of all to understand them. We "pre-war radicals" were just like all the other politicians; we were more interested in bossing people than in knowing them; we wanted to boss our neighbors into our own little plans for goodness, or efficiency, or justice. We did not understand that growth does not come from without or above, but from within and deep down.

Don't blame us then because we are no longer so sure as we were, or so noisy; think of us as having gone back to get acquainted with life, of liking better for a while to ask questions than to answer them; of *trying to understand*. And don't worry; you will hear of us again later (not us in any personal or egotistical sense, but of us who believe that understanding is the key-note of civilization); we shall be coming up from the soil all muscular with new power. For this is the truth of the matter: people are infinitely worth knowing, worth living among, worth working with; they are the only material we have out of which to build a New Earth. This is the greatest of all creative adventures; and better worth while than ever it was before in history; for the material is more alive, more malleable, more interesting. That it cannot at once, overnight, be shaped to our ideas of perfection, is no cause for sickly disillusionment, but for new enthusiasm and new effort. The true creator sees that while the stone is harder than he thought, the image within it is vastly greater, and nobler.

RAY STANNARD BAKER

Ray Stannard Baker has been called America's "star reporter" since the days of "the old McClure's." He followed the white plume of Wilson to Paris, directed the American Press Bureau at the Peace Conference, and is now at work on the authoritative biography of Wilson.

If the editor of The Survey is inquiring after pre-war radicals because he thinks they may have lost their zeal or changed their objectives, let him write a book claiming that some favorite corporate scape-goat is not and never has been guilty of certain sins with which he is charged—moreover that for twenty-five years he has carried on a valiant struggle to correct the said sins in the field where he had authority. The storm of bricks from pre-war radicals and their post-war imitators that will greet his effort will convince him that the tribe still thrives and is as jealous as ever of its ammunition dump.

The writer of these paragraphs has just applied this test and can guarantee its efficacy. The pre-war radical who considers it as treasonable to discover good among the "interests" as his enemy, the pre-war conservative, considers it treasonable to point out evil there, is still with us.

The group is not in my judgment seriously depleted. To be sure a few killed themselves for public usefulness sometime ago by self-imitation. They knew but one theme—one method of attack. When that was no longer effective with the easily bored public their following left them. They usually charged the desertion to the "interests" but their own in-

flexibility—their ignorance of the bigness and complexity of the problems with which they dealt—had much more to do with it than the
hostility of those who disagreed with their views and disliked their
methods, and whom they should have expected to oppose them—
until they could convince or overthrow them.

The fact is that the pre-war radical was often not a wise man—an
experienced or patient man. He knew little about human beings, and
what as individuals and herds they can be counted on to do under
certain circumstances, when his denunciation, his righteous indignation at the stupidities injustices and wrongs that complicate the
daily affairs of the nation, his demonstrations—for often they were
just that—that simpler, more rational procedure could be followed if
people would unite for it—when all this had given him an advantage,
he frequently lost it because he did not know how to take the next
step, did not understand the need of practical cooperation with all
men.

Some of the kind destroyed themselves by allowing their campaigns
to degenerate into sensationalism. That was what killed the aggressive
popular magazine, starting with careful investigation and temperate,
if often severe exposition—having a passion for facts and their meaning, these journals flourished, were listened to, but imitators interested
not in the whole truth of things but the half-truths which served their
theories, rose. The school was soon wallowing in sensation. Much of
it deserved the title of muck-raking which Mr. Roosevelt gave it. The
careful and serious editor and writer were tarred by the abuse of their
method, and finally a form of journalism capable of continued usefulness was done to death—by those in its own ranks—not by bankers
afraid of its influence as so often charged.

These casualties aside, the mass of pre-war radicals are still as large,
and if less vociferous still in their own way useful. Some of them like
Fred Howe, the lovable reformer whose confessions gave The Survey
the text for its question, are flitting from one exciting outbreak to
another, though few have landed as happily as he—the head of a sub-
limated gab-fest on his own ocean front in summer, an intellectual
flaneur in Paris in winter. Don't tell me the reformer does not know
how to provide oases for himself!

Not a few—probably most of the pre-war radicals have found new
themes. They know that their old problems are still unsolved, though
if they are candid they know that their efforts have led to a better
understanding and many corrections. If their temper was less mel-

ancholy they would rejoice that something has been accomplished. They see the need of new tools, new approaches, new and larger attitudes of mind. Many of them have come to believe that the present imperative duty of those interested in fixing up the world is to learn how to stop quarrelling—to do away with wars and strikes and lockouts—to suspect their opponent less and their own infallibility more—to be willing to peg away at the thing that comes to their hand —not asking that the nation stop in its tracks and listen to their voice —but convinced that if they are doing as well as they can what seems a useful thing, they are doing the only really radical thing man is capable of.

Iᴅᴀ M. Tᴀʀʙᴇʟʟ

Ida M. Tarbell, dean of American women journalists, was associated with McClure's from 1894 to 1906, and with The American from 1906 to 1915. Her Inside History of the Standard Oil Company was the first outstanding example of large scale magazine fact-gathering.

What has become of the pre-war "radicals"?

Well, what is a "radical"?

I used to think that a "radical" was a person who, like Thomas Jefferson, stood out valiantly—and even a bit wildly and frantically— against all avoidable encroachments upon individual life by that archfoe of individuality and personality, that greatest of all necessary evils, the State.

I used to think that a "radical" was a person who wished to wrest from the State its habitual traditional custom of throwing its weight— its coercion—into the scales in favor of the powerful against the weak.

The electing of legislators who would not give undue and excessive tariffs and franchises to manufacturers and investors; the electing of executives who would not use their administrative powers to check the growth of new expression in political philosophy, in literature, in motion pictures; the choosing of judges who would not use the rod of the injunction to repeal the constitutional rights of strikers—such I thought to be, in principle, in illustration, the motivating impulses and objectives of the "radical."

I have lived to see my error. The "radical" of this moment—dominantly—is not so much interested in trying to weaken the power of the State to enslave the thinker and the worker as he is in vainly trying to strengthen the power of the State to enslave the manager and the capitalist.

I say "vainly." At Washington we see bureau after bureau, commission after commission, funded by the energies of "radicals" and dominated now—and used against "radicals"—by "reactionaries."

This is so; and it is bound to be so; for the plain simple reason that more "reactionaries" than "radicals" can pay their railroad fare to Washington to see to it.

Those who take the sword will perish by the sword; and those who lay hold of government excessively to serve their purposes will ultimately perish excessively by government; for government in essence is nothing but coercion, nothing but the sword.

Contemporary "radicalism," trying governmentally to enslave its enemies, can end only by enslaving itself. It needs to transfer its emphasis from more commissions to more emancipations, from more bureaus of governmental inquiry to more equalities of governmental behavior, from more laws to more repeals of more laws.

"Radicalism," from being a grand wild dragon, has gone and become a thing in which the only "redness' is that it is a red-tape-worm.

I await its re-birth out of the cocoon into which it is winding itself. I shall then want to ride on its wings, just for a few trips, toward the sun, before I die, I hope.

WILLIAM HARD

William Hard, better known as Bill, one of the galaxy that made the old Everybody's Magazine a power in the land, now interprets Washington to the world and lets in lots of light.

Granted that a certain group of liberals have more or less disintegrated I do not find it possible to become hectic over their lessened prominence. Things happen in history. Wilson executed most of his own program and that of the Bull Moose, which gave us a chance to see how much our cures were worth. The war came along and handed us new problems of considerable magnitude.

The greatest world-problem now is peace. Labor elements and liberal elements in England, France, and Germany are attending to that. The greatest American problem I cannot pick out, because there does not seem to be any. For my part, free speech and free thought interest me more than any other issue and I find an active group of people to work with along those lines, most of these people being pre-war.

The hard difficulty we encountered in the La Follette campaign was lack of an issue. A definite cure was offered for the too much readiness of the Supreme Court to upset certain kinds of legislation, and the cure was probably wrong. At least it is likely that the soundest cure is time and circumstance. An old-fashioned cure for the problem of monopoly was pressed, and convinced almost nobody. The government ownership of railroads was trotted out of the stable but failed to cause excitement.

I went on the stump for La Follette and would do it tomorrow for his son. But it is the spirit I should be supporting, the honesty, the indifference to wealth. With most of the definite conceptions, such as the form of farm relief, the method of curbing trusts, isolationism, I should disagree.

Many of those of whom you are asking the question have found matters about which to remain busy. Eugene Debs has done a noble job, in jail and out. Roger Baldwin never sleeps in his work for old-fashioned Jeffersonian freedom. Victor Berger is in Congress and is trying to have Russia recognized. I do not know that Ray Stannard Baker was ever any better employed than now that he is in large part studying other sources of progress than political ones. Will Irwin gives his life to peace. Lincoln Steffens sticks to some views that the world cares little for, but I am perfectly satisfied to leave some of his years to his baby. The baby is worth it, and so is the wife.

It is true that the United States is happy making money. Labor has higher real wages than ever before. Figures are easy to fight with it but I believe at least skilled labor gets 20 or 25 per cent more than it did in 1913 for the same effort. It is a mechanical age. The muck-raking in which I took part in the year before 1912 was an asset in its place and time. But there is no use crying because our particular medicine is not needed forever. Other jobs approach and they will be seen through by other men.

NORMAN HAPGOOD

Norman Hapgood was editor of Collier's Weekly when it ousted Ballinger and spread the doctrine of conservation. He discovered Gifford Pinchot. Robert Collier, S. S. McClure, Erdman J. Ridgeway, John S. Phillips, John O'Hara Cosgrave were leaders who broke with tradition and made the cheap periodical a force in American life.

The political radicals Fred Howe talks about were gripped by the romantic notion that "the People could rule." They voiced the old American faith that privileged classes could be controlled by the

"Public." As a humble member of the reformers' crew of those hopeful days, I believed it too. Most of us have since been as disillusioned as Howe.

There is no "Public"; the "People" as a political party are unorganizable. Only economic classes can be organized. The only power that works is class power. The "combined manufacturers and bankers of the United States," as Woodrow Wilson put it, is the class that politically controls us. The world has lost faith in parliaments; political democracy is recognized only as a form under which capitalism controls society, just as feudalism controlled it through kings. Political liberalism is dead.

There can be no more reformers of the Tom Johnson, Sam Jones school; no more crusades for the initiative, referendum and other devices for popular control; no more political muck-raking. The pre-war radicals have been put out of business by the industrial autocrats. Political democracy and industrial autocracy can't exist together.

But a new radicalism has taken the place of the old. It is the radicalism of a new class rising to power on the failures of capitalism and on the democratic urge. That class is the organized producers—labor and the farmers. Fred Howe finally identified himself with them. He saw that radicals of today must put their roots into that class, not into a phantom public. Hundreds of others who want to serve their generation, and who ten or twenty years ago would have gone into political reform or social work, now tie up with labor and its allied interests. The pre-war radicals in the working class still carry on. Recruits from youth constantly add to their number, despite the discouragement of these days of reaction.

The same fine faith and love of their fellow men which marked Fred Howe's friends in the days of political reform find expression in these new working-class movements. Radicalism does not die: its forms change.

Roger N. Baldwin

Roger Baldwin is known best for his spirited work in organizing the American Civil Liberties Union. He arrived there by way of law, social and civic work in St. Louis. His nine months in jail in 1918 was for his conscience's sake; he refused to be examined for the draft.

Of the radicals I knew some have remained fixed, as the Single Taxers, still satisfied with their theory but perhaps more tired: some have plunged from Socialism to Communism—a long leap, or from Pacifism to Bolshevism—a longer one; some are sufficiently occupied with Birth Control; others wallow in Freudian Psychoanalysis, which has the combined advantages of wide popular appeal in its subject matter, an imposing technology, and profitable use as a business.

There are many who are discouraged by the war and its effects, who feel that social advance is hopelessly checked, at least for the present, and who have taken refuge in a more personal philosophy. There is something very soothing in the vast reaches of New, or even Old, Thought; wherein we may wander alone and reach prodigious heights of attainment which even if we can not prove, at least no one else can disprove.

The group I know the best, Socialists but not Marxians, who see in Socialism a gradually introduced change in business methods working for the good of the whole community, recognize but too clearly how this normal advance is delayed by the Bolshevist performance, and hold their fire for the present.

Some have attained what they worked for, as the Prohibitionists and Equal Suffragists, and if they had no further purposes they are quiet; though hardly contented with the results. The more advantages secured the harder it is to rouse the public to see the need of anything further. Neither does the exercise of power attained give any assurance that "Labor" *per se* is any wiser or more disinterested than "Capital."

For myself there is a definite relief in being free from the work demanded by the various "causes" now won or temporarily in abeyance, and able at last to write and lecture on my own lines of social philosophy. To the average mind a Socialist or a Suffragist can be nothing else, talk of nothing else. But now, when the ballot does not free woman from economic dependence, and then economic independence can not be maintained by the wife and mother until her household labor is professionalized, that immense structural and functional change in our economic base, the home, begins to loom large before us.

CHARLOTTE PERKINS GILMAN

Charlotte Perkins Gilman was a socialist, suffragist and feminist before liberalism was popular in the parlor—a social philosopher with a fighting edge.

I have no doubt but what the world war is largely responsible for the reactionary tendency of the day. This is a condition that has followed all great wars. To engage in such a contest requires a cultivation of intense patriotism. When nations begin mobilizing, they start with the liars. They write about their enemies and they write about themselves. Everything is good at home and bad with their enemies. Some fairly intelligent people do not know any better than to believe it. I believed part of it myself, but am gradually getting over it. After the war, the spirit of super-patriotism remains. This is easily used to the advantage of the strong. Religious superstitions likewise grow; the leaders have a positive doctrine which involves unlimited promises. Then too, people are generally prosperous, or seem to be, during a great war. All the slack is taken up. Every man is busy. Production is great. Wages and commodities are high. Every one likes it until they wake up, which is several years after.

Following the War of the Rebellion, it was eight years before the people began to realize that somebody had to pay.

One must always remember that human beings do not reason— enough to hurt. They live from their emotions and so far as they do reason, this is controlled by their emotions. They are patriotic when they are getting plenty to eat and begin to grumble when times are hard. The grumbling will come later—not very much later; and after that, again will bragging, blustering and one hundred per cent patriotism, and so on—world without end.

CLARENCE DARROW

Clarence Darrow, Chicago lawyer, the attorney for the defense in cases as varied as they have been famous—from the McNamara trial in Los Angeles to the Scopes case in Tennessee where he locked horns over evolution with Willam Jennings Bryan.

Them was the days! When the muckrakers were best sellers, when trust busters were swinging their lariats over every state capitol, when "priviledge" shook in its shoes, when God was behind the initiative, the referendum and the recall—and the devil shrieked when he saw the short ballot, when the Masses was at the height of its glory, and Utopia was just around the corner.

...Now look at the damned thing. You could put the avowed Socialists into a roomy new house, the muckrakers have joined the breadlines, Mr. Coolidge is compared favorably to Lincoln, the short ballot is as defunct as Mah Jong, Mr. Eastman writes triolets in France, Mr. Steffens has bought him a castle in Italy, and Mr. Howe digs turnips in Nantucket.

Shall we lay a wreath on the Uplift Movement in America? I

suppose we might as well. For the Uplift as a crusading spirit, as a dedication, as a religion, is comatose if not completely ossified—strangled both by the war and its own ineptitude. It was inept because its moral judgments took the place of sound analysis. It dealt in blacks and whites; it deified a muzzy and mystical conception of democracy, and found horns underneath every plug hat; it was too logic and not sufficiently psychological; it was cursed with political-mindedness.

But it was a gallant adventure, and before its chieftains and its martyrs we stand at the salute. Furthermore, it has left its enduring mark on the mores—even under the cold douches of Cooligism, even under the holy wheel of rotary. It shovelled the classicists of American art and letters into the dust bin—where they have since happily remained. Wall Street dodged the brickbats, only to have Longfellow and Lowell and Howells mowed down behind it.

Though the main purposes for which Mr. Howe dedicated his life are perhaps no nearer fruition, certain sparks which he flung in the byways have grown into raging conflagrations. The novel, the theater, architecture, decoration, poetry, the form of the essay, sex, the family, religion, history, even clothes, have been modified and liberated since Tom Johnson and the "interests" wrestled naked in the public streets of Cleveland.

But it was economics which the Uplifters cared about most, and it is precisely in the economic field that their effect has been the slightest. Why? Because they did not understand either their goals or the technique for achieving them. They fought valiantly—but in a circle. They were too moral, they were too sure. They knew little about the realities of production and distribution, and nothing about the springs of human behavior. They had no science to give body to their emotions—and today nothing remains but a cloud of steam, somewhere in the upper atmosphere.

To that cloud, I did from 1912 to 1920 contribute my quota. I went through the Uplift from settlement house to socialist party. But before Nantucket claims me, I want to take Wall Street to pieces the way Jacques Loeb took a starfish, I want to find out what makes men act the way they do. I want to grow ever more radical by getting ever nearer the roots.

Stuart Chase

Stuart Chase, who is one of the Labor Bureau group, has just written a book on Waste. He began as a certified public accountant, and is bent on finding out what economics has to do with happiness.

27

MR. DOOLEY

Reform—with a Grain of Salt

What follows is hardly a balanced view of the progressive movement. It is a fragment of conversation from a saloon on Chicago's South Side,
and expresses a perspective on reform and reformers from a layer of society
somewhat lower than the stratum where reformers were recruited. As usual,
Finley Peter Dunne's bartender, Mister Dooley, had a sense of the massive
inertia of human life that made him a better prophet at the turn of the century
than the enthusiasts of reform.

"Why is it," asked Mr. Hennessy, "that a rayform administhration
always goes to th' bad?"

I'll tell ye," said Mr. Dooley. "I tell ye ivrything an' I'll tell ye
this. In th' first place 'tis a gr-reat mistake to think that annywan ra-
aly wants to rayform. Ye niver heerd iv a man rayformin' himsilf.
He'll rayform other people gladly. He likes to do it. But a healthy
man'll niver rayform while he has th' strenth. A man doesn't rayform
till his will has been impaired so he hasn't power to resist what th' pa-
apers calls th' blandishments iv th' timpter. An' that's thruer in politics
thin annywhere else.

"But a rayformer don't see it. A rayformer thinks he was ilicted
because he was a rayformer, whin th' thruth iv th' matter is he was
ilicted because no wan knew him. Ye can always ilict a man in this
counthry on that platform. If I was runnin' f'r office, I'd change me
name, an' have printed on me cards: 'Give him a chanst; he can't be
worse.' He's ilicted because th' people don't know him an' do know
th' other la-ad; because Mrs. Casey's oldest boy was clubbed be a
polisman, because we cudden't get wather above th' third story wan
day, because th' sthreet car didn't stop f'r us, because th' Flan-
nigans bought a pianny, because we was near run over be a mail
wagon, because th' saloons are open Sundah night, because they're not
open all day an' because we're tired seein' th' same face at th' window
whin we go down to pay th' wather taxes. Th' rayformer don't know
this. He thinks you an' me, Hinnissy, has been watchin' his spotless
career f'r twenty years, that we've read all he had to say on th' evils iv
pop'lar suffrage befure th' Society f'r the Bewildhermint iv th' Poor,

Louis Filler ed., *The World of Mr. Dooley* (New York: P. F. Collier, Inc.,
1962), pp. 130–33. Reprinted with permission.

an' that we're achin' in ivry joint to have him dhrag us be th' hair iv th' head fr'm th' flowin' bowl an' th' short card game, make good citizens iv us an' sind us to th' pinitinchry. So th' minyit he gets into th' job he begins a furyous attimpt to convart us into what we've been thryin' not to be iver since we come into th' wurruld.

"In th' coorse iv th' twinty years that he spint attimptin' to get office, he managed to poke a few warrum laws conthrollin' th' pleasures iv th' poor into th' stachoo book, because no wan cared about thim or because they made business betther f'r th' polis, an' whin he's in office, he calls up th' Cap'n iv the polis an' says he: "If these laws ar-re bad laws th' way to end thim is to enfoorce thim.' Somebody told him that, Hinnissy. It isn't thrue, d'ye mind. I don't care who said it, not if 'twas Willum Shakespere. It isn't thrue. Laws ar-re made to throuble people an' th' more throuble they make th' longer they stay on th' stachoo book. But th' polis don't ast anny question: Says they: 'They'll be less money in th' job but we need some recreation,' an' that night a big copper comes down th' sthreet, sees me settin' out on th' front stoop with me countenance dhraped with a tin pail, fans me with his club an' runs me in. Th' woman nex' dure is licked up f'r sthringin' a clothes line on th' roof, Hannigan's boy Tim gets tin days f'r keepin' a goat, th' polis resarves are called out to protict th' vested rights iv property against th' haynyous pushcart man, th' stations is crowded with felons charged with maintainin' a hose conthrary to th' stachoos made an' provided, an' th' tindherline is all over town. A rayformer don't think annything has been accomplished if they'se a vacant bedroom in th' pinitinchry. His motto is 'Arrest that man.'

"Whin a rayformer is ilicted he promises ye a business administhration. Some people want that but I don't. Th' American business man is too fly. He's all right, d'ye mind. I don't say annything again' him. He is what Hogan calls th' boolwarks iv pro-gress, an' we cudden't get on without him even if his scales are a little too quick on th' dhrop. But he ought to be left to dale with his akels. 'Tis a shame to give him a place where he can put th' comether on millions iv people that has had no business thrainin' beyond occassionally handin' a piece iv debased money to a car conductor on a cold day. A reg'lar pollytician can't give away an alley without blushin', but a business man who is in pollytics jus' to see that th' civil sarvice law gets thurly enfoorced, will give Lincoln Park an' th' public libr'y to th' beef thrust, charge an admission price to th' lake front an' make it a fellony f'r annywan to buy stove polish outside iv his store, an' have it all put down to public improvemints with a pitcher iv him in th' corner stone.

"Fortchnitly, Hinnissy, a rayformer is seldom a business man. He thinks he is, but business men know diff'rent. They know what he is. He thinks business an' honesty is th' same thing. He does, indeed. He's got thim mixed because they dhress alike. His idee is that all he has to do to make a business administhration is to have honest men ar-round him. Wrong. I'm not sayin', mind ye, that a man can't do good work an' be honest at th' same time. But whin I'm hirin' a la-ad I find out first whether he is onto his job, an' afther a few years I begin to suspect that he is honest, too. Manny a dishonest man can lay brick sthraight an' manny a man that wudden't steal ye'er spoons will break ye'er furniture. I don't want Father Kelly to hear me, but I'd rather have a competint man who wud steal if I give him a chanst, but I won't, do me plumbin' thin a person that wud scorn to help himsilf but didn't know how to wipe a joint. Ivry man ought to be honest to start with, but to give a man an office jus' because he's honest is like ilictin' him to Congress because he's a pathrite, because he don't bate his wife or because he always wears a right boot in th' right foot. A man ought to be honest to start with an' after that he ought to be crafty. A pollytician who's on'y honest is jus' th' same as bein' out in a winther storm without anny clothes on.

"Another thing about rayform administhrations is they always think th' on'y man that ought to hold a job is a lawyer. Th' raison is that in th' coorse iv his thrainin' a lawyer larns enough about ivrything to make a good front on anny subject to annybody who doesn't know abut it. So whin th' raform administhration comes in th' mayor says: 'Who'll we make chief iv polis in place iv th' misguided ruffyan who has held th' job f'r twinty years?' 'Th' man f'r th' place,' says th' mayor's adviser, 'is Arthur Lightout,' he says. 'He's an ixcillent lawyer, Yale, '95, an' is well up polis matthers. Las' year he read a paper on "The fine polis foorce iv London" befure th' annyal meetin' iv th' S'ciety f'r Ladin' th' Mulligan Fam'ly to a Better an' Harder Life. Besides,' he says, 'he's been in th' milishy an' th' foorce needs a man who'll be afraid not to shoot in case iv public disturbance.' So Arthur takes hold iv th' constabulary an' in a year th' poils can all read Emerson an' th' burglars begin puttin' up laddhers an' block an' tackles before eight A.M. An' so it is on ivry side. A lawyer has charge iv the city horse-shoein', another wan is clanin' th' sthreets, th' author iv 'Gasamagoo on torts' is thryin' to dispose iv th' ashes be throwin' thim in th' air on a windy day, an' th' bright boy that took th' silver ware f'r th' essay in *ne exeats* an' their relation to life is plannin' a uniform that will be sarviceable an' constitchoochinal f'r th' brave men that wurruks on th' city dumps. An' wan day th' main rayformer goes out expictin' to rayceive th' thanks iv th' community an' th' public that has jus' got out iv jail f'r lettin' th' wather run too long in th' bath tub rises up an' cries: 'Back to th' Univarsity Settlemint.' Th' man with th' di'mon' in his shirt front comes home an' pushes th' honest lawyers down th' steps, an' a dishonest horse shoer shoes th' city's horses well, an' a crooked plumber does th' city's plumbin' securely, an' a rascally polisman that may not be avars to pickin' up a bet but will always find out whin Pathrolman Scanlan slept on his beat, takes hold iv th' polis foorce, an' we raysume our nachral condition iv illagal merrimint. An th' rayformer spinds th' rest iv his life tellin' us where we are wrong. He's good at that. On'y he don't undherstand that people wud rather be wrong an' comfortable thin right in jail."

"I don't like a rayformer," said Mr. Hennessy.

"Or anny other raypublican," said Mr. Dooley.

28

FRANKLIN D. ROOSEVELT

The Perspective from the 1930s

The gentleman who made the following remarks in an address to the Young Democratic Clubs on August 24, 1935, had high qualifications as a commentator on the progressive movement. He had been an insurgent legislator in New York State and a member of the Wilson administration, and by 1935 he was a leading expert in American social problems.

Whatever his party affiliations may be, the President of the United States, in addressing the youth of the country—even when speaking to the younger citizens of his own party—should speak as President of the whole people. It is true that the Presidency carries with it, for the time being, the leadership of a political party as well. But the Presidency carries with it a far higher obligation than this—the duty of analyzing and setting forth national needs and ideals which transcend and cut across all lines of party affiliation. Therefore, what I am about to say to you, members of the Young Democratic Clubs, is precisely—word for word—what I would say were I addressing a convention of the youth of the Republican Party.

A man of my generation comes to the councils of the younger war-riors in a very different spirit from that in which the older men ad-dressed the youth of my time. Party or professional leaders who talked to us twenty-five or thirty years ago almost inevitably spoke in a mood of achievement and of exultation. They addressed us with the air of those who had won the secret of success for themselves and of per-manence of achievement for their country for all generations to come. They assumed that there was a guarantee of final accomplish-ment for the people of this country and that the grim specter of in-security and want among the great masses would never haunt this land of plenty as it had widely visited other portions of the world. And so the elders of that day used to tell us, in effect, that the job of youth was merely to copy them and thereby to preserve the great things they had won for us.

I have no desire to underestimate the achievements of the past. We have no right to speak slightingly of the heritage, spiritual and mate-rial, that comes down to us. There are lessons that it teaches that we abandon only at our own peril. "Hold fast to that which is per-manently true" is still a counsel of wisdom.

While my elders were talking to me about the perfection of America, I did not know then of the lack of opportunity, the lack of education, the lack of many of the essential needs of civilization which existed among millions of our people who lived not alone in the slums of the great cities and in the forgotten corners of rural America but even under the very noses of those who had the advantages and the power of Government of those days.

I say from my heart that no man of my generation has any business to address youth unless he comes to that task not in a spirit of exulta-tion, but in a spirit of humility. I cannot expect you of a newer genera-tion to believe me, of an older generation, if I do not frankly acknowledge that had the generation that brought you into the world been wiser and more provident and more unselfish, you would have been saved from needless difficult problems and needless pain and suffering. We may not have failed you in good intentions but we have certainly not been adequate in results. Your task, therefore, is not only to maintain the best in your heritage, but to labor to lift from the shoulders of the American people some of the burdens that the mis-takes of a past generation have placed there.

Franklin D. Roosevelt, speech to the Young Democratic Clubs, August 24, 1935, in Samuel I. Rosenman, ed., *The Public Papers and Addresses of Franklin D. Roosevelt*, (New York: Random House, 1938), IV, pp. 337–38.

index